FREYBERG

Churchill's Salamander

FREYBERG

Churchill's Salamander

Laurie Barber

John Tonkin-Covell

Hutchinson

To those who soldiered, and soldier, in the service of New Zealand

This edition first published in Great Britain
in 1990 by Hutchinson, an imprint of
Century Hutchinson Ltd
62-65 Chandos Place, Covent Garden, London WC2N 4NW

Century Hutchinson Australia Pty Ltd
20 Alfred Street, Milsons Point, Sydney, N.S.W. 2061

Century Hutchinson New Zealand Ltd
187 Archers Road, Glenfield, Auckland 10

Century Hutchinson South Africa Pty Ltd
P.O. Box 337, Bergvlei 2012, South Africa

First published 1989

Printed in Singapore

ISBN 1 86941 052 1

CONTENTS

FOREWORD

War is an unforgettable experience, a time of dislocation, turmoil, and tragedy. Yet there is another side which makes for easier remembrance — a feeling of unity of purpose, sharpened by shared dangers and sustained by reliance on one's comrades. No dependence, in that sense, can be greater than that felt towards a leader who has the ultimate responsibility for the morale and well-being of those under his command.

It is a pleasure for us, accordingly, as two officers who served on General Freyberg's headquarters staff during the Second World War, to be asked to contribute a brief foreword to this book. He undoubtedly left on us, as on so many, an indelible impression of the quality of his leadership as we observed at first hand his methods and achievements, and his personal ways. But almost fifty years have passed since the dramatic events recounted here, and we believe that we may claim a certain objectivity.

The authors explain that *Freyberg: Churchill's Salamander* is not intended to cover the whole history of Freyberg's command of the 2nd New Zealand Division in the Middle East and Italy from 1939 to 1945. They have concentrated on two battles when the fortunes of war went against him, attracting criticism by some modern historians. The book examines some of these criticisms, and also criticisms of the Tebaga Gap battle. In particular, it seeks to answer the claim that Freyberg revealed limitations in his command ability when controlling forces larger than a normal division of fifteen to eighteen thousand men.

This is a most timely work. The authors have captured well the tense atmosphere of Freyberg's many battles and dealt faithfully with the decisions he had to make. We do not agree with every inference drawn or conclusion reached — for example, that Freyberg's reputation was gravely injured by criticisms after Crete, or that his relations with the New Zealand Government were seriously impaired. Further, caution is necessary in reaching conclusions concerning actions taken by individual commanders in the heat of battle, especially when all of the facts may not be known or the circumstances at this time fully appreciated.

We are glad the battles of Crete, Mareth, and Cassino have been carefully studied and researched in depth, using information from many sources including Ultra intercepts. It has been the authors' aim to base their conclusions regarding Freyberg on a methodical analysis of such evidence. It is our hope that other historians will be encouraged to examine further instances of Freyberg's exercise of command during five long years of war, and the response of the men he led.

It has been said that the greatest test of courage is to bear defeat without losing heart. Whether or not readers are convinced by the arguments so cogently marshalled in these pages, all will agree that in this sense Freyberg's leadership stands unchallenged. Field Marshal Wavell, a renowned fighting commander himself, would have concurred; he placed 'robustness' as the paramount quality of generalship. Winston Churchill wrote that a senior commander must have 'massive commonsense and reasoning power. . . but also an element of legerdemain'. All of these were facets of General Freyberg's outstanding and sometimes decisive leadership. For his qualities and especially for his unconquerable spirit, all who served with him, and indeed all New Zealanders, have cause to be grateful.

Sir Leonard Thornton
Sir John White

PREFACE

One of the most unfortunate catch-phrases of the 1980s is 'it's history!' This slick epithet is used to close discussion on any person or event that has moved from the present to the past. Its stupid presupposition is that the past is of no concern to the present and the future. Those who glibly employ the catch-phrase ignore the reality that the past fashions our present and future, and that without knowledge of who we are and what our forebears were we have an inadequate knowledge of ourselves.

This book is about a man who died in 1963, whose most consequential years were 1941 to 1945. The book's subject, Bernard Freyberg, New Zealand's most famous general, is indeed history. Yet, despite appraisal in numerous books, articles, and lectures, although his leadership capacity has been analysed by Winston Churchill and Bernard Montgomery, the authors of this book are convinced there is yet more to say about New Zealand's premier World War II commander. We believe the ledger of history is never closed and that its balance must be reappraised whenever new evidence is offered or new questions are raised.

This book is not an exercise in demythologizing. Our intent is not to cut down a tall poppy, and it will be seen that Freyberg's reputation is enhanced by our offering. This book does not pretend to examine exhaustively Freyberg's career and assess his every battle experience. Its examination is deliberately selective. Our aim is to reassess Freyberg's command capability in the light of his awareness of the 'Ultra' résumés of dispatches, the intelligence reports showing German plans, movements, and strengths, made available to him from the Crete campaign onwards. A further intent is to assess Freyberg's competence as the commander of corps-sized formations, to answer the charges that Freyberg was no intellectual, and that he reached his ceiling with his promotion to divisional command.

This critique of Freyberg the commander offers no offence to its subject. Winston Churchill, Britain's war leader, in a tribute to Freyberg, dubbed him 'the salamander of the British Empire'. Churchill, the supreme word crafter, was not liking the General to a harmless amphibian, but to the mythical lizard believed able to live and move in the heart of the fire. Freyberg, the salamander, can hardly be injured by being placed over the refining fire of history.

Laurie Barber
John Tonkin-Covell
University of Waikato
1989

ACKNOWLEDGEMENTS

The authors are indebted to a number of people and institutions. Very special thanks must go to Sir John White and Sir Leonard Thornton. Valuable assistance and perspectives were given by Professor Sir Harry Hinsley, Mr Walter Gibbons, Mr John Renwick, Mr Roy Lomas, and Mr Rab Campbell. The staff of the New Zealand National Archives, the Public Record Office of the United Kingdom, the National Library of New Zealand, the British Army Museum, the Queen Elizabeth II Army Museum, the Imperial War Museum, the Cabinet Rooms Museum, and the University of Waikato Library gave help in locating material. The General Staff of the New Zealand Army gave archival access to one of the authors who has been engaged on long term military history research. Quoted material is reproduced with the kind permission of the Controller of Her Majesty's Stationery Office and of Hamish Hamilton. Mrs Sandra Toner did a huge amount of draft typing, Mrs Lorraine Brown and her staff worked assiduously typing the tome, Ms Janette Wells typed the Appendices, and Mrs Ross Clayton and Mrs Wendy Peel prepared the photographic collection. Thanks are also due to Mr Ray Richards of Ray Richards Literary Agency, and to Mr David Ling of Century Hutchinson.

To all these people and others who made the enterprise possible, especially Susan Coubrough and Janet Tonkin-Covell, the authors wish to extend a heartfelt gratitude.

Laurie Barber
John Tonkin-Covell
University of Waikato
1989

A NOTE ON THE PHOTOGRAPHS

The photographs for this book belong to the collection of the Honourable Sir John White. Sir John White was Lord Freyberg's Personal Assistant for the years of the Second World War, and during that period took the opportunity to record on 35mm film the General and 2 New Zealand Division in the great Allied cause. From Greece through the Western Desert and thence to Italy and Trieste, it is a remarkable record. It is also important to note that Sir John White was responsible, as part of his duties, for keeping the GOC's diary from September 1941 to the cessation of hostilities in 1945. The entries were checked by the General at the end of each day, and annotations were made if so desired. From this photographic and daily documentary record emerge perspectives on Lord Freyberg without which we would most certainly be the poorer. The authors wish to record their gratitude to Sir John White for permission to use his unique pictorial material, and also for his valuable perspectives on the commander he served for five years of war.

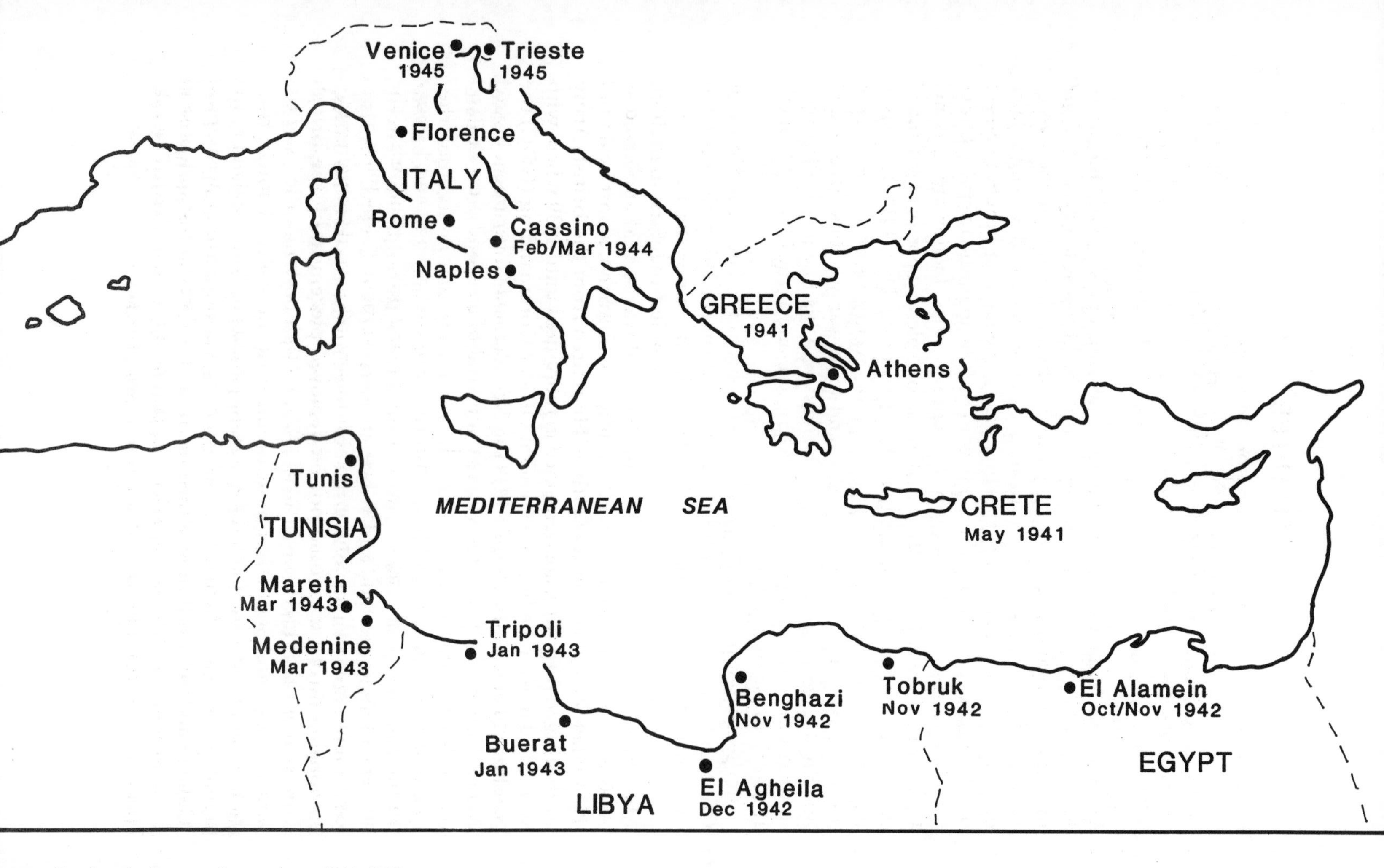

Freyberg's theatre of operations, 1941–1945.

CHAPTER 1

The War Horse Returns

Lieutenant-General Baron Freyberg of Wellington, VC, GCMG, KCB, KBE, DSO (1889-1963), is without doubt the best-known New Zealand military commander. Freyberg became a living legend on the eve of ANZAC day 1915 when he swam ashore in the Dardenelles to light false beacons in a plan to deceive the Turks as to the landing beaches chosen by the allied expeditionary force. He won the Distinguished Service Order for that exploit. In France, in November 1916, Lieutenant-Colonel Freyberg was awarded the Victoria Cross, for 'splendid personal gallantry' and 'utter contempt for danger'. By Armistice Day 1918 he was a temporary brigadier-general, at the age of twenty-eight, and a veteran with two bars to his DSO, a CMG, and nine war wounds. Streets and buildings have been named in his honour and his likeness is displayed in statues in New Zealand's capital, Wellington, and at the Queen Elizabeth II Army Museum, Waiouru.

In the inter-war years Freyberg failed in his bid to enter the House of Commons as a Liberal candidate in 1922, but succeeded in his courtship of an attractive widow, Barbara Maclaren, in the same year. Reduced by peacetime to a substantive rank, he commanded the First Battalion, Manchester Regiment, from 1929 to 1931, and was in 1931 appointed as Assistant Quartermaster-General, Southern Command, a post held until 1933 when he joined the War Office. He retired from the British Army in 1934, aged forty-five, and remained in retirement until 1939 when, with war's declaration, he became General Officer Commanding (GOC) the Salisbury Plains. At the close of 1939 the New Zealand Government invited Major-General Freyberg to assume command of a second New Zealand Expeditionary Force.

Freyberg's selection by Prime Minister Michael Savage and Deputy Prime Minister Peter Fraser followed cautious and probing enquiries. The leaders of New Zealand's first Labour Government (1935-1949) were determined that any New Zealand expeditionary force would remain under national control, and would not be deployed piecemeal by the British Government as it had been in World War I. High ranking officers of the Imperial General Staff strongly recommended Freyberg. Though born in London he accompanied his emigrant parents to New Zealand at the age of two. His secondary school education took place at Wellington College and he was first commissioned as an officer whilst a dentist in Morrinsville in 1912 — as a second lieutenant in the Sixth Hauraki Regiment, a territorial army unit. He rode with Massey's 'Cossacks' against

Wellington waterfront strikers in 1913.[1]

Beside his youthful experience of New Zealand and New Zealanders, Freyberg's reputation as a sportsman (especially in swimming), and as a brave but sensible World War I commander, well fitted him for the command of New Zealand's Second Division. Before his appointment he was made well aware of Savage and Fraser's insistence that his command would be a national force, subject to national oversight. He was issued with a charter that required him to maintain the closest links with the New Zealand Government and allowed him discretion to disregard orders from military superiors who might needlessly jeopardize his troops.

When the Second New Zealand Expeditionary Force departed by sea convoy to Egypt, its commander, Freyberg, was quickly accepted as the right man for the job. With the physique of an All Black forward, standing over six feet, confident in his leadership, and with a high pitched voice which was easily mimicked, Freyberg's bearing and humour endeared him to his troops. This was the leader who was to advise a British general who complained of an absence of salutes by the New Zealanders that they would always wave back. 'Tiny' Freyberg was quickly accepted by the division's officers and other ranks as a general who knew his business.

But did Freyberg know his business? Pre-eminent though Freyberg is among New Zealand commanders, his conduct of military operations at higher command level has long been the subject of vigorous debate. From 1941 to 1945 Freyberg faced criticism from powerful political and military leaders. General Sir Claude Auchinleck, General Officer Commanding [GOC] Middle East, argued that Freyberg sometimes intervened at too low a level of command.[2] General Mark Clark, United States 5th Army Commander in Italy, saw him as a prima donna who claimed special privileges for his New Zealand division.[3] One of Freyberg's own brigadiers, James Hargest, criticized his general's handling of the Greek and Crete campaigns.[4] Hargest was a Member of Parliament and made his complaint directly to Prime Minister Peter Fraser. Lindsay Inglis, another brigadier, reinforced these criticisms in a verbal report to Winston Churchill.[5] Montgomery of Alamein regarded Freyberg as his best divisional commander but was reserved about his capacity to command corps-sized formations.[6] Brigadier W. G. Stevens, commander of 2 NZ Division's administrative headquarters, regarded Freyberg as occasionally too cautious.[7] Major-General F. Tuker, commander of the 4th Indian Division at Cassino, argued that his corps commander, Freyberg, was barely competent.[8]

Freyberg's defenders were as numerous as those who attacked him. Churchill was amongst the foremost and bestowed on him the epithet given in this book's title, 'the Salamander of the British Empire'.[9] Montgomery esteemed Freyberg as the 8th Army's most reliable divisional commander, a judgement that was reinforced by Montgomery's battle placement of the New Zealand Division.[10] Brian Horrocks, sometime Freyberg's corps commander, deferred to Freyberg's experience and military judgement.[11] General F. M. Richardson regarded Freyberg as having what Napoleon called 'two o'clock in the morning courage', in common with great commanders — an ability to remain 'calm and unruffled' in the face of 'sudden unexpected catastrophe'.[12] Colonel (later Sir Leonard) Thornton consistently argued that his general was a highly able commander.[13] Of his enemies, both Field Marshal Erwin Rommel and Oberst von Mellenthin agreed that he was a commander with drive, and was opportunistic and aggressive.[14] General Sir Archibald Wavell firmly supported Freyberg's performance in Greece and Crete.[15]

Freyberg's best brigade commander, Howard Kippenberger, was in his latter days mercurial in his appreciation of his former commander's operational decisions.[16] Contemporary military historians are just as divided.[17]

This book addresses the question of Freyberg's capacity as a commander of corps-sized formations. It does not range over the entire gamut of Freyberg's military career but concentrates carefully on several significant battles wherein Freyberg's capacity for higher command should be open to accurate assessment. Crete, Alamein, Mareth, and Cassino are the touchstones of Freyberg's generalship. With reference to these battles, analysis is made of Freyberg's ability to use the carefully protected but uniquely advantageous intelligence gleaned by broken signal traffic. The argument that he made insufficient use of 'Ultra' (British intelligence summaries of German coded information, initially known as BONIFACE) is rejected.

While Freyberg most certainly preferred to command his New Zealand Division on those occasions wherein he was entrusted with corps-sized formations it is argued that he acquitted himself well. Freyberg was no 'template' commander, but a lateral thinker well able to apply his enemy's tactics to his enemy's disadvantage. His operational prescience was well demonstrated in his capacity to plan and direct combined air–land operations. He learned quickly from his enemy's *blitzkrieg* and panzer tactics, and at Mareth he was able to apply these lessons with success. His involvement with multi-national forces in Crete, North Africa, and Italy is discussed, with particular attention to his conflict with Mark Clark.

His Achilles heel was his loyalty to subordinates, even when betrayed by them. He did not pursue personal vendettas. Though a Briton by birth he thought and acted as a New Zealander throughout the war, ever true to the charter the New Zealand Government had granted to him.

Complicating Freyberg's divisional and higher-echelon decision making was his continuous and time consuming role as commander of New Zealand Middle East land forces — a task involving the attributes of a military politician. Few, if any, commanders of World War II were forced to combine such a task with their operational command. Montgomery left that to Alexander, and Bradley could depend in that area on Eisenhower.

That Freyberg was consistent in his personal bravery is undisputed. His war wounds, his forward battle headquarters, his appearances in the heart of the battle, and his steady attention to his duties while others took cover are all well known. This assessment demonstrates that unremitting professionalism and high command aptitude accompanied that bravery. On the battlefield Freyberg had many limitations imposed upon him by superior commanders, the enemy, and by circumstances. He dealt with these vigorously, tenaciously, and capably. Few could have performed better.

In 1940 Freyberg's concern to hone his Division quickly into an effective fighting force was frustrated by the slowness of home training and provision of equipment, by irregular convoy arrangements, and then by the fall of France. The three brigades of 2 New Zealand Division (4, 5, and 6) departed for Egypt at three-to-four month intervals, from January 1940. With the fall of France, 5 Brigade was diverted to Britain and remained on anti-invasion duty until early 1941. Whilst his Division was arriving and training, piecemeal, taking eighteen months to assemble, the Axis forces were on the march. An Italian invasion of Greece was repulsed by Greek forces. Hitler came to Italy's aid and German forces entered Bulgaria early March 1941 and moved towards the north-eastern border of Greece.

Aware that a German invasion of Greece was only a matter of time, allied forces were deployed to Greece throughout March. Freyberg received instructions from Wavell on 17 February with an order to tell no one of the Greek expedition. In response to Freyberg's enquiry whether the New Zealand Government had been informed, Wavell replied that it had. In fact, the New Zealand Government did not receive a request for New Zealand troops from Greece until 23 February. By the close of March most of the New Zealand Division was in Greece. The Germans knew they were coming. Not yet at war with Greece, they had sent their military attaché in Athens to greet the New Zealand transport as they arrived in the Piraeus.

On 5 April 1941 Freyberg's Division was placed under the command of 1 Australian Corps, commanded by Lieutenant-General Thomas Blamey. On 5 April the British and Commonwealth force commander in Greece, Lieutenant-General Sir Henry Wilson, was informed that the German attack on Greece would take place at 0530, 6 April (later amended to 0600) — information gleaned from the breaking of secret German codes.

Freyberg's force, on the eve of the German attack, was placed on the Aliakmon Line, a series of passes, through steep mountains, with flats on its flanks, the latter a godsend to enemy armour. Its terrain rendered reinforcement, from one pass to another, difficult. It needed more divisions than the British Imperial and Greek forces possessed to hold it properly.

Freyberg's Division was employed in 'W force', in the Aliakmon Line, with little armour, minimal air support, and aided by a patriotic but ill-equipped Greek army. 4 and 6 Brigades were posted to the coastal sector of the line, a twenty-four kilometre flank north of Mount Olympus, to a task more suited for two divisions rather than two brigades. 5 Brigade was tasked with guarding the passes on the slopes of Mount Olympus.

The German attack began, as promised by Ultra, on 6 April. Robin Higham's appreciation is a succinct and horrifying account of allied failure:

> The story of the next three weeks is quickly told. The Germans attacked with standard blitzkrieg, professional tactics; the exhausted Greeks reeled back; and the totally inadequate British forces, which had never got dug in, simply were forced to withdraw in good order as their pitifully small airforce was decimated, often on the ground at unprotected airfields. And all of this happened in steadily improving weather, though in northern Greece wet roads meant slow, slick driving until after the 18th.[18]

A decision to abandon the Aliakmon Line was ordered on 7 April. The long fighting withdrawal, 320 kilometres southwards down the Greek peninsula, began. The retreat became a rout, with troops harassed by Luftwaffe dive-bombers. Freyberg's soldiers were forced to move only by night and where possible by mountain tracks. On 17 April mountain mist fortunately hid 5 Brigade from the Luftwaffe as it retreated. From 19-20 April Blamey's corps withdrew to the Thermopylae Line, behind the Sperkhios River, with Freyberg's Division on the coastal strip. The line did not hold and on 22 April ANZAC Operational Order No. 2 instructed the evacuation of Greece. Over the next three days the Thermopylae position was abandoned.

Even in retreat the New Zealand Division hit hard. 4 Brigade, the rear guard, delayed the German advance near Kreikouki to allow other units of the division to embark, and engaged the enemy again on 27 April, close to Porto Rafti. But Freyberg's troops had experienced their first defeat. They left behind spiked guns, immobilized transport, and 1,614 New Zealand troops who could not be evacuated from the beaches south of Sparta and near Athens and who became prisoners of war.

On 28 April Freyberg was evacuated to Crete. He had disregarded an earlier order directing him to leave Greece on 23 April, insisting to his staff that he would not leave until his troops had preceded him. In Crete Freyberg and his soldiers licked their wounds. The troops of 4 and 5 Brigades had left Greece with only their uniforms and personal weapons. 2 Division had suffered 890 casualties in its first campaign, with 291 killed in action. Freyberg had survived — but with nine staff cars shot from under him during the campaign. His desire was to withdraw the entire division to Egypt, complete divisional training, and begin operations in the North African theatre.

Freyberg's force had taken a drubbing in the Greek campaign but high command and politicians eventually agreed that Freyberg had done all that was asked of him. As a divisional commander, Freyberg had shown, despite the dispersal of his division, that he was a cool, competent, and resolute leader. At Crete he was to be tested as to whether he was more.

CHAPTER 2

'Crete will be Held'

After the debilitating fiasco of the Greek campaign, Winston Churchill was determined that Crete would be held. Crete, 8,288 square kilometres in area, 257 kilometres long, and from 11 to 56 kilometres wide, 100 kilometres south-east of mainland Greece, rugged and poor, was a prize Churchill intended to keep. Crete could be a vital submarine and air base in the battle for the Mediterranean. Control of Crete could confine German sea and air forces and restrict their damage to the supply of Britain's North African army. Crete, with its population of 400,000 swollen by Greek military and civilian refugees, including the King of the Hellenes, and with Australian, British, and New Zealand troops camped on its coastal plains and lower hills, beneath its backbone of snow-encrusted mountains, was to be defended against the southward moving Germans.

The allied force in Crete (known as 'Creforce') was 42,500 strong, but deficient in artillery, armour, transport, tactical communications equipment, automatic weapons, and air support. Creforce's senior officer was a Royal Marine, General Weston. In response to a query from Churchill as to whether Weston was the right man to hold Crete, General Sir Archibald Wavell, Britain's General Officer Commanding Middle East, sought advice from the Chief of the Imperial General Staff (CIGS), Sir John Dill. Sir John stated his preference for Major-General Bernard Freyberg, and Wavell flew to Crete to implement the change. Freyberg's account of his meeting with Wavell is undisputed:

> We met in a small villa between Maleme and Canea and set to work at 11.30. General Wavell had arrived by air and looked drawn and tired and more weary than any of us. Just prior to sitting down General Wavell and General Wilson had a heart-to-heart talk in one corner and then the C-in-C [Commander in Chief] called me over. He took me by the arm and said: 'I want to tell you how well I think the New Zealand Division has done in Greece. I do not believe any other division would have carried out those withdrawals as well.' His next words came as a complete surprise. He said he wanted me to take command of the forces in Crete and went on to say that he considered Crete would be attacked in the next few days. I told him that I wanted to get back to Egypt to concentrate the Division and train and re-equip it, and I added that my Government would never agree to the division being split permanently. He then said that he considered it my duty to remain and take on the job. I could do nothing but accept. With that over we

> sat down round the table on the flat-topped roof in the open air under an awning. The only subject on the agenda was the defence of Crete... There was not very much to discuss. We were told that Crete would be held. The scale of attack envisaged was five to six thousand airborne troops plus a seaborne attack. The primary objectives of this attack were considered to be Heraklion and Maleme Aerodromes..[1]

Although Freyberg was kept in ignorance, his commander-in-chief was the bearer of accurate information gleaned from the enemy's communication network. Whilst the military balance seemed at first sight to be against the new commander of Creforce and his patchwork multinational force, a flaw in the ether redistributed the chances of victory or defeat. At the Government Code and Cypher School at Bletchley Park, in England, the team of code-breakers had won a regular though fragile entrée into several German army, Luftwaffe, and Reichsbahn (railway) ciphers. The fragility of their source was centred on the ability of the code-breakers to decipher signals and prepare résumés in time for tactical use. By maintaining high levels of competence and extraordinary working days, Bletchley Park's cryptanalysts generally succeeded in producing solutions to the major cyphers within twenty-four hours.[2]

Wavell's knowledge of a German invasion plan originated from hut three at Bletchley Park. All signals from Bletchley Park were paraphrases of the original 'Enigma' German signals: they stated what the Germans were saying to, and about, themselves. These summaries were then transmitted to the director, Combined Bureau Middle East (CBME), who then briefed the commander-in-chief and his chief of staff. The director was responsible for the maintenance of tight security of these summaries, well aware that if the Germans suspected their cyphers had been broken, they would change them, perhaps permanently shutting down this source of information.[3]

The Greek campaign saw the first operational use of the new German intercepts when the commander-in-chief and the chief of staff had both been fully briefed. It had been proposed as early as November 1940 that signals intelligence from the German Enigma transmissions should go directly to the Middle East, but because Whitehall did not wish to lose its monitoring role this did not occur until 13 March 1941. Thereafter, a new and limiting rule was applied to this new extension — that knowledge of sources was to be withheld even from the immediate recipients.[4] The recipients were informed that the source was 'completely reliable'[5] and cover stories were told of secret agents highly placed in German headquarters.

The special signal service to the Middle East was introduced only one month and seven days before German parachutists debouched on Maleme and its environs.[6] However, the growth in demand for Enigma-based intelligence stretched Bletchley Park's cryptanalysts to their limits.

Shortages of trained typists, fatigue, increased volume of intercepts, bureaucratic haggling over territory, and increased security intervention[7] imperilled the flow of intelligence to the battlefields.

Between 30 March and 26 April Ultra intercepts provided growing indications that German interest in Crete was increasing.[8] Wavell was still uncertain as to where the Germans would strike, and he hypothesized on 29 April that Crete might simply be a feint for serious German assaults on Cyprus or Syria. On 30 April the British chiefs of staff in London were still in two minds about the Crete information, and on 3 May Churchill himself was unsure whether Crete was a German cover plan, or not.[9]

Although Hitler did not approve operation 'Merkur' (Mercury) until 25 April 1941, the first indications of German airborne activity occurred on 25 March. Fliegerkorps XI collected Junkers Ju52 transports for glider-training, and ordered five or six *gruppen* of Ju52s to Poldiv. British military intelligence confirmed the arrival of 250 transport aircraft in the Balkans. On 13 March 'Detachment Süssmann' arrived at Poldiv. General Süssman was associated with Fliegerdivision Seven, the crack airborne formation of Fliegerkorps XI that had in 1940 carried out landings in Holland. British military intelligence warned that large-scale airborne operations were being prepared for somewhere in south-east Europe. There was no certainty, just speculation, that the targets could be the Greek Islands, Limnos, or Salonika. The possibility of air assaults on Syria and Iraq were also considered.[10]

From 26 April it became increasingly clear that the probable target was Crete. Intercepts revealed that Fliegerkorps XI was given priority on fuel supplies, and a reference was made to the importance of moving fuel supplies to Fliegerkorps XI's area by 5 May. At the same time, 26 April, German Railway Enigma revealed a large-scale movement from Germany to the Balkans, code-named 'Flying Dutchman'.[11] Parallel Enigma evidence showed this was the transfer of Fliegerdivison 7, scheduled to begin on 27 April. Moreover, Luftwaffe Enigma now referred specifically to Crete. Luftflotte IV referred to the choosing of airfields for operation 'Crete', and Fliegerkorps VIII asked for maps and photographs of Crete. Enigma, and augmenting intelligence, confirmed the air support function of Fliegerkorps VIII.[12]

With Bletchley Park and Cairo aware of a likely German airborne invasion of Crete, what clarity of information was passed to the commander of Creforce? The parameters of Freyberg's knowledge and assumptions on 1 May were communicated to the New Zealand Government:

> A German attack on Crete by simultaneous airborne and seaborne expeditions is believed to be imminent. The scale of airborne attack is estimated at 3,000–4,000 parachutists, or airborne troops, in the first

> sortie. Two or three sorties per day are possible from Greece and three to four from Rhodes if Rhodes is not used as a dive-bomber base. All the above with fighter escort. Heavy bombing attacks are to be expected immediately prior to the arrival of air and seaborne troops. The main fighter and dive-bombing support will probably be based on Rhodes. The following is our estimate based on the establishment of operational aircraft available in the Balkans for all purposes: 315 long range bombers, 60 twin-engine fighters, 240 dive-bombers and 270 single-engined fighters. The last two categories would require extra tanks if operated from the north of the Corinth canal. Only very small attacks can be expected from points south of this owing to the shortage of aerodromes in Morea, but some 60 to 90 dive-bombers and a similar number of single-engined fighters could operate from Rhodes, provided that the aerodromes in Rhodes are not required for other operations. It is estimated that both troops and shipping are ample for a seaborne operation and lighters for the transport of tanks are also believed to be available, hence the scale of seaborne attack is dependent on the extent to which the enemy can evade our naval forces. Reinforcements of enemy naval forces and shipping from Italy are possible, but would involve using the hazardous route round Cape Matapan if the Corinth canal is unusable.[13]

Freyberg's cable covered all the points of the intelligence communication, numbered JIC (41) 181 and entitled 'Scale of Attack on Crete', sent on 27 April from the Joint Intelligence Sub-committee of the Chiefs of Staff in London and used by Freyberg within four days of its arrival. The route from Whitehall to Crete, via the Middle East, was working well and with speed, although the general headquarters Middle East (GHQME) attempted to down play the size of the enemy force predicted by JIC (41) 181.[14]

Freyberg prepared for the worst. On 1 May 1941, the new commander of Creforce opened his day at 0900 hours with a conference of his officers. He outlined the new and serious situation he found himself in, commanding a rather more than corps-sized garrison, strung out over an island at points along a thin winding road. The commander of Creforce issued a Special Order of the Day to his garrison. In part it read:

> The threat of a landing is not a new one... We have in the last month learned a certain amount about the enemy air methods... We are to stand now and fight him back. Keep yourself fit and be ready for immediate action.[15]

Freyberg was already aware that the island's successful defence depended upon the denial of several vulnerable points to any invasion force. At all costs enemy forces must be destroyed wherever they threatened to secure a lodgement that would allow re-supply and reinforcement. In spite of being well informed as to the enemy's intentions, and faced with the manifest deficiencies of a dispersed garrison in three distant main areas, Freyberg was compelled by geography to leave the initiative to the Germans. Effective countermeasures designed to meet the tactics outlined in intercepted German plans made dispersion necessary. Command of the sea, his most effective bastion against the German army, lay with the Royal Navy and the Royal Air Force. Freyberg had no control of that battle and made his land dispositions as best as possible. The likely destruction of the seaborne invaders, given the intelligence available and the proximity of powerful surface units of the Mediterranean fleet, was tempered by an inexorable logic that a high cost in Royal Navy warships was inevitable. Naval intervention meant the exposure of naval units to air attack in the daylight hours. The navy could not intervene north of Crete (where the invasion convoys would be) and remain out of range of the Luftwaffe after daybreak. It was by no means certain than an utter débâcle at sea might not ensue. Freyberg realized that if the navy failed to intercept the enemy sea expedition, the chances of resisting simultaneous air and sea invasions were slim, particularly given the level of the evident air support freely available to the Germans.

The Creforce plans to meet the enemy involved two elements, mobility of reserves and fixed defence which might tend to work against each other. One essential ingredient was that the invaders must be counter-attacked immediately to prevent them securing an advantageous lodgement — an airfield or a port permitting re-supply. The other was that the vulnerable points useful to the enemy, the airfields and the main port, must be occupied and defended. This formula was dangerous in that it envisaged a basically static defence. To offset this the more or less static defenders were ordered to hold vital points against all comers and the laterally mobile forces were ordered to move to support selected defended localities should the need arise.

There must be an expectation of realizable assistance. To allow this the laterally mobile forces were instructed to reconnoitre routes to allow speedy help when static defenders called for assistance. Above all, emphasis was placed on low level initiative. Company, battalion, and brigade commanders must be prepared to make decisions that would bring about the destruction of the enemy's concentrations. In this way the initiative would be stolen from the land assault troops. Initially, the garrison must sit and wait, and respond to the German moves. But, as soon as possible, the airborne German forces would be compelled to respond to the garrison's dynamic defence. Cohesion among newly dropped paratroops and landed glider troops would at all times be prevented. While the garrison seemed to be at an initial disadvantage, the very dispersed and semi-random nature of airborne assault left the aerial invaders immediately, but only for a short period, physically vulnerable. This phase could not last long and every advantage must be wrung from it. After that, the invasion could be defeated by a consolidation of the static forces' defences and an increasing seeking out of the invaders by mobile forces. Destruction of the invaders near the airfields and the main ports was a *sine qua non* of the defence plan.

Even before Freyberg took command of Creforce, it is clear that the defence of the aerodromes was uppermost in the minds[16] of those at Creforce headquarters. Creforce Operation Order No. 2, issued on 29 April 1941, stated the intention to reinforce aerodrome defence at 'HERAKLION, RETIMO and MALEME'. At Maleme, soon to be the crux of Crete's defence, 5 NZ Infantry Brigade was to move two battalions to 'reinforce existing Battalion at Malene [*sic*] by 1600 tomorrow 30 April'. The 5 Brigade commander was to 'appoint a subordinate Officer to command troops MALENE [*sic*] AERODROME, reporting name to these H.Q.' — meaning Creforce headquarters.

Under item 6, 'DEFENCE OF AERODROMES', there is a note to refer to an instruction attached as Appendix A. Creforce Operation Order No. 2 is signed 'J. H. Willis, GS01 [general staff officer 1] CREFORCE'. The distribution of this order went to Freyberg and to garrison airfield defence units, but to only one New Zealand unit, 5 NZ Infantry Brigade.

Appendix A made clear that each static formation would be supported by a holding formation poised to intervene should the need arise.

> It is considered that the best method of defending an Aerodrome against air-borne attack is to combine perimeter defence with a mobile column.
>
> A suitable disposition is TWO battalions or similar proportion for perimeter defence, and a third battalion mobile.
>
> 2. The best location for the mobile battalion is such a distance outside the perimeter that they are comparatively immune from the preliminary air attacks on the Aerodrome and the perimeter. When these attacks are completed, the Commander of the Mobile column must use his judgement as to the best moment to move into attack.[17]

At Maleme on invasion day, 20 May, there was one airfield defence battalion with one and half battalions held back ready to support. The support battalions were the 23rd Battalion at near full strength, and a half strength 21st Battalion. A counter-attack plan to destroy an enemy lodgement threatening the airfield defence formation was provided for even in the early Creforce Operations Order, and it was noted in this plan that the commander of the supporting troops 'must use his judgement as to the best moment to move into the attack'.

According to the unit location sheet for the New Zealand Division for 1 May 1941,[18] the deployment of 5 NZ Infantry Brigade on Crete was as follows:

HQ 5 Inf Bde	PLATANIAS
21 Bn	1 mile west of PLATANIAS
22 Bn	MALENE [*sic*] Aerodrome
23 Bn	PLATANIAS
28 Bn	2 miles south of PLATANIAS

The location sheet for 2 May remained the same. The position of three out of four infantry battalions at or around Platanias, several miles from Maleme airfield, was unsatisfactory. In the event of an attack, no effective help could come quickly to the 22nd Battalion's aid. This arrangement flew in the face of Creforce Operation Order No. 2 with its concern for aerodrome defence. It has already been noted that 5 Brigade was the only New Zealand formation on the distribution list, receiving Copy No. 2. Despite this the Brigade did not carry out the order.

This omission on Brigadier Hargest's part is less serious only because the Germans did not attack then and there. Creforce Operation Order No. 2 was superseded on 3 May by Creforce Operation Instruction No. 10, which became essentially the basis of Freyberg's plans for the island's defence. Hargest's failure was later rectified by intervention by the General himself, to re-deploy the infantry battalions of 5 Brigade.

The order at the heart of Freyberg's plan for ground force defence of the island reflected the most precise intelligence and read:

Creforce Operation Instruction No. 10 *SECRET*
Copy No. 21
3rd May 1941

APPRECIATION

1. Enemy airborne attack on CRETE can be expected at any time. It will probably take the following forms:-
   (a) Intensive bombing and M.G. [machine-gun] attack on aerodromes and vicinity.
   (b) Landing by parachutists to clear obstacles and seize aerodromes.
   (c) Landing by troops in tp [troop] carrying aircraft. It is possible, although unlikely that landings may be made at places other than aerodromes.
2. Seaborne attack must also be expected. This will probably be attempted on beaches close to aerodromes and/or to SUDA BAY.
3. With the forces at our disposal, it is not possible to oppose the enemy at every place where he might land. The scheme of defence will therefore be based on defending the three aerodromes, HERAKLION, RETIMO and MALEME, and the area SUDA BAY, with a centrally placed Force reserve ready to move in any direction.

INTENTION

4. CRETE will be denied to the enemy.

5. *HERAKLION Sector*

Comd [commander] Brig [Brigadier] Chappel
Tps [troops] 14 Inf bde [Infantry Brigade] less 1 Welch
7 Med Regt RA (rifles)
2/4 Aust Bn [Australian Battalion]
156 Lt AA Bty [Light Anti-Aircraft Battery] less two tps (in support)
One tp and one sec 7 Aust Lt AA Bty (in support)
One sec B Bty 15 Coast Regt (in support)
Two Greek Bns

6. *RETIMO Sector*

Comd Brig Vasey
Tps 19 Aust Bde HQ
2/1 Aust Bn
2/7 Aust Bn
2/11 Aust Bn
1 Aust MG Coy [Australian Machine-Gun Company]
Two Greek Bns

Left boundary all incl: ARMYRO (Georgeoupolis, B 3340) — ASKIFOU, (B 2362).

7. *SUDA BAY Sector*

Comd Maj-Gen Weston
Tps MNDBO
1 Welch
NH
2/8 Aus Bn [2 rifle companies only]
151 Hy AA Bty
234 Hy AA Bty
129 Lt AA Bty
7 Aust Lt AA Bty, less two tps and one sec.
304 S/L Bty
15 Coast Regt, less one sec Base Sub Area
1 Greek Bn.

8. *MALEME Sector*

Comd Brig Puttick
Tps NZ Div
4 NZ Bde
5 NZ Bde
Oakes Force
Two tps 156 Lt AA Bty (in support)
One tp 7 Aust Lt AA Bty (in support)

Three Greek Bns.

9. *Force Reserve*
 1 Welch in SUDA BAY sector and 4 NZ Bde less one bn in MALEME sector are in Force Reserve. They will be administered by respective Sector Comds, but will be kept concentrated and ready to move at short notice on orders from Force HQ. Comd 1 Welch will be in close touch with Comd 4 NZ Bde.
10. *Policy of Defence*
 Sector Comds will organise their sectors so that of the troops allotted to the defence of aerodromes, one third is disposed on or around the landing ground, and two thirds are kept at such a distance that they will be outside the area which will be attacked in the first instance.
11. Possible landing areas other than aerodromes will also be protected in similar manner on a smaller scale.
12. In addition, possible sea landing places will be watched, and if resources permit held by troops.
13. It is important that each sector should have a sector reserve.

A.A. DEFENCE

14. Concealment is of paramount importance. All tps whether in reserve or in forward positions must be well dug in. During air attack, *both weapons* and men must be under cover.
15. Tps in concealed areas will NOT open small arms fire on aircraft unless they have been located and are attacked by aircraft, or the aircraft is about to land.
16. Major General Weston will co-ordinate all A.A. arty on the island.

STATE OF READINESS

17. Attention is directed to CREFORCE Operation Instruction No. 4. Irrespective of the degree of readiness in force, all tps will "stand to" at dawn and dusk.

R.E. STORES

18. R.E. Stores are allotted as follows:-

Sector	Wire (coils)	Pickets Short	Long	Shovels
HERAKLION Sector	1000	1200	1000	75
RETIMO Sector	1000	1500	1000	90
SUDA BAY Sector	700	900	700	60
MALEME Sector	2800	3000	2800	200

Sectors will draw direct from R.E. Stores, 42 Street, road SUDA-CANEA, as required.

19. *ADMINISTRATION*
 Issued Separately

INTERCOMMUNICATION

20. In future all correspondence, orders, etc., will be addressed to Sector Comds and NOT to units of formations.[19]

The role for Greek troops in this defence plan was set out in an addition to Creforce Operation Instruction No. 10 the following day. Section 13 of the instruction directed that each sector should hold a reserve. The Greeks were to fill this role and were intended for beach defence. British officers were attached to Greek battalions as advisers and were instructed to initiate intensive training.[20]

The promise of Creforce Operation Instruction No. 10 was that as Creforce was not of sufficient strength 'to oppose the enemy at every place where he might land', Creforce would be deployed to defend the main airfields and the port of Suda Bay. The operational objective of German seaborne forces would most likely be the aerodromes and the port, thus beaches close by were likely landing places. When account is taken of the amendments made to allocate Greek troops to man invasion beaches in the event of an attack, plus the assumption that the operational objective of German seaborne and airborne forces were the same, it is obvious that the General regarded the airborne threat as the greater. The Greeks needed training — it is inconceivable that Freyberg would have suggested a beach defence role had he thought a seaborne landing would be the main attack. Moreover, he had decided his priorities already: the Navy was to deal with an amphibious landing by destroying the invasion convoys *en route*. Provided the Navy could remove the sea threat, the airborne attack would be dealt with by the garrison.

The overall object of the German assault would be to secure a lodgement for reinforcement and re-supply — an aerodrome or a port. If this was denied, the island could be held. To deal with the possibility that the enemy might concentrate on one promising area, Freyberg created a brigade group of trained infantry battalions (the 18th and 19th Battalions of 4 Brigade and the 1st Welch Battalion). As Force Reserve, this was a centrally located brigade group, 'kept concentrated and ready to move at short notice on orders from Force HQ'.[21] Although the armoured support available at the time of the actual invasion had not yet arrived, their later deployment reflected the General's intention. Ten light tanks were placed with Force Reserve. While pairs of heavy British Matilda Infantry support ('I') tanks were placed near the airfields, for close armoured support, six other light tanks were sent to Heraklion. While Heraklion was too far away for a centrally located reserve to reach it easily if the need arose, Freyberg ensured that enough resources were deployed there to meet any likely eventuality. The implication was that the Force Reserve was intended for use in the Maleme or Retimo areas of the island, while being held close to Suda and Canea.

There is no doubt that Freyberg saw the demand of airstrip defence as urgent and crucial. The *War Diary* of the 2nd NZ Division notes that on 3 May the: 'G.O.C. Crete [General Officer Commanding, Freyberg] visited these HQ. Dispositions of 5 Inf Bde altered in order to place more tps near MALEME aerodrome.'[22] Here was the commander of Creforce himself intervening in the deployment of infantry battalions in the 5 Brigade area. Hargest had not carried out the earlier order — Creforce Operation Order No. 2. Freyberg now made sure that adequate support would be available to 22nd Battalion, the formation defending Maleme aerodrome. To this end the 23rd and 21st Battalions were moved to take up positions near to the airfield, while the 28th Maori Battalion stayed at Platanias. The General made sure that at Maleme his defence plan, for a third of the defending troops to be located about the airfield, and two-thirds in reserve but close at hand, was carried out.

Freyberg went to the Maleme sector on 4 May, the day that Creforce Operation Instruction No. 10 came into force: 'Message recd [received] from PM NZ [Prime Minister of New Zealand] and sent to troops — say and addressed 28 Bn, 21 Bn, 22 Bn, 23 Bn — RE [Royal Engineers], A/Tk [anti-tank], 7th Fd Coy [Field Company], 5 Fd Regt.'[23] He visited the units involved in the airfield's defence. Most important were the infantry battalions that would bear the brunt of the assault: the 22nd, the 23rd, the 21st grouped around the aerodrome, and the Maori Battalion at 5 Brigade headquarters at Platanias. When Freyberg spoke to the officers and non-commissioned officers (NCOs) of the 22nd Battalion on 4 May:

> He spoke in terms of praise of the work we had done and outlined our probable future. He warned us that we would have to withstand and counter intensive aerial recce, strafing and bombing of areas known or likely to be occupied by troops follow[ed] by attack from parachute and glider troops and later from surface craft and troop carrying planes.[24]

It was a timely warning. To 'withstand and counter intensive aerial reece' meant remaining concealed from the Luftwaffe's reconnaissance aircraft for a very obvious reason: an airdrop on to well-hidden infantry might result in the annihilation of the paratroops before they had time to concentrate and be effective.

From the General's Creforce headquarters, located in the Suda Bay sector, above Canea, Freyberg had travelled to and inspected preparations in all three airfield localities and the main port area by the end of 4 May. On Monday 5 May, the General cabled Wavell on the state of the Greek troops on the island, and also Churchill to reassure him that the garrison could cope with an airborne assault, but warned there were still doubts about stopping a combined air–sea attack.[25] To Wavell he signalled:

> There are some 10,000 other ranks here without arms and with little or no employment other than getting into trouble with the civil population. Can these men be evacuated as soon as possible? Between the Greeks and ourselves an excellent relationship exists, but it will be imperilled unless we can quickly get rid of our surplus personnel.
>
> By Royal proclamation of the King of Greece what remains of the Greek Army are now placed under my command. Sooner or later the question of feeding, clothing, and equipment will become a problem that must be considered. Am I right to take over the remnants of the Greek Army and re-form them...
>
> Meanwhile, I am proceeding with the job of reorganisation. I have asked the [Greek] Prime Minister to pick a young Commander and work through him. I am going to pick a small staff of officers to administer the eight battalions that exist. I intend putting in Brigadier Salisbury-Jones and a number of British officers to help them with their training. What I am doing is, I know, very irregular... I would now be glad if guidance can be given me before I embark upon a full-scale policy. Can I also be told what arms can be spared and when I can expect them for the eight existing Greek battalions?[26]

Also on 5 May, Freyberg replied to an enquiry from the British Prime Minister:

> Many thanks for your cable. Cannot understand nervousness. I am not in the least anxious about an airborne attack. I have made my dispositions and feel that with the troops now at my disposal I can cope adequately. However, a combination of seaborne and airborne attack is different. If that comes before I can get the guns and transport here the situation will be difficult. Even so, provided the Navy can help, I trust that all will be well.
>
> When we get our equipment and transport, and with a few extra fighter aircraft, it should be possible to hold Crete. Meanwhile, there will be a period here during which we shall be vulnerable...[27]

By the close of 5 May, Freyberg had consulted with all the senior officers of the major British, Australian, New Zealand, and Greek formations on the island, and promulgated a role for each of the nationalities in the island's defence.

What of German preparations? Enigma summaries of 4 and 5 May revealed that reconnaissance of ports and airfields on Crete was a Luftwaffe priority, and that Fliegerkorps VIII did not plan moving from Poldiv to Athens till 8 May.[28] This last intercept provided a vital clue — that the attack would be later than 8 May. The identification of reconnaissance targets confirmed the enemy's objectives.

British intelligence historians affirm that on 6 May Enigma traffic revealed the completion date of their preparations along with complete operational orders for the attack. This communication is cited with the BONIFACE identification code CX/JQ 911.[29] However, there are grounds for holding that this was not the date on which Freyberg received this vital information. Enigma summary texts were identified by 'Orange Leonard' (OL) designations, and an OL text, identical in content, is dated 13 May 1941 and was sent at 1745 hours GMT. Messages sent from Bletchley Park experienced a certain delay before being sent to Middle East commands. Besides, the actual opening of the OL text states that a communication 'has been sent to Major General Freyberg', perhaps implying a pre-13 May dispatch. As the letter/numeral buried within the 13 May text is 'Orange Leonard three nought two' — a device used apparently in some other texts to number them — and that letter/numeral 'fits' in with the dates and letter/numerals of other OL texts, then it is implied that OL302 is dated 13 May. The suspected OL302 of 13/5/41[30] lies between OL278 of 11/5/41[31] and OL319 of 14/5/41.[32] All this merely identifies OL302 of 13/5/41 as identical in content to CX/JQ911. We have no way of knowing if the version that General Freyberg apparently received was on this later date, or sometime earlier: say, for instance, when a senior officer from General Headquarters Middle East was sent to the General to underline the authoritative nature of the intelligence being received from what may have been put to the General as 'an agent in Athens'.

This points to the dilemma: the possibility that CX/JQ911 did not get to the commander of the garrison on Crete until 13 May, seven days after having been manufactured as a summary of operational orders from the broken original cipher text of the Luftwaffe radio traffic.

The likelihood of a seven days' delay is simply an unlikely 'worst case' possibility. If the visiting senior officer from General Headquarters Middle East had the text of the summary with him, this would date the version that Freyberg received as 11 May: the date this officer visited Crete being recorded in the General's diary. It is unlikely that the information was received by Freyberg on 6 May, though a day or two later could easily be the date. This is speculation. What is really of consequence is not the identification of the day the intelligence was received, but that Freyberg did actually appraise the information before the date the Germans completed their preparations. There can be no doubt over that: the text of 13 May would not otherwise have referred to the fact that the intelligence had been sent to the General. For convenience, then, it is to be assumed that OL302 is CX/JQ911 and that the date of dispatch was 13 May, although what the General received may have been obtained some two days earlier.

There was no doubt that invasion was imminent. Given the urgency of every defensive preparation and the intelligence feast at Freyberg's disposal, were Freyberg's appreciations and orders unambiguously filtered down to lower commands?

In 23rd Battalion Operation Instruction No. 3, dated 5 May 1941, the 23rd and 21st Battalions were ordered to prepare for a support role to the airfield defence battalion, 22nd Battalion:

> (4) 23 Bn in its present area and 21 Bn immediately to the SOUTH are disposed in concealment and are primarily available in a counter-attacking role to go to the assistance of 22Bn at AERODROME if the need arise [*sic*]... [then details position of Battalion companies and platoons]
>
> (8) 23 Bn will maintain its present position under cover and will be prepared to counter-attack the enemy if he effects a landing on the beach or at MALEME AERODROME. Officer [*sic*] and N.C.O.s will recce cross country covered approaches to the AERODROME forthwith. Coy Commanders will be prepared to carry out a practice move forwards at an early date WHEN ORDERED.[33]

The reconnaissance of the terrain was underlined in a supplementary order that followed the next day:

> SECRET
> 23 (Cant. Otago Bn)
> 6 May '41
>
> *Ref. Operation Instruction No. 3 Dated 5 May 1941*
> The following... are issued in amplification...
>
> 2(d) ... Depending on the situation the coys may be requested to counter attack the enemy either on the aerodrome, on the beach, or on the foothills. The requisite recce, to enable efficient performance of any of these tasks will be carried out forthwith.[34]

This laid out a mobile role for the infantry companies of 23rd Battalion, not simply static defence of their particular position based on Dhaskaliana village. To effect this order one would expect all company commanders and platoon officers to take part in reconnaissance at least in staggered groups on different days. Indeed, without the carrying out of such a reconnaissance 'forthwith', it is difficult to see how the reinforcement procedure in 23rd Battalion Operation Instruction No. 3 could be implemented. No officer-familiarization with the ground occurred, and the reconnaissance was in such a truncated form as to be effectively useless. On 15 May, the *War Dairy* records that:

> 2/i/c and I.O. [intelligence officer] reconnoitre routes to TAVRONITIS

> R. [River] and ridge west of it and 22 BN position, in preparation for 23 Bn's possible c. [counter] attack role in this direction.[35]

Only two officers reconnoitred the ground. Unless the Battalion's second-in-command, Major Fyfe, and the intelligence officer 2nd-Lieutenant Dan Davin (the future New Zealand official historian of Crete) were ordered to command troops moving forward to support the airfield battalion, there would be no officer who knew the way in detail. Should that take place after dark, to give immunity from air attack, sound knowledge of the ground over which the supporting troops must move would be vital. In the event, the darkness on the nights of the campaign turned out to be dark indeed — a new moon period.[36] To move effectively with some stealth in darkness towards an area, where to take a wrong direction might lead into the enemy, demanded prior reconnaissance and familiarity with the terrain. The practice move, outlined in 23rd Battalion's Operation Instruction No. 3 of 5 May 1941, clearly had not been undertaken. Was it to be this glaring omission that later confused the company sent to Colonel Andrew on 20 May so that they took over-long to cover perhaps a mile and three-quarters of unmined ground under cover of darkness? And had the company commander, Captain Carl Watson, been that way before, even in daylight?

On 7 May Freyberg expressed surprised optimism in replying to Wavell's offer to reinforce Crete with the British 16 Infantry Brigade. His priority was equipment, not troops.

> First. Agree not desirable at this juncture to attempt to land 16th Inf. Bde and broadly speaking do not require additional personnel of any arm as a first priority. Prefer concentrate on landing essential equipment and stores. Second. Agree infantry tanks with crews and light tanks valuable also carriers. Third. Ample artillery personnel available also sights and directors without stands. 25pr [pounder] ammunition could be unloaded... if guns available. Otherwise hasten despatch of 75mm guns. Tractors and artillery signal equipment will also be needed. Fourth. Other weapons required. Vickers guns and belts complete at least 24. Tripods for existing guns 30. Bren guns with magazines all possible to meet existing shortage of 300 and magazines for existing 300 guns. Rifles and bayonets 5,000 for British plus 500 for Greeks...[37]

Freyberg's priorities were apposite: armoured fighting vehicles; 25 pounder or 75mm guns plus sights and towing vehicles; heavy and light machine-guns; ammunition; and rifles. This ordinance would patch some of the holes in the garrison's equipment.

On 6 or 7 May Freyberg tied up the loose ends of his preparations to meet the projected attack. For the troops in the New Zealand Division he ordered:

Training Directive
for 5 Bde
Russell Force
Oakes Force
20 Bn.

1. Each unit to have training prog. submit 1 wk at time.
2. Drill — quality not quantity.
3. Subjects
   P & RT [physical and recreational training]
   Route marching
   Fire orders
   Fire discipline training
   Training in all Infantry weapon partic. practice of concealment & protection from the air.
   Unit & formation Sig. [signal] exercises, partic. with improvised visual means of signalling.
   Movement by night
   Pl Coy & Bn in the attack
   Pl Coy & Bn in the occupn. [occupation] of a defensive posn. [position]
4. Exercises will be held in areas where units are likely to be employed against air and airborne attack e.g. advances will probably have to be made across country in small colns [columns] rather than on rds [roads]; sections in the attack will have to move in very extended order rather than colns. Concealment from the air will be practised at all time.

Field
7 May 41
Copy to NZE
4 Inf Bde

Lt. Col.
General Staff
New Zealand Div.

The 23rd Battalion did not follow this directive with much energy. Even the runners were restricted when they sought to familiarize themselves with the terrain over which they would be expected to move in the likely event of line communications being disrupted by enemy assault:

Walter Gibbons, a runner in 23rd Battalion, later recalled:

> Our training at Maleme was platoon parades, route marches and desultory digging. . . We had no signalling equipment and messages of necessity were carried by runner. It is easy to be wise afterwards, but as runners we had too little knowledge of the area we were to serve. What was regarded as finding our way round was regarded in quite other lights by our officers. Consequently we learned the hard way. . . Two signalmen were posted to B. coy. H.Q.: Martin Svenson and me.

> B. Coy H.Q. was under a large and spreading fig tree and at the junction of tracks flanked by low stone fences. To our front the land sloped away gently, and to the front right there was a field of barley already about 12-15 [feet?] high. All around were scattered olive trees, as was usual on the whole north coast. (9231) Captain J.B. Gray was OC of B Coy. My first task was to carry messages for him, to and from battalion headquarters, and to the various NCOs and men under his command.[39]

The training syllabus for 23rd Battalion for the week before the attack, 12 to 18 May, gave the Monday, Wednesday, and Friday afternoons over to swimming, while Saturday and Sunday were to be generally free.[40] In the 22nd Battalion, training appears to have been more intensive,[41] presumably because the battalion realized it was the linchpin of the island's defence.

On 8 May, Freyberg held conferences and then reported to the New Zealand Minister of Defence on the last part of the mainland campaign, when what was left of the New Zealand Division in Greece — 6th Infantry Brigade and Divisional Headquarters — was south of the Corinth Canal. In this report he outlined the final confusion of the end of the mainland adventure. At 7 p.m. Freyberg met with Greek and British officers at headquarters.[42] In the meantime, the German preparations continued to be revealed in their unwittingly indiscreet signals' traffic. At 2105 hours on 8 May, Enigma, in the form of OL 258, disclosed orders for aerial reconnaissance of Kastelli and a requirement for oblique photographs of the area south and south-west of Canea for Fliegerkorps XI (the airborne ground forces).[43] On 10 May, German Enigma traffic revealed, in OL262, that the arrival of air transport units under Fliegerkorps XI was expected in the Athens area from the 14 May, including three Staffel of glider-towing Junkers Ju52s. It was also noted that this was within the time-scale in readiness for an attack by 17 May.[44]

For the Germans, the schedule was tightening. They were only allowing three days to have all their transport aircraft in the region of embarkation before preparations were to be complete. Like Freyberg, they were up against a timetable which was closing in on their projected assault date. As events would show, their haste would be curbed by a fundamental obstacle — aviation fuel supplies. Yet their problems were of their own making: for the Germans the timing of the attack was their choice. Any pressure on that was a matter of more remote expansionist predelictions, in particular operation 'Barbarossa' — Hitler's directive for the invasion of Russia.

Freyberg had exactly the opposite problem to the Germans. His preparations were of necessity restrained by his intelligence of German intentions and any known projected assault date. Unlike the enemy he was short of equipment, and so was the source of that equipment — Middle East Command. His supply route was vulnerable in daylight to enemy interdiction; he was engaged in an uphill struggle.

While the Germans' problems were those of their own making and their own time-scale, Freyberg's problems were from the start inherited and efforts to overcome them were lengthened by an increasing foreknowledge of the size and timing of enemy initiatives. The Creforce commander's task was to bring the enemy's initiatives to nought — this could only be done by an immediate response to a lodgement. Total destruction of the opposition ground forces must take second place to the immediate elimination of that fraction of the German forces committed to winning a landing ground.

From 11 May, the pace quickened, Freyberg racing the Germans, the Germans racing themselves. On 11 May Freyberg promulgated detailed orders for Force Reserve, the brigade group designated in Creforce Operation Instruction No. 10 of 3 May. In a new Creforce Operation Instruction No. 11, a brigade group known as the Composite Brigade, centred on the experienced 20th Battalion, would be formed to bring the New Zealand infantry strength in the Maleme Sector up to two brigades, to allow the brigade group designated as Force Reserve more flexibility of employment. This flexible role for Force Reserve, including local defence around Canea and Suda, and intervention elsewhere, was spelt out in further orders on 15 May.[45]

The 11 May order read:

Creforce Operation Instruction No. 11

SECRET
Copy No. 22
11th May 1941

INTENTION

1. It is intended to enclose SUDA BAY AREA in a defensive perimeter, and to locate within this perimeter a mobile reserve of one bde gp.

METHOD

2. *Force Res.* Comd — 4 NZ Inf Bde
Tps — 4 NZ Inf Bde (less 20 NZ Bn)
1 WELCH (temp under comd Force HQ)
1 Lt Tp RA (four 3.7 hows [howitzers] mobile)
Tp Carrying Tpt. — M.T. [military transport] for lifting marching personnel is being provided.
Location — To be notified later.

3. *Composite Bde* — In order to free 4 NZ Inf Bde, NZ Div will form Composite Allied Bde as under:
Comd to be selected by NZ Div
Tps. — Bde Bde [*sic*] HQ (to be formed by NZ Div)
20 NZ Inf Bn
One Composite Bn, to be formed from NZ details

One Greek Inf.

Role Occupation of a defensive posn facing WEST on a general North and South line through GALATOS and will be responsible for defence of coast to excl CANEA. Posn to be dug and wired...

6. *Mine Policy* Preliminary Allotment:

Sector	A.Tk Mines	Mines Shrapnel	Detonators, Mines Shrapnel
HERAKLION	450	1000	2000
RETIMO	450	1800	2000
SUDA BAY	200	900	1000
MALEME	400	1500	1700

A.Tk [anti-tank] Mines adapted for use on aerodromes are being made. Sectors will apply for numbers required. Before mines are laid anywhere else than on beaches, approval of Force H.Q. will first be obtained. Accurate details of all minefields will be recorded and reported to Force H.Q. All minefields will be guarded continuously.[46]

The switch of the 20th Battalion to form the heart of the Composite Brigade, and the transfer of 1st Welch to 4 Brigade may seem unnecessarily complicated. The alternatives were less than satisfactory. Without the 20th Battalion, the Composite Brigade would have no solid core of trained infantry. Had 1st Welch been placed in the new formation this would have created immediate difficulties. The most experienced officers in the Composite Brigade would then have been British, and they could be expected to receive the command appointments in the new brigade. Besides, 1st Welch would then no longer be located in the Canea–Suda area. Instead, one of 4 Brigade's New Zealand infantry battalions would have to do the job. This would not be impossible, but it would mean that if 20th Battalion was used in this role it might have come under the immediate control of new commanders for the stated extra purpose of local defence. As the commander of the Composite Brigade was the former commanding officer of the 20th Battalion, Colonel Howard Kippenberger, it made more sense to make the improvised brigade's core the 20th. The new brigade's officers could then be drawn from personnel who knew each other and each others' capabilities. There would be enough problems turning the improvised infantry into fighting soldiers of some basic effectiveness without officer appointment changes as well.

Broadly speaking, Creforce Operation Instruction No. 11 refined the basic premises of Creforce Operation Instruction No. 10 of 3 May. The local protection of the port was provided for, the use of 4 Brigade as a mobile reserve was developed, and the establishment of an improvised infantry brigade group to plug the gap in the Maleme sector left by the removal of 4 Brigade was strenthened by the inclusion of an experienced battalion as its core. The choice of Colonel Kippenberger as a temporary brigade commander was fortunate, not merely in terms of compatibility with 20th Battalion, but also because the new brigade commander would prove himself the most talented senior New Zealand brigadier in the Mediterranean theatre.

The use of mines was associated in the 11 May order, and local commanders were given discretion over the mining of beaches. Some 1,500 shrapnel mines and 400 anti-tank mines were allotted to the Maleme sector and it is suprising that none appear to have been used on the beach areas near the airfield. The presence of mines could have prevented the landing of transport aircraft in dead ground. A more extensive use of mines was undesirable because the local Cretan population were scattered throughout the island, and minefields would be a danger to them.

On 11 May the Creforce commander engaged in two roles: as general officer commanding 2 NZEF; and as Creforce commander. The General now sent a response to Prime Minister Fraser, on the proposal that Freyberg command an ANZAC Corps in the future. This would be the junction of 6 Australian Division and 2 New Zealand Division as an ANZAC Corps, with Freyberg as commander.

> I have to thank you for your message of 9 May. While fully appreciating the honour of commanding the ANZAC Corps and while realising that the association of Anzac has much to recommend it from an operational point of view, I would personally prefer to stay with the New Zealand Division. However, if the New Zealand and Commonwealth Governments so desire, I am prepared to accept the appointment provided that I can remain a servant of the New Zealand Government by continuing to be GOC 2nd NZEF, and provided the New Zealand Division remains part of the Corps I command. It may be possible for me to fly to Egypt and back in a day so that I could discuss this and other matters with the Prime Minister personally. Meanwhile, in accordance with the British Government's request, I must of course remain here with our two New Zealand brigades until we are relieved or until the danger to Crete is past. Our troops are in good form.[47]

The offer of the command of a corps was not an easy matter for Freyberg to accept. He preferred to retain command of the New Zealand Division, and he was apprehensive that he might be slotted into a permanent position as a corps commander. For one thing, as an ANZAC Corps commander on a New Zealand Army appointment, the General would not only have to be concerned with troops of two different countries, but with dealings with three governments — the British, the New Zealand,

and the Australian. As two of those would continually need to be informed of the commitment of the corps to various operations, it could become difficult if there was any disagreement over a task given the corps. Moreover, there was the small matter that the commander of the Australian 6 Division would in any case be free, unless his government deemed otherwise, to go beyond Freyberg to his government if he disagreed with him. There is no reason to believe that such considerations could not be sorted out. But it is important to note that the General viewed the prospect of commanding an ANZAC Corps with something less than unbounded enthusiasm. Freyberg also sent a cable to Egypt requesting a senior New Zealand officer to command the 4 New Zealand Brigade, or Force Reserve. The commander sent was Brigadier Lindsay Inglis.

At 1000 hours on 11 May, Freyberg spoke to Major Thompson and Brigadier Salisbury-Jones, presumably about the Greek troops: Salisbury-Jones was involved in the training programme for Greek formations. An hour later he saw General Scoutas, General Kapatius, and Colonel Ceravtis of the Greek Army, along with the Creforce staff.[48] As a result of this conference Freyberg cabled General Smith at general headquarters, Cairo, on a number of proposals regarding the size and organization of the Greek forces on Crete:

> . . . I put forward the following proposals which were agreed to in principle:
>
> Firstly, that the Greek Army should be organised on British war establishments.
>
> Secondly, that Greek troops should be brigaded with British troops and that Greek commanders should serve directly under the command of British brigadiers and staffs, and that the British commander in Crete should have the right to draft Greek soldiers into technical units, such as British artillery, engineers, medical, and other services, with a view to forming Greek technical units eventually. I also suggested that the British Commander-in-Chief should also have the right to send Greek officers and NCOs to Egypt for instruction.
>
> Thirdly, I suggested that in questions of procedure and detail of drill and training, &c., Greek practices should as far as possible apply. . .
>
> Fourthly, that the Greek Army should be under Greek Army Headquarters for discipline. . .
>
> I have worked out that in all we shall require twelve Greek battalions and three Greek field batteries, and I consider that we should go ahead and raise these as soon as it is possible to arm and equip them. . . I send you this information because it is necessary to start reorganisation at once. I am moving certain Greek battalions to dig defensive positions and have allotted them minor operational roles. These men are as yet mostly untrained, but I think the material will be good.[49]

The reference to minor operational roles included the use of Greek troops for beach defence and further confirms Freyberg's attitude to the seaborne option: it would have to be dealt with by the Navy. Creforce would concentrate its efforts on the airborne attack.

Also on 11 May a senior liaison officer arrived from Wavell. This officer may have been Brigadier Alexander Galloway. Freyberg called a conference, and present were the General, the Air Officer Commanding (AOC) Crete, the Senior Naval Officer (SNO), Crete, and the visitor.[50] The importance of the visit had less to do with the meeting, than with bringing Creforce up to date with the Cairo perspective. It is probable that the visit had to do with Enigma material being received by Freyberg from the Combined Bureau, Middle East — the radio clearing house for the Bletchley Park summaries.

On the previous day, 10 May, Churchill had sent a Personal Minute to the Chief of the Imperial General Staff, the First Sea Lord, and the Chief of Air Staff — Dill, Pound, and Portal — about Crete. It was full of optimistic interference. Anxious that the aerodromes should not fall easily into enemy hands, the Prime Minister suggested that when landings from the air began, tanks and special assault parties concealed near by should attack the enemy and destroy them. (In principle, this is not too different from what the commander of Creforce had planned: if the enemy attempted to secure a lodgement, they were to be immediately counter-attacked from concealed positions.) Regarding signals' intercepts, Churchill suggested:

> ... it would be well to send a special officer by air to see General Freyberg and show him personally the actual texts of all the messages bearing upon this subject. These messages could then be destroyed by fire.[51]

Disarmingly, the Prime Minister argued that the officer bearing the documents would answer for their destruction in the event of engine failure, and nobody was to see the texts but the General. This of course constituted a tremendous risk. The individual Crete intercepts, or summaries, by themselves might not constitute an indication that the Luftwaffe's ciphers were compromised: but, if they were found collected together, there could be little doubt. Wavell sent his senior liaison officer to Freyberg the next day, 11 May. On 12 May, this message was sent to the Prime Minister:

> OFFICE OF THE MINISTER OF DEFENCE
> *MOST SECRET*
> *PRIME MINISTER*
> ... 2 The Commander-in-Chief has accepted these suggestions and

has sent a special officer by air to see General Freyberg (see telegram, Flag 'C').

12 May 1941[52] L. C. Hollis

What is not clear is whether the Prime Minister's request was carried out to the letter. Perhaps it is more likely that the authoritative nature of the messages was stressed, though the cover story — the agent in Athens — was retained. It seems on balance doubtful that any officer would take the collective sheaf of summaries to Crete (even less the raw intercepts — these would probably not be available in the Middle East in any case). If such a sheaf of intercept summaries was ever passed to Freyberg, then the impact of the information would most certainly be underlined. If the Enigma summaries were only seen individually — as they came — the General himself would need to be very alert to take full advantage of their growing, if sporadic, significance. This would be particularly so if he, and he alone, made sure such messages were destroyed once he had read them. Whether or not Freyberg identified the source remains only of peripheral interest: the use he made of Enigma-source information in the deployment of his forces to meet the enemy clearly demonstrated that he made good use of this intelligence.

On 11 May, Enigma revealed some highly valuable information. OL 268 at 1025 hours referred to orders for the speedy transport of fuel to Corinth, and it was noted that petrol was due at Patras that day. In the evening, OL 277 of 2130 hours mentioned supplies of heavy bombs (types named) for Fliegerkorps VIII airfields. At 2230 hours, OL 278 revealed that some 27,000 tons of shipping, twelve ships, were being assembled for the Crete attack including rations and munitions.[53]

In Crete, on 11 May, a conference of 5 Brigade unit commanders took place at Maleme Court House. Albeit unknown to the participants, the orders given at this conference were pivotal to the success or failure of Creforce defence of the island. Brigadier Hargest in a diary entry the night before introspected on the crisis ahead:

> ... I know that my death would be a calamity just now... I know I am trusted and I know that in a crisis my judgement is sound and my instincts right and that mostly I am without personal fear... in a senior job only judgement counts in a crisis...[54]

Hargest's crucial role in Crete's defence makes it pertinent to ask how the Brigadier came to command 5 Brigade in the Maleme sector on Crete. Initially on Crete, Freyberg had only two brigadiers, Puttick and Hargest. Inglis and Barraclough were back in Egypt. Puttick, the commander of 4 Brigade, was the natural choice for acting divisional commander when Freyberg was made commander of Creforce. Colonel Kippenberger, the emerging talent of the Division and commander of the 20th Battalion, was given the task of building the improvised Composite Brigade around his own experienced 20th Battalion. As Hargest had commanded 5 Brigade thus far, it was perhaps only natural that he should continue to do so, in the absence of surplus talented brigadiers. It was only in battle that Kippenberger's competence as a fighting brigade commander would be revealed. When Inglis was recalled, he took over 4 Brigade, which, minus the 20th Battalion, became Force Reserve with several roles in the western sector.

Verbal orders to all 5 Brigade units and sub-units were issued by Hargest at the conference at 1100 hours. The intent was 'to co-ordinate defences so that confusion would not result in the event of an attack'.[55] These orders were confirmed by written instructions given the following Sunday, 18 May. The key decisions were that:

a. 5 Inf Bde will maintain a defensive line running east and west from PLATANIAS to TAVRONITIS River with special regard to the defence of MALEME aerodrome.
b. In the event of the enemy making an airborne or seaborne attack on any part of the area, to counter-attack and destroy him immediately.
c. The whole essence of the bde's work is a spirited defence.[56]

The Brigade would 'defend its position at all costs',[57] and should the enemy attack any part of the Brigade area between Platanias and the Tavronitis River, the Brigade's units were to 'counter-attack and destroy him immediately'.[58]

In 5 Brigade Operation Instruction No. 4, 22nd Battalion had immediate defence of the airfield as its main task, and, to that end, its support and reserve companies were to be used for 'Immediate counter-attack under cover of mortars and M.G. [machine-gun] fire.'[59]

Hargest's orders appear to show an ignorance of the likely problems facing the airfield defence battalion. Three-fifths of Andrew's companies ('C', 'D', and Headquarter's Companies) defended the Tavronitis River flat, the airfield (and beach), and the coast road through Pirgos, respectively. Two companies ('A' and 'B') held the dominating physical feature — Kavzakia Hill (point 107). None of these companies could move from those positions without vacating them. To move platoons or sections would weaken the area the platoon or section came from. Mutual support could be provided only by fire from adjacent troops and be effective only if they were not otherwise engaged (by enemy ground troops, or by air attack).

It could be argued that the premise behind the orders for 22nd Battalion relied on two possibilities, both of which obviated to some extent the above objections. The first possibility was that not all the battalion would be engaged at any one time. The response here is that the known plan of attack made such a fortuitous eventuality unlikely — and on the day this was borne out (even later on the first day Andrew was reluctant to take 'A' and 'B' Companies forward and risk losing the hill). The second possibility was that in any case another battalion, (21st or 23rd or 28th Battalion) would come to the 22nd's aid.

The orders continued that 22nd Battalion could expect that: 'If necessary, support will be called for from 23 Bn. and should telephonic means of comn fail here the call will be by "verey" signal [or Very, a light flash sequence] (WHITE-GREEN-WHITE).'[60] The orders of the 23rd Battalion were clear: '23 Bn. will maintain its present position and be prepared to counter-attack if enemy effects a landing (a) on the beach or at Maleme aerodrome, (b) on area occupied by Det N.Z.E. West of Platanias.'[61] The 23rd was to stand in a flexible readiness-to-attack posture. Either eventuality — an attack on the airfield or a landing among the Engineers' detachment — necessitated both a preparedness and a willingness to respond swiftly.

The 11 May Maleme Court House conference was not merely for the army units in the Maleme sector: Air Force and Naval units were represented as well. At least some of 5 Brigade's defensive plan must have been understood by the naval and air commanders. Yet, the co-operation the army received from RAF and Royal Navy units (including the Royal Marine gunners who had some Australian anti-aircraft troops under their operational command as well) was less than the situation demanded, and in part cut across the objects of the infantry battalions' operational plans. How far this affected the defence of the aerodrome will be seen in due course.

On Monday, 12 May, Freyberg received another cable from Wavell. The day opened at: '. . . 0900 hrs conference with SNO AOC and C-in-C [Crete] re co-operation during battle. LO Mid East took off to C-in-C [Wavell] our requirements.'[62]

Apart from the narrow issues of the conduct of counter-invasion ground operations, the meeting touched on the expected intervention of the Navy against seaborne forces, the level of support that could be expected from RAF resources, especially RAF capability to deal with concentrations of enemy aircraft gathering on the islands and mainland to the north. It was probable that Freyberg, by this stage, realized that tactical air support for the defenders would be slight. Wavell's liaison officer left with a priority 'shopping-list'. A letter to Wavell, carried back by the senior liaison officer, read in part:

> If they come as an airborne attack against our aerodromes, I feel sure we should be able to stop him if he attacks after the 16th. If however he makes a combined operation of it with a beach landing with tanks, then we shall not be in a strong position . . .[63]

An *Appreciation — German Plan For Attack on Crete* was issued on 12 May by the Creforce Brigadier General Staff (BGS). Labelled *'Most Secret'* and *'When Read, This Paper Will Be Destroyed By Fire',* this paper of at least forty-five copies firmly established that the airfields were the main enemy targets. The relevant portions read:

> 2. The first objective will most certainly be the three aerodromes, HERAKLION, RETIMO, and MALEME, the possession of which is an essential preliminary for the landing of troop carrying aircraft.
> 3. The second objective will be the seizure of SUDA BAY and HERAKLION ports to enable ships to land further troops and heavy equipment required for the complete occupation of the island.
> 4. . . .
>   (*g*) *D[day] 2.* Having seized and provisioned aerodromes, this day will be devoted to securing with the aid of further airborne troops, the ports of HERAKLION and SUDA BAY. Dive bombers will operate in close support of ground tps.
>   *D.3 and subsequently*
>   (h) Ships will commence to arrive on this day, and the complete occupation of the island will follow as quickly as possible.
> 5. From the above appreciation, it will be noted that the entire plan is based on the capture of the aerodromes. If the aerodromes hold out, as they will, the whole plan will fail. . .
> 7. It is to be further noted, that up to the present, the aerodromes have not been bombed, nor have the ports been mined. The obvious deduction is that the Germans hope to use both themselves in the near future.
> 8. Although this appreciation has not mentioned sea landings on beaches, the possibility of these attacks must not be overlooked; but they will be of secondary importance to those from the air.[64]

The airfields were of first importance: without them, the enemy attack would fail. The whole defence posture had been based on the principle of immediate counter-attack. Now the brigade commanders had the priorities of the defence underlined.

Further consultation with the RAF and Navy on Crete took place on Tuesday, 13 May, a week before the invasion became a reality. At this stage it is important to remember that the expected date of attack was 17 May. An extremely important Orange Leonard summary was transmitted on 13 May at 1745 hours GMT (Crete being about an hour in advance of Greenwich Mean Time). Because of its resemblance to the British summation of CX/JQ 911,[65] it is likely that this 13 May text is CX/JQ 911. Although the top of the available microfilm in DEFE 3/686 is unreadable, an OL number buried in the summary, OL 302, is probably the correct

OL numeral. (This number fits the date and numerical sequence of the other available OL texts — it goes between OL 278 of 11 May and OL 319 of 14 May.) To understand the significance of this summary of the orders for operation 'Mercury', we must first turn to the German situation. During the third week in May, Colonel von der Heydte, a battalion commander of the Storm Regiment of the Air Landing Division, was ordered to an 11 a.m. conference at the Grande Bretagne Hotel in Athens:

> One look at the hermetically-sealed and shuttered room in the Hotel Grande Bretagne, where the commanders of all the paratroop regiments and battalions were gathered to receive their orders, was sufficient to dispel the secret of our target; a large map of Crete was prominently displayed upon the wall.
>
> In a quiet but clear and slightly vibrant voice General Student explained the plan of attack. It was his own personal plan. He had devised it, had struggled hard against heavy opposition for its acceptance, and had worked out all the details. One could perceive that this plan had become a part of him, a part of his life. He believed in it . . .
>
> When the General had finished, the corps intelligence officer rose to speak. He sketched a broad picture of the enemy's situation. On the island were the remnants of two or three Greek divisions, much weakened by the battles of the mainland, and a British force of divisional strength consisting mainly of dominion troops under command of the well-known General Freyberg. A proportion of the population would be sympathetic towards a German attack . . .[66]

All the elaborate security measures surrounding the final German operational briefing were for nought. The radio intercept services, the cryptanalysts at Bletchley Park, the link to the Middle East, and the link to Crete ensured that Freyberg was cut-in on the distribution of the German orders. Here is the 13 May OL 302 summary which is probably CX/JQ 911:

> . . . communicated to you in this series has been sent to Major-General Freyberg.
>
> 1. The island of Crete will be captured by the 11th Air Corps and the 7th Air Division, and the operation will be under the control of the 11th Air Corps.
> 2. All preparations, including the assembly of transport aircraft, fighter aircraft, and dive bombing aircraft, as well as of troops to be carried both by air and sea transport, will be completed on 17th May.
> 3. Transport of seaborne troops will be in co-operation with Admiral South-East, who will ensure the protection of German and Italian

transport vessels (about 12 ships) by Italian light naval forces. These troops will come under the orders of the 11th Air corps immediately on their landing in Crete.

4. A sharp attack by bomber and (Director for all Orange Leonard 302) heavy fighter units to deal with the Allied air forces on the ground, as well as with their anti-aircraft defences and military camps, will precede the operation.
5. The following operations will be carried out as from Day 1:
   - i) The 7th Air Division will make a parachute landing and seize Maleme, Candia and Retimo.
   - ii) Dive bombers and fighters (about 100 aircraft of each type) will move by air to Maleme and Candia.
   - iii) Air landing of 11th Air Corps, including Corps Headquarters and elements of the army placed under its command, probably including the 22nd Division.
   - iv) Arrival of the seaborne contingent consisting of anti-aircraft batteries as well as of more troops and supplies.
6. In addition the 12th Army will allot 3 Mountain Regiments as instructed. Further elements consisting of motorcyclists, armoured units, anti-tank units will also be allotted...

[7.] Also as the result of air reconnaissance, the aerodrome of Kastelli south-east of Candia and the district west and south-west of Canea will be specially dealt with, in which case separate instructions will be included in detailed operation orders.

8. Transport aircraft, of which a sufficient number — about 600 — will be allotted for this operation, will be assembled on aerodromes in the Athens area. The first sortie will probably carry parachute troops only. Further sorties will be concerned with the transport of the air-landing contingent, equipment and supplies, and will probably include aircraft towing gliders.
9. With a view to providing fighter protection for the operations, the possibility of establishing a fighter base on Skarpanto will be examined.
10. The Quartermaster-General's Branch will ensure that adequate fuel supplies for the whole operation are available to the Athens area in good time, and an Italian tanker will be arriving at the Piraeus before May 17th. This tanker will probably also be available to transport fuel supplies to Crete. In assembling supplies and equipment for invading force it will be borne in mind that it will consist of some thirty to thirty-five thousand men, of which some 12,000 will be the parachute landing contingent, and 10,000 will be transported by sea. The strength of the long range bomber and heavy fighter force which will prepare the invasion by attacking before Day 1 will be of approximately 150 long range bombers and 100 heavy fighters.

11. Orders have been issued that Suda Bay is not to be mined, nor will Cretan aerodromes be destroyed, so as not to interfere with the operations intended.
12. Plottings prepared from air photographs of Crete on 1/10,000 scale will be issued to units participating in the operation.

1745 13/5/41 GMT[67]

With this communiqué it was scarcely possible for Freyberg to have a clearer picture of the enemy intentions. His previous commitment of units was well suited to repulse the enemy forces designated to target areas. His dispersed deployment of the island's garrison in the 3 May orders was confirmed in its wisdom, as the targets of the airborne forces were those very areas. The seaborne convoys would have to be dealt with by the Navy, and he had definitely downgraded this form of attack as secondary to the airborne threat.[68] It now remained for him to refine his measures. Armour and some extra infantry would need to be deployed before 17 May.

An interesting feature of the German orders was the subordination of command of all ground forces to Fliegerkorps XI, a Luftwaffe unit. For the first time in history the air force was to engage in a large-scale assault on an island, and take responsibility for the fortunes of the soliders it would disgorge. From this time on until 20 May, the Luftwaffe increased the level of its daylight bombing and strafing sorties to soften up the garrison before the main assault.

On 14 May, the Creforce commander yet again put the question of the departure of the King of Greece to the Foreign Office, but without success. Freyberg received a cable from Wavell, and was notified of the arrival in Cairo of the New Zealand Prime Minister, Peter Fraser.[69] Freyberg was now engaged in his final inspections of island defences, as the enemy was expected on 17 May. The question of placing troops in the unoccupied ground west of the 22nd Battalion's aerodrome defences arose. According to Geoffrey Cox:

> One point . . . particularly disturbed Puttick. There was a gap . . . the high ridge which commanded Maleme airfield from the west, a ridge rising above the stony riverbed of the Tavronitis River. He suggested to Freyberg that the 1st Greek Regiment, stationed . . . at . . . Kastelli, should be moved to this ridge. But the Greeks were under the command of their own authorities . . . By the time the permission of the Greek High Command had been secured, invasion seemed close, and the move was not made. This left a gap . . . fatal to the defence of Maleme . . .[70]

We have already seen a counter-argument to the movement of 1 Greek Regiment from Kastelli. Freyberg put the problem this way:

It is a mis-statement to say that we could not move the 1st Greek Regiment without permission from the Greek authorities. As far as I can remember the facts were these: Owing to policy matters holding me at H.Q. and the fact that Heraklion was looked on as the most important aerodrome, I inspected their defences first, and it was not until late in the period of preparation that I got to Maleme. . . I discussed the whole question with General Puttick [then Brigadier], and I was in favour (and so, I think, was he) of moving the 1st Greek Regiment up to the area west of the aerodrome. It was only when he looked at the surface of the ground, and took into account the shortage of tools, that we realised that it would be impossible to do it and have them dug in before the attack came.[71]

The New Zealand brigadiers were also busy with their inspections. Brigadier Hargest had noted in his diary for 13 May:

Brig Puttick came and we spent the morning inspecting the defences at the western end of area at Maleme and he seemed pleased. I addressed the Bde HQ men on the job in hand and spurred on the officers here. Visited all but 21st Bn — see them tomorrow.[72]

The General himself was rapidly drawing his preparations to a close. On the morning of 15 May, he went yet again to isolated, vulnerable Heraklion. He noted the 'I' tanks were at Heraklion, a pair being allocated to each airfield, and that five more bren-gun carriers were on the way.[73]

In the meantime, Enigma traffic provided additional details. The previous evening, 14 May at 1840 hours, OL 319 noted there was no confirmation that gliders would be used, as only one unit of thirty-six towing aircraft had been so far identified. (This was to prove misleading.) The numbers of men in the parachute regiments consisted of 1,600 to 1,800 men, battalions around 550, and companies of 120. The paratroops were said to be armed with machine-guns, sub-machine-guns, and rifles. The Air Landing Division's support weapons included anti-aircraft guns, anti-tank guns, 31mm mortars, and 75mm guns. The Ju52 transport aircraft might carry light tanks up to 3.5 tons.[74]

This was reasonably accurate. In the battle that followed, the infantry's comparative weaponry showed that in the 22nd Battalion rifle companies, automatic weapons averaged around six bren-guns and six Thompson sub-machine-guns per company. Some companies possessed an anti-tank rifle and, or, a 2 inch mortar. Ammunition for these weapons varied, and grenades were not over-abundant: some were simply home-made adaptions of tins, with hunks of concrete and gelignite thoughtfully provided by the nearby NZ Engineers.[75]

The German paratroop companies relied on a 'dropped' strength of around 156 men, equipped with one pistol per man, one Mauser carbine per man below non-commissioned officer, some twenty-two light machine-guns, three light anti-tank guns, and three light mortars. A 'heavy' paratroop company would have 135 men, the same small arms equipment, but different automatic weapons: eight heavy machine-guns, eight medium mortars, two light artillery pieces.[76]

On 15 May, two days before the assault, Freyberg issued his orders refining the roles of Force Reserve — the 4 NZ Brigade under Brigadier Inglis. The matters of mobility, areas of operation in order of priority, and the attachment of light armoured forces were covered. Creforce Operation Instruction No. 13 delineated the Force Reserve brigade group: it comprised 4 NZ Brigade (less 20th Battalion), 1st Welch Regiment, supporting artillery units, and ten light tanks of 3 Hussars. This motorized mobile force was ordered to be ready to operate in the Canea–Maleme–Suda areas as a priority, Retimo and Heraklion being much less likely.[77] (The last-named had more armour than the other localities because of geographical isolation.)

Three days later, Creforce Operation Instruction No. 16 of 18 May detailed the available military transport for the new reserve. Sufficient 3-ton lorries were now with 231 Reserve Military Transport Company to move Brigade headquarters and two battalions, amounting then to two-thirds of an infantry brigade. Thirty were assigned to the 18th Battalion, twenty-seven to the 19th Battalion. These fifty-seven trucks included the transport for Brigade headquarters and the Light Troop of Royal Artillery.[68]

While some limitations had been placed on Force Reserve because of a lack of lorried transport, most of Force Reserve could be moved fairly quickly. Moreover, the priority areas for Force Reserve were reasonably close at hand, Maleme being the extremity of the Maleme–Suda axis.

On 15 May the two 'I' tanks were concealed at Maleme, handily placed to intervene on the airfield, from the forward slopes of Hill 107. Meantime, on the same day, the 21st Battalion reconnoitred forward of its position to place two platoons near the Tavronitis, north of Vlakheronitissa, in preparation for a support-role movement: to cover the rear of the 22nd Battalion's area, and in particular the left flank of 'D' Company's river bank positions.[79] However, the positions of the 22nd Battalion at Maleme did not maintain a continuous wide perimeter of the small airfield and the surrounding features. On the conventional maps the truncated company positions indicate the presence of troops of a particular company on or near that piece of ground. The maps could not indicate fields of fire in clear weather or in the smoke and dust of aerial bombardment. There are some clear indications of the roles of each company in their placement on the Maleme topography, on the beach, the coast road, the Tavronitis River bed and the bridge, the hill features dominated by Point 107, the small villages of Pirgos and Vlakheronitissa, Maleme, Xamoudhokhori, and the small Sfakoriako Stream.

'C' Company, 22nd Battalion, sat astride the airfield: 13 Platoon guarded the beach front on the northern side of the aerodrome; and 15 Platoon occupied the north-western end of the airfield, overlooking the flat expanse of the air base and the sea end of the wide flat of the Tavronitis. 15 Platoon were the only troops in any position to command the area below the Tavronitis bridge. Any attack encompassing airborne troops landing simultaneously on both the airfield itself and across the river would probably disastrously reduce any response 15 Platoon could be expected to make. If such pressures were combined with the diverting attentions of enemy fighter aircraft and dive-bombers, 15 Platoon could not be expected to remain intact for very long. 14 Platoon commanded the southern long side of Maleme aerodrome and the coast road running alongside at this point. Lying in front of a canal at the base of the hill feature Point 107, this platoon's attention would be centred on preventing enemy forces from occupying the airfield. The rear of 14 Platoon was secured by the presence of 'A' Company, 22nd Battalion, on the forward Point 107 slopes, and two dug-in and camouflaged Matilda tanks of the 'B' Squadron detachment of 7 Royal Tank Regiment. 14 Platoon's left was end-on to the heavy modern girder bridge over the Tavronitis. Neither 14 nor 15 Platoons could be expected to provide immediate and substantial fire against an attacking force from over the Tavronitis bridge without largely abandoning their immediate airfield defence functions. Under such circumstances reliance would need to be placed on the northern platoon of 'D' Company, 22nd Battalion, to break up an across-bridge sortie by the enemy. Yet, as 'D' Company was itself largely end-on to the bridge and had not secured it, such a remedy might not be so easy. Nor did the existence of the RAF camp and administrative buildings, between 'D' and 'C' Companies, help. In the general confusion of smoke and dust, and with the shattering sounds from weapons, bombs, shells, and aircraft engines at high revolutions, the chances of perceiving, responding, and successfully eliminating an opposing eastbound thrust might be substantially reduced.

In summary then, 'C' Company's deployment had a single purpose — to prevent the airfield being used to land enemy troops and supplies. This fixed-denial function and the determination of positions by the surrounding terrain go some way to explain the rest of 22nd Battalion's positions. All were aimed at either direct fire support of 'C' Company — for 'A' Company on Point 107 — or flank protection; 'D' Company to the south and west — the bank of the Tavronitis; Headquarters Company to the east in the village of Pirgos astride the coast road; 'B' Company remained on high ground to the south and east behind point 107, more as a semi-reserve company role, a secure anchor for the holders of Kavzakia Hill. A forward platoon of 21st Battalion covered another portion of the upper Tavronitis south of 'D' Company's position. The only way directly to 'C' Company, without coming under fire from other 22nd Battalion troops, was from the west over the Tavronitis, north of the bridge. And this was under the muzzles of the naval guns deployed on Kavzakia Hill.

Clues as to the actual placement of 22 Battalion's defences may be gleaned from the Battalion's *War Diary*. The copy in the Public Record Office notes the destruction of all secret documents on 20 May, so the period 1 to 19 May 1941 is not a day-by-day record. It is an after-battle account, compiled with matters fresh in mind, presumably in Egypt, and therefore written in hindsight. It nonetheless provides a picture of the vital ground that suggests a defending tactician's nightmare:

> The broken terrain, the olive grove and the vineyards made it impossible to find a spot which gave a view of the whole battalion area, and prevented the complete development of assisting fire.[80]

The large 8 kilometre perimeter and small 3 to 11 metres deep ravines running from the eastern spur to the coast are mentioned.

22nd Battalion's commander, Colonel Andrew, faced a dilemma. If the trees and vines were cleared (by explosives, fire, etc.) to form an open glacia down the slopes of Kavzakia Hill to allow direct fire, his concealment would end. The presence of his large formation would be revealed, and of course cover on the slopes destroyed. Concealment was the prerequisite of surprise. The foliage was left to lull enemy suspicions.

Concealment was all important to Freyberg's plan to trap and destroy the enemy on arrival. Two 'I' tanks of the 7 Royal Tank Regiment were dug in by the 22nd Battalion on the forward slopes of Kavzakia Hill. Commanded by Captain Braddock 'who was for operational purposes responsible to 5 Inf Bde', these tanks were to deal with German transport aircraft arriving on the airfield.[81] Andrew had the discretion to use them as he saw fit. Supporting artillery, of the 27th Field Battery, were dispersed 2 to 3 miles east of the airfield. 'A' Troop, 27 Field Battery, had its two 3.7 inch howitzers located behind Vineyard Ridge in 21st Battalion's area; 'B' Troop was located in 23rd Battalion's area with three Italian 75mm guns; 'C' Troop had four French 75mm guns immediately south of the engineers-turned-infantry of 7 Field Company on the coast road.[82]

Machine-guns were concentrated to fire over the aerodrome from Kavzakia Hill. Machine-guns from the 27th Machine-Gun Battalion were located as follows: 2nd Lieutenant Macdonald's four guns (1 Platoon) were located above the canal immediately south of 22nd Battalion's positions in Pirgos, to cover the beach and the airfield.

Lieutenant Luxton, with half a platoon, was on a spur above Maleme village, covering the airfield and the beach. There was a shortage of proper tripod mountings — five arrived at 23rd Battalion on the night of 19/20 May, but were not delivered when the invasion began next morning. Some six Browning machine-guns removed from destroyed RAF aircraft were 'mounted for A.A. [anti-aircraft] work and were in positions on the slopes overlooking the 'drome'.[83]

However, the Bofors anti-aircraft guns were not concealed. Major-General Weston, the Royal Marine commander, had been made responsible for all anti-aircraft defences (by Creforce Operation Instruction No. 10, section 16). At Maleme this brought all ten Bofors guns, two 3 inch anti-aircraft guns, and two 4 inch coast defence guns under the command of a Royal Marine officer, Major Kay.

In direct contravention of Creforce Operation Instruction No. 10, section 14, wherein concealment of anti-aircraft guns was required, Major Kay deployed the Bofors guns openly to suit the defensive purposes of the RAF. This provided a theoretical cone of fire to protect the aircraft pens constructed around the airfield, but on invasion day there would be no RAF operational aircraft left at Maleme.

> All ten guns [six Royal Marine and four Australian] were sited on the immediate perimeter of the landing ground. None of the guns had a silent reserve role — in fact none could have been so used if desired as positions were obvious and not concealed.
>
> A.A. shooting was not very effective. There were literally hundreds of targets at less than 2,000′, but the Bofors did not seem to be able to cope with Me109's [Messerschmidts] and 110's flying 50 to 200 feet over them at speed.[84]

Another observer noted that: 'the Bofors guns, terribly prominent in their sandbagged positions, marked the perimeter of the field'.[85]

The lack of concealment and the exposure of the luckless gunners was to be fully exploited by the Luftwaffe. The week-long Luftwaffe attacks used as a 'softening-up' period before 20 May, plus an unfortunate order, resulted in almost total failure by these weapons on invasion day. The mistaken shooting down of an RAF Hurricane fighter days before the attack had resulted in orders from Major Kay that fire was to be held until positive identification was made.[86] This merely made a bad situation worse. Positively identifying low level attacking aircraft that inconveniently appeared more than one at a time, and not all from the same direction, made firing under such circumstances impossible.

By Friday, 16 May, Freyberg was feeling more confident, even with the daily air activity over Crete. He cabled Wavell:

> My plans for the defence of Crete have been completed, and I have just returned from a final tour of the defences. The visits have encouraged me greatly. Everywhere all ranks are fit and morale is now high. All the defences have been strengthened and the positions wired as much as possible. We have forty-five field guns in action with adequate ammunition dumped. There are two infantry tanks at each aerodrome. Carriers and transport are still being unloaded and delivered.

> The 2nd Battalion, Leicesters, have arrived and will make Heraklion stronger. Although I do not wish to seem over-confident, I feel that at least we will give an excellent account of ourselves, and with the help of the Royal Navy I trust that Crete will be held.[87]

The defences were as ready as could be expected. The gods seemed to smile, for now the Germans had a crisis, only part of which was revealed in Enigma summaries on 16 May. OL 339 at 0805 hours suggested that although the opening of the attack might still be the 17 May, there was a possibility of it being postponed for forty-eight hours. OL 341 at 1340 hours said further that the 19 May looked now to be the earliest date for the assault. Both OL messages note the information was sent independently to General Freyberg.[88]

According to Conrad Seibt, the corps supply and administration officer for Fliegerkorps XI, problems arose over the supply of aviation fuel for the transport squadrons in the days immediately preceding the attack:

> In Pireaus a quantity of aviation fuel had been found in a fuel storage installation and was transported to the airfields. The chief supply of fuel, however, had still to arrive. The freighter carrying 8,000 barrels and the tanker were both en route from Italy and there had to pass through the Corinthian [*sic*] Canal to reach Pireaus. Because of the explosion on 26 April, however, the canal was still blocked by debris [from the bridge], despite attempts by Greek divers to clear it. In agreement with the naval headquarters at Pireaus I requested German divers and better equipment to be sent from Kiel by plane. They arrived on 13 May and began working in continuous shifts. On 17 May the canal was cleared, but the ships' captains then demanded that it be swept for mines.
>
> Meanwhile 20 May had been established as D-Day, and to have sufficient fuel available in time I had to insist that both ships pass through the canal on 17 May. I immediately dispatched Lieutenant Specht by plane to the western end of the canal with orders to enforce my demand. By evening he phoned me that both ships had reached the eastern exit.
>
> . . . By noon of 18 May both ships had arrived at Pireaus. Under the command of Generalmajor Mackensen every effort was made to distribute the fuel to the airfields in the Athens area. In the evening of 18 May I was still worried that sufficient fuel for three sorties would not be available at the aerodomes by the night of 19 May in accordance with the demands of higher headquarters. . . but by the evening of 19 May. . . the last barrels of fuel were en route to the airfields.[89]

Freyberg had now made every preparation essential to his plan. 17 May passed with Freyberg at his headquarters, working on administrative matters. A series of cables were sent to Cairo, concerning the visit of the New Zealand Prime Minister and the nomination of a successor in command should the General become a casualty. The previous day yet another cable had gone to Wavell over preparations for the evacuation of the King of Greece. Air attacks had increased in intensity and on 17 May, the General noted in his diary the 'bad air raids on Suda Bay'.[90]

On 17 May at 1045 hours, OL 354 revealed that a Luftwaffe photo reconnaissance of all aerodromes for operation 'Colorado' [the British code-name for the German attack] had been ordered, as well as for Suda Bay and the tented camp eight miles south-west of Canea. The summary noted in its usual form: 'Director for all Orange Leonard Three Five Four sent independently to General Freyberg.'[91]

By 18 May, Freyberg had made arrangements for the evacuation of the King of Greece to the hills, where, in an emergency, he could be removed to a southern port for removal to Egypt. Freyberg was also on the move again, showing himself to his troops, checking positions:

> ... Series of air raids... __ in afternoon visited Suda Pt and Georgiopolis [*sic*] __ saw Vasey and had a much wanted swim in Armyro Bay __ Evening talked to Inglis and gave him his unenviable role __ saw ADC [AOC?] who asked to be allowed to send few fighters to Egypt. Wanted to bring his personnel to Suda which I could not recommend __ Winston sent us a telegram.[92]

On this day, the written order confirming the verbal orders given to the various unit commanders at the Maleme Court House conference on 11 May were promulgated by Brigadier Hargest of 5 Brigade. Of immediate tactical concern were those for the commanders of the three infantry battalions in the proximity of the airfield: the 21st, 22nd, and 23rd Battalions — Allen, Andrew, and Leckie. Of these, Allen and Leckie, while formerly battalion officers (Leckie, for instance, had been the 23rd's second-in-command), had only been commanding officers for a short time. Leckie had become commanding officer of the 23rd with the departure of Colonel Falconer for Egypt; Allen had succeeded Macky on Freyberg's personal intervention: the reputation of the 21st in Greece where they had received heavy casualties in the Pinios Gorge was under a cloud.

At 0150 hours on 19 May, an OL summary (OL 370) of Luftwaffe Enigma traffic said that a conference of commanders of German air force units would be held that day at Eleusis airfield. Maleme, Canea, Heraklion, and Retimo were specifically mentioned, and reference was made to strafing attacks at Maleme. It was noted that today was 'Day minus One', and also that OL 370 was sent to General Freyberg.[93]

The Luftwaffe had concentrated its striking power for operation 'Mercury', and in the week before 20 May the aircraft of Fliegerkorps

VIII, in their cumulative softening-up attacks on the island, built up a useful reservoir of experience. Operating over a sea approach, co-ordinating attacks, and establishing smooth turn-arounds in the re-arming and refuelling of aircraft required considerable organizational skill. Apart from the small-scale nuisance attacks that the RAF was occasionally able to mount, the absence of effective opposition assisted the Germans. The Junkers Ju87, dive-bombers, and Messerschmidt Me109 fighters were forward, mainly at Molaoi, Milos, and Skarpanto, and used Argos and Corinth as base airfields. Me110s — twin-engined fighters — operated from the Athens area. Long-range bombers and reconnaissance aircraft flew on from as far away as Rhodes, Salonika, and Bulgaria.[94] The Ju52 transports and the airborne forces of Fliegerkorps XI waited on the airfields of Eleusis, Megara, Corinth, Mylene, Phaleron, Tanagra, Topolia, Dadion, Almiros, and Tatoi.[95] At midday on 19 May, the airborne troops learned that they were to invade Crete on 20 May. As Walter Gericke, the commander of IV Battalion of the Storm Regiment, wrote:

> With strong formations of parachutists and assault troops XI Air Corps will capture by storm the three usable airfields upon Crete, at Maleme, Retimo and Heraklion, and will then be reinforced by further formations of parachutists and mountain troops both from the air and by sea.[96]

The Luftwaffe had now concentrated over 1,150 aircraft on its various airfields: at least 280 long-range bombers, ninety single-engined fighters, ninety twin-engined fighters, forty reconnaissance aircraft, 150 dive-bombers, and over 500 transports. There were eight main types: Heinkel He111s, Dornier Do17s, Dornier Do21s, Messerschmidt Me109s, Messerschmidt Me110s, Junkers Ju87s, Junkers Ju88s, and Junkers Ju52s.[97]

The RAF's incapacity to deal with these concentrations of enemy aircraft during the week before the invasion shows the weakness of RAF strength. RAF attacks were mainly carried out at night, by level bombers at a time when accuracy by level bombing was notoriously unreliable. The numbers of aircraft involved in the raids speak for themselves.

On the night of 13/14 May, four Wellingtons attacked two airfields. On the night of 14/15 May, six Wellingtons attacked three airfields. The next night, eighteen Wellingtons attacked five airfields. The following morning of 17 May, eight Beaufighters took off from Heraklion on Crete, where they had arrived at dusk the previous evening, and: '. . . attacked concentrations of aircraft at MALAOI [*sic*] ARGOS and HASSANI aerodromes'.[98] On the night of 17/18 May one lone Wellington bombed the airfield on Rhodes. On 18/19 May, three Wellingtons raided Hassani and Eleusis aerodromes. The raids were but pin-pricks to the Luftwaffe. The tankers, temporarily stalled at Corinth Canal while carrying vital aviation fuel, whose presence had been revealed by Luftwaffe Enigma traffic, were left alone.

On 19 May, on Crete, Freyberg was going through a frustrating time of waiting. The air attacks continued, the Greek King was a distracting issue, and Middle East Command sent a cable suggesting the invasion might not come, then later cancelled this message. The General had in the meantime received the OL 370 message setting the assault day as 20 May:

> Slept in clothes at Battle HQ __ expected enemy to carry an attack __ Bombardment of Suda Bay and Maleme early __ also bombardment of Heraklion __ had the usual letter from Gen. Heywood about how perturbed he was about posn of the King and showing me a letter he proposed to send to C-in-C and CIGS. I took the line that it was a purely diplomatic question and C-in-C ought not to be bothered __ scale of air attack has been increased but thanks to our arrangement I believe the dive-bombers on Suda Bay have been prevented from bombing the pier __ smoke from fire Suda obscures Canea Plain and Maleme __ cable from C-in-C suggesting that attack on Crete might not come[.] Later in day cancelled.[99]

Freyberg had now only a few more hours to wait.

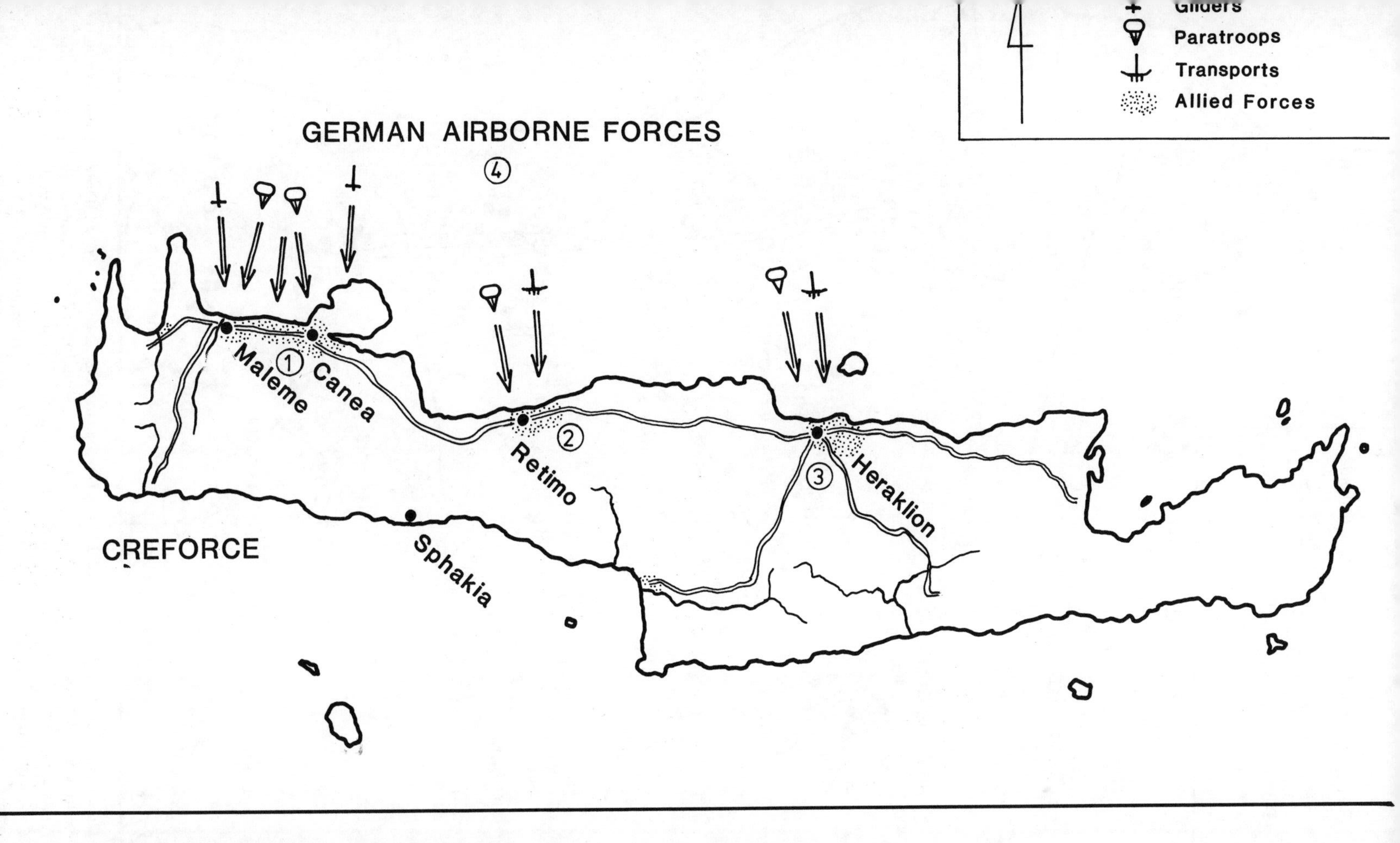

The Crete invasion, 20 May 1941. Key: 1 — NZ and Greek forces; 2 — Australian and Cretan forces; 3 — British and Greek forces; 4 — Fliegerkorps XI.

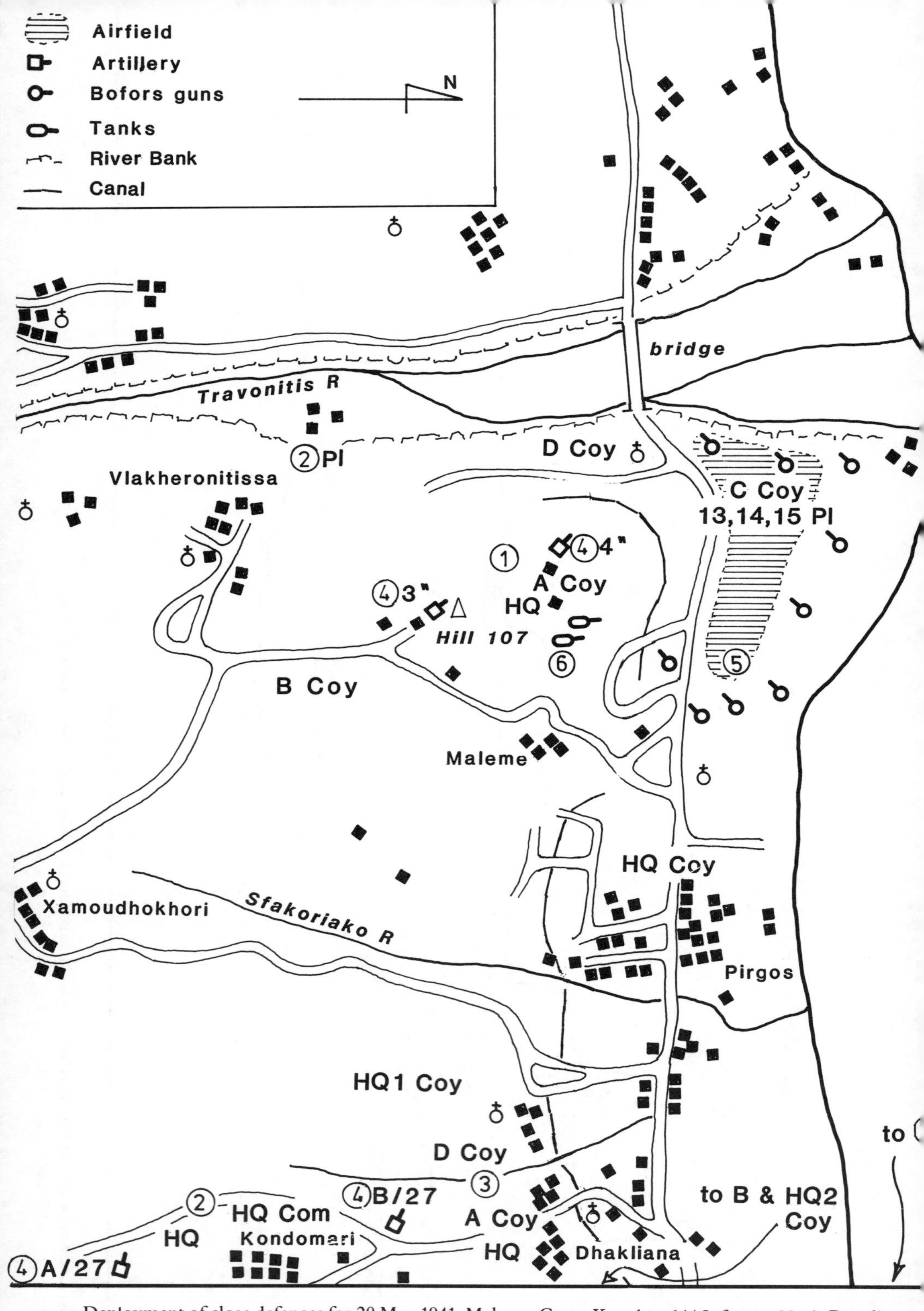

Deployment of close defences for 20 May 1941, Maleme, Crete. Key: 1 — 644 Infantry, 22nd Battalion, Andrew; 2 — 376 Infantry, 21st Battalion, Allen; 3 — 5 71 Infantry, 23rd Battalion, Leckie; 4 — artillery, Army and Naval; 5 — anti-aircraft guns on Maleme Airfield perimeter; 6 — Matilda tanks (2); 7 — 619 Infantry, 28th Maori Battalion, located with Brigade headquarters at Platanias.

CHAPTER 3

The Battle for Crete

In the early hours of Tuesday, 20 May 1941, there was a great stirring on the Greek island and mainland airfields to the north of Crete. In a huge crescent-shaped span, the personnel and aircraft of Fliegerkorps VIII and Fliegerkorps XI were making final preparations prior to their departure for Crete. Three days late because of the difficulties in obtaining adequate fuel supplies, the assault was on, monitored each step of the way by the code-breakers of Bletchley Park.

For the fighters, bombers, and dive-bombers of Fliegerkorps VIII, the task was now easier. All effective aerial opposition had been swept from the skies over the island. In addition, the softening-up attacks of the previous week had solved any problems the close support aircraft had in co-ordinating tactics. For the transport and glider crews the experience of a massive air-drop against defended positions was about to commence. Although assured and highly trained, they were unaware that their staff officers had critically underestimated the strength of the defending garrison, and its deployment; a deployment, moreover, carefully based upon intelligence assessment of their own plans of attack.

Years later, Arnhem won notoriety as the cardinal disaster for British airborne forces. It is ironical that the Cretan assault, where German paratroops suffered much greater losses right at the start, is not portrayed as a greater strategic blunder.

The German invasion was planned in two phases. The Tuesday morning of 20 May was to be devoted to subduing the western sectors — from Kastelli through Maleme and Canea to Suda — to seizing the aerodrome at Maleme and also the landing ground at Kastelli. The afternoon would be given over to Retimo and Heraklion.

On the island, the infantry of the 22nd Battalion waited in well-dispersed company positions. During the past week as air attacks had intensified, with bombing and strafing twice a day, casualties in the battalion were slight. On Monday 19 May a great number of bombs fell on 'C' and 'D' Company positions in the space of five minutes. Total battalion casualties from the bombing raids had been one killed and two wounded — all casualties from the aerodrome defence troops ('C' Company). Given their exposed positions, more might have been expected.[1] 22nd Battalion, the strongest battalion in 5 Brigade with 644 officers and men, waited for what was to come.[2]

Well under a mile from the 22nd Battalion lay the 571 soldiers of the 23rd Battalion and 376 men of the 21st Battalion. Less than four miles away were another 619 troops of the 28th Maori Battalion, at Brigade headquarters around Platanias, while some 364 engineers improvised as infantry held the coast road between 28th and 23rd Battalions. Near the airfield, over 1550 infantry were deployed in three battalions, detailed to deny the aerodrome to enemy airborne forces.

Some time before 7 a.m., 20 May, the Ju52s left the airfields of occupied Greece, rose steadily into the air, then turned to form up at aerial rendezvous points before commencing the outbound journey over the Aegean Sea. On the island itself, the regular morning 'daily hate' was already taking place with a 7 a.m. bombing and ground strafing, though with little real effect.[3]

For Pilot Officer R. K. Crowther of 30 Squadron, RAF, at Maleme, the opening of the invasion was eventful:

> At 0430 hours on 20th May, the defence officers inspected all positions and satisfied themselves that everyone was on the alert. A second inspection was carried out at 0600 hours. At 0700 the alarm was sounded and within a few minutes very severe and prolonged bombing of the defence positions started. The Bofors crews as the result of sustained bombing and machine-gunning attacks during the past seven days were by this time almost completely unnerved, and on this particular morning soon gave up firing. One Bofors gun was seen to go into action again but the shooting was rather inaccurate. While the [RAF] Camp was being bombed, enemy fighters made prolonged machine-gunning attacks on the Bofors positions and inflicted heavy casualties. At the same time there was intensive ground strafing of troops over a wide area in the locality.[4]

At 7.45 a.m. the air raid warning sounded once more, and the rumble of approaching aircraft filled the air. From a slit trench on the forward slope of Kavzakia Hill above Maleme aerodrome, Squadron-Leader Howell observed:

> The first formations of bombers — Junkers 88's — were in sight now and wheeling in to run up over us... That meant we were the target. We waited till we heard the whistle and whine of several scores of heavy bombs on their way down, and then we went flat in the bottom of our trench. The bombs struck in twelves, earth spouted to the heavens, the crump and shock of impact crept closer up the hill. The noise was indescribable. The ground shuddered and shook under us as the bomb pattern passed over and beyond.
>
> The whole area was shrouded in thick choking dust, and earth and stones were falling everywhere. We could not see more than a few yards. But we heard the whistle of more bombs on their way down and we kept below ground...bombs bursting close to us shook in the sides

> of the trench. We were covered in earth. Our eyes and mouths were full of grit. And it still went on. We were shaken . . . Debris continued to crash around us . . . We lost count of time.[5]

The sounds of the Bofors positions taking a pounding on the edge of Maleme airfield were long remembered by Howell:

> . . . Long bursts of cannon and machinegun fire as low-flying fighters came in to attack the anti-aircraft gun pits. These were already silent under the terrific weight of attack with the exception of one Bofors gun down by the beach. This went on firing for some time till a host of Stukas and Me 109s fastened on it and shot and blasted it out of existence.[6]

The *War Diary* of 22nd Battalion records bombing and strafing attacks going on for ninety minutes with no respite. The main areas of the battalion's defences under attack were those of 'C' Company on the airfield, 'D' Company by the Tavronitis, and the 'terraces' (the forward hill slopes of Hill 107, running back from the airfield to battalion headquarters).[7] Dust and smoke rose to several hundred feet and obscured the view of most of Maleme's defenders.[8] As the bombing eased, about sixty gliders swept in to the Akrotiri Peninsula (Canea–Suda), the Prison Valley, and to Maleme.[9] Nearly half the glider force landed near Maleme. Elements of the headquarters of the Storm Regiment, along with elements of III Battalion in nine gliders under the command of Major Braun, landed south of the Tavronitis bridge. The headquarters of I Battalion and 3 and 4 Companies, under the command of Major Koch, were to land in more than twenty gliders.[10] 3 Company was headed for the mouth of Tavronitis; I Battalion headquarters and 4 Company were to land on Kavzakia Hill.[11] It was all neatly timed and co-ordinated.

Most of the aerial bombardment ceased to allow the gliders to land. Now as they crashed their way on to the island, the first of the Ju52s carrying paratroops commenced to swing in low over the western sectors to drop parachutists from Group West and part of Group Centre.

General Meindl, commanding Group West, had been tasked to take Maleme airfield and reconnoitre west to Kastelli, south and east of Maleme, and make contact with Group Centre, which was to be in Canea. The aerodrome at Maleme, once it was safely in German hands, was to be used immediately to land troop carriers. The paratroops in the Maleme area were carefully deployed to this end. Four companies of II Battalion (numbers 5, 6, 7, 8), under Major Stentzler, were to land far to the west, south of Kolimbari, where with no garrison forces in the area they would be unmolested. A seventy-two man detachment, under Lieutenant Muerbe, would land three miles from Kastelli where they would run into 1st Greek Regiment and be cut to pieces. Numbers 9, 10, 11, and 12

Companies of III Battalion under Major Scherber were to be dropped east of Maleme airfield along the road in the direction of Platanias: directly over the 23rd Battalion and the NZ Engineers' units, on the mistaken assumption that no Allied troops occupied the area. Of IV Battalion, under Captain Gericke, 13, 14, and 15 Companies were to drop west of the Tavronitis bridge beyond the 22nd Battalion's perimeter, though within the range of the 4 inch guns of 'Z' Battery, Royal Marines, sited up on the slopes of Kavzakia Hill above 'D' Company, 22nd Battalion. 16 Company of IV Battalion was to be landed south-west of Kavzakia Hill.[12]

Designed for a quick seizure of commanding areas by *coup de main,* with a capacity for only a slow build up in quieter areas, the German operation now became seriously endangered. The parachutists, vulnerable to ground fire, were seriously handicapped as they tumbled from the low-flying Ju52s. Unlike the British X-Type parachute harness that allowed the jumper to steer directionally, using arms to manipulate the lift webs, the German paratrooper was a prisoner of his falling parachute. The German RZ 16 parachute harness converged its rigging lines to a central ring behind and above the paratrooper. The paratrooper fell very much at the mercy of gravity and could not steer out of the way of obstacles.[13] Once landed, the paratrooper was momentarily vulnerable as he struggled from his harness. Creforce defenders soon learnt to make the most of these German disadvantages.

The glider troops at Maleme had mixed fortunes as they tumbled from their grounded DFS 230s. Those landing on the slopes of Kavzakia Hill suffered heavy casualties. While those in the Tavronitis River bed also suffered losses, they managed to seize and hold the bridge adjacent to the weak point in the defence perimeter — the RAF encampment. Key officers became casualties. Braun, in the Tavronitis, was killed, and Koch, on Kavzakia Hill, was severely wounded.[14]

For General Freyberg, the invasion of Crete was the test of careful preparation. He had deployed his garrison in widely scattered localities, and relied upon his brigade and battalion commanders to engage and counter-attack enemy concentrations immediately. He, like General Student far across the water in Greece, could only await news as events unfolded. Freyberg later wrote:

> I stood out on the hill with other members of my staff enthralled by the magnitude of the operation. While we were still watching the bombers we suddenly became aware of a greater throbbing in the moments of comparative quiet, and looking out to sea with the glasses, I picked out hundreds of slow-moving troop-carriers with the loads we were expecting. First we watched them circle counter-clockwise over Maleme aerodrome and then, when they were only a few hundred feet above the ground, as if by magic, white specks mixed with other colours floated slowly to earth.[15]

He remarked that the enemy was 'dead on time'. Six German gliders swept in over the heads of the officers, towards landing objectives further along Akrotiri Peninsula. At 9 a.m. on that Tuesday morning, a situation report to General Headquarters, Middle East, from Creforce, read:

> Attack started. Troops landed by parachute and glider. Estimate approximately 500 parachutists south-west of Canea. Approximately 50 troop-carrying aircraft. More now approaching. Situation obscure.[16]

The enemy was landing his paratroops and glider troops along the western sectors, from Kastelli to Suda. Around this time communications with Heraklion were temporarily severed.[17]

Hindsight is the historians friend and from hindsight attention is focused on the critical area of battle, the western sectors. What is clear now was not clear at the time, to the garrison or to the enemy. It was only good luck that allowed General Student critical advantage in the days ahead. While Maleme's defence emerged as crucial, it should not be imagined that initially the defence of Retimo and Heraklion was any less important. The successful defences of both localities ably demonstrates the care with which Freyberg's plans were put into action, despite only limited resources.

The paratroops of III Battalion came down for the most part on the concealed New Zealand infantry. They confronted Captain Carl Watson, 'A' Company commander, 23rd Battalion:

> The first lot seemed to curl over us and land on the 'drome, the second lot seemed to go over the back of us towards 21 Bn, and we began shooting, though most of these were out of our range.
>
> Suddenly, they came amongst us. I was watching the 21 Bn area and a pair of feet appeared through a nearby olive tree. They were right on top of us. Around me rifles were cracking. I had a Tommy gun and it was just like duck shooting.[18]

Walter Gibbons, a runner in 'B' Company, 23rd Battalion, had a harrowing time as the attack came in:

> There was no room in the slit trench for me so I spent the whole softening up process under a banana tree with my hands behind my head... The noise of bombs, machine guns, aircraft engines and screamers was indescribable, along with the dust and smoke and all manner of desultory firing at aircraft. We did get back to our HQ — just a few yards — before the paratroops began to jump over our area. The parachutes seem scarcely to open before the invaders hit the ground. Some appeared to attempt to steer their landings between the nearby stone walls. It was an open season. And it was a slaughter of some magnitude... Here in Crete there was no front line; for the

> Germans and for us it was kill or be killed. It took but a moment to discover the parachutist was vulnerable as he touched the ground, and as he struggled to free himself from his harness. One Bren gunner somewhat behind and above our fig-tree promptly disposed of five or six Germans between the stone walls immediately behind us... Each trip to Bn HQ necessitated clambering over the bodies... We were aware there were odd paratroopers in the cornfield on our right front. By evening they had crept closer...[19]

The 23rd Battalion smashed the III Battalion paratroopers that fell within their area. By the end of the morning, hundreds of corpses littered the 23rd's position.

When General Meindl made his parachute jump, around 8.30 a.m., it became clear to him that instead of an easy victory, something akin to a disaster had befallen many of the troops of the Storm Regiment. The glider troops, the bulk of them under the command of Major Koch and Lieutenant Plessen, had been exterminated upon arrival. Their commanders had been killed, as the various remnants of the Tavronitis groups had retreated back west of the river, though the bridge remained in German hands. Captain Gericke's three IV Battalion companies — machine-gun, anti-tank, and mortar companies, without supporting infantry — had been collected by their commander and brought to a position west of the river bank. Meindl had reacted vigorously to the threatening situation. He sent two II Battalion companies under Major Stentzler south, in a protracted flank march, to move to the rear of the New Zealand infantry on Kavzakia Hill. Besides the glider troops, the remaining company from II Battalion, and the three companies of IV Battalion, he had only 700 troops left, a still formidable force well equipped with automatic weapons and mortars.[20]

Meindl's speedy intervention was crucial, for an estimated two-thirds of III Battalion had been killed, including all the officers. The battalion had dropped on to the concealed infantry of 21st and 23rd Battalions, and on a detachment of NZ Engineers.[21] But Meindl's improvisations and reorganization had not gone unnoticed. His preparations to attack from beyond the western perimeter of 22nd Battalion's defences prompted reaction from the commander of 'D' Company, Captain Campbell:

> The 4″ coast defence guns just east of this area [the slopes above 'D' Company, 22nd Battalion] were contacted at 1030 in an attempt to have the mortars and machine gun concentration West of the TAVRONITIS engaged with direct fire. O.C. detachment was not willing to deal with the target.[22]

This refusal of gun support was from 'Z' Battery, Royal Marines. The Germans, clearly visible in Polemarkhi and Ropaniana, were out of effective small-arms range but could easily have been dealt severe blows by the naval battery. The grounds for refusing were that the guns were sited for sea targets.[23] The implication was that close fire, over open sights, would disturb the guns' sighting, or reveal the guns' locations to the Luftwaffe. The Marines had previously had no qualms about placing their Bofors batteries in very exposed positions around Maleme airfield.

This was the kind of frustration that began to dog the Battalion's defence of the aerodrome area for most of the day. Contact with Colonel Andrew at Battalion headquarters was made by 'D' Company, for a request was sent to the Brigadier by the Battalion at 1030 — the same time as the Marine refusal: '22 Bn asked area EAST of ROPONIANA village to be searched by arty fire. Order given to 27 Bty [NZ Artillery] in N.Z.E. area [C battery]. Shelling very accurate.'[24] The first mass aerial invasion in history was now in furious contest. The defenders seemed saturated: dropped on by enemy soldiers arriving apparently at random right over and across all defensive positions around the aerodrome, and on the holding locations of the support infantry battalions, concealed though they were for the most part under the cover of foliage.[25] It was a similar battle for other elements of the garrison attacked that day. This new mode of warfare, never before attempted on a large scale, astounded the defenders but did not suppress resistance. It is ironical that a military success by the Creforce garrison, and a military failure by the Luftwaffe, should finally work in favour of the Germans.

The garrison had managed to keep itself well concealed prior to the invasion on 20 May. The German Air Force failed to detect the size of the defence force. It also failed to discover the garrison's deployment. Superior camouflage and concealment, unrevealed by reconnaissance, allowed the airborne troops to fall into the hands of the enemy. This, in itself, accounted for the destruction of many of the invaders. But this ground-to-air firing also magnified the confusion and the fears and anxieties of the defending ground forces.

In three key formations in 5 Brigade, the 21st, 22nd, and 23rd Battalions, no one knew immediately how many German troops had landed. Nor was it at once apparent where they had concentrated, or where they were dispersed. The defenders felt the enemy's nearness — a dangerous and lethal omnipresence.

This fear was well manifested on 20 May.[26] It made for a paralysis of tactical command decisions. Far beyond the immediate range of a soldier's vision, let alone small arms range, nobody, locally, could be sure where the Germans' strength lay. From the time of the first parachute jumps, every man in every locality, be they Private Smith, Lieutenant Davin, Captain Watson, or Colonel Leckie, was personally engaged with the enemy, who were literally, at times, only feet away. There was no time for the luxury of looking about to see where other Germans landed. Anyone who did usually died. The dust of bombing, the smoke of battle, the foliage that remained, and the incessant interminable noise prevented the senses from being otherwise occupied in observation.

The very success of the battalions around Maleme, in exacting a fearful slaughter from concealment, increased a temporary tactical blindness at an important stage of the opening attack. It sometimes led to uncertainty over the enemy's whereabouts and relative strengths: even where he had most dangerously concentrated. This influenced decisions on troop movements, which in the absence of radio contact, added to the dangers and to the risks taken. Ignorance and uncertainty led to paralysis of command, particularly when a task included moving sizeable bodies of troops to other areas. Taking risks involved the possibility of making wrong decisions, with unknown incalculable results. The defending battalion commanders at Maleme were compelled to 'read' the action compounded by a literal 'fog of war' descending on the battlefield, by the smoke and dust of bombing, which obscured any visual communications. The defending commanders lacked radio equipment on a useful scale, and of convenient size, weight, and reliability. This lack and the visual obstructions of smoke and dust meant nearly all the infantry, from privates to battalion commanders, fought at close quarters — blind.

The unique mode of the German airborne assault, supported by fierce air support, prevented the preparation for Freyberg of an accurate and encompassing situation report. The landings, wherein the Germans were almost completely vulnerable, were masked from fatal exposure. At Maleme, many paratroops and glider troops landed amongst the well-concealed major deployment of the garrison, and paid the price in blood. Although the heavily engaged New Zealand infantry did not realize it, Freyberg's trap had slammed shut on the invaders.

Although General Freyberg had been offered a decisive tactical advantage by his private perusal of the Enigma summaries of German intentions, British incompetence now assisted the enemy. The RAF, with a record of non-cooperation at Maleme, provided the Germans with an intelligence coup of immediate tactical usefulness. When Meindl's paratroops captured the bridge and made headway by taking some buildings in the RAF camp, they not only discovered a tactical flaw in the defence perimeter, they gained something better than ground. In spite of knowing full well that the invasion was imminent, the local RAF staff officers failed to destroy their code books. The battle report of Fliegerkorps XI, *Einsatz Kreta* noted their capture:

> The main source for the enemy order of battle is contained in a list of code names dated 20 May 1941, which was captured on the first day of the attack and gave all the units and battalions, including the Greek battalions.[27]

For the officers of the Storm Regiment, the fog began to lift. They had been surprised completely by the garrison's strength. This disadvantage could have been compounded for some time. Given the opposition thus far met, the paratroops' commanders could not be certain from which direction the next counter-blow might be struck. They did not know what other concentrations might lie concealed in close proximity. With the capture of the Creforce code books, fear was to a large degree eliminated. It was not too difficult to work out what the approximate actual local defence strengths were, by comparing the Allied units listed with the experiences of airborne troops already landed. The Germans read the tactical radio traffic through their efficient network of sets, and the size of Freyberg's units in each vicinity was readily assessed. Defence intentions were quickly assessed and where possible countered. German intelligence had unknowingly checkmated the intelligence that Freyberg had used to deploy his troops, and the German gain was of use in battle conditions. It was sufficient to encourage tired troops and their commanders to fight on, rather than surrender. This security breach was the nadir of RAF support on Crete.

For 5 Brigade, 23rd Battalion, this German gain was particularly harmful. According to the 23rd Battalion *War Diary,* the battalion was cut off from radio communication with 5 Brigade headquarters and the 22nd Battalion early in the first day.[28] The link with 5 Brigade was restored later that morning; that with the 22nd Battalion was not. Throughout the day, 23rd Battalion was in constant touch with 21st Battalion headquarters by telephone.[29] As these two formations were the principal support forces available to assist the airfield battalion's defence, this was to be expected.

The breakdown of communication between the forward infantry and the support battalions was potentially serious. At best, messages were sent by company and battalion runners, or by the even more dubious expedient of flares. The only radio link depended on 5 Brigade headquarters at Platanias. The 22nd's radio had weak batteries and their contact with Brigade remained tenuous. When the 23rd's link with 5 Brigade was restored, much depended on decisions made by Brigadier Hargest. In particular, he would either have to decide himself when support battalions would be needed by the 22nd Battalion, or he must act as an indirect intermediary between his battalion commanders, Andrew, Leckie of the 23rd, and Allen of ther 21st. If he chose the former course, he would be evaluating the forward situation from four miles in the rear. Although the airborne assault on the western sectors was initially 'frontless' — with troops dropped everywhere — Freyberg's deployment meant that the airfields and the port areas remained the crucial goals. Without them, the Germans could have no secure lodgement.

For Colonel Andrew of the 22nd Battalion, the problem of communications, both within his formation and with other units, became acute from the time of the opening preliminary air bombardment. The telephone lines from his Battalion headquarters to his scattered companies were immediately severed, leaving him with little alternative to the risky expedient of employing runners. Line contact with Brigade and the other battalions had disappeared with the attack. His entire communication with 5 Brigade was interrupted for nearly an hour, and there was no direct link with the 23rd Battalion, or the 21st, for the same period.

Some time after 10 a.m., radio contact with Brigade was re-established, and the 22nd reported that hundreds of paratroops had landed south and west of their positions.[30] Some twenty minutes later, the 22nd made a request for the artillery support.[31] Close to 11 a.m., the 22nd relayed a message that communications between Battalion headquarters and the forward companies had broken down, and that nothing had been heard from the 22nd's Headquarters Company in Pirgos. Andrew made a request that the 23rd try to contact his Headquarters Company. The 22nd reported they were holding the line, in the face of 400 parachutists.[32] Andrew later wrote:

> I endeavoured to contact HQ Coy myself, and was fired at by Germans in the valley and under trees between Bn.H.Q., H.Q. Coy and B Coy. I went to ground and before withdrawing counted eight enemy.[33]

The 22nd Battalion during the course of Tuesday morning came under pressure at five main points.[34] The glider landings along the Tavronitis had been a problem for 'D' Company. While two gliders were destroyed on the left, No. 18, the right flank platoon, had been unable to deal with all the glider troops amongst it, with the result that by about 10 a.m. all of 18 Platoon's forward posts were captured. (This allowed the Germans to take possession of the RAF administrative buildings and the code books mentioned earlier.)

The west flank of 'C' Company's area, the Tavronitis side of the airfield, was critical. For here 15 Platoon was hopelessly outnumbered by glider troops and paratroops in the river bed, and the platoon was under heavy fire from machine-gun and mortars located at the western end of the Tavronitis bridge. At around 10 a.m., 15 Platoon's flank was penetrated. Again the capture of the RAF administrative block figured: enemy fire was coming from near the rear of 15 Platoon. A number of the platoon's positions were captured early in the assault — all the rest were taken by midday.

The south-west positions of 22nd's Headquarters Company in Pirgos came under fire. Street fighting took place in Maleme village. Heavy machine-guns were used by the enemy throughout Tuesday to thwart runner-contact attempts by both Beaven of Headquarters Company and Colonel Andrew who was atop Kavzakia Hill.

The result of the capture of the RAF buildings, in the weakest point of the defence perimeter, gave succour to the German survivors of I

Battalion of the Storm Regiment on the lower slopes of Kavzakia Hill. Two attacks were mounted up the slopes of Kavzakia Hill, in the morning, almost behind 'D' Company, but the situation had been restored by Battalion headquarters personnel. (During this exchange the 'shield' incident took place, where captured Allied prisoners were driven before the German infantry's guns in the mistaken belief that the New Zealand infantry would not fire.)

In the afternoon, in spite of heavy German casualties, the 22nd's situation appeared to deteriorate further. In the meantime, at around 11.40 a.m., 23rd Battalion reported to 5 Brigade headquarters, by radio, that it had cleared its area of enemy forces.[35] This was of considerable significance when the 22nd later asked for the planned counter-attack from support battalions. By now, small groups of Germans kept up sufficient fire to stop a number of runner messages from getting through, either from the forward companies, or from Battalion headquarters. German control of the area about Maleme village and the RAF encampment sealed off company commanders from their battalion commander, and vice versa. Odd messages still slipped through, but not enough for officers to form a satisfactory picture of the situation.

Maintaining communications became a growing problem, which should not be belittled even though 'D' and 'C' Companies were only a few hundred yards distant, and all the tracks in the area had been well-traversed by runners who had three weeks to become familiar with them.[36] While movement in the open was risky, it was a risk that the Germans were facing all the time, but the Germans found that they had landed in exposed positions in the immediate presence of a hitherto concealed garrison, and they must simply move or die. In Crete individual runners were easy targets for scattered groups of airborne troops. One particular 22nd Battalion runner, who seemed to bear a charmed life on the first day, was captured whilst carrying a report that might have brought considerable relief to Andrew and his forward Headquarters Company. Andrew himself, as we have already seen, was prevented from going forward to assess the situation by enemy small-arms fire. Like exposed soldiers, runners took their chances — getting through not only involved skill in moving through enemy-held areas, it also involved luck.

When luck ran out disaster fell. Lieutenant Beaven, of Headquarters Company in Pirgos, sent off runners to 22nd Battalion headquarters and to 'B' Company, but none returned, nor it seems, got through. At 3.50 p.m. Beaven sent off Frank Wan, a 22nd Battalion runner who had traversed part of the battlefield that day. The message read:

> Paratroops landed East, South and West of Coy area at approx 0745 hrs today. Strength estimated 250. On our N.E. front 2 enemy snipers left. Unfinished square red roof house south of sig terminal housing enemy MG plus 2 snipers. We have a small field gun plus 12 rounds

manned by Aussies. Mr Clapham's two fwd and two back secs O.K. No word of Matheson's pl except Cpl Hall and Cowling.

Troops in HQ area O.K.

Mr Wadey reports all quiet. No observation of enemy paratroops who landed approx 5 mls south of his position [the AMES post from whence Frank Wan had come].

Casualties: killed Bloomfield
wounded Lt Clapham, Sgt Flashoff, Cpl Hall,
Pte Cowling, Brown.

Attached plans taken off Jerry.

1650 hrs

G. Beaven, Lt.
OC HQ Coy.[37]

Wan was captured but hid his message until the war was over. His undelivered message contained the intelligence Andrew needed, for it conveyed that Headquarters Company was still in position, and had not taken too many casualties. The base for a counter-attack from Pirgos near the airfield was still fairly secure. This message was sent late in the afternoon[38] when the Battalion's position seemed to Andrew to be becoming increasingly precarious. At the time Beaven's message was sent, Andrew was starting to worry about enemy contact from his rear — the south-west.

On Tuesday afternoon the position of the 22nd's companies deteriorated. Having lost regular contact with the three forward companies, every pressure on 'A' Company on Kavzakia Hill increased Andrew's anxiety. Mortar and heavy machine-gun fire from the Germans in the Tavronitis area made many of 'A' Company's forward posts untenable.[39] The company was forced to pull back from the summit of the hill towards the 'B' Company ridge.

Brigadier Hargest, at Platanias, in the early afternoon, felt no cause for concern. A message transmitted from 5 Brigade headquarters to 23rd Battalion at 2.25 p.m. was clear and succinct: 'Glad of your message of 11.40 hours. Will NOT call on you for counter-attacking unless position very serious. So far everything is in hand and reports from other units satisfactory. . .'[40] The lack of pressure in the 23rd Battalion's area left the main support formation free:

> At Maleme the 23rd did little all day on the 20 May, after destroying the initial landing. There were some small pockets to be cleared out. There was no reason why aid should not have been offered to the hard pressed 22 Bn. Watson, the commander of A Company, made some tentative moves himself, but his superiors' general inertia meant no positive steps were taken.[41]

By Tuesday afternoon the commanders of the 22nd and 23rd Battalions could not communicate with each other directly, and were entirely reliant upon Brigade headquarters, far to the rear, for information about each other. Of this, there was not much forthcoming. Andrew knew nothing of Hargest's message of the 23rd assuring the latter that 'everything is in hand'; Leckie could not know how serious Andrew felt the 22nd's position was. Nor, initially, did Brigadier Hargest.

The realization by the 22nd, around 11 a.m., that communication with the forward companies had broken down may have been disquieting, but it was not more than that. Close to mid-afternoon, at 2.55 p.m., Brigade headquarters received a message from the 22nd that the enemy had penetrated into the Battalion headquarters' area.[42] This alarming turn of events was followed less than one hour later with a further report from the 22nd that its left flank had given way, but with reassurance that the situation was in hand. A signal included a request for news of the Headquarters Company in Pirgos as 'reinforcements were badly needed.'[43]

Here was exactly the template situation that General Freyberg had provided for in his orders for the defence of the aerodromes. Clearly this was the time, as Davin suggested, for Hargest, at the very least, to issue warning orders to the 23rd and 21st Battalions, to make preparations to move by companies or whole battalions to the assistance of the 22nd, if required.[44] This did not happen. The one person who knew what both Andrew and Leckie had reported during the course of the day was physically far removed from the action — yet it was only the Brigade commander who could make the decision to intervene.

The option envisaged earlier, in Creforce Operation Order No. 2 Appendix 'A', stated: '. . . the Commander of the Mobile Column must use his judgement as to the best moment to move into the attack.'[45] Without an order from Hargest, the only circumstances when the 23rd might have been justified in coming to the 22nd's assistance without direction was if emergency flares from the 22nd were sighted, or if a runner from Andrew reached the support battalions requesting immediate help. The 'white-green-white' Very flares were fired some time before 5 p.m. by the 22nd, but they were not seen by the 23rd's observers (possibly because of dust and smoke).[46] Leckie may have been misled as to the 22nd's position, because of an earlier request from Andrew, via 5 Brigade. Some of the 23rd were sent to contact the Headquarters Company of the 22nd in Pirgos. Their approach was fired on by some of the 22nd's infantry — they failed to make contact and win intelligence for Andrew. Andrew was not informed of this turn of events it seems. The implication of this might have been that the 22nd's Headquarters Company were in good enough shape to provide a sharp defence.[47] It could conversely be reasoned by Leckie that as the company in Pirgos was still capable of resistance, the 22nd's position was not so bad at all. Hargest's earlier signal regarding a counter-attack as unlikely certainly supported this view.

All this is somewhat in the realm of speculation. What is really clear is that Andrew did not get the message through to his Brigade commander that he definitely needed assistance. Leckie, under the impression that there was nothing to worry about, was compelled to rely on an absent Brigade commander on a weak radio link. Much reliance needed to be placed on Hargest's judgement. It was, perhaps in the stress of battle, faulty judgement.

The crisis of the first day's battle had arrived. Yet it is such simply in hindsight: even Andrew, perturbed by the turn of events could not have seen, in the unravelling unfortunate chain of circumstances that followed, that the road to defeat had begun.

The German pressure was increasing. Unknown to Colonel Andrew, No. 17 Platoon of 'D' Company, the forward platoon by the Tavronitis, was ordered by Captain Campbell to retire further up the slopes of Kavzakia Hill to escape an apparent pincer movement on both flanks.[48] This was close to 5 p.m. Around this time, Andrew ran into troubles of his own with his Brigade commander.

Before we consider those difficulties, we must deal with an even more extraordinary turn of events. Sometime during the Tuesday afternoon, Major Thomason of the 23rd Battalion recalled:

> Col. Andrew came to our Battalion headquarters in person and asked for help. He was first guided to me by one of my men. I knew Les Andrew well, he and I were good friends. He was very shaken and disturbed and I personally took him down to Battalion headquarters. I don't know the outcome of his visit except that his request was not granted. This took place fairly early in the afternoon. I cannot state the exact time.[49]

This turn of events is not alluded to in the Battalion *War Diaries,* the Brigade *War Diary,* or in the text of the *Report of the Inter-services Inquiry on Crete.* While not crucial, it is nonetheless important.

The request from Andrew himself was for help. Clearly this came within the parameters of the arrangements upon which the deployments of the support battalions had been based. There was no point to the placement of the 23rd Battalion if it was not going to carry out this support function. Yet the request was refused.

It may be that Hargest's 2.25 p.m. message had been received by this time, and Leckie decided that he was to wait for orders from the Brigadier. If so, it was a very short-sighted view. If Thomason is correct, not only about the visit, but about Andrew's appearance — 'shaken and disturbed' — then the refusal is even less explicable. Andrew was not noted for being flappable, quite the reverse.[50] This was not a runner who had arrived fortuitously, but the commander of the airfield defence battalion. He had taken the risks that his own battalion runners ran, to get assistance personally. This in itself should have underscored the importance Andrew attached to it.

There was rivalry between the 22nd and 23rd Battalions, animosity existed between Leckie and Andrew, there were differences in approaches to discipline and to alcohol, there was North–South rivalry. But all this does not greatly add to the understanding of this refusal of aid. Nor is it very useful to note that Leckie had only become battalion commander of the 23rd a short time before (though it is of interest to recall that Allen had become commander of the 21st Battalion only since arriving on Crete, too). What is really important are the implications for Andrew that were now apparent.

If Andrew was shaken when he arrived at the 23rd's headquarters, he must have felt extremely dispirited when he made his way back to the 22nd Battalion. The plan that embraced support would, if it was to function in any way, depend very clearly upon the decisions of the absent brigade commander at Platanias. The defence of the airfield in the interim, until such orders were given by Hargest, was simply in the hands of the 22nd Battalion, by itself. Leckie would not help, the 22nd was alone. Leckie could easily have sent back even at least one platoon with Andrew, on the understanding that runners be sent back to the 23rd to report on the current situation of the airfield defence battalion. The main defence tactic envisaged by Freyberg — counter-attack by the untouched forces some distance away (less than a mile from the 22nd's supposed perimeter) — was withheld by the battalion commander responsible for mounting such an attack.

This unfortunate meeting of the two infantry battalion commanders set the scene effectively for the rest of Tuesday. By 5 p.m., Andrew was again in radio contact with Brigadier Hargest. Colonel Andrew put to Hargest that the time had indeed arrived for assistance from the 23rd Battalion. Incredibly, the brigade commander was to reply that, according to Andrew's account, the '23rd could not attack as they were engaged with paratroops'.[52]

The brigade commander's refusal to implement the agreed operational plan led Andrew to a final expedient to stem the enemy near the foot of Kavzakia Hill, in the RAF encampment, and the Tavronitis bridge. There was obviously no point in sending further runners to Leckie. Unless the brigadier himself would give the orders for the support battalions to assist, Andrew must solve his own problems.

Andrew could now be sure only that he retained the two companies on the hill, 'A' and 'B', plus the remnants of 'C' Company that could be still contacted: what was left of 13 and 14 Platoons. It would be folly to send either of the companies on the heights forward, for the vital hold on the hill would be less secure. The infantry to be sent to attack the Germans in the river were to have a supporting role for what Andrew had in mind: a small armoured assault using the two heavy tanks concealed on the forward slope of Kavzakia Hill.

The two tanks of the detachment of 'B' Squadron, the 7th Royal Tank Regiment, set forth on their brief journey supported by the two remaining sections of 14 Platoon under Lieutenant Donald, and six gunners from 156 Light Anti-Aircraft Battery.[53] Difficult terrain and the numbers of Germans around the Tavronitis bridge area made the little attack a forlorn hope. As matters turned out, one tank ingloriously turned back after the luckless crew found the two pounder ammunition would not fit into the breech of the turret gun. The remaining tank turned off down the bank into the river bed, proceeded under the bridge, firing as it went, but became irretrievably stuck in boulders.[54] The gallant sections of infantry accompanying the tanks were cut to pieces. The arrival of Andrew's armour on the scene caused consternation among the airborne troops, and for a few minutes the Germans found themselves fighting forces immune to their small-arms fire. Given the importance of Maleme why were light armoured vehicles not deployed with the tanks in the Maleme area?

There is an ambivalence about the role designated for the bren-gun carriers within the 5 Brigade area.[55] It was expected that 22nd Battalion would have seven. Three had come from 1st Welch, and four more were expected. It is unclear how many carriers 22nd Battalion had.[56] As lightly armoured vehicles that were relatively vulnerable, they could provide a useful adjunct to a tanks-and-infantry attack. With two Matilda tanks, the later afternoon attack on the first day could have been undertaken by at least five tracked fighting vehicles plus infantry. Andrew, in the confusion of battle, does not seem to have considered this possibility. As to their vulnerability to air attack, the bren carriers on the road up in the hills survived intact by the simple expedient of draping fallen parachutes over the vehicles.[57] The airfield battalion's carriers *were* operational during the critical period, for they were disabled and abandoned by the New Zealanders when the battalion withdrew.[58]

A clue to the neglect in these vehicles' use may be found in the suggestion that both the 23rd Battalion and 5 Brigade headquarters used two bren carriers as communications vehicles, and for the transport of wounded. Major Leggat, Andrew's second-in-command, apparently commandeered a 23rd Battalion carrier to Platanias to give Hargest the news of the 22nd's withdrawal on the first night.[59] Similarly, Dawson, Brigade-Major, 5 Brigade, made a return journey from Platanias to Leckie's headquarters in the early hours of 21 May. Captain Ken Cramer, 'B' Company commander, 22nd Battalion, used a vehicle with his company to keep in touch with Andrew and 'A' Company: 'Communications with A Company were visual and by liaison. We had a carrier which had made two trips to Battalion Headquarters by early afternoon.'[60]

By the end of daylight on 20 May, the four bren carriers were back with 'B' Company. Two of them had been used during the day; firing on the enemy between 'B' Company and Headquarters Company, or on paratroops in the latter company's area.[61] On the road the carriers escaped attention, disguised with draped parachutes.[62] As battle intensified, the bren-gun carriers were abandoned and made unserviceable, which underlines the little value placed on them.[63] They remained until nearly dawn.[64]

It has been suggested that on Crete there was insufficient armour. No doubt the dispersal of the six Matilda 'I' tanks, deployed in pairs at the main airfields, inevitably lessened any impact that tanks might have. The dubious state of repair they were in added to this. Yet the ubiquitous bren-gun carriers, plus the light-tank detachments (like Farran's 3 Hussars), would surely have offset these weaknesses, particularly if combined with a strong infantry assault. One platoon section and two tanks at Maleme could not do much, and underlined Colonel Andrew's predicament — lack of infantry reinforcements. There was only one tank, later at Galatas, supplementing a strong infantry assault that gave useful support. Two heavy tanks, three light tanks (there were ten available), four bren-gun carriers, and three companies from the 23rd Battalion might well have dislodged the German position at the Tavronitis bridge, and at the edge of the aerodrome. The actual appearance of the two Matildas caused consternation at the bridge.[65]

The failure of the tank attack, and the depletion of 14 Platoon, left the 'C' Company commander, Captain Johnson, with less than half of 13 Platoon, beside his cooks, runners, and stretcher-bearers; a force scarcely sufficient to hold the remaining side of the airfield. He informed Andrew that he must be reinforced after dark, and was ordered by the battalion commander to 'hold on at all costs'.[66] The battalion commander determined that something must be done. Andrew once more made radio contact with Hargest and reported that if there was to be no support from the 23rd, withdrawal was necessary as casualties had reduced his infantry to a strength capable of holding his perimeter only as far as 'B' Company ridge — out of sight of the airfield. Hargest's rejoinder was: 'If you must, you must.'[67] Within a few minutes, 5 Brigade at last signalled to Andrew that two companies of infantry were being sent to the beleagured 22nd. It is clear that Colonel Andrew understood these troops to be on their way, and would arrive 'almost immediately'.[68]

With apparent disregard for the crisis at hand, Hargest selected one of his reinforcement companies from the Maori Battalion at Platanias, hours away from Andrew. This was 'B' Company of the 28th Battalion, under Captain Royal. The other company was 'A' Company, 23rd Battalion, a little over a mile as the crow flies from the 22nd's 'B' Company positions behind the top of Kavzakia Hill. Andrew was not told from where the companies were coming.

At the 23rd's headquarters at the time Andrew mooted his withdrawal back from the top of Kavzakia Hill, there was little apprehension about the 22nd's position. Andrew's earlier visit had not alarmed the commander of the 23rd. Walter Gibbons, the 'B' Company runner, recounted:

> . . .Our communications were by runner. I was stationed on the right flank of the 23 Bn with Captain Gray and . . . B Coy. . . We had a good view of the aerodrome and could hear the progress of the battle on 20 May. It seemed to be going against the 22nd, so about 6 p.m. Gray ordered me to go to 23 Bn HQ to get an appreciation of the situation. The light was fading and I made the journey without too much difficulty. Bn HQ seemed to be in a state of disorder in the gully. What was alarming was that some elements of the 22nd Bn seemed to be retreating through the gully in some disorder.
>
> I found Davin, who was the Bn Intelligence Officer for the 23rd and gave him Gray's message, expressing apprehension, and asking for information for Gray. I note that in none of Davin's history does he make reference to my request on behalf of Gray. Despite the fleeing members of 22 Bn Davin assured me for Gray that the situation on the aerodrome was completely under control and mopping up operations were continuing. I returned to Gray with the information, which he questioned since the sounds of battle were now near the eastern perimeter of the aerodrome.[69]

The 23rd had coped with the ferocity of the initial assault from the paratroopers, and it could well be that sanguine feelings engendered by the morning's success made the 23rd's commander less than sympathetic towards Andrew's afternoon visit. The hint here, and it is no more than that, is that the 23rd's headquarters' staff thought the 22nd were engaged in mopping-up operations. Leckie, at this stage, did not consider that the time to go to the 22nd's aid had arrived. He would wait until ordered to do so.

For General Freyberg, this was a trying day. The critical areas, apart from Suda Bay, were distant from his headquarters. Of necessity he was isolated from the fighting at the danger points. He was not assisted by poor communication links, but if the enemy's intentions had been read correctly, Creforce would have to fight in self-contained localities, and their General would have to put up with a temporary limited perspective. He summed up his view that night in a cable to Wavell in Cairo:

> Today has been a hard one. We have been hard pressed. I believe that so far we hold the aerodromes at Maleme, Heraklion, and Retimo and the two harbours. The margin by which we hold them is a bare one and it would be wrong of me to paint an optimistic picture. The fighting has been heavy and large numbers of Germans have been killed. Communications are most difficult. The scale of air attack upon us

has been severe. Everybody here realises the vital issue and we will fight it out.

Later: A German operation order with most ambitious objectives, all of which failed, has just been captured.[70]

The German operation order, referred to in the cable, was discovered almost by chance by the sometime editor of the garrison newspaper, Geoffrey Cox. It was an interesting discovery:

Bell had taken over the night shift . . . I stayed to help him, spreading out my sleeping bag at the back of the dugout. By the doorway stood two canvas bags filled with captured enemy documents, ready for onward shipment to the experts in GHQ in Cairo by a destroyer due to sail from Suda in the small hours. Before turning in to sleep I decided to glance through some of this mass of maps, aerial photographs, paybooks, code books and military papers. This led me to a document which was to have some influence on the battle . . .

It was a faded carbon copy, line upon line of close packed typescript, in places stained with blood, of the Operation Order for 3rd Parachute Regiment, the formation charged with the attacks on Maleme, Canea and Retimo. As I made my way through it, picking out the more difficult words with the help of a pocket German dictionary . . . I realised that it set out in considerable detail the German plan of attack. Its importance was underlined by instruction that it was to be burnt once it had been read, and was not to be taken into action.

The General sat behind a bare wooden trestle table in his dugout. On the table lay a hand grenade, ready for use against any enemy intruder. With John White holding a torch for me to read by, I made a rough translation of the order. It not only gave in detail the plans for 3rd Parachute Regiment, but also a summary of the invasion plan for the whole island, including the attack on Retimo and Heraklion. In the Canea area the town was to be surrounded, and then occupied by nightfall. Galatas was to be stormed, and the Canea–Maleme road blocked. The attack was to be pressed towards Retimo. None of these objectives had been achieved.

Even more important was the estimate of our strength on the island which the document gave. This showed that the German Intelligence was extremely poor. They set the British garrison as no more than 5,000, of whom there were 400 at Heraklion, and none at Retimo. This was roughly the size of the garrison before any of the troops evacuated from Greece reached the island. The Germans had apparently failed altogether to learn of the considerable number of New Zealand and Australian troops from Greece who had stayed on Crete, or of the fresh British units brought in to Heraklion. The total number of British and Greek troops under Freyberg's command was nearly six times the

German estimate... some 20,000 of these were in the fighting units...

The German knowledge of the terrain was also faulty. They had either not bothered with extensive air photography or had misinterpreted what surveys they had undertaken. Areas full of hazards were marked as suitable for parachutists and gliders... From these smudged and grubby pages leapt the fact that we had a much better chance of winning this battle than could have seemed possible twenty-four hours earlier.

I put the document back into the bag for Cairo, and it went off that night. At the same time Freyberg added a postscript to his despatch to Wavell, saying that an important enemy document had been found. It revealed the main German objectives, none of which had been attained. At the end of his long day the General could seek some sleep with the feeling that the situation was reasonably well in hand...[71]

Cox's discovery was very pertinent indeed. If it is true that Freyberg had heeded the very lucid information provided by the Enigma summaries from Bletchley Park, then Cox's rough translation of the captured orders must have relieved any vestiges of uncertainty the General felt about that intelligence. The great mistake in the German assessment of the British order of battle was revealed. This not only meant a fundamental underestimation by the invaders of the garrison's numbers, it also signified that Freyberg's deployment of his fighting infantry and main artillery batteries had gone unnoticed. In itself, this said a good deal for the camouflage and concealment of Freyberg's troops, particularly as Enigma had revealed that extensive aerial reconnaissance had indeed been laid on (OL 260 of 9 May and OL 302 of 13 May, for example). He had based his defence on the enemy's plans — the Germans had been completely in the dark as to Freyberg's.

This fortuitously captured document did not cloud the General's judgement: his cable to Wavell spoke of a bare margin, and that the troops had been hard pressed. He was as yet unaware that circumstances at Maleme were about to take a turn for the worse. He was also unaware that the Germans in the west were now able to correct their appreciation of the garrison. This was not merely because of the ferocity of the defence in so many unexpected places. The Germans' own capture of the tactical code-names of the British order of battle, of all units including the Greeks, could refocus their attacks and reorganization. The General sent a short cable to Fraser, who had recently arrived in Cairo:

We have had a hard day. Everything depends on the next few hours. The whole of my force has been in action. The importance of the battle is realised by us all. The men are in great form and fighting well.[72]

In the GOC's diary, the entry for 20 May was written at the earliest on 21 May, for the movement of the airfield troops was unknown to Freyberg even late at night on 20 May. The full entry reads:

> Battle for Crete Begins — Blitz at 0800 hrs, more or less continuous for day — Parachutes, gliders — all points attacked during day — hospital and guns (3.7) lost and recaptured — captured document shows enemy's objective for day in Canea area: none[*sic*] achieved — POWs indicate surprise at resistance — Maleme attacked heavily, bombers, fighters, paras, but aerodrome held — 22 Bn forced to withdraw during night, but aerodrome remains covered by fire — Heraklion and Retimo both attacked by bombers in morning — parachute attacks in afternoon — aerodromes remain denied to enemy — fighting on plain of Canea towards prison and Cemetery Hill — King of Hellenes nearly captured; escapes with escort to south — Brit[ish] Min[ister] leaves — estimated total enemy landed; Canea 1890, Maleme 1770, Retimo 1770, Herak[lion] 2000 — RAF cable re Wellingtons 'giving all available help'.[73]

While Freyberg pondered, the crucial battle for Maleme was fought and lost.

After the failure of the tanks and the infantry of 'C' Company's 14 Platoon, Colonel Andrew received word from one of his runners, Peter Butler, that 'C' Company was in bad shape. Of the platoons, 14 Platoon had only three fit men, 13 Platoon had less than half its men, and 15 Platoon had not been heard of for some time and was probably overrun.[74] Of 'D' Company, nothing was known; no word had come from Headquarters Company. Time had passed and it was not clear that the promised reinforcements would not arrive quickly, though for a while, Andrew and his officers waited in grim expectation. The reinforcements had been promised by Brigade soon after 6 p.m. At 7.25 p.m. Andrew sent a radio message to Brigade. According to the Brigade *War Diary*, 'They asked for immediate assistance and reported their casualties as heavy. Also that 'I' tanks had been in action for a short time only.'[75] An hour later, around 8.30 p.m., Andrew sent a last message on the No. 18 radio set, the batteries about to expire. It was to Hargest and to the point: '[I] told him I would have to withdraw to 'B' Company ridge.'[76]

There was no recorded reply to this. Moreover, the commander of the airfield defence battalion was now out of radio contact with the rest of 5 Brigade. With communications broken, and given the day's experiences, the 22nd was alone.

The withdrawal to the 'B' Company ridge placed Andrew and his two companies in an awkward position. Although the rear of the hill dominated the aerodrome, the ground in the 'B' Company area was too hard to dig in, and was overlooked by the command post atop Kavzakia Hill. Effective small-arms fire on the airfield could no longer be applied and enemy pressure from the south-west indicated that troops on 'B'

Company ridge alone could be neatly enfiladed the following morning should the Germans also take the summit posts. Yet to pull back from the top of Kavzakia Hill was seen to be necessary. The 22nd Battalion *War Diary* puts Andrew's position by 9 p.m. on 20 May this way:

> By this hour the enemy was between Coy and Bn HQ. He had worked up the eastern ridge and so cut off the line of communication with D Coy. Maleme village was in his hands and no contact had been made with HQ Coy. A D Coy man reported that all the rest of D Coy was either killed or prisoners of war. The enemy was holding the area between Vlakheronitissa and Xamoudhokhori in force and threatened to push between our East and West ridges.[77]

Andrew felt an intense isolation. 'D' Company had apparently been overrun — if that was the case there was nothing between the hilltop and the Tavronitis. 'C' Company had been reduced to a handful of survivors. And of Headquarters Company nothing had been heard for many hours now. No sizeable reinforcement materialized from his rear sufficient to make up for the three apparently smashed forward rifle companies. The enemy was now probing the south-west flank of 'A' and 'B' Companies on the heights.

While the defence crumpled, a company finally arrived from the 23rd Battalion, nearly three hours after Andrew had been assured by Brigade that two companies would be sent. One now arrived, hours late. The support, well meant no doubt, was insufficient. Of the other company, there was no news at all.

The report that 'D' Company of the 22nd had been wiped out was false, although they had suffered considerable casualties, estimated as forty per cent.[78] The attack on the forward defence line overlooking Vlakheronitissa was intense and Andrew withdrew his battalion to the eastern ridge of its sector.[79] Andrew judged that the pressure on 'A' Company was increasing, while movement from the east (presumably from the Maleme village area) posed the threat that the companies might be cut off from the 21st and 23rd Battalions' areas.

> Even had we not been cut off, the position could not have been held next day as we were overlooked by the Western ridge [the former command post] and moreover with no opportunity of digging in and on one of the barest parts of the area few would have survived the heavy morning air attacks. Accordingly Lt. Col. ANDREW ordered an immediate withdrawal to the 21-23 area. Meanwhile the counter-attacking party of the 23rd arrived and it was decided that they should cover the withdrawal.[80]

Andrew's own view of his decision to withdraw, recorded in his

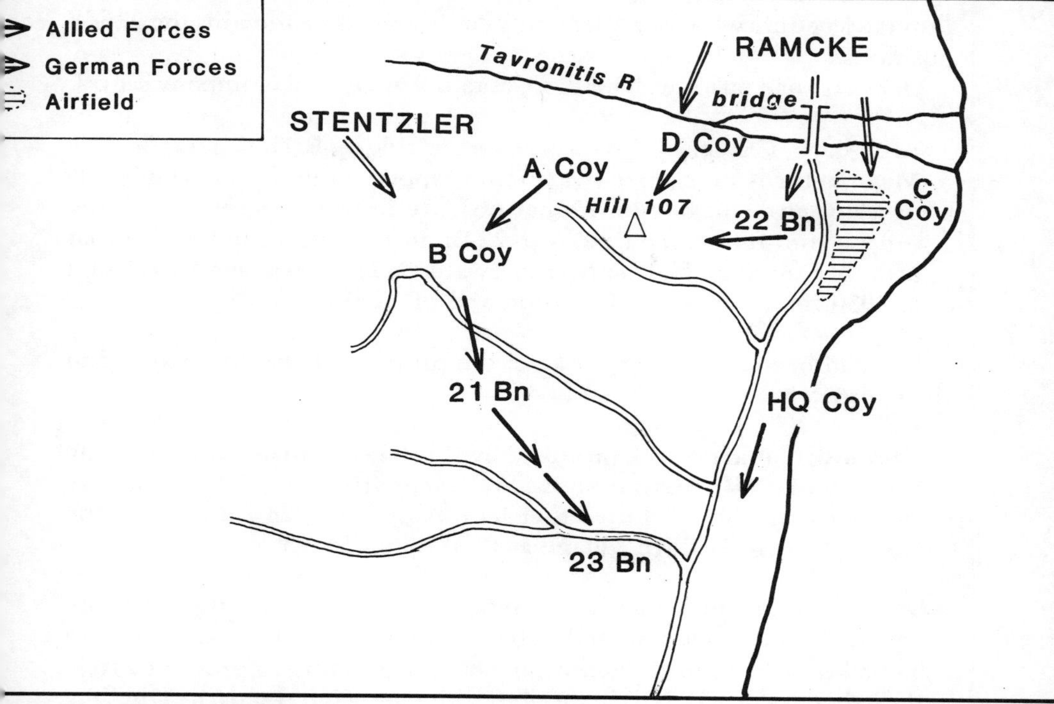

Andrew retires, 20/21 May 1941.

handwriting in the 22nd's *War Diary,* is definite:

> The withdrawal from Maleme aerodrome and the surrounding country was carried out following a wireless report to Bde. and was made on my recommendation. The position was such that if I had not withdrawn my small force that night I would not have been able to do so in the morning. Even if the position could have been restored by a counter attack it could not have been held even by a fresh battalion. Looking back now and knowing more of the facts I am convinced that the withdrawal at the time was the only possible action to take.[81]

At his headquarters the commander of Creforce was unaware of this fateful decision of final withdrawal, and would remain so for quite some time.

It had taken Captain Watson's 'A' Company from the 23rd quite a while to get to Andrew. The route taken, via the 21st Battalion positions, made a dog's leg — perhaps a necessary precaution for moving up at night, but it seems to have added to the commander of the 22nd Battalion's uncertainty. Confusion reigned. The 23rd Battalion had no news that a Maori Company was on its way from Platanias: when these troops under Captain Rangi Royal arrived at the 23rd, the latter were surprised, but provided a guide who took them on a circuitous route towards the 22nd's positions.

Darkness had fallen well before Captain Watson's 'A' Company set off.

> After dark, CO sends situation report to Bde by Bren Carrier. . . Bde Major returns by carrier [why?] and reports situation in other parts of island in hand but somewhat obscure in some sectors. . . Under orders from Bde to send a Coy to 22 Bn to assist in the defence of that area, 'A' Coy (Capt Watson) went forward via 21 Bn area and WD station at 1930 hrs to come under command of 22 Bn.[82]

There had been a time lag between the promise of the companies and their dispatch:

> The dusk counter-attack promised by Bde failed to materialise. Actually one coy of 23 Bn arrived on B Coy's ridge [the rear of 22 Battalion's positions] at 2100, and the other [company] from 28 Bn reached the outskirts of MALEME village at 0100 on 21 May.[83]

These two accounts suggest that it took over an hour for the 5 Brigade orders to be translated into action by 'A' Company, 23rd Battalion. Also it had taken 'A' Company about one and a half hours to proceed a mile and a half at most (via 21 Battalion's positions). Was it too dark? Did they find it hard to find their way? Had too little attention been given to the difficulties of moving forward at night?

Much later, on 2 July 1941, General Ismay responded to a demand from Churchill for a report on conditions that night on Crete:

> The moon was two days into its last quarter when the attack started on the 20th May and was new about half way through the battle. The Germans thus had very nearly dark nights throughout. These conditions favoured the approach of sea-borne forces: but reports all agree that the Germans took no action either in the air or on the ground, during the hours of darkness. No paratroops were dropped except in daylight. There was no night bombing and no use was made of the darkness to stage night attacks.
>
> This seems to be in accordance with German tactics in all theatres of war up to the present.[84]

Darkness was a potentially valuable ally to the garrison of the western sector — to cover a withdrawal on the first night and allow opportunity for counter-attack immune from aerial intervention.

Shortly after midnight on the night of 20/21 May there was a surprise:

> At 0030 hours Lt Col Andrew with part of his Bn arrived at 23 Bn

> HQ reporting that all surviving troops from his defensive psn. were withdrawing, 'A' Coy. 23 Bn acting as rearguard. Col Andrew reported that a large concentration of the enemy was formed up in the TAVRONITIS area.[85]

With the New Zealand infantry support plan inoperative, the airfield was already lost. Help had been refused by Brigadier Hargest. No assistance was forthcoming from the support role battalions, the 21st and 23rd Battalions. The commander of the airfield battalion had lost contact with his forward companies. The dangerous hinge between 'C' and 'D' Companies caused by RAF intransigence had been forced open. Elements of the savaged attack force were scattered in awkward places — in Maleme village and in buildings about Pirgos. Across the shingle bed of the Tavronitis, and below the bridge, the airborne attackers posed critical problems for the western perimeter defence that were only partially perceived by Colonel Andrew atop Kavzakia Hill.

The defenders were now besieged. The airfield battalion had three-fifths of its infantry companies pinned down. They could not move without surrendering vital ground. Any movement by what remained of the 'C' Company platoons necessitated the evacuation of close fire positions about the airfield itself. Movement by 'D' Company would further open the hinge between it and 'C' Company or allow the Germans further ground along the eastern bank of the river. Movement by Beaven's Headquarters' Company involved giving up buildings in Pirgos and the paratroops were already demonstrating the good use they could make of solid houses as strong points for their automatic weapons. Finally, 'A' Company on the hill could not advance to the forward companies without first exposing itself to the enemy ground troops or to air attack. More than that, it would leave the hill in the hands of only one company and there was no guarantee that an enemy outflanking movement to the south-west might not expand. It had been better to stay on the heights, hold on, and continue requests for assistance.

The delay in arrival of the support battalions' rifle companies ensured that the forward companies of the 22nd Battalion remained pinned, checked without the reinforcing fire of counter-attacking friendly infantry. In this predicament the two tanks were a late forlorn hope rather than a trump card. The end was nigh. The subsequent withdrawal by two-fifths of Andrew's infantry strength (not counting 'A' Company of the 23rd), of all that he believed remained (what was left of his forward companies came later, extricating themselves piecemeal), was merely an epitaph to a paralysed defence plan.

Who was to blame? It was the Brigade commander, Hargest, and the battalion commanders, Leckie and Allen, who were responsible for this unfortunate state of affairs. Their response, when Andrew and his troops retired, gave a clue to the extent of their paralysis. No orders were given for an immediate counter-attack under cover of darkness with all available troops. Hargest had not been left in ignorance by Andrew. Leckie had seen and refused Andrew in the afternoon. Davin, at the 23rd's headquarters, had taken no notice of Gibbon's message from Gray, though this was not vital. What was vital was that when the withdrawal from the airfield was revealed, the support battalions remained where they were.

Hargest had let Freyberg down. Strange almost fateful processions now moved over the top of Kavzakia Hill and Andrew's command post. Firstly, Andrew's own 'A' Company moved out from these positions. The late arrival of around only a hundred infantry, expected hours earlier after repeated requests, ensured that retreat must sensibly be the only course for the remaining two-fifths of the 22nd. Carl Watson's 'A' Company, having held Andrew's posts for a time, moved out as the rearguard of Andrew's formation in the early hours of 21 May. Captain Royal's guide from 'B' Company, 28th Battalion, came upon the deserted hilltop command post, then returned to the reinforcements, reporting the departure of 22nd Battalion. Ironically, the 28th had lost their way, come round the bottom of Kavzakia Hill, through Pirgos, and reached the silent airfield. They went through the 22nd's Headquarters Company, observed by a few of the troops not sleeping. The 22nd soldiers thought they were Germans, and stayed quiet, having fought to exhaustion.

A little later, elements of 'D' Company of the 22nd made their way to Andrew's former command post, where, to his chagrin, Captain Campbell found empty entrenchments.[86] A lack of timely support for the 22nd had led inexorably to the dominating hill feature above the small aerodrome falling by default to the now exhausted German paratroopers.

Andrew's arrival at the 23rd Battalion's positions had immediate consequences. The 23rd were shocked by his unexpected presence. The signal line to Platanias having broken down again, Major Leggat, the second-in-command of the 22nd, set off by carrier to Brigadier Hargest. Leggat reported that Andrew had pulled back from Hill 107, and they did not know the whereabouts of his three forward rifle companies. Andrew had arrived at the 23rd's headquarters at around 2 a.m. Leggat went to Platanias, and Hargest in pyjamas was roused from sleep at about 3 a.m. to hear Leggat.

At the same time, at 3 a.m., the three battalion commanders — Leckie, Andrew, and Allen — plus the artillery commander, Major Philp — met at the 23rd's headquarters near Dhaskaliana to discuss the situation. Of what was said at this meeting little is known. Major Philp noted the haggard exhausted appearance of Colonel Andrew and inferred that the airfield battalion must have had a rough passage. All Andrew could tell them was that his forward companies had apparently gone, and the 'details of enemy strength and dispositions' were 'just not known'. Leckie's later inclination, we are told, was to blame Andrew for having withdrawn.[87]

Next day it was not simply a question of dominating the airfield from

Kavzakia Hill. The arrival of Watson's 'A' Company from the 23rd brought Andrew to around half the strength he had begun the previous day with. Then he had had five companies, now he had three; surveying the situation on Tuesday night he faced the prospect of taking on further German assaults from the ground, and from the Luftwaffe the next morning. If the airfield had gone, the enemy must nullify the hill, and all their attention would be given to this task. Aware how hard the fighting had been to hold the heights that day, the silence from two of his three forward companies was ominous. If they had gone, and 'C' Company had obviously been shattered, how would three more companies on one increasingly exposed feature fair the next day? He had no way of knowing that the Germans' hold was tenuous, even desperate. No other single battalion or its commander on Crete was to face such an onslaught alone. The 22nd had done its job: held on throughout the day at all costs. Slightly wounded by a splinter earlier in the day under bombardment, out of touch with the immediate defenders of Pirgos, the bridge, and the riverbank, perhaps distracted by a lack of response to sundry pleas for assistance by radio, Very flares, and a personal visit to the 23rd, he can hardly be blamed for deciding late in the evening to cut his losses and pull back with his remaining troops.

'I well remember that all looked to Colonel Andrew', wrote Major Philp of the meeting at the 23rd's headquarters in the small hours of 21 May.[88] For what? It can hardly have been for direction. Andrew had asked for help for a considerable part of the afternoon and early evening, and got none. There was obviously no determination on the part of Leckie and Allen to take their battalions and Andrew's depleted companies back and retake the high ground above the aerodrome before dawn. It is not that they could have that is important — obviously a counter-attack in strength of at least two battalions would have made the German grip on Kavzakia Hill at worst precarious, at best non-existent. What is really important is that these units would not now go without direct orders. The Brigade commander, Hargest, was just rising from bed in Platanias as the battalion commander's meeting began, and his costly lack of action persisted. Hargest would not go forward, even as far as the 23rd's headquarters to see for himself. The 23rd Battalion was going nowhere. Neither was the 21st Battalion. Apart from 'A' Company of the 23rd, they had not been going anywhere all day.

The 21st and 23rd would not help on the Tuesday night because the battalion commanders and the brigade commander continued to reinforce the unpalatable truth of the day — that the brigade plan for the defence of the airfield had broken down: the 22nd Battalion had received no help at all, or got too little too late. The Brigade Operation Instructions and the Creforce Operation Instructions, central to the defence, had been abrogated. Freyberg's principal tenet to prevent the securement of an enemy lodgement that would lead to large-scale re-supply and reinforcement — immediate counter-attack — had been disobeyed.

To blame the 22nd and Andrew for the loss of Maleme is to fly in the face of events. He and his troops had held the airfield and the heights better than even he believed they could. The denial of assistance brought the withdrawal possibility to a head for Andrew. The poor materialization of that support — one company — may have underscored it, rather than dispelled that possibility. The lateness of Captain Royal's Company from the 28th Battalion is hardly surprising, given the distance from Platanias and the fact that they lost their way, going to Pirgos instead of Kavzakia Hill. The withdrawal, and the crisis caused by it at Maleme, were the direct result of acts of omission by the brigade commander, and by Leckie and Allen on that Tuesday. Doing nothing to provide timely help for the 22nd meant that the airfield fell to an exhausted enemy by the narrowest of margins. The substance of their inaction meant their presence in the brigade plan was superfluous — they acted only locally, to destroy the Germans dropped in their own immediate area. The initiative still rested with the New Zealand troops, but with the passing hours it began to slip from them. Apart from the opening hours when all units were engaged subduing the paratroops and glider troops that arrived in their locality, inaction or piecemeal commitment to company-sized movements (scarcely counter-attacks) were a feature of all 5 Brigade infantry battalions, with the exception of the embattled 22nd Battalion.

The invaders made the most of this failure to reinforce. The remaining German troops who had outlasted the day's attrition in the aerodrome's environs now began, in spite of all losses, to adjust their positions to advantage under cover of darkness. It was in this way that the vacated Kavzakia Hill, known to the troops as Hill 107, fell to the paratroopers. In the 23rd, the reaction was understandable, if unfair:

> It is sufficient to say that no counter-attack eventuated, nor did the 23 Bn take the initiative at first light to act independently. There was general condemnation of the 22 Bn when it became known the paratroopers had control of the aerodrome.[89]

And what of Freyberg? He remained for the moment in ignorance of the state of the defences at Maleme. Certain that the cool imperturbable Andrew and his battalion would have given a good account of themselves, he was as yet at 3 a.m. on the early morning of 21 May unaware of the vacancy of Kavzakia Hill, the Tavronitis riverbank, and the airfield. As yet, Puttick, acting commander of the New Zealand Division, like his superior at Creforce, remained oblivious of the slow reversal of fortunes. At 4.30 a.m., Hargest informed the New Zealand Division:

> At 430 5 Inf Bde reported that 22 Bn had left their posn about the aerodrome and reformed to the West of 21 and 23 Bns. Brig. stated

> that there could be no question of replacing this Bn. . .?[90]

Until he was informed, there could be no basis for any tactical intervention by Freyberg. His original dictum — swift counter-attack — still stood. In 5 Brigade, this sensible key to the battle was being ignored.

Following the meeting of the three battalion commanders and the artillery commander (on whom would now fall the primary responsibility for gunfire to be played upon Maleme airfield once the sun came up and so prevent the landing of transport aircraft), Andrew set off to Platanias. He arrived at 5 a.m. His battalion's casualties had been very heavy, it was thought:

> Lt Col. Andrew, 22 Bn, called at Bde HQ and said he had been able to collect only four officers and about two companies from his battalion. . . He withdrew during the night 20/21 May to left flank of line held by 23 Bn and sent out patrols to contact his missing companies. B.M. [Brigade Major — Captain Dawson] returned to front with Col. Andrew.[91]

It was now too late to do anything before dawn allowed Luftwaffe activity. While Freyberg's defence plan was mismanaged at Maleme it was effectively operational in other parts of Crete.

For the Germans, the aerial invasion attempted on 20 May had been a costly failure. No airfield or harbour had been captured. The morning drops and landings by paratroops and glider troops in the New Zealand sector and around Canea and Suda had not achieved any significant military objectives. 3 Parachute Regiment, whose operational order had been captured and translated for Freyberg's benefit, had been spread inland in the area of the Prison Valley, and were to preoccupy Colonel Kippenberger and the garrison troops of 10 Composite Brigade and significant portions of the Force Reserve, particularly the 18th and 19th New Zealand Battalions, on that day and in the days ahead. They posed no immediate threat, but they had the potential ultimately to cut off 5 Brigade if not contained. They would be dangerous if the Germans succeeded in taking Maleme airfield and drove 5 Brigade eastwards. I Battalion, under Heidrich landed *en bloc* near the prison and had virtually no opposition — not surprisingly, because the area was unimportant. The bulk of II Battalion dropped close to Galatas, and took heavy casualties: Karl Neuhoff, a company sergeant-major, estimated that only thirty-five men survived the landing and immediate post-landing minutes.[92] III Battalion, under Major Heilmann, were widely scattered while the Engineer Battalion became involved in a hand to hand battle with Greek troops and Cretan civilians near Alikianou, both sides suffering sizeable casualties.

The other half of I Battalion, the Storm Regiment, two companies under

Captain Altmann and Lieutenant Gentz, was to land on the Akrotiri Peninsula and south of Canea, respectively. Altmann's glider troops had bad landings and were roughly handled by the Northumberland Hussars near Creforce headquarters. Cut off in groups, they were forced to surrender for lack of supplies after a few days.[93] Gentz's glider troops had better landings, but were forced eventually to fight their way through to 3 Parachute Regiment, down to a strength of twenty-seven from ninety.[94]

The headquarters of 7 Airlanding Division arrived in four gliders. Three of these suffered bad landings, killing most of the occupants. The remaining glider crashed on Aegina, its wings falling off in flight. This glider contained the commander of 7 Airlanding Division, General Suessmann, who died with the rest. Colonel Heidrich of 3 Parachute Regiment now became commander of 7 Airlanding Division.[95] In the west, then, the opening day of what the Germans had hoped to be an easy victory was for Creforce a day of apparent defensive success.

The German invasion of the eastern sectors, of Retimo–Georgeopoulis and Heraklion, were disconnected not merely by the accident of geography of space and distance, but by time as well. Luck would finally give victory to the invaders, but at Heraklion and Retimo, disaster fell upon the defenders. For then only one bright spot would emerge, by accident, and the by-product of a débâcle.

The morning's operations in the west, from Maleme to Suda, had been paralleled by air attacks in the eastern areas. These inflicted little damage but were costly, and in conjunction with the invasion going on in the west may have been the cause of a dislocation of the Luftwaffe's plans. There can be little doubt that losses in aircraft, the requirements of refuelling, reloading, and (in the case of fighter and bombing aircraft) rearming, plus the considerable variation in flight distances to and from the spread of airfields needed a co-ordination that proved to be beyond the capabilities of Fliegerkorps XI and Fliegerkorps VIII. The different distances between flying to and from a mainland aerodrome like Eleusis to the western sector on Crete (over 160 miles) was more than double that from Milos to the same area (over eighty miles). (Ironically, the Scarpanto airfields which might be regarded as 'forward' landing grounds were, because of the length of the island of Crete, nearly as distant from Maleme as Eleusis.) The distance variation was compounded by the difference in performance of aircraft types, particularly in terms of speed and range. A slow Ju52 would take far longer than a Me109 over any flight path; the greater range of the Ju52 meant that more time would be available to it over the target area than for a shorter-range fighter. None of this was unknown to the Luftwaffe. The short loiter-time for fighters over England during the Battle of Britain had been a useful factor in the defender's favour.

Initially the morning's operations had gone well for the Luftwaffe. Now, overstretched with more troops to land at Heraklion and Retimo in the course of the afternoon, troop transport and air support lost co-ordination. According to Fliegerkorps XI's battle report:

> The formations started in incorrect tactical sequence, and arrived over their target areas between sixteen and nineteen hundred hours not closed up but in successive formation and at the most by squadrons. The bulk of the forces had to land without fighter protection. Moreover in the end, the force delivered was some six hundred men less than had been intended.[96]

The shambles that resulted in nearly 600 German parachutists stranded on Greek aerodromes would in the end be extremely useful for General Student. At Heraklion, their absence simply compounded the disaster.

The Creforce troops at Heraklion under the command of 14 Infantry Brigade were around 8,000 strong.[97] The core of trained infantry, some 2,799 men in four battalions, (the 2nd Yorks and Lancs, the 2nd Black Watch, the 2nd Leicesters, and the 2/4 Australian Infantry Battalion) was formidable. The remainder consisted of about 1,000 British troops of varying degrees of usefulness, and three Greek battalions. The anti-aircraft guns were better dug in than at Maleme and would perform some useful tasks on the first day, in contrast to the Bofors gunners at the other end of the island. Armour consisted of the usual pair of Matilda tanks, plus a small number of light tanks of the 3 Hussars. The principle of immediate counter-attack had been underlined by the Brigade commander.

The Germans had underestimated the size of the opposition and expected a maximum of five battalions (three British and two Greek) and a few tanks. The Heraklion garrison was reinforced with 655 trained infantry during the battle, by the 2nd Battalion of Argyll and Sutherland Highlanders from Tymbaki.

The Germans sent against Heraklion an estimated 2,000 paratroops, but no gliders. The preliminary air attacks, not of the intensity of those at Maleme and therefore raising little of the dust and smoke that bedevilled the defenders there, subsided before the transports arrived. The Ju52s themselves did not come all at once and some of the companies were widely scattered in the drops. Moreover, the transports became vulnerable to ground fire as they lumbered unprotected by fighter escorts. The *War Diary* of the 2nd Black Watch recording the destruction at 7.07 p.m. notes the destruction of 'eight of them at one time'.[98]

The German force comprised 1 Parachute Regiment plus II Battalion of 2 Parachute Regiment. The assault plan had been to land with fighter protection, but this was no longer available. II Battalion of 1 Parachute Regiment was designated to take the airfield. They dropped in two groups, but did not land together. 5 and 8 Companies landed east of the aerodrome: one of the officers survived with around sixty men. 6 and 7 Companies and an anti-aircraft machine-gun company dropped west of the airfield. They ran into very heavy fire from 2/4 Australian Battalion, and were then attacked by tanks of the 3 Hussars and the 7 Royal Tank Regiment. An hour from the opening drop of II Battalion, the unit losses were large: twelve officers and 300 men killed, plus eight officers and 100 wounded.[99]

I Battalion was dropped over five miles east of the airfield; 3 Company landed on time with no opposition; 1 and 2 Companies were three hours late (near dusk); 4 Company never came at all.[105] Colonel Brauer, the commander of 1 Parachute Regiment landed with I Battalion — far to the east and unable to command his battle.

III Battalion landed late and attacked west and south of Heraklion town. They had been spread out, and became embroiled in fierce encounters with the Greeks, with elements of the 2nd Yorks and Lancs and other units. Some small groups of III Battalion penetrated the town and dock area, but most of the troops landed were forced to retire to positions south-west of Heraklion.[100]

While II Battalion of the 2nd Parachute Regiment landed unopposed further to the west, two of its four companies failed to arrive — without transport they remained at the Greek airfields.[101] In short, the Germans at Heraklion achieved little on the first night. They had sustained heavy losses by enemy action and their force was not up to strength. Colonel Brauer was unaware that some 600 of his invasion force had been left behind.

Whereas at Heraklion the invaders had been outnumbered, at Retimo the garrison faced invaders a few hundred stronger. This was offset by two factors. Firstly, the Australian troops were the most battle-hardened of the troops on the island, and secondly the circumstances of the German's descent on Heraklion were happily repeated at Retimo.[102] Lieutenant-Colonel Ian Campbell of the Australian Imperial Forces had two Australian battalions: the 2/1 Battalion and the 2/11 Battalion, over 1,200 experienced infantry. About 800 Cretan Police, an efficient fighting force, held Retimo town itself. In addition there were around 2,300 Greeks, some unarmed; those with weapons had little ammunition as well as grenades. Even the rifle ammunition was not oversupplied.[103] The Germans, under Colonel Sturm, had about 1,500 men — troops of I and III Battalions of 2 Parachute Regiment. They were experienced airborne troops and their most recent assignment had been the drop on New Zealand 6 Brigade at Corinth Canal.

The terrain favoured the defence: a narrow coastal strip half a mile wide at the most with overlooking high ground. Campbell made defence of the landing ground his priority. The added advantage of plenty of foliage for concealment meant that the enemy failed to learn the actual strength of the garrison. As elsewhere on Crete, Freyberg's dictum of shielding his forces from German reconnaissance paid off.

At about 4 p.m. twenty fighters and light bombers attacked but failed to make any impact on the concealed infantry. The Ju52s began dropping troops at 4.15 p.m. and seven were immediately shot down. The air drops were generally prolonged and spread out, which, along with the by now standard ambush of some companies landing on their foes muzzles, made for serious casualties among the invaders. This time there was air support overhead, but because of the close fighting, the pilots refrained from attempting machine-gun and bombing attacks: they could not tell friend from foe.[104]

At Retimo, as at Heraklion, the shambles of the Luftwaffe's air/ground co-ordinations was to some extent compounded by the lateness of the assaults. Not only were the drops strung out, but the garrison had only to endure a relatively few hours before darkness set in. They would not have to last a day without reinforcement, as Andrew's 22nd had at Maleme.

The German assault troops made good use of the few hours and light. By nightfall it seemed that they might at first light be able to dominate Hill 'A' overlooking the landing ground. Two companies of parachutists, later reinforcements, had all but pushed off the Australian infantry holding it, and Campbell, starved of help, had been informed over the radio by Freyberg's headquarters, 'Regret unable to send help. Good luck.'[105]

He therefore planned a counter-attack at dawn.

> The first attack by Channell [one of Campbell's Company commanders] was at dawn. When that failed I led round my remaining Company and told Captain Moriarty to take most of the troops in the area and clear Hill A at about 10 hrs.[106]

On noticing a German aircraft dropping bombs on paratroopers on the hilltop just before 8 a.m., Moriarty determined to attack at once. The Australians were immediately successful. This was followed later on 21 May by Australian destruction of the German remnant. Colonel Sturm and his staff were taken prisoner, and Sturm's orders were captured. The tanks that had come to grief the previous evening were salvaged. It had taken five attacks, three on the evening of 20 May, two the next morning, to retake Hill 'A'.[107] Yet, by persisting, the Australians had been successful. The German forces in the coastal strip near the defence positions were out of the fight.

The shambles of the afternoon of 20 May that had been the feature of the ill-timed and ill-co-ordinated assaults on Heraklion and Retimo left General Student with a reserve of only 600 paratroopers. After these were gone, there were only two ways to commit further German ground forces to the island: by sea, or by landing aircraft on airfields. Student in Athens was as blind as the headquarters of Creforce as to the situation at Maleme and its possibilities.

In the face of likely disaster it was decided to send a seaborne invasion force, in spite of the Italian fleet's decision not to sail in its support. This was a desperate and dangerous expedient, for units of the British Mediterranean Fleet were already at sea, ready to meet such an eventuality.

Student was later to claim that by the evening of 20 May, he was able to assess the situation sufficiently to know that the *Schwerpunkt* of the attack would have to be Maleme.[108] While radio contact had been lost with the 2 Parachute Regiment at Retimo, Gericke quotes Student as being generally well informed:

> With the other three attacking groups at Maleme, Chania and Heraklion, radio contact was good from the first... the parachute regiments came through soon after dropping and then gave their regular situation reports to Athens.[109]

Bletchley Park was privy to these signals, but with a battle raging and with the ever present danger of German recognition that their codes were broken, the cryptanalysts were timid over the further distribution of tactical material to the commander of Creforce.

On the other hand, Student was not sanguine enough to initiate measures he had in mind without more information. Gericke quotes Student:

> During the night I sent for Captain Kleye, a bold go-getting character on my staff, and told him to take a Junkers 52 and land at Maleme in order to get a personal feeling of how things were going with the Storm Regiment... he managed to land on the airfield and also to get off again although fired at by the enemy. In this way he was able to bring back the important information that the western edge of the airstrip lay in dead ground.[110]

It was a bold stroke although the loss of one more Ju52 by this time would have been neither here nor there. Student's reaction to Kleye's news was to send six Ju52s loaded with ammunition and supplies to put down on the beach in the dead zone. This was a measure of desperation. About 8 a.m. on Wednesday 21 May, 350 paratroops were safely dropped west of the Tavronitis to bolster the ground forces.[111]

This was only the beginning. Later on that day, more landings were ordered, heedless of the casualties, for the Germans realized that for their ground forces, it had come down to a matter of win ground or surrender. It was a crude strategy but it was made necessary by the cumulative catastrophes of the abortive Tuesday assaults. Creforce defence appeared to be holding. The success of Freyberg's defence of the island had ruptured the enemy's invasion, and it seemed likely the Royal Navy would wreck the German efforts by sea. It was the inaction and lack of enterprise of the rear support battalions of 5 Brigade, and the indecisiveness of Brigadier Hargest that turned the tide and allowed Fliegerkorps XI its opportunity.

New Zealand Division was informed at 4.30 a.m. on 21 May that the 22nd Battalion no longer held the airfield at Maleme. Given the inclinations of the battalion commanders and the brigade commander of 5 Brigade, nothing could now be done in terms of countermoves until dark on the Wednesday night. Early in the morning of 21 May, Freyberg himself had gone from Creforce headquarters to ascertain what was happening in the New Zealand sector: 'GOC in C arrived at Div HQ at 0850 hrs for a conference with Div Comd and Staff.'[112] The upshot of this meeting seems to have been that a conference of brigadiers and Freyberg himself would take place in the afternoon at Freyberg's headquarters.

Apart from the arrival of the six transports with ammunition during the morning and the relatively small drop of paratroops, no further activity would take place until the afternoon, although the garrison was not to know that.

The conference on the Wednesday afternoon at Freyberg's headquarters was chaired by the General and attended by Brigadiers Puttick, Inglis, Vasey (of the Australian Brigade), plus Stewart. Hargest did not attend. Perhaps Puttick thought that the commander of 5 Brigade should remain with his troops. Any expression of Hargest's views would be made by the acting Divisional commander, Puttick. Similarly, Puttick was the filter by which Hargest would learn the outcome of the meeting. It may be speculated that had Hargest been there, Freyberg could well have ascertained that matters were less than satisfactory within 5 Brigade.

Countermeasures were decided. A two-battalion counter-attack was determined, using the New Zealand Divisions' reserve battalion, the 20th, along with the rear-most formation of 5 Brigade, the 28th Maori Battalion — two fresh strong infantry formations. An Australian battalion from Georgeopoulis would move west that night to take over the positions of the 20th New Zealand Battalion. The latter, using Australian transport, would move up to Platanias, where they would join the 28th for the counter-attack. As the seaborne attack was expected during the night, the 20th were to remain until the 2/7th Australian Battalion came up.[113] When Lieutenant-Colonel Walker, the commander of the 2/7th Australian Battalion, raised the possibility that the Australian relief might be delayed in the darkness, Inglis dismissed this, asserting that 'a well trained battalion' would be able to relieve the 20th in an hour.[114] The plan was set.

While Freyberg and his senior officers were considering the night's operations to retake the aerodrome, the Germans attempted to drop still more paratroops, and to force their way on to the airfield. Around midday on 21 May, the last two companies of paratroops descended along roughly the line of the coast road between Pirgos and Platanias.[115] In spite of, or perhaps because of, the decimation of III Battalion of the Storm Regiment the previous day, the German commanders sending these troops remained unaware that this whole area was occupied in force by the garrison. This may have been because the destruction of III Battalion on 20 May had been so complete. Whatever the reason for the drop, it was needlessly expensive of human life: there was no reason why the two companies could not have been dropped well west of the Tavronitis in safety. Some fell in the sea; those on land deposited themselves on the Maori Battalion or the two engineer units further west. The desperate scenes of the previous day were repeated in miniature:

> . . . a Hun dropped not ten feet away [wrote Captain Anderson]. I had my pistol in my hand . . . and without really knowing what I was doing let him have it while he was still on the ground. I had hardly got over the shock when another came down almost on top of me and I plugged him too while he was untangling himself. Not cricket I know but there it is.[116]

These companies suffered the same fate as the unfortunates who had fallen unsuspectingly on the concealed 23rd Battalion the day before. Few lived.

More seriously for the defenders, Student had ordered a battalion-sized unit of 800 mountain troops to be landed on Maleme aerodrome regardless of the cost. It was a bold move. A close perimeter defence and artillery fire might have decimated this attack. It is a tribute to the skill of the pilots that the Germans got away with it:

> The landing was carried out with the greatest dash and determination by JU formations of Battle Squadron (Special Duties) 3, in spite of enemy artillery fire and, to begin with, also machine-gun fire. A number of JUs were shot to pieces or burnt out on the beach and on the airfield. Extensive losses of mountain riflemen were avoided through the presence of mind of the pilots.[117]

In a real sense, the successful arrival of these troops and the paratroops dropped in the west earlier on that Wednesday, some 1,150 men in all, transformed the German situation on the ground. The remnants of the Storm Regiment had been relieved with fresh troops, who unlike their predecessors, or the nearby New Zealand infantry, had not undergone the maelstrom of 20 May. The slender, fragile clinging lodgement of the night was now not impregnable, but certainly firmer. At around 7 p.m. Colonel Ramcke, a decisive commander, landed at Maleme. Losses of Ju52s were around one-third of those landed, but this was not translated into infantry casualties as well.

Maleme, in German hands, was still contested on 22 May. Creforce artillery was exacting its price in the accumulation of obstructive wreckage. To clear wreckage from the aerodrome's landing and take-off areas prisoners of war were used ruthlessly. Major Reinhard Wenning of 5 Mountain Division reported on his arrival over the airfield on 22 May:

> Maleme [was] covered in vast smoke and dust clouds, a large number of Ju52s circling above it. Coming closer we realise the reason for this circling. On the airfield, which is extremely small there are lying a number of crashed planes and some of these are burning. One Ju52 which is landing collides with one of these wrecks, spins around and lies motionless in the middle of the narrow and inadequate landing strip. This diminishes our chances of landing especially as I can count ten other planes in the air which were circling before we arrived. Despite this my pilot tries to land three times without success because during each approach to the strip suddenly another plane turns in from the side, cutting us off. On the airfield itself we can see shells exploding. The enemy artillery is pouring an accurate fire on to the runway... already this morning several Ju52s suffered direct hits while landing...[118]

Once landed, Wenning found on the aerodrome:

> ...numerous burnt out or still burning remains of planes. Planes were continuously landing, spitting out their men and material, despite the shells exploding around them. It was chaotic. In the air were still about twenty planes looking for the opportunity to come in. The landing strip had to be continuously cleared of all the crashed aircraft. This was hard work done with the help of prisoners, who were already numerous. A very energetic officer was handling this job.[119]

The officer, identified as Major Snowatzki, ensured the co-operation of the captured members of the garrison. When they first refused to work at clearing wreckage, he had three of them shot. This was later verified at the war crimes trials at Nuremberg.

The Germans were clearly prepared to hold Maleme and transform the airstrip into a usable field at any cost. The RAF's veto of Creforce plans for demolition before the invasion had reduced the task of their ground parties to the clearing of landing paths. Had the surface been thoroughly disrupted by ploughing, judiciously spread obstructions, and by mining, Maleme would have remained inoperable much longer. Clearing a useful operational aerodrome is altogether a different proposition to beginning to restore a completely non-operational wrecked airfield. By 22 May there was no longer direct small arms and machine-gun fire on to the airfield. While the clearing parties of prisoners and enemy personnel had to work exposed to the hazards of artillery fire, the chances of their being wiped out completely were reduced.

A gaping hole now yawned in the island's defences, the direct result of 5 Brigade's failure to carry out brigade battle plans and Freyberg's orders. It is easy, though not entirely idle, to envisage a different and decidedly more dangerous situation for the Germans. The Wednesday morning could have opened with the rifle companies of the 23rd Battalion, perhaps a company from the 22nd and one from the 21st, flung forward around Maleme. The 23rd might have partially taken Kavzakia Hill, reoccupied Pirgos, and the whole force of some five to six infantry companies might have reduced the enemy's hold to the Tavronitis side of the airfield. So long as the airfield itself remained inoperable, the Germans could not expand through large-scale re-supply and large-scale reinforcement. At the very least there would have been a drawn battle with the total outcome in the balance. As each hour passed, the dwindling of the German's supplies of paratroops, arms, and ammunition would continue without the continuous arrival and unloading of transports.

It was, of course, not like that at all because the battalion commanders and the brigade commander had not swung their troops into action to restore the situation. The New Zealand officers on the spot had deferred a counter-attack until the Wednesday night at the earliest. Once first light had come, and the Luftwaffe with it, on the morning of 21 May, nothing effective could be done by the infantry without exposure to aerial intervention. In similarly inauspicious circumstances, logic implacably compelled the Germans to take the risks of large-scale casualties in men and material. Not to do so meant, in the long run, inevitable defeat. They took the risks this entailed because, without an airfield, their ground forces already landed were headed for annihilation.

To Walter Gibbons of 'B' Company, 23rd Battalion, the night had not been easy and daylight on 21 May was frustrating:

> There was little sleep at night. Any dozing was abruptly terminated by outbreaks of firing. Tracer indicated a rather mixed dispersion of enemy and defenders.
>
> On the 21 May there was little fighting within the 23 Bn area. We expected we would be called on to counter-attack. Instead we watched the enemy get control of the aerodrome and begin landing troop transport planes, disembarking troops and flying off. There was nothing we could do but watch. There was some enemy pressure on the B Coy positions during the day after the withdrawal of 22 Bn. . .[120]

The orders for the awaited counter-attack, planned during the afternoon of 21 May, were not sent out to those units out of radio contact with their headquarters until evening, probably partly for ease of distribution under the cloak of dusk or darkness.

5 Brigade's orders for the counter-attack were:

1. Starting Time for Advance 0100 hrs 22 May 41
2. Starting Time for Attack 0400 hrs 22 May 41
3. Line of Advance: 20 Bn on right of rd, but when past MALEME CEMETERY and on to AERODROME, the left of the Bn will move under the terrace, 100 yds left of the rd.

4. 28 Bn to move to left of rd, and when nearing objective will make certain its left is on top of KAVZAKIA HILL (107).
5. On completion of task, 20 Bn will move back to ridge in front of MALEME village with posts thrust forward to command the AERODROME. Thence approximately along line of rd to Pt 107.
6. 28 Bn as soon as task is finished and it has handed over to 20 Bn will withdraw to its location at PLATANIAS by covered routes.
7. 21 Bn will occupy a line from Pt 107 back to wireless station.
8. Bde Report Centre at Old Bde H.Q. PLATANIAS VILLAGE.

Headquarters,
5 Inf Bde,
FIELD,
21 May 41.[121]

A copy for 23rd Battalion of this order arrived at 10.45 p.m. of necessity in a 3 Hussars' tank, for the wireless telegraphy link was put out of action in the afternoon.[122] The 23rd Battalion had been given no role in the attack other than, according to Dawson (the Brigade-Major) and Mason (Staff Captain, 5 Brigade), a ' "mopping up role" after the attack passed through [the] immediate position'.[123]

The role of the 20th Battalion, the reserve unit of the New Zealand Division, had become more significant because two-thirds of the nominated Force Reserve had already been given to and committed by Puttick to defending the area west of Canea. This basically meant containing 3 Parachute Regiment in the Prison Valley, with the 18th and 19th Battalions of 4 Brigade under Brigadier Inglis assisting the composite formations under Colonel Kippenberger. The one reserve battalion in the New Zealand Division area had been allotted a role in the repelling of a seaborne invasion known to be scheduled for the night of 21/22 May. This battalion was restricted to its holding area until the 2/7th Australian Battalion from Georgeopoulis relieved it. This was ordered by Freyberg himself, in response to the Australian battalion commander's concern over the contingency of delay. Inglis had dismissed Walker's worries. He should not have for the Australians were late.

According to Burrows, the commander of the 20th, the arrangements were that:

> The Bn was to be relieved... at about 2000 hrs that night, and making use of the Australian transport I was to take the 20th on to report to and receive orders from Brigadier HARGEST.
>
> The Australian Bn... arrived nearly three hours late. Between 2200 hrs and approx 0100 hrs... I twice rang Bde for instructions... I was told to remain in position until relieved.[124]

Should the 20th have been moved given the Royal Navy's destruction of the seaborne invasion convoys? The invasion convoy closest to Crete came within eighteen miles of the coast nearest the Maleme sector before being sunk. Until it had been removed, the threat was real given that the seaborne forces consisted of not only more troops, but heavy weapons as well. Also, the extent of the Australian delay could not be predicted, and delay needs to take account of the hour to hour factor: they might appear at any moment, and the 20th could be on its way. It is argued, however, that holding the start of the 28th Battalion at Platanias until the 20th came up was not the only option for Brigadier Hargest.

Davin has speculated on the substitution of the conveniently placed 23rd Battalion to accompany the 28th Battalion on the counter-attack, leaving the 20th to come up later and either take over the 23rd's positions, or join the drive forward.[125] In the darkness would it have been difficult to extract the 23rd from their positions? However, Watson's 'A' Company had moved in the darkness the night before, and 'B' Company of the 28th had passed through also on its fruitless journey. The order arrived late — at around 10.45 p.m. at the 23rd Battalion headquarters. The companies had then to be warned that troops would later be passing in the darkness. Not a pleasant prospect, creeping around in the dark, but not impossible. Gibbons, as a runner, was tasked in 'B' Company:

> In the night I had to find several section posts and warn them of the long delayed counter-attack. I must say I was pretty scared all the time anyway — none of the bravery rubbed off on me. . .[126]

If it was possible to get messages around the battalion in the dark, then it was also possible to get messages around to move troops. After all, if the 28th and 20th Battalions were able, if belatedly, to advance from Platanias then the relatively small amount of movement necessary to form up the 23rd for an attack could be done. Unlike the 20th Battalion, the 23rd were at least on familiar ground. The success of both the 28th and the 20th in the advance, until daylight brought the inevitable aerial intervention of the Luftwaffe, clearly demonstrates that the option was practicable. There is no evidence that this was considered by Puttick or Hargest. Yet faced with the delay, particularly as the start time of 0100 hours on 22 May approached, it should have been an option that almost suggested itself.

However, it was dark and late. Hargest asked Puttick if the attack had to go in, given the lateness of the start time. He was told it must. He seems to have been tired, and perhaps despairing. When James Booth of 7 Anti-Tank Regiment dined with a 3 Hussars officer in Cairo shortly after Crete, the officer turned out to be Roy Farran — the tank commander who was to fight well at Galatas. The name 'Hargest' was mentioned:

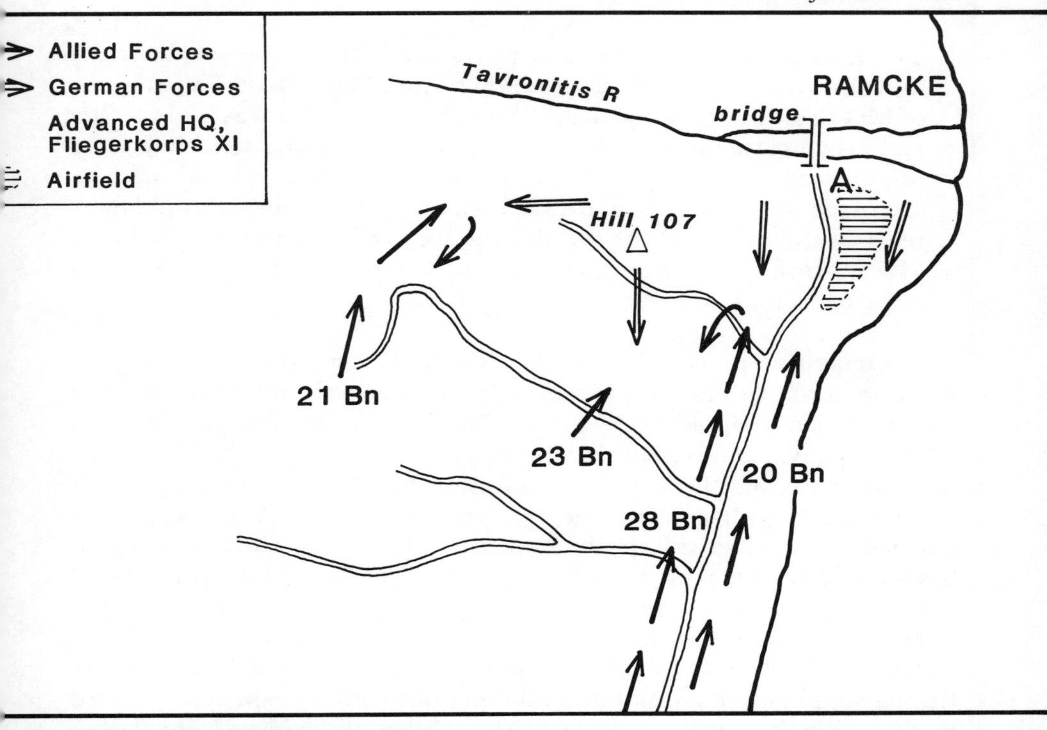

The counter-attack fails, 22 May 1941.

> He [Farran] had taken three tanks to assist in the counter-attack on Maleme aerodrome and had reported to Hargest for instructions on their deployment. Hargest said he was too tired and was going to bed and would talk to him in the morning.[127]

This was an unexpected reaction from a brigade commander who had been given the chance to retake a vital position, using fresh formations sent to him.

The delayed start took place with the 20th and 28th Battalions at around 3.30 a.m. Even then, only two companies of the 20th, 'C' and 'D', were available at that stage. The three other companies followed later. The 20th moved along more or less north of the coast road, while the Maori Battalion companies moved west, south of the road. The infantry met pockets of the enemy, and as they moved further west, resistance became more intense. The then Lieutenant Upham of 'C' Company, 20th Battalion, wrote vividly:

> Went on meeting resistance in depth — in ditches, behind hedges, in the top and bottom of village buildings, fields and gardens on road beside drome. The wire of 5 Bde hindered our advance. . . There was

> T.G. [sub-machinegun fire] and pistol and plenty of grenades and a lot of bayonet work which you don't often get in war. The amount of MG fire was never equalled. Fortunately a lot of it was high . . . We had heavy casualties but the Germans had much heavier. They were unprepared. Some were without trousers, some had no boots on. The Germans were helpless in the dark. With another hour we could have reached the other side of the 'drome. We captured, as it was, a lot of MGs, 2 Bofors pits were overrun and the guns destroyed. The Pws went back to 5 Bde.[128]

Lieutenant-Colonel Allen of the 21st Battalion, still in his original position, took the initiative and his infantry forward, and by 10 a.m. had captured Xamoudhokhori.[129] Some of his troops, including elements of 'D' Company, 22nd Battalion, who had been attached to the 21st, made it as far as the old 'D' Company positions by the Tavronitis. By about 11.30 a.m., Allen heard that the 28th and 20th had been held up, so he decided to maintain his positions rather than push further forward. Sometime after 3.30 p.m., he retired upon his old Vineyard Ridge positions. It was a remarkable effort, against fresh German troops, but it would have been more useful the day before, in the afternoon.

The attack failed, and the Germans were therefore free to bring in more troops, supplies, and ammunition, though not without some cost exacted by the remaining artillery of Major Philp. What of the Navy? The flashes of the naval gunfire at sea had been thankfully received by Freyberg and his staff, leading to his famous remark: 'It's been a great responsibility — a great responsibility.'[130] There can be little doubt that the General believed a great weight taken from his shoulders. He had planned to hold Crete on the basis that the Royal Navy would stop the German seaborne forces. Unavoidably, the Navy had kept him in suspense. But now the ships of Admiral King and Admiral Glennie had, over a longer period than that one night, nullified the German amphibious effort.

The vital naval task in the early part of the struggle for the island — the interception and destruction of the invasion convoys — was successfully completed following contact at 2330 hours on the night of the 21st May. This was followed later, in the early hours of Thursday morning (22nd May), by a flotilla sweep into Kissima and Canea Bays with five destroyers — HMS *Kelly, Kashmir, Kipling, Kelvin,* and *Jackal.* Of this force sent by Admiral Rawlings — in part to look for survivors of earlier sinkings of Royal Navy warships — HMS *Kelly* and *Kashmir* proceeded briefly to bombard Maleme airfield with 4.7 inch guns.[131] More effective than the fragile RAF raids launched from Egypt, the cost exacted was high. The next morning caught by Stukas of I/StG2, under Hauptmann Hitscold,[132] *Kelly* and *Kashmir* were sunk, bringing to nine the number of warships sunk locally since 20 May.

From Freyberg's viewpoint, the Navy had done its job well. The seaborne threat was removed, and an infantry attack by two fresh battalions was moving to retake Maleme, with sizeable infantry formations, namely the 21st and 23rd Battalions, available close at hand for support if needed. He did not know that Puttick's pedantic interpretation of his orders concerning the relief of the 20th Battalion had stalled the attack so that it would not be able to be completed until daylight. He could not know that Hargest's handling of both days since the assault opened had been less than effective.

At 0330 hours GMT, a signal was sent to the Middle East from Bletchley Park. Summary OL404 looked to be, on the face of it, the useful signal that a commander in Freyberg's position should have been sent immediately. OL404 stated that the Germans' main current objective was to consolidate Maleme in preparation for further landings, detailing as first expected arrivals the 1st Battalion of 85 Mountain Regiment, plus the Mountain Pioneer Battalion. This in itself was useful: more troops were to be expected; but perhaps the presence of the Pioneer Battalion implied engineering works were wanted to clear the airfield, making the lodgement more secure. The crunch in the message was that the: 'ADVANCED HEADQUARTERS OF ELEVENTH FLIEGERKORPS IS AT BRIDGE IMMEDIATELY TO WEST OF AERODROME.'[133] This was vital information. It underlined definitely that the Germans were very serious about Maleme. Freyberg would know that Fl.XI was the ground formation in charge of the invasion. It had been noted earlier that the seaborne forces were to come under its auspices immediately upon a successful landing.

The rub was that OL404 contained a specific instruction that General Freyberg was not to be informed of the contents of the summary. The timing of the message's receipt would be around the time the troops were moving off to the attack. Had it been seen by Freyberg it could have given the attacking forces an objective supplementary to the aerodrome. It would also have explained why the area around the bridge would be very strongly defended.

This is not the whole story. Crete's time is two hours in front of London's, so 3.30 a.m. London would be about 5.30 a.m. on the island. The forward troops would have been well gone, and given the state of Allied tactical communications at this juncture, the chances for any messages getting through were clearly nil.

It does not end there, though. Seven hours later than 0330 hours GMT, it was decided that OL404 and other messages should be passed to General Freyberg. This decision is revealed in OL411 of 1030 hours GMT, on 22nd May (that is, about 12.30 p.m. on Crete).[134] The counter-attack had failed by this time, although ironically the 21st Battalion was still lingering round behind Kavzakia Hill near the Tavronitis.

The necessary nervousness that inevitably accompanied the reading of the enemy's own current signals was based on the underlying fear that the Germans might suddenly unexpectedly realize they had been compromised. That could lead to the end of 'Most Secret Sources'. Security of Enigma-based material was to the forefront in the distribution arrangements currently in force in the Middle East for BONIFACE (the code-name for signals intelligence). The contents of OL404 was in its own way slightly alarming. The analysts would know that Fl.XI was in charge of the invasion. The mention of a headquarters for Fl.XI could be an indication that the small German lodgement was consolidating and was slipping from Freyberg's hands. A glance at a map would show that Freyberg's own headquarters above Canea was not too far from Maleme and raised the issue of the risk of sending further material to Freyberg. The decision to restrict the circulation of the intercepts was reversed. It would be interesting to know whose hand intervened. One might suspect a Churchillian hand — it was he after all who earlier wanted to send all raw intercepts to Freyberg on Crete.

For Freyberg, the events of the next day were a bitter blow. That he well understood the importance of the failure of the counter-attack is revealed in his battle diary:

> 22 [May] D3 Fine and clear — Heraklion and Retimo remain clear but road communications severed from Suda — no further landings Maleme, main attack continues — fantastic story of Hun leaving by tp carrier [this was a Hargest invention borne of wishful thinking] — tp carriers come in at rate of 20 per hour — Plan to recapture aerodrome by c/attack changed to withdrawal and forming of defensive posn owing to threat against rear from force S/W of Canea [presumably 3rd Parachute Regiment] and severe casualties of 5 Bde [a feature Hargest was now inclined to exaggerate] — So Maleme becomes an operational aerodrome — question of maintenance of Creforce — cables pass — . . . in evening 5 Bde withdraws — has to fight way, some guns lost — infiltration of enemy communications — Naval action in Canea Bay, and Maleme shelled — . . . cable from C-in-C on situation — preparation of report for C-in-C — Lull in morning due to German attack on Navy with loss of cruisers 5 destroyers and battleships damaged.[135]

The implications for the defence of the island were now clear. At the sharp end, it was no less so.

Gibbons, at 'B' Company headquarters, 23rd Battalion, recounts:

> All day on the 22nd May we watched the planes flying in and disgorging men and material. There was also some concentrated and penetrating pressure on our forward posts. It was decided to withdraw the Brigade. The information came to us just before daylight on 23 May. I had to advise several section posts. It went well, but I did find the enemy

> already in one. Since we were to disengage and move quickly, firing was frowned on.
>
> Most of the battalion moved inland to retire to the Platanias area. After warning my sections I returned to B. Coy HQ to find they had gone. But our signals officer Noel Jones (7207) and Charlie Davies (10053) were coming there. The three of us decided to reach Platanias via the canal. On the way we found the Engineer Detachments had already moved back.[136]

They were in fact the last New Zealand infantry retiring in front of the enemy.

Freyberg's reaction to the failure of the counter-attack was to have a staff conference and to plan for another counter-attack, this time by 18th Battalion and the 2/7th Australian Battalion. 4 Brigade was to be moved forward as well, and there was a possibility that 5 Brigade battalions would also take part. The object of the attack was as before: to retake the aerodrome.[137] This took place around 5 p.m.

Puttick left the conference and returned to Division, and then went on to 4 Brigade headquarters. Transport was ready there to take him on to Platanias, and 5 Brigade headquarters. He was not to go to Platanias — the road had been temporarily cut by elements of the German 3 Parachute Regiment.

The problem posed by the paratroopers in the Prison Valley had occupied the attentions of 4 Brigade for some time. There was the fear that 5 Brigade might become cut off and therefore encircled by the Germans who were still pouring more troops in through Maleme. This no doubt occupied the reflections of Brigadier Hargest at Platanias. Hargest, presumably by radio, got a message through to Puttick, and 'represented that his troops had been severely attacked, were considerably exhausted, and certainly not fit to make a further attack'.[138] Puttick could not go forward to Platanias to see for himself. He could not know that the 5 Brigade units were not in the dire straits outlined by Hargest. Hargest himself had not moved from his more comfortable position at Platanias to learn at first hand how his forward battalions were really faring. Puttick contacted Freyberg at Creforce and urged that rather than attack, the position was such that it would be better that 5 Brigade withdraw before it was cut off.

The General informed Puttick that he was to talk to Brigadier Stewart. The latter would be at New Zealand Division headquarters with authority from Freyberg to take what action was necessary. Puttick and Stewart met at 9 p.m. and decided to withdraw 5 Brigade. According to the New Zealand Division *War Diary:* '5 Inf Bde warned at 2230 hrs to be prepared to withdraw during night 22/23 May.'[139] This was followed by: 'Orders for withdrawal of 5 Inf Bde issued 0015 hrs [23 May].'[140] The result of this move left the 5 Brigade battalions still about Platanias, but too far back from the airfield to interfere with the German build-up. The brigade commander on the spot knew the situation on the ground as did the divisional commander. Freyberg, because of his distance from the battle needed to trust their judgement. Clearly the aerodrome was for the moment lost. Freyberg trusted his subordinates.

The alacrity with which 5 Brigade retreated to the Platanias area has already been a matter of comment. The 23rd Battalion, which had remained in a fixed position since the opening of the invasion (leaving aside company-sized movements like 'A' Company's march to the 22nd's defences), now moved with such rapidity that Walter Gibbons, on completing his round of warning his section posts of the movement, returned to 'B' Company headquarters to find it empty of personnel. Gibbons, Jones, and Davies were by accident the last of the 23rd to pull out.

The retreat, to Platanias, did not stop there. A further withdrawal by 5 Brigade right back through the positions of 4 Brigade and 10 Composite Brigade, in front of Galatas, prevented the following enemy from outflanking and cutting off 5 Brigade. It also compounded the problems for the defence. At least three battalions of 100 Mountain Regiment and 85 Mountain Regiment exploiting the unopposed freedom of movement offered in the south were able to move towards, and join up with, formations of 3 Parachute Regiment, in the Prison Valley. The inland German forces were now considerable, no longer in danger of being cut off and withering from lack of support. Each mile gained, while it lengthened the German line of communications, conversely increased the distance of the New Zealand infantry from the airfield at Maleme. The hopes of retaking Maleme were now utterly dashed. The senior officers of 5 Brigade had no stomach left for any countermoves against the airfield, and the brigade commander had persuaded the acting-commander of the New Zealand Division to concur with the shift to the east. The whole move, from the forward battalion positions well west of Platanias to the area in the rear of 4 Brigade, represented the *de facto* surrender of the operationally most important region of the western sector to the enemy. Any countermoves from here on represent attempts to slow down the impetus of the German advance. Maleme aerodrome had now irrevocably gone to Fliegerkorps XI.

The tenor of Freyberg's cables to Wavell, on 23 May, betrayed a mounting alarm at the deterioration of the tactical situation at Maleme.

> *No. 416, 23 May 1941*
> Reference your telegram of 22 May (no. 414). The situation at Maleme is really serious. Send all available air help. A full report follows.[141]
> *No. 417, 23 May 1941*
> The following is a report on the situation as at 10 p.m. GMT, 22 May. The position is clear at Heraklion and also at Retimo, but the enemy have withdrawn at the flanks and have blown the road. Heraklion is

now in touch by road with the Argyll and Sutherland Highlanders and I have ordered them to concentrate a battalion and tanks at Heraklion preparatory to reinforcing the Suda garrison, if possible by road. Enemy action has prevented road communication between Force [Headquarters] and Retimo and also, I believe, between Retimo and Heraklion. Retimo has no transport. I have ordered the two garrisons concerned to clear up the situation and they will do so provided the enemy do not carry out any further landing against them.

At Maleme the enemy have been most active. I want you to get the true picture so that our difficulties can be appreciated. They have continued to land troop carriers, not only on the aerodromes under our shellfire but also on the beaches and a strip to the west, in the most methodical way. In all, fifty-nine landed between 1 p.m. and 4 p.m. today, and this rate of arrival can be taken as the approximate guide for today, 22nd, and yesterday. To deny Maleme aerodrome to the enemy meant holding a long and vulnerable area. He is in strength in an area on the road south-west of Canea, and by attacking in the direction of the coast this evening he cut off the troops at Maleme. It was my intention to attack the aerodrome again tonight but the threat to my rear has forced my hand. I have decided to readjust the present insecure position and make ready for secure defence. The serious situation is that Maleme becomes an operational aerodrome within 20,000 metres of Suda Bay.

Small ships landed Germans on the peninsula behind Canea today and this may become a problem. Parachute and beach landings can cut any of our routes at any moment. All these questions have to be considered and I have decided firstly, that I cannot continue to chance all the rear areas and coastline, and, secondly, that the troops cannot fight without a rest. Therefore I am taking up a line which will lessen my responsibilities. The enemy is now approaching equality in numbers. We shall continue to fight here and at other points in Crete, and we can fight on as long as maintenance does not break down. Everything depends on maintenance in the finish.

In my opinion we must continue to use Suda. The only southern ports open are Tymbaki and Sphakia; the road to the latter is not completed and both must be protected, while further transport is essential before they can be used.

Later: 4.30 a.m. GMT, 23 May. Reference your telegram of 22 May (No. 414). I have already cabled you regarding Maleme and the air assistance required. A cable from my AOC, No. A.35, deals with landing grounds and refuelling. Our approximate line runs north-west and south-east 200 yards west of Galatas. I consider that RAF help, especially fighters, may alter the outlook and it is for very deep consideration whether this help can be made available and maintained for the next few days, which are critical. Enemy troop carriers continue to arrive today.[142]

The New Zealand Division's position was deteriorating. The Germans were now bringing in men and supplies and weapons at will, with close support aircraft and at least an emergency forward aerodrome virtually on the front line in flying terms, underlining the complete switch in the military fortunes of the invaders and the garrison. The defenders were holding, but only just. The Germans would press on knowing that every metre yielded by the New Zealanders increased the security of their lodgement. What Freyberg had feared most of all, what his plan of the island's defence had had as its main objective, had now happened — an airfield had been lost and there had been no immediate riposte at Maleme. There had been excuses for not carrying out orders. There had been little initiative at brigade and battalion level, and now there was little of it at division — with the New Zealand Colonel, Kippenberger, as an exception.

The commander Creforce's battle diary noted some RAF activity — light bombers and fighters around Maleme — but also that the Ju52s continued to arrive.[143] The New Zealand Division had re-formed on a new defence line and was subjected to a severe bombing attack. Heraklion and Retimo were also secure but cut-off and bombed.

Essentially the garrison was not yet defeated, but unless something could be done to assure a very serious German reverse on the battlefield and cut-off their re-supply, the tenure of Allied troops on Crete must be limited. Time was now solidly on the side of the Germans.

In a cable to Wavell, Freyberg reviewed the situation on 24 May 1941:

> An enemy attack upon us here [Galatas] seems to be indicated. Since our move back our dispositions are on a better basis. We are in depth and more capable to withstand attack.
>
> As I feel we are on the eve of an attack I want you to know the full picture of the last four days. The fighting has been very fierce and we can definitely say that the much-vaunted parachutists have been heavily defeated. I cannot believe that they will be used again for a similar objective.
>
> The total casualties of Creforce since 20 May are 1909, as follows: killed 396, wounded 1118, missing 395. Three-quarters of these are from the New Zealand Division at Maleme. The German casualties are, however, much higher: at Heraklion — 790 killed, 20 wounded, and 178 prisoners; at Retimo — approximately 500 dead, 300 wounded, and 50 prisoners. Maleme and the surrounding country saw the hardest fighting of all. At the aerodrome there was a shambles of German dead and burning planes and, I am afraid, a large number of our 22nd Battalion. Estimated [enemy] killed were over 1000, prisoners 320, wounded 80 (making no allowance for wounded left in their hands). Thus the total enemy losses are in the vicinity of 3340.
>
> As I have said, the fighting has been savage and man for man we

have beaten him. I feel that you should know that the scale of air attack we have been faced with has been far worse than anything I had visualised. It has been savage. Further, our men are very tired. Indications today are that the Germans will attempt to blast their way through using 500-pound bombs. We have seen the result of this during the last two days. I know that men will do their best but with the lack of any air support whatsoever the result with tired troops must always be in the balance. I have not discussed this question with anyone and you can count on us to do our best. Anything you can do to neutralise the air situation would help us materially.[144]

The General's entry in his battle diary was equally bleak. 24 May had passed with light cloud and fresh breeze:

. . . Blitz on front line and savage attack on Canea town; fires started — All psns hold, no major attacks — Force HQ moves at short notice at night — 6 inch opens on enemy — . . . Retimo cut off and short of supplies; LO [Liaison Officer] reports parachutists no success there — Navy shell Maleme during night 24/25 — First part Commando arrive. . .[145]

5 Brigade had withdrawn behind the positions of 4 Brigade during the night of 24/25 May. The battalions of 5 Brigade had no sooner reached semi-reserve positions when they were called on to fight once more. The 19th Australian Brigade, under Brigadier Vasey, was now operating on the left of the New Zealand Division's line. The infantry of 4 Brigade were steadily pushed back by ground, and co-ordinated air attacks, through 25 May. At around 8.30 p.m., the Germans broke through the Composite Battalion and captured Galatas, only being stopped at the other side of the village by artillery brought swiftly into action by the quick thinking of Major Bull, firing over open sights at close range.

Freyberg cabled Wavell:

No. 426, 25 May 1941

Today has been one of great anxiety for me here. Last night the enemy carried out one small attack and again this afternoon he attacked with little success. At 5 p.m. this evening bombers, dive bombers, and ground strafers came over and bombed our forward troops and then his ground troops launched an attack. It is still in progress and I am awaiting news.

Later: Puttick has informed me that the line has gone and we are trying to stabilise. I do not know if they will be able to and I am apprehensive. I will send messages as I can later.[146]

The situation at Galatas was restored by the personal intervention of Colonel Kippenberger. The Germans needed to be checked strongly if they were not to break through the centre of the New Zealand Division, with potential serious consequences for the infantry on either flank. Reinforcements from 5 Brigade had been sent for. Two of 3 Hussars light tanks under Lieutenant Farran turned up where Kippenberger was waiting:

> Farran stopped and spoke to me and I told him to go into the village and see what was there. He clattered off and we would hear him firing briskly, when two more companies of the 23rd arrived, C and D, under Harvey and Manson, each about eighty strong. They halted on the road near me. The men looked tired, but fit to fight and resolute. It was no use trying to patch the line any more; obviously we must hit or everything would crumble away. I told the two company commanders they would have to retake Galatos with the help of the two tanks. No, there was no time for reconnaissance; they must move straight in up the road, one company either side in single file behind the tanks, and take everything with them. Stragglers and walking wounded were still streaming past. Some stopped to join in as did Carson and the last four of his party. The men fixed bayonets and waited grimly.[147]

What then took place is famous in the annals of 2 New Zealand Division. The two companies of the 23rd Battalion and the two tanks of 3 Hussars attacked up the road into the village. They were accompanied from the left by elements of the 18th Battalion under Colonel Gray and some other infantry. It was not yet dark:

> . . . as the tanks disappeared as a cloud of dust into the first buildings of the village the whole line seemed to break spontaneously into the most blood curdling of shouts and battle cries.[148]

Colonel Gray could '. . . never forget the deep-throated wild beast noise of the yelling, charging men as the 23rd swept up the road'.[149] In one of the fiercest assaults of the war, the infantry companies of the 23rd stormed into Galatas and furiously drove the Germans from the village at the point of the bayonet, along with grenades, rifle fire, and bren-guns. It became a rout. Lieutenant Thomas described his experiences:

> . . . stepping over groaning forms, and those which rose against us fell to our bayonets, and bayonets with their eighteen inches of steel entering throats and chests with the same. . . hesitant ease as we had used them on the straw-packed dummies in Burnham. . . The Hun seemed in full flight. From doors, windows and roofs they swarmed wildly, falling over one another to clear our relentless line. There was little aimed fire against us now.[150]

After days of frustration, of tiredness, of retreat, of impotence in the face of the fighters and dive-bombers, the infantry of the 23rd demonstrated with terrible exactitude just what New Zealand infantry could do. The temporary brigade commander of 10 Brigade, Colonel Kippenberger had intervened decisively at a very dangerous moment, and had countered the enemy threat by using an immediate assault to shatter the enemy's momentum. This had been used to some extent at Heraklion, and most definitely by Campbell at Retimo. It was of course that central axiom of the defence laid down by Freyberg: immediate counter-attack.

The success of the Galatas riposte ensured that the battalions of 4 Brigade could retire behind those of 5 Brigade during the night without further interference by the Germans.

Freyberg noted in his battle diary in spite of air attacks, positions had been held.[151] He had received bad news from Brigadier Puttick:

> . . . message from Brig Puttick arrives night 25/26 at 0140 hrs stating that 2000 hrs on 25th our line was broken; expressed doubt whether he can hold enemy on 26th.

Puttick's expression of doubt was a harbinger of disaster. At 2.45 a.m. on Monday 26 May, Puttick sent Hargest a letter that envisaged a withdrawal by the New Zealand Division to the east:

> My dear Hargest,
>
> I think you and Inglis have done splendidly in most difficult situation. All I have time to write now is to say that in the unfortunate event of our being forced to withdraw, we must avoid CANEA and move well south of it towards SUDA. Brig. STEWART says he will in that event try to organise a covering force across the head of SUDA BAY through which we would pass, south of the Bay, of course. This information is highly confidential to you but will indicate a line to follow in the event of dire necessity.
>
> Would you kindly pass one copy to INGLIS.
>
> Good Luck.
>
> Yours ever,
> E. PUTTICK.[152]

Kippenberger was not one of the addressees of Puttick's missive.

General Freyberg had already come to the conclusion that holding the island was now untenable. Freyberg cabled Wavell, and was blunt and to the point. The defence of the island was past the point of no return. It remained to try and ensure some kind of orderly withdrawal:

26 May 1941

I regret to have to report that in my opinion the troops under my command here at Suda Bay have reached the limit of endurance. No matter what decision is taken by the Commanders-in-Chief, from a military point of view our position here is hopeless. A small, ill-equipped, and immobile force such as ours cannot stand up against the concentrated bombing that we have been faced with during the last seven days. I feel you should be informed that from an administrative point of view the difficulties of extricating this force in full are now insuperable. A certain proportion of the force might be embarked provided a decision is reached at once. Once this sector has been reduced, the reduction of Retimo and Heraklion by the same methods will only be a matter of time. With the exception of the Welch Regiment and the Commando, the troops we have are past any offensive action. If, in view of the whole Middle East position, you decide that hours help, we will carry on. I would have to consider how this would best be achieved. Suda Bay may be under fire within twenty-four hours. Further, our casualties have been heavy and we have lost the majority of our immobile guns.[153]

There was a necessity now for Freyberg to make decisions that would bring about orderly retirement, without the enemy breaking through, or being encouraged to do so. At around 4 a.m. on 26 May, Freyberg sent Puttick, now commanding the New Zealand Division and 19 Australian Brigade, the following message:

Dear Puttick,

I have read through your report on the situation. I am not surprised that the line broke. Your battalions were very weak and the areas they were given were too large. On the shorter line you should be able to hold them. In any case there will not be that infiltration that started before. You must hold them on that line and counter-attack if any part of it should go. It is imperative that he should not break through.

I have seen Stewart and I am sending this plan by G2 who will tell you of my plan. I hope we shall get through tomorrow without any further trouble.

B. Freyberg.[154]

Having made a small criticism of Puttick's handling of the situation, the General regarded the pull-back as sufficient, and gave an imperative order to hold the line. The Germans must be delayed, even if this involved a counter-attack. Major Saville took the letter to Puttick, reporting to him at around 5.40 a.m. on 26 May. He gave Puttick Freyberg's instructions that Puttick and Weston were to establish a joint headquarters near Suda, and that Brigadier Inglis was to report to General Freyberg immediately.[155]

Several hours earlier, we have noted, Puttick had already put into Hargest's mind the possibility of withdrawal from west of Canea to Suda, a sizeable distance. For Hargest, the suggestion of withdrawal was a goad to action. In his diary he noted:

> Early on Monday I moved my HQ to the old Div HQ on the hills before Canea — it was larger. . . and I could get in touch with my neighbours the Australians.
>
> When I arrive Div had gone but Brig Inglis was asleep there and one or two of his staff but he went off to his Bde in rear. I was here in telephonic touch with Div HQ and the 19 Aust Bde and our artillery. Quite early we had reports of enemy pressure and heavy attacks occurred all day. The Aust Brigadier Brig Vasey came over and we met. . . he was to be my comrade for one week and a good one. . .[156]

According to the 23rd Battalion *War Diary,* there was a brigade conference of commanding officers at 0900 hours attended by commanding officers of 19th, 21st, 22nd, 23rd and 28th Battalions.[157] As a result, the 22nd Battalion 'received orders to be prepared to withdraw that evening'.[158] This was around 11 a.m. At about 2.20 p.m. a message was sent out to the 5 Brigade battalions, and to the 19th Battalion:

> *19 Bn*
> Conference of COs at Bde HQ at 1500 hrs.
>
> Note: We are working with the Australians and a British Covering Force — the night's operation should be an easy one.
>
> R.B. Dawson, Capt.[159]

Brigadier Hargest took no chances that his brigade would be left behind. According to the after battle report of 4 New Zealand Brigade, it was recorded that on 26 May:

> During the afternoon orders were received from Force HQ that Brig Inglis was to take command of a Composite Brigade consisting of 1 Welch, Rangers, and some Marines with the object of covering the withdrawal of the New Zealand and Australian brigades.[160]

This was in fact a new Force Reserve created by Freyberg. Inglis had commanded the previous Force Reserve, so it was natural that the commander of Creforce would wish to have an experienced brigadier in command.

The 19 Australian Brigade had been having a brisk day of it. The 2/8th Battalion had had contact with the Germans at around 11.26 a.m., but by 12.15 p.m. this attack had dissipated. The 19 Brigade's *War Diary* records news at 3.20 p.m. that 5 NZ Brigade's right flank had been penetrated.[161] A quarter of an hour later, at 3.45 p.m., it was recorded in the *War Diary* that:

> The left flank of 2/8 Bn was penetrated and the CO was advised to stabilise the attack by putting one pl[atoon] in gap and contacting army tps coy NZE[ngineers] on their left.

At around 4 p.m., Major Peart, the quartermaster-general and assistant adjutant-general of the New Zealand Division, sent a message to Creforce:

> RUCK [19 Australian Brigade] reports enemy working round his left flank WUNA [5 Brigade] reports situation dangerous counter attacking with one bn Comd DUKE [NZ Division commander — Puttick] had left on foot to visit you before situation deteriorated. Is it possible form rear line with fresh troops in event withdrawal being forced.[162]

About forty-five minutes later, Puttick signalled to Creforce headquarters: 'RUCK [19 Bde] reports situation on left very unsatisfactory inform LIFT [Suda Bay Sector] urgently.'[163] Puttick later related that between 4.40 p.m. and 5.30 p.m., both Brigadier Hargest and Brigadier Vasey made strong representations over the telephone for a retreat.[164]

Puttick's absence earlier was because he had made a journey on foot to see General Freyberg. He suggested that the New Zealand Division be withdrawn to the head of Suda Bay, and Force Reserve and the Commandos could be used as a covering force. Freyberg understood this preference, but reasoned it would bring the Germans too close to the Suda dock area and thus endanger the expected night landing of further Commandos and supplies. Freyberg therefore insisted that the line presently occupied be held. He also informed Puttick that General Weston of the Royal Marines was now in charge of the western line, and the troops including Force Reserve and 19 Australian Brigade were under his command.[165]

Inglis was left in no doubt over his duty:

> I told him that the line must be stabilised and that I proposed to put him in command of Force Reserve with his Brigade Staff and send them forward to relieve the N.Z. Division. I visualised them taking over the position which the Welch Regt and themselves prepared astride the road to the west of Canea.[166]

Of the commanding officers of the three formations comprising Force Reserve, namely 1st Welch, the Rangers, and the Northumberland Hussars, only Major Boileau of the Rangers had arrived at Force headquarters. A short while later, Inglis went back to the New Zealand Division. The point to note at this stage is that Inglis had been given command of Force Reserve by the General himself, and that he had already met one of the commanding officers — Boileau.

When Puttick made his way back to the headquarters of the New Zealand Division, it was not on foot. He got a lift from the commander of 1st Welch, Lieutenant-Colonel Duncan, who was heading that way in his car to see Inglis.[167] Inglis was certainly present at that destination while Duncan was there. The commander of Force Reserve had met two of his three commanding officers of his new brigade — and as 1st Welch was by far the most numerous formation, it is fair to say that Inglis should now have seen the most important officers of Force Reserve.

Just prior to Puttick reaching Creforce headquarters, Freyberg:

> . . . informed General Weston of the orders I had given Brigadier Inglis and I advised him to put in the Force Reserve to stabilise the line and relieve the N.Z. Division that night.[168]

Weston then went to Puttick to assess the situation at the front. At around 5.45 p.m., Weston and Wills (his staff officer) saw Puttick at Divisional headquarters. Puttick had just prepared a message to send to Creforce, which was now shown to Wills and Weston. Worried about the flanks of his brigades and the severity of air attack, Puttick suggested a considerable withdrawal.[169]

Weston then checked with Brigadier Vasey of 19 Brigade: Vasey himself spoke to Weston. The 19 Brigade *War Diary* verified Vasey's concern:

> The Bde Comd then told Gen WESTON he thinks it impossible to hold on for 24 hours. The right Bn is strong, the enemy has come through the Greeks, the centre bn has swung around and joined up with the RMs weak spot. The Bde Comd thinks that too many old tps in this area are not worth anything now. He proposed to retire and make a short line East of SUDA BAY. Gen WESTON cannot give a decision yet.[170]

This entry was annotated by Vasey, 'I had previously discussed this plan with Comd NZ Div.'

The conversation between Vasey and Weston took place at around 6.05 p.m. Brigadier Vasey, it seems, had determined to go. The warning orders and conferences of officers of 5 Brigade confirmed a similar intent by Brigadier Hargest. Yet Freyberg had stated, both in written orders to Puttick, and verbally face-to-face, that the line must be held. He had made sure that his cable to Wavell had not become known by his subordinate commanders. In his own words, 'Once the word "withdrawal" is used no more fighting takes place.'[171]

Weston, having heard both Puttick's and Vasey's views, judiciously declared he could not make the decision to withdraw on his own initiative, and intimated that he would go to see General Freyberg. Colonel Duncan of 1st Welch noted that:

> There was some strong language at the Conference. I was hanging about on the fringe and heard some of it. Everyone, including Inglis, pressed for the holding of the rear line. In fact Inglis informed me that he had made a recce of it. Weston would not alter his wish to hold the forward line. It was pointed out to him (Weston) that if he sent Force Reserve forward he would never see them again.[172]

As Weston was about to depart for Freyberg's headquarters, Inglis asked him about his new command:

> As Weston was about to go, I tackled him about the 'new brigade'. He was hurried and worried, and very short with me; but I gathered that he intended to use these troops himself and not through me. In any event, neither then nor at any other time did he give them orders through me, and I did not attempt to make confusion worse confounded by giving them any myself.[173]

Here, then, was the setting for a first-class disaster. The Creforce commander had given orders for the line to be held. Although the fighting had died down, the concerns of the two brigadiers, Hargest and Vasey, had prompted Puttick to seek clarification from the General himself. This had been categorical: the line must be held. The arrival of Weston at the headquarters of the New Zealand Division raised the issue again. The commander of Force Reserve, the unit which was to be moved up, decided not to go to his new command, but to wait at Division for orders. In addition, battalion commanders in 5 Brigade had received warning orders of a retreat early in the day, and there had been meetings to make arrangements for the withdrawal.

The confusion continued. At 7 p.m., the battalion commander of 2/7th Australian Battalion phoned Brigade headquarters to say he had been told that the Maori Battalion had been withdrawn from his right. Vasey's Brigade Major phone 5 Brigade who said this was not so.

Around 7.30 p.m.:

> Brig. VASEY rang SUDA BAY sector Comd and G(I) being absent he spoke to Staff Offr and explained to him the situation, telling him very forcibly his opinion of the situation as he had done previously.[174]

Around the same time Vasey was back on to Puttick:

> Comd phoned Div Comd and discussed with him action he thought

ought to be taken in default of orders from higher authority. Comd stated his view that a retirement to the vicinity of Suda Bay was necessary to prevent the enemy coming into contact before first light. It was agreed that if NO orders were received by 2330 hrs, a decision would be made. . .[175]

The message of retreat, contrary to the orders of the Creforce commander, continued to filter through to more units. Around 8 p.m., Sergeant Philpott of 27th New Zealand Machine-Gun Battalion was at headquarters, 5 Brigade. He asked Brigadier Hargest if the two guns under his command could be moved. Philpott was informed that all troops would be pulling out at midnight, to an area three miles beyond Suda Bay.[176] Similarly, the *War Diary* of 'C' Squadron, the King's Own Hussars recorded on 26 May:

[We] now came under 5th Brigade. . . At 20.45 orders were received from Brigade that they were withdrawing to a line just north of SUDA and that we were to cover their withdrawal and then lie up in an area in rear of Bde. They could not tell us where Brigade HQ would be. . .[177]

From about 9 p.m. both Hargest and Vasey were in constant touch with Puttick by phone for orders. Puttick was waiting for a reply from Weston, but none came. Hargest put the situation as he saw it in this way in his diary:

. . . About 9.30 he [Vasey] said he would have to go. I pointed out that whatever happened we must keep together and he agreed. . . about 9.30 a representative from div came — Major Peart came [*sic*] and said Brig. Puttick could not get permission for me to go or move, but I was to do so with Vasey. . .

It was no good to me and I rang again and told them I wanted orders — to go or to stay. Brig Puttick said 'Go' and help form a line at Suda about six miles east through Canea.

All arrangements had been made and at about 10.30 we moved each Bn on its route with the Australians on our flanks to the south. . .[178]

The infantry brigadiers were persuading Puttick that their situation was so untenable that he would have simply to disobey Freyberg's orders and move if no reply was received from Weston, Creforce headquarters, or Freyberg. In 5 Brigade, having made all his preparations throughout the day, Hargest was determined to push ahead.

The signal sent from 5 Brigade at 10.15 p.m., 26 May, was explicit:

A line is being formed two miles West of SOUDA [*sic*]at approx the junct of two converging roads. Beyond this line all tps must go. units will keep close together, liaise where possible to guard against sniper attack. 5 Bde units in general will hide up in area along road between SOUDA and STYLOS turn-off. Hide up areas for units will be allotted by 'G' staff on side of road after passing through SOUDA. Bde HQ will close present location at 2300 hrs and travel at head of column. Will then set up adjacent to STYLOS turn-off. A dump of rations boxes already opened is situated near the main bridge on main CANEA road also some still at DID. Help yourself. It is regretted that NO further tpt [transport] is available for evacuation of wounded. It is desirable that MOs should travel with tps. There is possibility of amn. being on roadside near Main Ordnance dump. Take supplies as you pass.[179]

At 10.30 p.m. Puttick gave his orders to the two brigadiers by telephone, about an hour before the retreat would begin. The Force Intelligence Officer, Captain R. M. Bell, happened to be at Division, and Puttick gave him a message for General Weston:

DUKE [N.Z. Division] urgently awaits your orders. Cannot wait any longer as bde comds represent situation on their front as most urgent. Propose retiring with or without orders by 11.30 hrs 26 May [11.30 p.m.] to line North and South through KHRISTOS 1553.[180]

Hargest and Vasey took Puttick at his word, and Inglis subsequently decided to refrain from joining his new command. Force Reserve would go, nominally leaderless, into a vacant forward position, under Colonel Duncan, expecting NZ Division units still to be in place on their south flank. Inglis, who could have easily informed them — after all, he had spent some time with the commander of 1st Welch, Colonel Duncan, earlier in the evening — deserted his post, preferring to stay with the NZ Division. This was to deprive 1st Welch of important tactical intelligence of some moment, for without it they would be engaged with German forces larger than themselves from unexpected (as well as expected) directions. In the bloody day that followed, 1st Welch would pay for Inglis' dereliction of his duty with their lives. It is to their lasting credit that they fought long and hard, for it was their effort that would prevent by delay a good proportion of the pressure from the Germans on the New Zealand and Australian rear. One more spontaneous action would take place, as we shall see, that would check the German advance. But to return to the night of the retreat.

Freyberg had been found by Weston, and Freyberg had not changed his mind. He insisted that the line must be held. There was a delay in the sending of Weston's reply to Puttick, although it is doubtful that had the message been received earlier, the latter would have rescinded his orders.

At last Weston sent the message to Puttick by dispatch-rider at 1.10 a.m., 27 May, setting out Freyberg's requirement that the NZ Division stay put until relieved:

> BRIG. PUTTICK
> GOC in C has ordered that 4 NZ Div must hold present positions tonight 26/27 May until relieved by 1 Welch, NH and 1 Rangers. These latter units received orders to move about 20.00 hrs and they should move up about midnight.
> 0110 hrs. W.H. Wills, Lt-Col GSO 1 Suda Area HQ's.[181]

An error — '4 NZ Div' — stands presumably for 2 NZ Division. The orders were quite clear. The real problem was that with the flurry of warning orders and preparations alluded to earlier, the battalions of the New Zealand Division were already on their way. Puttick and Lieutenant-Colonel Gentry, *en route* to General Weston, received the message about 1.45 a.m. 27 May.[182] The New Zealand infantry battalions had already been nearly three hours on the road.

The NZ Division *War Diary* is laconic in its record of the move.

> 4 Inf Bde had been under comd Col KIPPENBERGER during the day [26 May] but reverted to Brig INGLIS that night and 4 Inf Bde marched to an area about one mile south of STYLOS. Div HQ left by route march for the STYLOS area arriving in small parties at 0500 hrs. Comd and G1 visited Gen WESTON'S HQ at 42nd Street to notify him of the move that had been ordered. Comd met Brigs HARGEST and VASEY just outside Gen WESTON'S HQ and discussed rearguard posn. About 430 hrs Comd and G1 visited GOC at SUDA POINT. During discussion they were informed that Major General WESTON would command and organise the withdrawal of all fwd tps including ours.[183]

Brigadier Hargest viewed the move in somewhat less objective terms:

> . . .We reached the outskirts of Suda Bay — very tired — met Vasey and Gen Weston Royal Marines and laid off a line running from the head of Suda Bay. . . called 42nd Street. We held our conference beside a car's lamps and to my astonishment Puttick said that he was only 'a passenger' and that Gen Weston commanded. Ye Gods the NZ Division had gone out of commission — if the lower formations followed suit complete distintegration would follow. . . I determined to hold the Bde tighter than ever.[184]

Hargest had seen nothing wrong with his and Vasey's agitation of the previous day. The fact that Puttick had been bulldozed by the commander of 5 Brigade into disobeying Freyberg's orders escaped him. Hargest's views were the correct views — for Hargest. For him, 5 Brigade was the superior formation of the New Zealand Division. Had he not come to the rescue of 4 Brigade at the Galatas position?[185] He failed to accept that the New Zealand retreat had contributed to the loss of Force Reserve later that morning. He disregarded the fact that the New Zealand Division had left a great hole south of the position that was occupied by 1st Welch in the early hours of 27 May. For him, 'the Welch were foolishly thrown away'.[186] Indeed, he was quite sanguine about the matter:

> [He saw]... enemy bombers and fighters blasting away at a village, to our surprise, until we found that the Welch Regiment and Rangers who had gone out to beyond Canea with the mistaken idea that they could hold the line Vasey and I had left had been smashed to bits in a few minutes and had been driven up to the hill village where they were annihilated. Whoever sent them should have been shot.[187]

Actually, the troops of Force Reserve fought their delaying action longer than Hargest gave them credit. They were attacked by three enemy forces: frontally by the Ramcke Group and 100 Mountain Regiment, and outflanked in the south by the 3rd Parachute Regiment.

The large hole left by the withdrawal of the NZ Division and the 19th Australian Brigade allowed other German formations to sweep on, uninterrupted by the battle with Force Reserve in the north. 141 Mountain Regiment headed straight on towards 42nd Street, while 85 Mountain Regiment penetrated eastwards as well, but further south. The most forward troops of 141 Mountain Regiment were those of I Battalion, led by Colonel Jais. The NZ Maori Battalion, and elements of the 21st, the 19th, and the 22nd Battalions were strung along the sunken road that was 42nd Street. The 2/7th Australian Battalion was to their north, and the 2/8th Battalion further to the right, near the coast. Slightly to the rear this time was what remained of the 23rd NZ Battalion.

I Battalion of 141 Mountain Regiment failed to perceive the proximity of the concealed defenders (a pattern for the whole campaign). The arrival of aircraft low overhead heralded the approach of the Germans. There was:

> A ragged rattle of small arms fire, surprisingly close, and bullets mowing the leaves of trees... The Maori reaction was immediate — there was a glint of steel and a rattle as bayonets were fixed, then another rattle as magazines were filled and safety-catches released.[188]

To the tired, frustrated men of the Maori Battalion, the prodding and the probing of the Mountain troops was too much. The 28th Battalion had had a rough time of it on Crete, often being committed to battle piecemeal or in situations that held little prospect of success. Daylight had robbed them of triumph in the counter-attack on Maleme on 22 May.

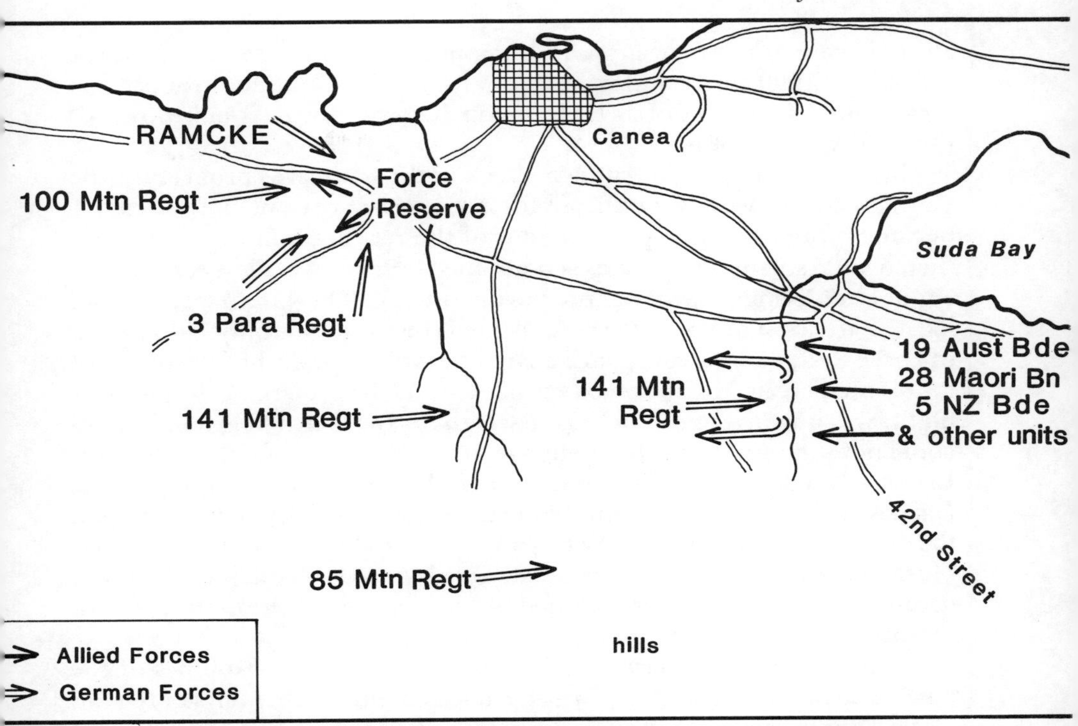

The defeat of the Force Reserve and the counter-attack at 42nd Street, Crete, 26 May 1941.

Now, something snapped: the 28th Battalion, in a terrible rush borne of anger, went up over the bank at the enemy. As 'B' Company were momentarily checked by enemy fire, 'A' Company:

> . . . Moved forward in extended formation through 'B' Company and into the attack. At first the enemy held and could only be overcome by Tommy-gun, bayonet and rifle. His force was well dispersed and approximately 600 yards in depth and by the time we met them their troops were no more than 150 yards from 42nd Street. They continued to put up a fierce resistance until we had penetrated some 250-300 yards. They then commenced to panic and as the troops from units on either side of us had now entered the fray it was not long before considerable numbers of the enemy were beating a hasty retreat. As we penetrated further their disorder became more marked and as men ran they first threw away their arms but shortly afterwards commenced throwing away their equipment as well and disappearing very quickly from the scene of battle. . .[189]

Companies of the 21st, 20th, 19th, and 22nd swept forward, inspired by the fury of the 28th Battalion, to close with the enemy who had had all the advantages of air support, equipment, and numbers. The attack moved over 600 yards, and wiped out at least 300 Mountain troops. The incautious I Battalion of 141 Mountain Regiment was knocked out of the battle.

This not inconsiderable sudden check to the eastwards progress of the German Group West is significant for a number of reasons. The Germans became more careful in their pursuit of the retiring infantry. Although there would still be some sharp actions, the Germans were less enthusiastic about attempting a headlong pressuring pursuit. The 42nd Street action, like the attrition of Force Reserve, slowed the pace. Not only did a group of Force Reserve survivors gain a chance to avoid capture, but the potential for disaster, created by the revolt of the ANZAC brigadiers on the previous night, was now averted. The whole weight of the German ground forces could not surround, cut-off, or engage the NZ Division and the Australian Brigade and attempt to overwhelm them by strength of numbers. Like Galatas, and Force Reserve, the 42nd Street encounter depended not upon the deliberations of the infantry brigade commanders, but upon common-sense responses to adverse circumstances by colonels, majors, captains, lieutenants, and non-commissioned officers, not to mention the spirit of the infantry themselves.

These three actions serve as a litmus paper for the capabilities of the New Zealand, Australian, and British troops on Crete. After days of retreat, battle, fatigue, lack of food, and numerous other deficiencies, these soldiers were still possessed of substantial offensive abilities. They conformed exactly to the infantry model Freyberg envisaged in his defence of the island: troops able to withstand assaults and capable of delivering immediate counter-attacks. It was higher, sometimes at battalion level, often at brigade or division, that the real Achilles heel of the defence showed up.

Kippenberger's post-war criticism was blunt and to the point:

> The failure in each case seems to me to have been that they answered all questions pessimistically, that they saw all dangers real, imagined or possible, that none made any effort to dictate or control events, that they were utterly without any offensive spirit, and that invariably in each case they adopted a course that made victory impossible. . . not the kind of mistakes that all commanders make, selecting unsatisfactory start-lines, making the rate of advance too fast or too slow, failing to tie up lanes for supporting any neighbouring formations, etc., but fundamental mistakes irretrievable by the valour and devotion of those under their command.[190]

For Freyberg the central problem on Crete was beyond all the manifest material shortcomings, a failure of command. Several brigadiers reported orders, fundamental to Freyberg's projected defence, as options to be considered, as battlefield possibilities. This, not a failure on Freyberg's part, not a disregarding of the priceless intelligence furnished by Boniface, not a failure of the ordinary infantry, was why the western sector crumpled while Retimo and Heraklion held fast. The German airborne forces had come at the outset within an ace of losing the entire air-dropped force without hope of recovery. Even in defeat Fliegerkorps XI had received heavy injury from which it would not recover, to be denied future employment. Hitler would ground these airborne forces, not realizing their failure rested on a colossal haemorrhage of intelligence that was fully exploited by an able opponent, despite that opponent's paucity of military resources.

The worst was yet to come for the retreating troops from the western sectors, in the shape of a tortuous march over the mountain to Sphakia, and the uncertain days of evacuation by the ubiquitous Royal Navy. In military terms the defence of the island was over. The isolated garrisons at Retimo and Heraklion had increasingly felt themselves hard-pressed as the Germans took full advantage of their forward airfield on Crete at Maleme. It was now inevitable that they should fall. It was merely a matter of how many troops could be evacuated before Crete was entirely subdued. The troops on the eastern end of the island were disadvantaged — Heraklion was the only large port apart from Suda (now in German hands): any Navy vessels going to or from Heraklion were vulnerable for much longer to Fliegerkorps VIII than those ships calling at the small port on the south coast.

Some 3,486 troops were evacuated from Heraklion on the night of 28/29 May; from Sphakia over four nights from 28/29 May to 1 June, the totals were 724, 6,029, 1,510, and 3,710, respectively. Around 17,000 troops were safely evacuated. Somewhere in the region of over 12,000 troops were captured: these included over 2,000 New Zealand troops, over 3,000 Australians, and over 6,000 British Army and Naval personnel.[191]

In terms of casualties, the British forces on Crete suffered 1,751 killed and 1,738 wounded. By far the largest numbers of killed were troops of the British Army (612) and the NZ Division (671). The British Army had 224 wounded, the Australian Imperial Forces 507, and the NZ Division 967. The total German casualties were estimated as being 4,000 killed and 2,600 wounded. Of those killed, about 2,500 were in the opening landings, and 900 for the ground forces subsequently. Flying and sea deaths were around 600. The total landed strength of the Germans seems to have been 23,120, of whom several thousand would not have been heavily involved with fighting.[192] The casualties for the Germans at the sharp end of the fight, particularly the airborne forces, were amongst the highest in the war.

CHAPTER 4

The Reason Why

Brigadier James Hargest, a much decorated officer hero of World War I, was no ordinary citizen soldier. He was also a Member of Parliament for Awarua, and although of the opposition National Party he communicated regularly and privately with Labour's Prime Minister Peter Fraser. In 1940 he had advised Fraser to come to England to investigate Freyberg's command capability, and after the fall of Crete he sought a personal interview with the Prime Minister.

Indifference to Freyberg's orders shown by Hargest on Crete and his incompetence as a brigade commander were compounded by his behaviour towards his commanding general. Member of Parliament or not, Hargest was bound by the channel of command. Though a political conservative he acted the role of a political commissar, using his status as a Member of Parliament to undermine Freyberg and to blame him for the loss of Crete. In June 1941 Hargest met Fraser in Cairo. Present at the meeting were Carl Berendsen, the permanent head of the Department of External Affairs, and Fred Waite, National Patriotic Fund Commissioner. Hargest wrote later of the meeting: 'Then in Fred Waite's room with only the four of us, Mr Fraser, Berendsen, Fred and myself, I told my story. I hope it will bear fruit.'[1]

Hargest was highly critical of the New Zealand withdrawal in Greece, alleging that Freyberg 'does not keep control over the conduct of operations which is essential for full supervision and coordination'.[2] Hargest insisted that Freyberg failed to take his senior officers into his confidence and that they were at times in doubt as to his intentions.[3] Hargest, aged fifty years and well practised in politics, knew well how to win merit from another's failure. But there was much he did not tell Fraser. He was not present at the conference attended by his Divisional Commander, Puttick, on 21 May. He did not see Freyberg, would not go forward from Platanias to intervene in the crisis at Maleme airfield, and would not move back until 5 Brigade fell back in general retreat. In close contact with Vasey, he had plagued Puttick through the day on 26 May, and issued starting orders to his 5 Brigade units that began a confused retreat to the 42nd Street positions, he himself ending further back at Stilos. His lethargy was decisive at Maleme; his actions and orders on 26 May created a hole, and began the retreat of the New Zealand division and an Australian brigade. It was merely fortunate that the consequent annihilation of Force Reserve took some time, and that the spontaneous counter-attack led by Maori Battalion troops at 42nd Street halted the German progress temporarily. Hargest's failure on Crete is hardly surprising, given his classification as unfit for active service, a classification that had been overridden by the intervention of the Prime Minister.

Hargest's use of parliamentary privilege disallowed any redress that Freyberg might have summoned from the reports of men of the calibre of Kippenberger. Hargest, and as we shall see Inglis too, was permitted to attack Freyberg in camera, and get away with it. Freyberg's charter, as an instrument to prevent the Division being committed to suicidal operations, protected New Zealand's interests — but not Freyberg's. Freyberg's authority and his military career were blighted, and he became more subject to the fickle will of his political masters, to the extent that he had great trouble maintaining the Division at near full strength for the rest of the war.

After the fall of Crete, Winston Churchill played his part in the search for a scapegoat. For Churchill defeat on Crete had been bitter as well as unexpected. His biographer, Martin Gilbert, noted that criticism of the Greek campaign was linked in Britain with criticism of the Prime Minister. Churchill had been told that Crete would be held and he himself had been at pains to ensure that Freyberg received transcripts of code-broken German signals. In a diary entry of 6 June 1941, Sir John Colville, a member of Churchill's private office, noted Churchill's anger:

> The P.M. dictated his speech for next Tuesday, rather cantankerous in tone and likely, unless substantially toned down, to cause a good deal of unfavourable comment. Pug [Major-General Ismay] says he thinks it is impossible to run a war efficiently if so much time has to be devoted to justifying one's actions in the House of Commons. At the risk of seeming smug he maintains that no error or misconception was made in the direction of the campaign in this end.[4]

Churchill spoke with the main newspaper editors, 'with a view to damping down their criticisms and explain the position'.[5] When he did address the House of Commons on 10 June he lambasted his critics and spoke for one and a half hours. He argued:

> . . . [what] if we had given up the island of Crete without firing a shot? We should have been told that this pusillanimous blight had surrendered the enemy key of the eastern Mediterranean. . . . [the fighting had] a severity and fierceness which the Germans have not previously encountered in their walk through Europe.[6]

Crete's fall was but one of Churchill's mental preoccupations of the time. He faced problems in the Middle East, where Air Vice-Marshal Longmore had already been replaced as head of the RAF, and where it was already in Churchill's mind to do something about Wavell, the Army Commander-in-Chief. There had been the narrow squeak of the *Bismarck* chase in the Atlantic Ocean during the Crete campaign, with the attendant loss of the battle-cruiser HMS *Hood* and the stretching of naval resources to trap the marauding German battleship. He was taxed by a concern to maintain and strengthen support from the Roosevelt administration in the United States, at a time when Britain, albeit temporarily, stood alone with her Empire against the almost invincible legions of Nazi Germany.

For all that, Churchill hated military failure and was determined to remove generals that were not providing victories. Some nine days before Germany invaded Russia (22 June 1941), Brigadier L. M. Inglis, of 2 NZ Division, reported to Churchill in London. Brigadier Inglis was appointed General Freyberg's emissary and entrusted with the mission of reporting on the Crete operation to the War Office.[7] Inglis met Churchill on the night of 13 June 1941. The next day Churchill, in a personal minute to the Chiefs of Staff Committee,[8] gave his reaction to this meeting:

10 Downing Street,
Whitehall.

MOST SECRET

GENERAL ISMAY FOR COS COMMITTEE.

Brigadier Inglis, with whom I had a long talk last night, gave a shocking account of the state of the troops in Crete before the battle. He stated that there were not above 10,000 men in the fighting units. None of the New Zealand battalions had been made up to strength or re-equipped after the Greek evacuation, except to a limited extent, such transport and light tanks as were available had to be fished up out of the sunken ship. There were no Mills grenades. The R.A.S.C., R.A.O.C. and other rearward troops were quite unarmed, thoroughly disorganised, and represented bouches inutiles. Even the artillery and gunners had no personal arms. The only field guns available were italian [*sic*]. The only well equipped troops which reached the island were some British troops and Royal Marines, none of which took part in the battle until the retreat began.

2. If the above statements are correct, and they must be searchingly tested, they contrast markedly with the statements made to us beforehand by General Wavell and General Freyberg, although in the latter case a robust view of the task set him is creditable. On April 18, according to General Wavell, Crete was warned that an attack was likely, and our warnings in most precise detail from April 30 onwards are on record. I cannot feel that there was any real grip shown by Middle East HQ upon this operation of the defence of Crete. They regarded

it as a tiresome commitment, while at the same time acquiescing in its strategic importance. No one in high authority seems to have sat down for two or three mornings together and endeavoured to take a full forward view of what would happen in the light of our information, so fully given, and the many telegrams sent to me and by the Chiefs of the Staff about SCORCHER. No one seems to have said 'we have got to hold the place with practically no air support. What then should be our policy of our air fields and the counter attacks of paratroops and other airborne landings? What supplies and equipment are necessary, and how do we get them in? The food difficulty was not mentioned to us. The non-removal of bouches inutiles was a great fault, although some I believe were taken off. It is true that some of the supplies were sunk en route. The slowness in acting upon the precise intelligence with which they were furnished, and the general evidence of lack of drive and precision filled me with disquiet about this Middle East staff. It is evident that very far reaching steps will have to be taken.

3. I am far from reassured about the tactical conduct of the defence by General Freyberg, although full allowance must be made for the many deficiencies noted above. There appears to have been no counter attack of any kind in the western sector, until more than thirty six hours after the airborne descents had begun. There was no attempt to form a mobile reserve with the best troops, be it only a couple of battalions. There is no attempt to obstruct the Maleme aerodrome, although General Freyberg knew that he would have no Air in the battle. The whole seems to have been a static defence of positions, instead of the rapid extirpation at all costs of the airborne landing party. It was lucky, however, that the troops got away when they did....

5. There will have to be a detailed inquiry into the Defence of Crete. We must, for our own information and future guidance, have all the facts established.

W.S.C.
14.6.41

Inglis had shown himself to be as disloyal as Hargest. Why did two New Zealand brigadiers seek to injure their General? W. C. McClymont, official historian of the Greek campaign, opined:

> [T]he military and political worlds were looking for someone to blame and Freyberg was criticised by many people more important than New Zealand officers. Mr Churchill was much concerned; Freyberg was very hurt at this attitude. I know this because Freyberg told me so himself.[9]

Churchill, as we have seen, was very much aware of the nature of the code-broken material and therefore of the relative completeness of the intelligence available to the commander of Crete's garrison. He had undertaken, and been assured by his own staff, that Freyberg had been fully briefed. Now he received an account from a senior officer of Freyberg's own command, the New Zealand Division, at variance to the views of Wavell and Freyberg. Inglis, for the second time in a month, had let Freyberg down, badly.

The substance of the criticism as minuted by Churchill was partly true, partly false, and wholly misleading. The number of men in the 'fighting units' and the strength and limited re-equipping of the New Zealand Infantry Battalions were not causes of failures. The transport and light tanks 'fished up out of a sunken ship' contributed little to the loss of Crete, although an impression of desperation is imparted in the story. It was not true that there were 'no Mills grenades' — clearly more would have been very useful. Non-combatant troops were not entirely 'thoroughly disorganised'. Some elements were. Nonetheless, 10 NZ Composite Brigade had been formed under Kippenberger from mostly non-infantry units. Some gunners had no small arms — some did. To be pedantic, not all the field guns were Italian, but some were.

It was inaccurate to allege that the 'only well equipped troops', 'some British troops and Royal Marines', only 'took part in the battle after the retreat began'. The commandos of Layforce arrived at the time of the 26 May débâcle, a defeat contributed to in no small way by Brigadier Inglis, and so could do no other than fight in the retreat. The Leicesters, the Argyll and Sutherland Highlanders, the Black Watch, and the 1st Welch were all present, and, like the rest of almost the entire garrison on the first day, took part in subduing the opening assault. It was, indeed, the 1st Welch that Inglis himself deserted on the night of 26 May.

The portfolio of intelligence warnings were known to Churchill in their entirety, but not to Inglis at all. Churchill had admitted to doubts, as late as 3 May, that the Germans might be 'only feinting on Crete'.[10] Churchill was easily persuaded of a lack of real grip by General Headquarters Middle East. Anxious to rid himself of Wavell he was pleased to hear that for that general headquarters, Crete was 'a tiresome commitment'.

Freyberg had certainly not ignored the intelligence that he was offered. All intelligence on Crete, apart from JIC(41)181 of 28 April, was essentially cumulative. JIC(41)181 summarized the April plans of the enemy — the other Enigma material including the celebrated CX/JQ911 came to light as the pace of the enemy's transmissions about build up of German formations increased. It was hard work and good fortune that brought Freyberg (unknowingly) in on the distribution of British summaries of German signals. There was no single time when all this material could have been placed together and considered. By the apparant transmission time of CX/JQ911 — 13 May 1941 — the Luftwaffe had commenced its daily interdiction to soften Crete's airborne target areas. It was clear to Freyberg that there was little available air support, even though the promise of it, if the ground troops could hold the aerodromes, had been made. Indeed it was this promise of air support that resulted in Freyberg leaving critical air fields relatively unobstructed. There is no doubt that Creforce Operation Orders took account of the measures needed for dealing with an airborne invasion — the main thrust of Creforce Operation Instruction No. 10 of 3 May deals with this precisely, as does the BGS's 'Appreciation of the Scale of Attack' of 12 May.

The alacrity of Freyberg's response to the communiqués stands in stark constrast to the allegations charging '. . . slowness in acting upon the precise intelligence with which they were furnished'. By 4 May clear orders set up the basis for dealing with airborne attacks. These went down to brigade and battalion. Equally unfair was the charge that 'there appears to have been no counter attack of any kind in the western sector until more than thirty six hours' after the assault opened. The first day had been spent everywhere reducing the incursions of the airborne invaders, and nowhere had they been singularly successful. Weak counters had been made, resulting in the pushing from Maleme of the 22nd Battalion. An ill-timed but significant counter-attack had been mounted the next night by two New Zealand infantry battalions (20th and 28th). It is significant that attached to this charge is no reference to the failure of 5 Brigade to carry out Creforce orders in force on the opening day of the battle.

That no 'mobile reserve', even of 'a couple of battalions' was formed was a travesty of the truth, especially as it came from Inglis. The Creforce orders after Creforce Operation Instruction 10 dealt particularly with the formation of a reserve under Inglis' command, centred on 4 Brigade. The details of how it should concentrate and move were clearly indicated, as well as provisions for operating with light-armoured support. In the event, the necessary formation of yet another Force Reserve under Inglis' command late in the campaign — the Welch, Northumberland Hussars, and Rangers — was not mentioned. This is not surprising as Inglis had disobeyed direct orders from Freyberg in the face of the enemy and had failed to take command of the new Force Reserve.

A strategy of 'static defence of positions' is attributed by Churchill to Freyberg, on Inglis' summation. Nothing was said about the failure and paralysis of command by Hargest, Inglis, and Puttick that had made defeat inevitable. What was obviously not clear to Churchill was that Freyberg had in fact given the German airborne forces a very bloody nose precisely because he had prepared to meet them on the basis of the precise intelligence sent to him. Instead, brigadier Inglis had misled Churchill into believing Freyberg had been incompetent on Crete, and had added further fuel to Churchill's manifest distrust of the Army Commander-in-Chief, Middle East.

Churchill's insistence on 'a detailed inquiry into the defence of Crete' was perhaps natural enough, but hardly well thought through. It would be difficult to carry out an inquiry which did not take into account the authoritative nature of the German Enigma material upon which the defence of the island was to have been based, without briefing the committee as to the nature of those top secret sources. For security reasons, this obviously could not be done. Freyberg himself had not been fully briefed. Given that the senior officer of the committee held only the rank of Brigadier, it is difficult to see how he could be briefed better than General Freyberg. Without the nature of the Enigma summaries being known, 'all the facts' could hardly be 'established'. Yet, ironically, without 'all the facts', the inquiry might fail. Brigadier Inglis had dropped Freyberg into hot water, hardly a desirable milieu even for a champion swimmer.

The Inter-Services Committee on Operations in Crete sat in Cairo in late June 1941 and was visited by the New Zealand Prime Minister, Peter Fraser. Fraser had two questions, 'raised by some officers of the New Zealand Division', one of which related to the evacuation from Kalamata in Greece, the other 'was directed to the divisional command'.[11] General Freyberg, Colonel Stewart (his General Staff Officer 1), and Brigadiers Puttick and Hargest appeared before the committee.

Hargest's self importance, very much that of a politician, revealed itself in his 'short diary' entry for 20 June 1941:

> Up into the Middle East Headquarters to give evidence before Crete commission. Colonel Andrew came with me and we gave good evidence. I produced an enlargement of the area — my orders written two days before the attack and my war diary giving moment to moment happenings — quite a fair type and they were pleased generally.[12]

Strangely, the officers of the inquiry committee were of fairly junior rank. Brigadier A. G. Salisbury-Jones, who had been involved with the training of Greek troops on Crete, chaired the committee. The other army officer was an artillery man, Lieutenant-Colonel G. E. R. Bastin, RA. Commander C. Wauchope, RN, represented the Navy, and Wing-Commander E. C. Huddleston the Royal Air Force. The secretary was Squadron-Leader P. Y. H. Smith, RAFVR.[13] All the officers were inferior in rank to the commander of Creforce, Freyberg, and to the Royal Marine commander on Crete, Weston, another Major-General. The senior officer had indeed been the subordinate to both.

Intelligence analysis was not an issue before the committee. None of the committee was privy to the source of the special signals intelligence, the Enigma material, to which only Freyberg and Wavell had been granted access. Freyberg, even though he must have thought it very good intelligence, could not emphasize that his deployment and refinement of his troop positions had been dependent upon this, without revealing the remarkable accuracy of his concealed source. Enigma, as signals traffic of the time, must have seemed extraordinary. Freyberg had been told that BONIFACE, an agent in Athens, was highly placed. This cover explanation of the source of his material seems to have been accepted by him without question.

The committee, and those before it, were blind to the advantages accruing from special intelligence and could not be expected to bring down findings that showed the island to be lost by the narrowest of margins. It is therefore unremarkable that the committee survey of pre-attack intelligence was somewhat circumscribed. Section number 4, in part 2, says that a warning of 29 April was repeated from Middle East Command predicting an airborne attack. The scale of attack was suggested to be about three to four thousand paratroops; the invasion of a German air division, a German Mountain division, and an Italian infantry division.[14] This fits well with JIC(41)181 of 27 April, except for the Italians. As the JIC appreciation was not an obvious intercept summary (unlike CX/JQ911) it seems that the assessment Freyberg initially received was open to the committee. In a sense, as Freyberg's main decisions were based on his appreciation of JIC(41)181, the picture is very accurate, but the committee was not appraised of the extensive updates that confirmed Freyberg's decision in the days that followed.

After an initial analysis of force deployment, the committee proceeded to examine the defence at Maleme. Hargest's evidence before the committee was quoted in detail:

> Since the brunt of the fighting fell upon the 5th Infantry Brigade, an outline of the instructions issued by their commander will be of interest. The Brigade was ordered to maintain a defensive position running east and west from Platanias into the Tavronitis River, with special regard to the defence of Maleme aerodrome. In the event of the enemy making an airborne or seaborne attack on any part of the area the brigade was to counter attack immediately. . . In the event of an enemy attack from west of the Tavronitis River, the 21st Battalion was to move and hold the line of the river facing west on the left of the 22nd Battalion. In the event of the 23rd Battalion being ordered forward, it was to be prepared to occupy that unit's position and launch a further counter attack on the beach or aerodrome.[15]

A distinction was being made by Hargest. The 21st Battalion was to respond in a particular circumstance. The 23rd Battalion was to move 'in the event of. . . being ordered forward'. The 22nd Battalion was primarily to defend the aerodrome and was instructed to cover the whole area of the aerodrome and approaches to it. Hargest admitted that 'in the event of a landing being made on the aerodrome, support and reserve companies were to be utilised for immediate counter attack under cover of mortar and machine gun fire'. 'I' tanks would be brought in to assist. In evidence he stated that 5 Brigade had three platoons of machine-guns, that artillery were to fire on the beach and airfield *in extremis,* and that bren-gun carriers 'were to search areas in the immediate vicinity of the brigade and to counter-attack'. This last instruction, given the size of 5 Brigade's area, is ludicrous, particularly when it is considered that the bren-gun carriers seemed mostly to have been used as officers' transport.

In part 3 of the report it is suggested that faultless reaction on the part of Hargest's brigade and his battalion commander took place.

> In all cases where parachutists landed in the vicinity of troops they were immediately dealt with. . .The enemy was quick to exploit his footing in the riverbed and throughout the day exerted heavy pressure against the western portion of the sector held by the 22nd Battalion. The difficulties of the battalion were increased by the infiltration southwards of troops who had crash landed on the beach near Maleme village. In spite of gallant counter attacks assisted by I tanks the situation became grave, and at nightfall the commanding officer considered his battalion in danger of being cut off. He therefore decided to withdraw to the general line occupied by 23rd and 21st Battalions.[16]

This is a travesty of what had actually occurred, but the committee had only the word of the officers of 5 Brigade as evidence. No one appeared to ask why the 21st Battalion did not fulfill its automatic response role as earlier agreed to by its brigade commanders. No mention is made of the dangerous gap created by the RAF camp area. Nothing is said as to why the 23rd Battalion was not ordered up, or why two widely separated companies from the 23rd and 28th Battalions eventually were sent after dark. The timing of the withdrawal is not mentioned — it was far later than 'nightfall'. Nor is it pointed out that only two-fifths of Andrew's companies (plus 'A' Company, 23rd Battalion) could respond to the order. The late counter-attack the following night is described in some detail, and daylight exposure to air attack is given as the main reason for failure. The withdrawal of 5 Brigade is intriguingly put down to the gap left by 20th Battalion, a battalion that had gone forward in the abortive counter-attack.

No mention is made of Brigadier Inglis and his failure to take command of Force Reserve, nor his hand in the improvised withdrawal of New Zealand troops. However, the report does note that Freyberg warned General Weston, on the morning of 26 May, that he proposed sending 1st Welch, the Northumberland Hussars, and the Rangers (his Force Reserve) to relieve the New Zealand Division. The position held was to be kept 'at all costs' to cover the arrival that night of Layforce commandos and certain essential stores coming by destroyer. The report notes that Weston told Puttick of the relief at 1800 hours, but Puttick said that his

From left to right: Freyberg, Russell, Puttick, Wellington 1940: the senior officer of 2 NZEF and the senior officer of 1 NZEF.

Below: the GOC inspects New Zealand infantry, Wellington. The GOC's new Personal Assistant is on the extreme left.

Greece, April 1941. Freyberg shares a joke with his officers; Colonel Stewart with the pipe. The staff car had been shot up. The General went through nine cars being strafed in Greece.

The Commander, Creforce, at his battle HQ on Crete above Canea. The aide-de-camp is Jack Griffiths.

Below: the Matilda 'I' tank, Freyberg looking on: desert picture. Matildas were employed in pairs at the aerodromes on Crete.

View from Freyberg's battle HQ over Canea in the direction of Maleme. Note the smoke from shelling and bombing.

Inside the cave HQ during the retreat at Sphakia: Freyberg centre, naval officer on right.

Location of the cave at the foot of an outcrop. Officer in left foreground is John White.

Aftermath: GOC Creforce on a cruiser in Alexandria Harbour. Puttick is behind the General.

Father and son: the GOC and Paul Freyberg.

The rugby spectator.

The General's Packard outside General Headquarters Middle East, Cairo, in April 1940. It was here that the Crete inquiry was held, in June 1941.

On the wireless in the rear of an armoured car; shellfire in the background.

Closer view of the man on the mike, different da

Staff car. Operation 'Crusader', Freyberg top left.

The 'near capture' photograph. The enemy is only a few hundred feet away. The General stands alone on 1 December 1941. He departed only when the Germans were close. It is the 'loneliness of command', when all has gone to pot. 6 Brigade gun line is being overrun.

New broom in North Africa. Visit of the new Army Commander, 8th Army, Lieutenant-General B. L. Montgomery to HQ, 2 NZ Division, in the desert. Brigadier Kippenberger third from left; Freyberg seventh; Monty in beret.

Handover: Horrocks takes over from Freyberg before Alam Halfa.

Practitioners of battle: the General and Kippenberger.

An unawed experienced Divisional Commander: the General talks with Monty, left, with Oliver Leese between.

Below: Freyberg and Horrocks at the 1942 handover.

troops could not hold out. Weston said he would have to refer this matter to Freyberg, and departed so to do. Over the crucial issue of withdrawal the report concludes:

> In the late afternoon the situation deteriorated rapidly. As orders were absent from General Weston, Puttick and Vasey decided to prevent encirclement by withdrawing to 42nd Street near Suda, making the decision about 2200 hours. Meanwhile General Freyberg had issued an order that the line was to be held, but the order was only received when the withdrawal had started.[17]

The report seems ignorant of the fact that had Inglis taken up his post, Force Reserve would have been fully appraised of this tactical situation and that its destruction might well have been prevented. Weston's failure of command and the brigade commanders' decision to take matters into their own hands is glossed over by the suggestion that communications broke down following the stealing of dispatch-riders' motorcycles by retreating troops. The most telling point in the report is its conclusion that 'by the morning of the 27th, General Freyberg realised that evacuation had become inevitable. . . his hand had been already forced'.[18] Acting in direct contravention of clear orders, Brigadiers Hargest, Inglis, and Puttick, with the Australian Brigadier Vasey abetting them, had issued their own instructions and withdrawn New Zealand and Australian troops. From hindsight the deterministic conclusion of the committee seems excessive. It found that:

> . . . the major lesson of this campaign was that to defend with a relatively small force an island as large as Crete, lying under the permanent domination of enemy fighter aircraft and out of range of our own was impossible.[19]

The word 'impossible' seems to do less than justice to the slight margin that allowed a German victory. The committee was not to know that because of detailed intelligence, and provision for immediate counter-attacks in the vital ground, the enemy could well have been brought to grief on the first day.

Hargest, before the committee, was cool, articulate, and the perfect politician. In his short diary entry for 25 June 1941 he demonstrated how far his political machinations against General Freyberg had gone. As one of his excuses for his failure to hold the airfield he insisted that he needed, for its defence, to have been given command of all weapon systems locally, including anti-aircraft guns and the coastal batteries. While control of these weapons away from the division was inconvenient, it was in fact a peripheral factor in the weakness of Crete's defences. It was not lack of command of guns that led to the loss of Maleme. His diary spoke of the above in the context of a meeting at NZ Division headquarters. An 'Excellent feeling prevailed...We discussed...quite candidly...My view...was supported.'[20]

Hargest was in his natural element before the Committee of Inquiry. This practised politican made his case well and he succeeded in sowing the seeds of suspicion to make Freyberg a suspect commander. Fraser now watched Freyberg with care and his brigadiers increased their power within the Division, knowing that the Prime Minister would in the last analysis back the unanimity of his New Zealand brigadiers over and against their British commander. The 'soviet' of brigadiers, ironically so-called by Freyberg, from now on could make its presence felt within divisional policy making. It was a measure of Freyberg's strength and skill that he could still impose command and offer leadership in the presence of this system, and given the political impossibility of removing an incompetent like Hargest, and an unreliable brigadier such as Inglis. Fraser, impressed and depressed by the criticisms of Freyberg that came from the brigadiers after the fall of Crete, began to search for an alternative commander. Dill, the Chief of the Imperial General Staff, referred a request for advice from Fraser to Freyberg's present and immediate past commanders in the Middle East, to Auchinleck and Wavell:

> New Zealand Prime Minister has had information from various sources which leads him to doubt if Freyberg is the right man to command New Zealand division. While Mr Fraser likes Freyberg and is keeping an open mind, this is causing him grave anxiety. It is clear that New Zealand's only division of such splendid men must have a really good commander. Could you let me have your opinions which I will communicate to Mr Fraser and if General Auchinleck is not satisfied I will ask him to initiate a confidential report.[21]

Wavell, to his credit, responded immediately, on the day of the receipt of his communication from the Chief of Imperial General Staff, on 21 August 1941:

> Freyberg produced one of the best trained, disciplined, fittest divisions I've ever seen and he must be given fullest credit for their exploits in Greece and Crete. I'm aware relations between him and his staff and subordinate commanders were not happy due to Freyberg's passion for detail and desire to do everything personally instead of letting his staff work. I think he wore himself out at Crete through this tendency. If Freyberg is replaced in New Zealand division, I should be very pleased to have him in India. I have no Lieutenant-General's appointment in sight but could give him command of one of the new divisions being raised.[22]

Six days later, Wavell sent a follow-up signal:

> Has any decision been taken about Freyberg as it may affect appointments here? I think Fraser would be most ill-advised to displace him as no man could have done more for division. On reflection think I was wrong what I said about relations with brigadiers. I only meant that he is not always an easy man to serve owing to his keenness. I propose to recommend for KBE for his work in Greece and Crete and repeat I should like him in India if New Zealand do not want him, though I think they will be wrong to lose him.[23]

Auchinleck took some little time to reply to Dill's query. On 2 September 1941 he signalled:

> After careful enquiry consider it would be great mistake to move Freyberg from command New Zealand Division to whose training and efficiency he has wholeheartedly devoted himself with excellent results. In action he is a first class commander. In peaceful periods he is apt perhaps to centralise and pay too much attention to detail which possibly irritates his subordinate commanders somewhat. This tendency probably due to his intense zeal for efficiency. On balance strongly recommend his retention in command division. Am not at present prepared to recommend him for higher command.[24]

Apart from India what 'higher command' could there have been for Freyberg in late 1941? The 19 Australian Brigade, under Brigadier Vasey, on Crete, was part of the Australian 6 Division. It was this formation that General Blamey thought should be melded with 2 New Zealand Division once they had returned to Egypt to form an ANZAC Corps. This ANZAC Corps would come under the command of General Bernard Freyberg. Blamey's recommendation went from the British Dominions' Office to the Australian Government on 7 May, 1941. The Australian War Cabinet looked at these proposals two days later. Fadden, as acting Prime Minister, reminded Blamey that the Australian Government had already cabled the Dominions' Office, on 18 April, asking for Australian troops to be placed under the command of the GOC, Australian Imperial Forces, and that Blamey's proposal would split this force (moreover that 7 and 9 Divisions would not be pleased). Blamey's reply on 15 May, five days before the invasion of Crete, proposed a regrouping of the Australasian contingents in the Middle East. Upon the approval of ANZAC Corps, he was to suggest that 7 and 9 Divisions form an Australian Corps, under Lavarack.

Thus a solid four-division Australasian force of two corps was being proposed. While Blamey would continue to argue for an Australian Corps, after Crete he changed his mind about Freyberg commanding ANZAC Corps. Two officers from the Australian Imperial Forces on Crete,

Brigadier Vasey and Colonel Cremor, had informed Blamey that Freyberg 'had bungled his task in Crete'.[25]

Vasey's evidence is suspect. Vasey had commanded his 19 Australian Brigade alongside Hargest's 5 Infantry Brigade during the last few days of the Crete campaign. His role in the 26 May fiasco has already been discussed. Hargest described Vasey immediately after a visit by the latter to 5 Brigade's headquarters, on the morning of 26 May:

> Tall, good looking, a soldierly type he was to be my comrade for one week and a good one. He said his troops were fresh and had not been engaged and could hang on indefinitely.[26]

It was the same Vasey, a few hours later on 26 May, who urged withdrawal and took the Australian Brigade out of the line when the New Zealand Division withdrew contrary to Freyberg's orders.

There is no doubt that Freyberg was injured by the political machinations of his brigadiers. To a lesser general, the grubby aftermath of politico-military intervention stimulated by military subordinates and abetted by the New Zealand Prime Minister could easily have been the last straw. Having defended Crete, despite serious deficiencies of resources, and to have come so close to victory and been robbed of it by failure in part by one of the very officers subsequently agitating for their commander's dismissal hardly encouraged Freyberg to stay on. Yet he did, even though he was saddled with an incompetent brigadier who, having Prime Minister Fraser's ear, remained in place with impunity until his capture by the Germans in November 1941. Freyberg soldiered on, the *de facto* political commissars of the New Zealand Division not withstanding.

CHAPTER 5

Reputation Recovered

For Freyberg and his 2 NZ Division the sea and roadway from Crete to victory was littered with the debris of failure and frustration. Crete was the lowest ebb in the General's fortunes, with 671 of his New Zealanders killed in action, and 2,180 taken as prisoners of war. Despite the award of the Victoria Cross to 2nd Lieutenant C. H. Upham and Sergeant A. C. Hulme, the Division's remnant, returned to Egypt for re-formation, the incorporation of reinforcements, and for divisional training, were chastened by defeat.

By September 1941 the Division was sufficiently repaired in body and spirit for movement to the Western Desert for more intensive training — in day and night attacks and movement in desert formations. Freyberg at last had his Division together to refine it into a precision tool. In November the Division began to move towards the Libyan frontier and into Cyrenaica, to take part in the 8th Army's operation 'Crusader'. The movement towards the operational zone was imposing. Brigadier Howard Kippenberger wrote:

> The whole 8th Army, 7th Armoured Division, 1st South African Division, and the 2nd New Zealand and 4th Indian Divisions moved westwards in an enormous column, the armour leading. The army moved south of Sidi Barrani, past the desolate Italian camps of the previous year, along the plateau south of the great escarpment, through the frontier wire into Libya, south of the enemy garrisons in the Sidi Omars, and wheeled north. Then, just as we were rejoicing in the conception of a massive move on Tobruk. . .the whole army broke up and departed different ways.[1]

Operation 'Crusader', the plan for the 8th Army's first offensive, was first mooted while Freyberg was still in Crete. When he entered into the discussions he was horrified by the plan's shortcomings. He at once made clear that, in his view, the goal was ill conceived, and that the plan's failure to bring tanks on to divisional command was appalling and would cause increased casualties. He also argued that air support was insufficient.

Freyberg's foreboding of further disasters created for him a battle of loyalties. His commanding General required the utmost secrecy over operation 'Crusader'. The New Zealand Government, in granting him his charter, required warning of any possible débâcles. He delayed communicating his misgivings to Fraser. When the Prime Minister became aware that a new operation was imminent he forwarded a check-list of pertinent but embarrassing questions to the Commander of 2 NZ Division, with a barb included:

> In view of experience in Greece and particularly in Crete I should be grateful if you telegraph me the information, if necessary after consultation with the C-C Middle East.[2]

General Sir Claude Auchinleck, Commander-in-Chief of Middle East Land Forces, disarmingly assured Freyberg that he must keep true to his charter and answer his Prime Minister's question, but Freyberg's answers, reduced to thin gruel by the 8th Army requirements for secrecy, told Prime Minister Fraser next to nothing. After failing to receive answers to questions asked of Churchill, the wily Fraser began to make open enquiries in London. At this point the embarrassed Auchinleck was forced to dispatch a senior New Zealand officer to London to convey to the Prime Minister a detailed and highly confidential résumé of 'Crusader'.

Auchinleck's plan in this operation was to outflank Halfaya Pass and strike towards Capuzzo. Freyberg's task in 'Crusader' was to destroy as much of the Axis force on the frontier as possible and then advance to the west. This was part of a total plan intended to entrap the entire Afrika Korps. While the Germans evaded the trap they were forced to withdraw to El Aghelia.

The first 'Crusader' battle, Sidi Rezegh, witnessed the emergence of a superior division on to the desert scene — 2 NZ Division. Significantly, Major-General F. V. Von Mellenthin, then GSO 1, Panzergruppe Afrika, consistently affirmed the aggressive and threatening attacks made by Freyberg's force throughout the battle. Of 21 November 1942 he recalled:

> Meanwhile ominous reports came in from the frontier areas. The New Zealand division was on the march, and on the afternoon of the 21st it thrust behind our frontier fortresses and crossed the Trigh Capuzzo on both sides in the Sidi Azeiz. This brought them dangerously close to Panzergruppe headquarters at Gambut, and Rommel ordered us to move to El Adem during the night.[3]

2 NZ Division's 6 Brigade advanced on 23 November to capture the Afrika Korps' headquarters near Bir Chleta. This brigade's persistence seduced Rommel from his battle oversight into control of a minor operation. Von Mellenthin opined of this:

> On 24th November we had fewer than 100 tanks fit for battle, and the rifle regiments had been decimated by the South Afrika force. Unfortunately Rommel overestimated his success and believed the moment had come to launch a general pursuit. Rommel had been away

> from his headquarters, engaged in fighting the 6th New Zealand brigade, near Pt. 175, and his knowledge of the situation south of Sidi Rezegh was necessarily limited.[4]

Von Mellanthin affirmed that on 25 November the 2 NZ Division appeared in force in the Sidi Rezegh area, and the Afrika Korps Division, which had been left, was placed in a critical position by the New Zealanders joining with the Tobruk garrison.

There is no doubt that Rommel regarded the New Zealanders as the most dangerous Division within 8th Army, a fact witnessed by his personal visit to Afrika Korp headquarters, on 28 November, to insist that the Division must be prevented from moving into Tobruk.[5]

Von Mellanthin dubbed 2 NZ Division's General 'their indomitable commander'.[8] However, the Division's success had been won against Rommel's 2nd Eleven. His three armoured divisions had all been in action on the frontier area and on their return they overwhelmed 2 NZ Division and forced Freyberg to engineer a fighting escape.

In the battle for the relief of Tobruk, the battle of Sidi Rezegh, Freyberg and 2 NZ Division had won the respect of the 8th Army and of their foe, but in four days had lost nearly 1,000 killed, 1,699 wounded, and nearly 2,000 as prisoners of war. By mid-December 1941 the bulk of 2 NZ Division was back in Egypt, and remained there until 23 February 1942 when they began a movement to Syria and Lebanon. In this new location, Freyberg was informed that he had been promoted Lieutenant-General with effect from 1 March 1942. In June 1942 the Division was recalled urgently from Syria to Libya following a decisive defeat of the 8th Army armour. The battle of Gazala ended on 15 June with the 8th Army in full retreat and the Panzerarmee moved up to Tobruk's outer defences. In less than eight days Freyberg's Division was in place at Mersa Matruh.

Rommel had crossed the Egyptian frontier and 2 NZ Division was part of the 8th Army force summoned to prevent outflanking by laying minefields and well prepared defensive boxes. Auchinleck's battle plan, in the face of this advance, was uncertain — he seemed more concerned to prevent envelopment than defeat his enemy, and his persistent refusal to place armour under divisional control reduced the impact of Freyberg's force. Even so, the Panzerarmee found the New Zealand block formidable. Rommel's mobile columns were held but Freyberg and his Division were surrounded and forced to retreat to the Alamein Line.

The Alamein Line has been well described by John Strawson as:

> . . . the only line in the desert with a top and a bottom. About forty miles across, it was flanked by the sea in the North and the Quattar Depression in the South. Rommel would have had to come through this line if he wished to reach Alexandria . . .[6]

Through July Rommel probed the Alamein Line and Auchinleck worked to expand and strengthen his defence perimeter. On the night of 14/15 July, 2 NZ Division was employed as part of a defence operation to sweep the Afrika Korps from Ruweisat Ridge, a dominant high point. The New Zealand brigade commanders were given a key role in this operation (Freyberg was absent from the battle in hospital). The New Zealanders captured Ruweisat Ridge, after a night attack, wherein they advanced more than 10 kilometres. Having gained their objective, 2 NZ Division found itself attacked in the rear by 15th Panzer, and in need of urgent armoured reinforcements. Whilst the position was being held in fierce contest, Brigadier Kippenberger attempted to enlist aid from nearby armoured units. His reception again points to the problem of poor co-operation and bad relations between infantry and tank commanders in the desert battles:

> After ages, perhaps 20 minutes, we reached a mass of tanks. In every turret someone was standing gazing through glasses at the smoke rising from Ruweisat Ridge four miles away. I found and spoke to a regimental commander, who referred me to his brigadier. The brigadier received me coolly. I did my best not to appear agitated, said that I was commander of 5 NZ Infantry Brigade, that we were on Ruweisat Ridge and were being attacked in the rear by tanks when I left an hour before. Would he move up and help? He said he would send a reconnaissance tank. I said there was no time. Would he move his whole brigade?
>
> While he was patiently explaining some difficulty, General Lumsden drove up. I gave him exactly the same explanation. Without answering he walked around to the back of his car, unfastened his shovel and with it killed a scorpion with several blows. Then he climbed up beside the brigadier, who was sitting on the turret of the tank. . .The general asked where we were and the brigadier pointed out the place on the map. 'But I told you to be there at first light'. General Lumsden then said, placing his finger on point 63.
>
> I jumped down and did not hear the rest of the conversation but in a few minutes the general got down and in a soothing manner which I resented said that the brigade would move as soon as possible.[7]

The New Zealanders retained the ridge, but at a cost of 1,405 casualties, of whom all but 290 were killed or captured.

It was now apparent to Rommel that his only way to break through the barrier Auchinleck had erected was to attempt to find a way around its flank. The battle of Alam el Halfa (3 August–7 September 1942) was a battle fought to win or prevent this attempt. On 31 August Rommel's forces broke through minefields between the New Zealand positions and the Qattara depression, and thrust in depth toward the Alam el Halfa position. Rommel's plan was to take the Alam el Halfa ridge and then advance 21 Panzer to Alexandria, and 15 Panzer together with 90 Light to Cairo. However, now Rommel was faced for the first time by a new 8th Army commander. On 13 August 2 NZ Division was informed that Lieutenant-General B. L. Montgomery had taken command of the 8th Army. The new broom swept clean. His well-conceived concentration of tanks and artillery, aided by air support, brought the German advance to a halt. 2 NZ Division attempted to capitalize on the German defeat with an attack towards Deiral Munassib on 3 September, but the German fighting retreat was consistent, and held them all. The El Alamein Line held and Rommel's last chance of reaching the Nile was denied him. On 8 September 1942 Freyberg's Division was moved to the west of Alexandria, to the sea, for a rest. The Division's strength was now reduced to 11,500 effective troops, and because of a manpower shortage in New Zealand, getting reinforcements was uncertain.

With Panzerarmee and the Afrika Korps stopped in their tracks and increasingly short of the *matériel* of war, Montgomery could prepare himself for his *pièce de résistance* — a decisive set-piece battle. In the second Battle of El Alamein, fought from 23 October 1942 until 11 November 1942, Freyberg and 2 NZ Division were a vital ingredient in Montgomery's recipe for victory. Alamein was not a corps or divisional battle, but an army battle, conceived and directed by its Army commander, and Freyberg's role was precisely indicated. Montgomery's decisions were well based on a plethora of intelligence. Ultra provided the Army commander with a high level of information about German supply problems and operational aims. David Irving's assessment is trenchant:

> Many of Rommel's top secret radio communications with his high command are reaching Montgomery as Ultra intercepts only hours later... Thus when Rommel radios the high command...about his illness, Montgomery got a copy of Professor Horster's diagnosis too. Each time Rommel reports his plans of attack, the Ultra intercepts enabled Montgomery to plan an appropriate defence.[8]

Ultra allowed Montgomery to master the mechanics of battle positioning. Rommel was doubly disadvantaged by the destruction of his intelligence cell in Cairo (which had been intercepting the signals of the United States military attaché) and by a decline in his personal health (blood pressure problems, stomach and intestinal catarrh, and nasal diptheria). On 19 September he was relieved by General Georg Stumme, and on 23 September he returned to Germany on sick leave, but was forced to return prematurely on 25 October after Stumme's death from a heart attack in battle.

Montgomery's plan, envisaging a massive artillery barrage followed by a breakthrough, allocated an assault division role to Freyberg's force. The Division, reduced to two infantry brigades in strength, was reinforced by 9 Armoured Brigade.

Freyberg's Division had nearly one month to prepare for this offensive. The General's account of divisional training demonstrates the high demand he placed on his men:

> Time being short, we started our training with a full scale divisional rehearsal under conditions as similar as possible to the actual attack we were to carry out later capture Miteiriya Ridge. . . Acţual minefields had been laid in positions, corresponding to those in which we expected to find them. . . Live shell was used, and we had one or two casualties, but all ranks gained confidence from the accuracy of the barrage.[9]

By mid-October Freyberg's divisional training programme was complete and after a brief 'beach holiday' 2 NZ Division was moved to its battle line-up position. On the night of 22/23 October the Division was moved forward, to positions immediately behind the starting line. On the morning of 23 December Freyberg held a commanders' conference, and gave his orders: 'The division had to advance to a depth of between 5,000 and 6,800 yards from its start line. . .The rate of advance was 100 in three minutes. . .'[10] After dusk, following a day of enforced silence, Freyberg's Division made its last preparations for battle. The General was highly excited:

> I have been writing up this diary as the hands of the clock move to zero hour. There are now five minutes to go before the biggest artillery bombardment any of us have ever heard commences at 2140 hours. . . It is away. . . flash after flash from in front, to left, to right, and from the mediums and heavies in the rear. . . A searchlight at the vertical, appears to the rear. Infantry are off. . .[11]

The artillery bombardment by 1,000 guns punched a hole in the enemy's position with the intention of allowing armour and mobile troops to move through the gaps blasted in the enemy minefields. Whilst Montgomery, his planning complete and his orders given, retired to his caravan to sleep, Freyberg achieved their goal on the Miteiriya Ridge and opened a south corridor.

However, Montgomery's battle plan quickly became unstuck. There were two problems — the armoured divisions were not fighting their way through the German minefields and 88mm anti-tank guns with sufficient drive, and the German minefields were greater in depth than had been estimated. By early 25 October, Freyberg had become exasperated with the delay in 10 Armoured Division's break-out. He complained to Lieutenant-General Sir Oliver Leese, XXX Corps commander, that the armoured division was not 'properly set up for the attack'[12] and at 9.15 a.m. he noted 'Commanding an armoured division from right back is not a success. . .There has got to be a great deal more spirit than there has been in the past.' He reported to Corps that 'M. Ridge situation is rapidly becoming static warfare.'[13]

At his commanders' conference, at 1600 hours on 25 October, Freyberg astutely observed that tanks seemed no longer to be the key asset for North African battles:

> From what I have seen I think the days of armour are rapidly passing. . .88 mm has almost paralysed the armour — they say they have an even chance in the moonlight.[14]

It took personal intervention from Montgomery to move the commander of 10th Armoured Division, who was 12 kilometres behind his leading armoured vehicles, to take charge of his battle — from the front.[15]

Without an in-depth armoured breakthrough, Freyberg's initiatives could no longer be the cutting edge of Montgomery's operation. Another plan was needed.

By 26 October it was apparent that Montgomery's master plan needed radical revision. Armour had not broken through to threaten the Panzerarmee's lines of communication. The attack was stalled and Montgomery needed to think again. Montgomery's biographer, Nigel Hamilton, observed that discussions with Freyberg took place before the new decision was made:

> At the New Zealand division headquarters shortly before midday on 25 October Bernard [Montgomery] assessed the local situation with Freyberg and then spoke to Leese and Lumsden . . . Freyberg, angered by the excessive caution of Gatehouse's armoured brigades, considered it impossible to go ahead now with the intended 'crumbling operation'. Equally he had no faith that Gatehouse would ever break out beyond the Miteiriya Ridge; he therefore advised the army commander to postpone further operations until the evening, and then allow the New Zealand infantry to mount an artillery-supported attack to gain the 'Pierson' line for the armour, about 4,000 yards beyond the ridge. The armour could then follow up. Lumsden agreed. General Montgomery did not.[16]

It is significant that in his diary Montgomery recalled the conference only in the briefest essentials and made no mention of the Freyberg–Lumsden proposal. However, it is clear that Freyberg was outspoken about the need for a new thrust. Michael Carver is convinced of Freyberg's soundness:

> Freyberg, who two days before had been proposing 'a new attack on a 3-divisional front, using the armour to provide a "firm base" by protecting the flanks and only joining battle if the enemy armour attacked away from his gun line', went to see Morshead that morning

> and then went on to lunch with Montgomery. The latter told him that he planned to use the New Zealand division to advance along the coast in exploitation of the Australian attack, Freyberg to use his armoured brigade to protect his left flank. 6 NZ Brigade would take over the Australian sector the night following the one of the latter's attack, that is 29/30th. Freyberg's attack would begin as soon as possible afterwards, probably the next night, the 30/31st. As the New Zealanders themselves could not provide any more infantry, he would be fed with a succession of British infantry brigades, first the 151st of 50th Division, the 152nd of the Highland, then 131 of the 44th and finally perhaps the Greek brigade.[17]

The New Zealanders were reduced to a secondary role, but Rommel's artillery, albeit with difficulty, brought the Australian attack to a halt. Montgomery's amended plan had also failed, and after six nights the 8th Army had not won the decisive victory its general had designed. A new direction was called for and after withdrawing himself from the battle, Montgomery returned with his new plan — 'Supercharge'. John Strawson succinctly clarifies Montgomery's purpose for this new variation on his original theme:

> Its aims were fourfold: to destroy Rommel's Panzer force; to oblige him to fight in the open and so use up precious fuel; to block his supply routes and prevent resupply, to force him from his forward airstrips; to cause the disintegration of the entire Panzerarmee.[18]

For 'Supercharge', Freyberg's 2 NZ Division was augmented by two infantry brigades, 1 Brigade and 52 Brigade, together with the newly equipped 9 Armoured Brigade. His task was to cut a passage to Tel el Acquqir to allow X Corps to attack the German rear with armoured cars, while the British armoured divisions divided Rommel's armour by driving north-west to the sea. But the New Zealanders were tired, the artillery exhausted by its moves from target to target and the deployments in critical areas were confused. Freyberg sought a postponement of this action, and Montgomery acceded to a short delay.

On 2 November, at five past one in the morning, the artillery of II British Corps (300 guns) began a creeping barrage — the second in the North African campaign. Freyberg's infantry was ready, but the British armour was unenterprising and sheltered behind the New Zealand support brigade. Exasperated, Freyberg repeatedly called his corps commander, asking him to intervene and speed up 1 Armoured Division's advance. The New Zealand commander's battle diary clarifies the New Zealand perspective of their armoured colleagues:

> At first light our people were on the high ground. They had been there

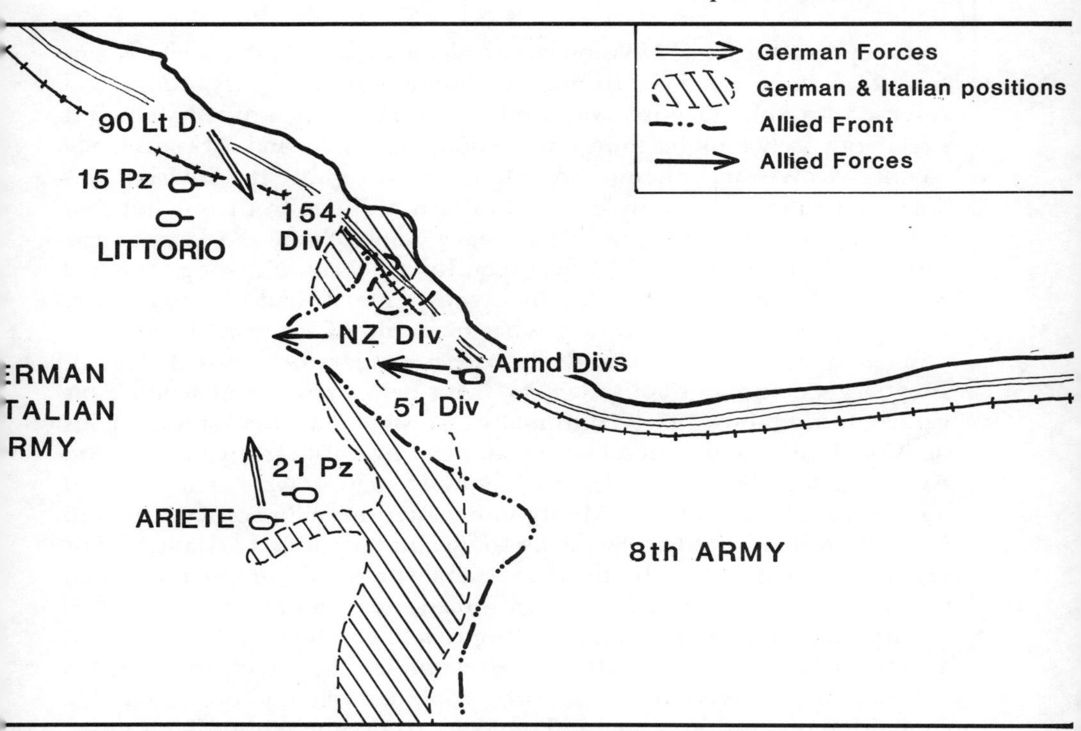

Operation 'Supercharge' at El Alamein.

> and in the middle had become a little disorganised. . .one armoured division came up but at the moment they are not across the road. . . It seems to me that one armoured division can do a little more. They are stopping all forward movement and the tanks are becoming dangerously congested.[19]

Freyberg's 9 Armoured Brigade made a dent in the German line and even before 1 Armoured Division belatedly came to reinforce them turned that dent into a hole, but suffered great casualties in so doing. On 2 November, from 11 a.m. until 1 p.m., a fierce tank battle raged between 1 Armoured Division and 15 and 21 Panzer Divisions. However, Montgomery's anti-tank shield, his field artillery, and his air support this time assured him of victory. By the close of 2 November, the Afrika Korps had but thirty-five heavy and medium tanks and twenty Italian light tanks still operational. Freyberg was amongst the first to appreciate the degree of success the 8th Army had gained. His battle diary records that at the close of 2 November he phoned his Commander, Royal Artillery (CRA) to warn him that he would have to think of mobility now the 'war is over in Africa and there will be no more decent battles here'.[20]

The pursuit that Montgomery had for so long sought was now possible and Freyberg and 2 NZ Division were ordered to prevent the Afrika Korps from reaching Fuka. 5 NZ Brigade, withdrawn from Miteiriya Ridge, and reserved for this purpose, was anxious to move out immediately, but Freyberg wisely took his time. Congestion, confusion, and darkness made a cohesive divisional pursuit difficult. On 5 November the Division was delayed again by a dummy minefield south of Fuka. In the pursuit that followed, lack of petrol and then heavy rain slowed and bogged the pursuers. On the night of 7 November, Rommel and his troops reached Sollum and some security. Rommel, with a metal road to retreat over, was given enough time to save what he could of his beaten army.

What does El Alamein, and the battles preparatory to it, tell us of Freyberg's command aptitude? Far from being a non-intellectual, his rigorous mind shows itself continually assessing and reassessing both his divisional tasks and general's role, and the overall effectiveness of 8th Army. His long battle to coalesce armour and infantry was based on sound doctrine, finally accepted by Montgomery after the failure of X Armoured Corps to fulfil its battle role during the second battle of El Alamein. His argument, early in that battle, that several thrusts should be made, and the successful attack heavily reinforced, was much sounder than Montgomery's 'eggs-in-one-basket' approach. Freyberg's adaption of air, armour, and motorized transport, to maximize the effectiveness of his Division as a precision operational tool, is well demonstrated. He capitalized on his experience and seniority to reinforce bluntly his views with corps and army commanders, albeit not always successfully.

There is little doubt that Montgomery regarded him as an exceptional and talented divisional leader. Michael Carver regards this as, in part, an explanation of 2 NZ Division's choice for the pursuit after the battle:

> The choice of the New Zealand division to lead the pursuit was a curious one and can be explained on the grounds of personal choice; that Freyberg was the only commander at that stage who Montgomery felt he could trust to be sufficiently thrusting; or on the grounds of caution; that he thought that the task of holding the retreating remnants of the Panzer Armee was one that required more infantry than an armoured division could provide.[21]

As a divisional commander, Freyberg showed flair, especially in the seizing of initiatives, and showed himself a splendid tactical commander in fluid, mobile battles, with more grasp of both battles than at least one of the 8th Army Corps commanders. Like Montgomery, he was calm and confident in battle, and his judgement appears on several occasions to be far more accurate than Montgomery's. When 2 NZ Division's attack plan was moved from a coastal to a inland attack, Freyberg's grunt was accompanied by the calm and sensible reflection — 'that's what I wanted to do originally'.[22]

CHAPTER 6

Mareth

On 23rd January 1943, 2 New Zealand Division, as part of the 8th Army, entered Tripoli. In the months from the beginning of the battle of El Alamein, Freyberg's Division had advanced over 2,200 kilometers. On 23rd January, Freyberg's victory day was almost his last. The GOC together with Brigadiers W. G. Gentry and W. W. MacD. Weir escaped from an ambush near Tripoli.

With the Libyan campaign at an end, Montgomery planned for a speedy reduction of the remaining Axis forces in North Africa and to this purpose 2 New Zealand Division was moved 240 kilometers westward in early March, 1943 to Medenine in South Tunisia. Montgomery was determined to force the Axis remnant into a battle on their Mareth Line.

Montgomery outlined his plan for the Mareth battle to a conference of his commanders on 9 March 1943 — a mere three days after 8th Army had suddenly turned back Rommel's attack at Medenine. The offensive was to be resumed with the Army in three corps, each with a very different role. Leese's XXX Corps, consisting of the 51 Highland Division (Wimberley), the 4 Indian Division (Tuker), and the 50 Northumbrian Division (Nichols), would assault the Mareth Line defences frontally. In addition to three infantry divisions, Montgomery was also able to deploy a Guards infantry brigade, an armoured brigade, and a full artillery corps. Horrocks' X Corps included 1 Armoured Division (160 tanks), reserved as an armoured exploitation force, to move through the breach made by XXX Corps.

For this battle, Freyberg was offered a new formation, centred on his own national command, the 2 NZ Division: it was called the New Zealand Corps. This Corps comprised a force of over 29,000 men (including a French contingent) and over 172 armoured fighting vehicles, of which 151 were tanks. To reach its battle station NZ Corps made a long inland march through the desert, outflanked the Mareth Line by passing south of it, headed beyond the Matmata Hills to Tebaga Gap (code-named Plum), and thrust through this valley to debouch into the rear area well behind the Mareth Line. Freyberg's Corps was part of an 8th Army of about 160,000 men, 610 tanks, and some 1,410 guns. This army faced Axis forces of less than 80,000 men, around 150 tanks (including 10 Panzer Division's tanks around Gafsa), and about 680 guns. Statistics, in war, are not everything; certainly they were not to be the instant guarantee of success at Mareth.

By sending Freyberg's NZ Corps so far inland to the rear of the Axis position, Montgomery hoped to divide the attentions of the enemy to produce a situation in which it was impossible for the latter to win. In his diary, on the eve of the battle, Montgomery observed:

> The enemy would find himself attacked in very great strength on both his flanks simultaneously; he was not strong enough to hold off both attacks at the same time; if he concentrated against one attack, then the other would make progress.[1]

There was of course a drawback to such a plan. If by some chance the enemy was able to hold the Mareth position after a fierce encounter with XXX Corps, and threaten to bleed it dry, NZ Corps might find itself a long way out in the desert. If the Axis infantry could hold the Mareth Line with only a little help from the Panzer Divisions, then Freyberg's outflanking force might find itself facing small but highly experienced German armoured forces — no less than the fighting arm of the Deutches Afrika Korps — the 15 and 21 Panzer Divisions.

Any assessment of General Freyberg's role in the Mareth battles must consider the strengths and weaknesses of his NZ Corps. How comprehensive or diverse was this large motorized formation entrusted with a threatening but tactically secondary role?

New Zealand Corps came into being at midnight 11/12 March 1942. It consisted of the following formations:

N.Z. CORPS Lieut-General Sir Bernard Freyberg

	2nd N.Z. Division	Freyberg
	8th Armoured Brigade	Brigadier C.B.C. Harvey
	King's Dragoon Guards	
25,600	64 Medium Regiment, Royal Artillery	
men	57 Anti-Tank Regiment, Royal Artillery, less one battery.	
	One battery 53 Light Anti-Aircraft Regiment Royal Artillery.	
	'L' Force	
3,500		General Leclerc
men	FFF Column	

8th Armoured Brigade tank strength:

76 Shermans
13 Grants
62 Crusaders
151 Total + 21 armoured cars.

KDG = armoured cars

'L' Force:

2 troops armoured cars
1 squadron self-propelled guns
11 other guns various types
Anti-tank regiment
Anti-aircraft guns
2 reconnaissance companies
5 lorried companies
1 Greek squadron

Free French Flying Column:

2 armoured car squadrons
1 tank company (11 Crusaders, 2 Shermans)
2 platoons infantry[2]

The NZ Division was by March 1943 what General Freyberg termed 'one of the New Type divisions' of the British Imperial Army, quite distinct from a traditional conventional infantry or armoured division. It was most suitable for a mobile form of warfare. According to Freyberg:

> It is an infantry division with one infantry brigade replaced by an armoured brigade. The two infantry brigades are lorry-borne but they are not to be confused with motor brigades. They are trained and equipped for attack and defence as ordinary infantry while the motor brigade is fitted for a more defensive role. The armoured brigade has three armoured regiments and a motor battalion. The whole force is thus completely motorized. All its brigade HQ are in ACVs [Armoured Command Vehicles] and can operate on the move. It carries with it 12 days rations and water at two quarts per man per day, 350 miles of POL [petrol oil and lubricants], and 360 rounds per gun for the divisional artillery. It is unlike its opposite number in the German Army, the 90 Light Division [*sic*] . . . We have 72 field guns to their 48. We have slightly more heavy and light machine guns and the same number of mortars. It is only in anti-tank guns that we have less. They have 200 plus and we have 130. We have three regiments of tanks and they have only one (which, incidentally, never operated with them). Further, we are fully equipped to do any tactical operation that the ordinary positional infantry can carry out. 90 Light have practically no assault infantry at all — they are weapon holders. The New Type Division is an extremely mobile and hardhitting force relying on three elements for its offensive power; its armour, its artillery, and its extreme mobility. Because of this the New Type Division, like the armoured division is a strategic weapon, specially suited for making surprise appearances

> upon the battlefield. Possessing these characteristics the New Zealand Division was the logical choice for the Left Hook operations.[3]

The armour, the artillery, the mobility of the force, and the availability of good assault infantry to grind the enemy down in close battle made for a powerful and well-balanced division.

Nonetheless, it would be a mistake to conclude that 2 NZ Division had become an all-powerful formation on the battlefield. Its mobility and armour brought a demand for its use in dangerous outflanking moves and the relative vulnerability of a single division operating far around the flank of strong enemy forces was considerable.

Depth of penetration could pay dividends in terms of threat to the Axis rear. But a single division remained an isolated formation; unless engaged with the enemy, it was 'off' the battlefield. If the opposition chose simply to contain it, the result might be more than a nullified threat; it could be dealt with piecemeal later. This ambivalent vulnerability — a matter of employment — is exemplified in Freyberg's remarks on the object of 'Left Hook' operations:

> It is simply an outflanking operation on a bold scale adapted to desert conditions. Its object is to turn the enemy out of a strong position by outflanking him to the left and so attacking him by surprise from the left flank or in the rear. The Left Hook involved in every case a long approach march over open country in desert formation, the force moving self-contained with no secure L of C [line of communications], ready to fight a defensive battle against the full strength of the German Panzer forces on our front.[4]

The key to this ambivalence is the tactic of fighting a 'defensive battle' in the enemy's rear. It in itself acknowledges implicitly the weakness of the lone division in the enemy rear. To fight more than a defensive battle needed more than a lone division with, at the very least, thin lines of communication with friendly supply formations. The 'defensive' action was a holding operation not a challenge to the main enemy strength. This latter consideration was clearly beyond the brief and capabilities of the NZ Division. The point was to draw the enemy rearwards so that once its force had become divided, the main forces of the 8th Army could press home a 'central' attack on an unbalanced opponent. It was to threaten the enemy's rear noisily, so as to draw units in that direction. Once dislodged, the main 8th Army could push the enemy along, increasing the momentum of retreat.

The execution of an offensive move around the flank to the enemy rear areas involved meticulous planning:

> The Left Hook has always been part of the Army plan, so that it has

> worked in with an Army directive, and the timing is fixed by Army. D. day is usually fixed as the day when the frontal attack is delivered against the main enemy position, usually in moonlight on D night. It will probably be on D plus 1 day when the outflanking force is expected to reach its objective so that all calculations in planning must be backwards from that day to the position of assembly before the approach march and deployment for battle must be planned, and it must be relied on for selecting a route which a division in desert formation can follow. From this information you must pick your objective which will fit in with the Army plan. If the enemy defences are compared to a pill-box with side windows and a back door, the question is whether you aim your shots in at the side windows or the back door. The decision to close the back door or not will depend on the degree of surprise likely to be gained and relative strength of guns and armour of the enemy mobile reserves and that of the outflanking column. If complete surprise is effected the outflanking force may take up its position without having to fight, but if not less favorable ground will have to be used. In picking an objective you aim at occupying ground that will embarrass the enemy to the highest degree and force him to react violently. The object must be sufficiently far from his occupied defences to force him to attack at once. The aim is to separate the enemy tanks from their anti-tank gun-line and force the enemy field guns off their survey.[5]

The tactical aim of the move was to provoke a substantial reaction that was enough to include an incautious separation of armour and gun line. The move would be threatening enough to tempt the opposition to do this hurriedly. Obviously, surprise would be a useful element, as well as the fear of disruption of line of communications. This is fine on paper, but is less easy to achieve in practice. Freyberg understood this very well.

> Surprise must have priority in planning. . . Rapidity of movement and concealment of it, especially from air reconnaissance are prerequisites of surprise. . . In calculating the areas in which it is safe to move by daylight the. . . state of the rival forces must be taken into consideration. Movement forward of the area which can be neutralised by our fighters must be carried out by night along lit routes. Thus, in an approach march of 115 miles it may be advisable for two of the moves forward to be by night. Moves by day in close proximity to the enemy should be carried out slowly to ensure the minimum dust is raised. Experience has shown that desert moves can be made without detection from air reconnaissance even without continuous air cover, but dust clouds and reflection of the sun and moon on windscreens are visible for a long distance and may give away a move. Wireless is another big factor. . . much can be learned from wireless traffic, and we have therefore come

> to the conclusion that the only safe way of preventing leakage through our wireless traffic is to close down altogether. This is in line with German teaching that wireless traffic, especially of armoured divisions, gives away movements of formations. Once contact is gained, of course, wireless is opened in full, and is used freely except with regard to any future operation. . .[6]

The slimming down of the logistics tail for an outflanking move was a delicate matter of balancing the needs of the fighting forces for handy petrol, supplies, and ammunition, against the vulnerability of those 'soft-skinned' formations to enemy action. As much as possible of the administrative group must be left behind to be called up when needed.

The division would move in two groups, with different requirements. The first line would have petrol for 250 miles, and rations and water for seven days; the second line would have petrol for 100 miles, rations and water for four days. If possible, dumps of petrol would be made forward so vehicles could be replenished at the end of the day.

Once the outflanking move was under way, the organization of what might loosely be called the column, became critical:

> Wherever possible movement will be in desert formation on a wide front with dispersion between vehicles of anything from 100 to 200 yards, depending on the air position. The column moves by Brigade Groups, everyone knowing the layout of his respective unit and the unit's position in its respective group. The axis of advance is marked by what is known as a thrust line. This consists of a visible sign (in our case a black diamond on an iron picket) put up every 700 yards along the road. It is laid by a navigator on a compass bearing with provost putting in the signs. When not in touch with the enemy the navigator moves ahead of the force and when in touch with the enemy he moves with the leading armoured element. In unknown, featureless country moving across country is always difficult. Moving by compass bearing, especially at night, is likely to result in error, but as long as all groups travel on the same axis, the error can be ascertained by astrafix each night and the thrust line corrected the next morning. This method of movement gives great flexibility. No matter what direction you are moving in, vehicles remain in the same relative position whether moving or halted. . . For a night move vehicles close in laterally and from front to rear visibility distance. The actual formation for movement differs slightly in each Brigade Group although the general principle is the same. The following is the system adopted by one Brigade Group which gives the general plan. The Field Regiment is always put out on the side away from the threatened flank, and small units, anti-tank battery, Field Ambulance, Machine Gun Coy etc are in the centre. The Group is on a 24 vehicle frontage. The main units

on left and right are in 9 columns each and the centre group in six. At normal dispersion the frontage is 2400 yards, to a depth of about 3,000. The organisation is flexible and if it is necessary to break down the frontage through bad going, the left column can go to the front, followed by the centre, followed by the right. All changes of formation are controlled by flag signs. It is noteworthy that if the Brigade Group were moving on a road at 100 yards dispersion, it would extend over 40 miles, whereas by this method its depth is reduced to under 3 miles. Carriers and 2-pounders anti-tank guns travel outside Brigade formation to a flank, to the front or to the rear according to the tactical situation. At night the brigade closes into vehicle visibility distance which is ten to twenty yards between vehicles, giving the Brigade a frontage of 300 to 400 yards, and the depth is proportionately decreased. In desert formation you can average 8 to 10 MIH [miles in an hour] in daylight and 75 to 100 miles in a day is a good day's march. Night speed depends on the going and the state of the moon. A good average speed is 4 MIH although up to 7 MIH has been done. A night march of 35 miles (we have never yet achieved this) [written after Mareth] would be very good.[7]

The handling of a division on the move became critical when the outflanking force came close to the enemy. Changes were made up front:

> . . . Reconnaissance ahead into the enemy country may be impossible and the Navigator must move with the forward unit. It is essential at this stage that the Commander of the force should move at the head of the column under cover of the light screen ready to change the thrust line in accordance with the tactical situation.[8]

The problem of lengthening flanks, an inevitable accompaniment to an outflanking thrust, was to a large extent avoided by either the employment of certain units for flank guard duties, or by the relatively quick response by the division to a threat by throwing out a 'gun line'. This undertaking illustrates organizational skill needed in handling a division on the move:

> The decision to put out a gun-line is made by the Divisional Commander at Tactical Headquarters. Code words indicate at once that a gun-line defence facing a certain direction is to be put out. On receipt of it the leading Brigade halts and rear elements close up as may be necessary, the whole division conforming at 100 yards dispersion. Meanwhile the Commander withdraws down the axis to the ACV at Main HQ. Alongside the ACV an AA gun fires in the direction in which the gun-line is to be put out. The Divisional Commander meets his Orders Group 2000 yards from the thrust line immediately under the point where the AA gun shells are bursting [but

which have ceased firing]. He there gives the general line on which the gun-line will be put out, details depending on the ground, cover etc. As soon as the general line has been indicated each Group Commander is in position to carry out his reconnaissance and give his own Orders Group their orders. The gun-line can cover a front of 14000 yards in considerable strength. This front is divided up by pre-arranged plan between the various groups in the formation. Each Brigade covers 6000 yards and the reserve group is responsible for 2000 yards. The whole division deploys first anti-tank guns and then sub-units. Field Artillery are deployed in the Brigade area. Regiments in the gun-group, if there is no mission with the armour, deploy in the centre of the Divisional Area. . . The artillery is placed on a divisional artillery grid as early as possible and controlled through HQ NZ. Reconnaissance starts at once beyond the gun-line and artillery OPs go out. All troop carrying transport is retained in the area. From the time orders are given for everybody to dig in up to the moment when the artillery is connected up and ready to open fire on a Divisional base will be 2½ to 3 hours. . .[9]

Because of the obvious vagaries of any particular situation, it was not possible to make rigid rules for each and every contact with the enemy. In part, in any event, contact with the opposition was not necessarily determined by one's own forces. Freyberg knew this when he summarized principles that could be applied to the tactical battle:

The timing of the attack to seize the vital ground selected as the objective depends on certain factors. If the going is good a well-trained force can move at night and appear on the objective at dawn. . . however, the approach march must be a short one and it must be possible to carry out a good reconnaissance beforehand. The aim should be to capture all objectives as soon after dawn as possible. The daylight move has distinct advantages. There is no disorganisation and the column can move much faster. A force must have three or four hours to deploy to fight a battle. When contact is gained [it] is usual for Divisional Tac HQ to be with the cavalry. At this stage the Brigadier commanding the leading Brigade should take over and the Divisional Commander must position himself so that he can control the whole battle. The battle must be fought as a Division and not as independent Brigade Groups. Both infantry Brigades will move on the thrust line to the objective to hold a front of from 8 to 10 miles. Very active reconnaissance will be pushed out in front to achieve maximum surprise. The armour may be given a new thrust line depending on the tactical situation. Two field regiments and the mediums will be deployed to cover the front, all three field regiments being ready to accompany the armour. The way in which the armour is used will

> depend upon the strength of the armoured component. The ideal situation is to be strong enough to use the armour offensively. The policy is to fight the armour as much as possible inside the area covered by the whole weight of the field and medium artillery. . . In the early stages of gaining contact, air support should play a large part. There is a stage when the enemy is disorganised, when his guns are separated from his tanks, and there is likely to be a considerable amount of thin skinned transport on the move. This situation can be anticipated and bomber support turned on in advance to take advantage of the targets which will be offered.[10]

The NZ Division, augmented by the inclusion of the French forces under General Leclerc, was as NZ Corps, a good-sized formation to go round the Axis flank at Mareth: it was of sufficient dimensions to cause the German and Italian commanders to be concerned about their rear once they were aware of NZ Corps' presence. NZ Corps was strong enough not to get into trouble quickly, and of such a size that it would only require the addition of other formations to transform threat into menace. It was to be a most convenient arrangement.

In Montgomery's plan for operation 'Pugilist', the objectives and the roles for the formations of the 8th Army were clear:

> 1 Object: The object of Operation 'PUGILIST' is to destroy the enemy now opposing Eighth Army in the Mareth position, and to advance and capture Sfax.
>
> For the troops of 30 Corps, their central role was defined:
>
> 8. . . .Object: To break into the Mareth position, to roll it up from the east and north, to destroy the enemy holding troops and prevent their escape, and subsequently to advance and capture Gabes.
>
> The supplementary role posed for NZ Corps was:
>
> 9. The task of NZ Corps will be to make a turning movement round the enemy western flank . . .
>
> The Corps will then advance northwards, will break through any enemy troops or switch lines, and will endeavour to establish itself astride the road Gabes–Matmata so as to cut off the enemy and prevent his escape.
>
> 10. The movement of NZ Corps will be so timed that by night 20/21 March it has begun to create a serious threat against the road Gabes–Matmata.

X Corps was to be in reserve, to be ready to exploit the XXX Corps drive through the Mareth Line. In the meantime it would protect the left and rear of XXX Corps before and during the attack itself.

The formations of NZ Corps commenced their long circuitous route on 11 March. The French forces remained where they were, out in the desert round Ksar Rhilane, ready to join the Corps on the way. The movement to the staging area, from Medenine via Ben Gardane to a point between Ben Gardane and Foum Tatahouine took place in daylight, and the first phase of this movement looked like a withdrawal to enemy reconnaissance aircraft.

The infantry moved on 11 and 12 March; the Artillery, 8 Armoured Brigade, and the Reserve Group moved on 14 March. Night moves were then made by the various formations from the staging area to the assembly area past Ben Amir through Wilder's Gap. The infantry brigades moved on the nights of the 11/12 March (6 Brigade) and 12/13 March (5 Brigade). The Artillery and the Reserve Group moved on the night of 14/15 March, and finally 8 Armoured Brigade on the night of 15/16 March.

The move was under way. Freyberg noted in his diary:

> *Mon 15th March*
> Perfect morning. Too perfect as excellent for Bosche Strat R plane... Breakfast at 0800... Had talk to G1 [GSO1] and CRE [Commander Royal Engineers] after breakfast. Saw LO [liaison officer] to Army. Told him we were up to schedule, and our only trouble at the moment was transporters [for tanks]. Think Bosche may be going, and we won't in that event be able to accelerate by 24 hours. Only possible if transporter situation is all right. We won't allow any movement by day. We can accelerate by 24 hours but it is doubtful whether we can do more as the stuff won't be up. We can leave at 1600 in the afternoon and get to the start line before dark. In short we can do our approach march here in one afternoon and one night. If we move by day we will need fighter cover... RAF RDF [radio direction-finding] people have joined up. Self contained to travel with NZ Corps... Spent the afternoon in the office. Talked to Gentry. Some difficulties are emerging in the going. Will consider leaving at 3 — getting into night formation at 6. Will require air cover. We could then push through and halt on the Bir Soltane Road, stay in our groups and open out at first light...
> *Tue, 16th March*
> Some mist about which was welcome as 8 Armd Bde Transport was still coming in. GS(I) Summary shows recce unit of 21 Pz [Panzer] is in Gafsa area. Part of 10 Pz is in Keirouan area. Rest probably north of it... Had a talk to Bonnifant [*sic*] at 0900 and then Harvey [8 Armoured Brigade]... Have decided to tell Army that difficulties are many... Mines being laid everywhere. Recce units over whole area. Question of the first 25 miles to be left open. We have until 1200 hrs on 20th to alter plans... Decided with G1 at lunch time to avoid the long night advance if possible. Orders to be issued but possibility of change will remain.[12]

The concentration of NZ Corps was now nearing completion. It was a powerful, balanced force, yet to be termed a corps, for it had at this stage only been augmented by the 3,500 French troops and the term 'corps' gave a misleading impression of its capabilities. A division with the addition of a single brigade differs from a corps of two or three divisions.

On the 17 March, the General briefed his officers for the great flanking move:

> This is a hastily composed force with a specialized mission. A lot of units have not fought under our command, and at the risk of repeating myself sometimes, I would like to make certain that various points of procedure are clear so that we shall think along the same lines. It is a fast moving operation, a surprise appearance on the battlefield, or we hope it will be a surprise appearance to a certain extent. The enemy is obviously nervous. He knows where we will strike but not how and when. The job is to turn the enemy out of the Mareth Line and advance to Sfax to capture the aerodromes to the west of that place. Our operation is timed to synchronise with the attack which is of the 20th. Our particular role is to turn the flank and advance to capture the aerodromes West of SFAX. We have a striking force composed of a recce element of two cavalry regts under the comd of the Force Commander. We have an armd bde. We have a strong gun group which starts off with a regt of arty under the 8th Armd Bde Commander, plus a fd arty regt and the medium arty of the 64 Med Regt [Medium Artillery Regiment]. Whenever the arty are brought into operation we can count on having two fd regts and a med regt. When the situation allows we can group the two fd regts with the 2 Inf Bde groups. We have a very strong striking force of armour and guns. In addition we have two inf bde groups, not strong in striking power, but strong indeed in defence, particularly against tank attack. Our Bde Group is capable of putting out a gun-line of between 10 and 15 thousand yards, or even more if necessary. They put out gun-lines either by day or by night, and they are capable of strong infantry offensive action with the bayonet. There is also Gen Le Clerc's [*sic*] force which, for the start, is guarding our L of C and later in the defence North of Gabes of our left flank. While we will continue the left hook he will do a right hook against the enemy in the Gafsa-Pichon area, and will be tapping in on our left. . . The first difficulty of the approach march is the Wadi El Arash which is a decided obstacle. The enemy realizes this and has got Armd Cs watching that area. In its existing state we could not get through and it will require work by the Sappers with bulldozers. Tomorrow night General Le Clerc [*sic*] will capture the feature and we shall send forward a Sapper party to clear the roads. It will take about 8 hours to get it clear. Very careful control will be necessary in that gap if it is to be done at night, and ack ack protection and air cover will be necessary if we are to cross it by day. There will be nine

> tracks on a 100 yd front. It can not be made any wider. At night all tracks will be lit. The Sappers will also clear any mines. To avoid a delay at the gap, vehicles must rush through and then open out again on the other side. A two hour delay might be decisive. From the gap there is a move of 42 miles across country which is intersected by wadis but not difficult to negotiate. . . The object is to get that manoeuvre over by dark. If that operation fails the battlegroup will cover the deployment of the gun group. The latter will deploy after daylight and will proceed with systematic registration of the enemy position. We shall then carry out an infantry and tank attack under bombardment with the object of clearing a way for the force to move on.[13]

Freyberg's briefing had contained a mixture of optimism and understandable caution. Well aware of the role of the outflanking force and the necessity for speed to rattle the confidence of the Axis commanders, the limited size of his NZ Corps meant that limits must be placed on its employment.

His purpose in moving quickly was in essence to magnify the threat posed by NZ Corps. A fast threatening envelopment might suggest to the opposition that the flank attack contained forces stronger than it really had at its disposal. The main tactical thrust was to induce the German divisions to react rapidly, separating the Axis armour from its guns. If this could be achieved, a battle could develop where the option for the German armour to retire behind a conveniently placed gun line of 88s no longer existed. The infantry of NZ Corps was to be held back for the awkward bits — where the terrain and the composition of the enemy imposed the need for a set-piece battle.

If the enemy was found, out in the open desert, then he was to be pinned down and outmanoeuvred. Where the enemy was in possession of a bottleneck like a defile, then the familiar use of artillery bombardment and infantry attacks under cover of darkness would be used.

There was a need for caution by the NZ Corps armour, mostly 8 Armoured Brigade. There was to be no rushing of an enemy gun line: that would be 'tank suicide'. Freyberg was well aware that heavy tank losses would leave him isolated, with two infantry brigades, far in advance of any potential assistance. The tactic for the tanks was to seek a flank; where there were no flanks because of the accidents of geography, there would be no option but to operate with infantry and tanks under cover of the corps' artillery.

In all of this, the rapidity of the advance limited the amount of ammunition and petrol that could be carried. Therefore it was essential to keep the lines of communications open to the rear. This was the priority task for Leclerc's French troops. This delegation reduced the drain on the NZ Division (including 8 Armoured Brigade), and the momentum of the outflanking advance could be maintained with no lessening of the

Corps hitting power.

It was hoped that as the NZ Corps unbalanced the enemy, the Axis reserves could not be committed in the uncertainty created, or alternatively that they would be pulled back from the Mareth Line once the presence of NZ Corps, hovering near Hamma and Gabes, was disclosed.

The major uncertainty was the whereabouts and intentions of the enemy 15 and 21 Panzer Divisions, and the 164 Light Division. Their probably location and intentions had been assessed, but the Afrika Korps was notoriously mercurial and adaptable. It would be dangerous to assume that they might not concentrate quickly against a threat from the rear.

Following the conference, Freyberg met General Leclerc, and then tightened his own preparations:

> Had a talk to Gen Le Clerc [*sic*] on his operation tomorrow night and decided to send up to him a bty of 55's. The General lunched with us. He does not speak English so we got on quite well in French. LO left for army in Stimson after conference. Had a long talk to G1 on plans during afternoon and worked in the office. LO from army got back before dusk. Stimson jolting a bit as it came in to land in the wind. 50 Div succeeded in their attack. Took PWs from young fascists [*sic*]. Gds Bde failed to take Kidney held by two regts of 90 Lt. The Gurkas raided a platoon post and took a PW from 164 Div. The American show went quite well. The Itys appear to have gone back about 10 miles. This advance might mean 21 Pz having to commit a regimental group on the Macknasey Road which will be all to the good. Rang Brigs and gave them information. Told Kippenberger to keep an eye on HQ during my absence tomorrow. Wrote letters and went to bed fairly early.[14]

On Thursday 18 March, the NZ Corps commander visited Montgomery and was brought up to date with final arrangements for the attack and for the deep outflanking movement. Freyberg's diary noted the weather on 19 March as cold and overcast, but probably improving. Air support depended of course on reasonable flying weather. After the morning conference, Freyberg discussed some of the possibilities with his CRA, Steve Weir:

> Gentry fancies a quick advance with tanks, and going for his gun line in daylight. I favour bringing in the whole thing and getting as much camouflage as we can, bombing the areas solidly all day and then picking a place, registering it, and doing a proper set piece attack at night.
>
> Query: Are 60 rounds enough?
>
> CRA: That depends on the depth. It won't take you very far. 60

> Rounds at three rounds per minute allowing five minutes on the opening line would take you 1500 yards.
>
> GOC: That is all we want to go. We have to hold that and bring in our tanks and guns through. We have to fight for the observation [point] and we have to refill with amn [ammunition] next morning. The second line will be behind 5 Bde, and if necessary the second line can be dumped at the guns when we decide what we are going to do. As soon as Bir Soltane is taken 100 rounds will be dumped there. I think that as soon as the thing develops he is either going to fight or go. If he fights it is going to develop into a long drawn-out business and we shall have to destroy a lot of the troops he has got.[15]

An improvement in the weather was noted and the move was postponed till later:

> Moved at 1800 and continued all night, some soft going but generally speaking fair. Many holdups due to Armd Bde B Echelon which appears to have very little idea of moving in desert formation. Received from Army 'Benghazi Minus' [enemy aware of the outflanking move but there has been no reaction].[16]

On 19 March Freyberg received important intelligence. Enigma traffic put the number of Axis tanks at 196. These consisted of the 10 Panzer Division with fifty-seven, the 15 Panzer Division thirty-eight, the 21 Panzer Division with seventy-four, and the Centauro Division with twenty-seven.[17] This knowledge did not dispel some uncertainty as to what the enemy might choose to do with this armour, but that evening a decrypt revealed that the 10 Panzer Division was to stay around Kairouan as a reserve, and that 21 Panzer Division and the Headquarters, Deutsche Afrika Korps, were to move to an area south-west of Gafsa. This meant the 10 Panzer were more than a day's march from the Mareth Line. Freyberg hoped that the American drive would lure the Germans into employing this armour against US II Corps.

By the early hours of 20 March NZ Corps had reached a position to the east of Ksar Rhilane, just before Wadi el Aredj. It was a time for decisions about the next moves. Freyberg noted:

> Reached destination at 0200 hrs and had a conference with Queree [the GS01]. In view of 'Benghazi Minus' decided to let men get breakfast and get away at 0800, KDGs [King's Dragoon Guards — armoured cars] at 0730. Hope to get forward against enemy by 1200, start survey [for artillery] and have a fire fight and attack by night. Decided to break wireless silence at 0700. Sent 'Tripoli 0730' which should bring air cover over wadi; ack ack protection also. 5 Bde guns to go forward... Armd Bde to move through gap five miles and concentrate. Army report no

> reaction to Gafsa operation and 21 Pz therefore able to operate against pugilist [*sic*]. Had great difficulty getting line communication. A great deal of movement on the axis [thrust line] owing to stuck vehicles coming forward into posn. Stand to at 0530. Shook out into some sort of dispersion which was difficult owing to the soft going. Left for Tac HQ at 0800. Certain amount of gunfire forward not yet identified.[18]

By now NZ Corps had the rising ground of El Outid to the right: to the left lay open desert. In front ahead lay Ksar Tarcine and Wadi el Hallouf — beyond that and to the west was Bir Soltane. The decision to move forward in daylight was sensible in view of the Benghazi Minus message from 8th Army. If the enemy was not going to react, it would be better to move forward rather than give time and extra space for him to marshal his forces. Resumption of wireless communication, needed to move the column, would underline the threat to the enemy flank.

The 21 Panzer Division made no move in reaction to US II Corps' threat towards Gafsa, nor did it head for Mareth, thereby giving evidence that the Axis commanders were prepared to await further developments. Conversely, the fact that 21 Panzer Division remained handily placed to operate against Freyberg or XXX Corps was a spur to press on towards Tebaga Gap. To await darkness on 20 March meant that not only would time pass, but that the twelve hours pause might nullify the outflanking move completely. Though thin numerically on the ground, the Axis forces had the usual advantages of operating on interior lines. That advantage could only be eroded by a significant threat to the rear. It was important now for the enemy to see the danger slowly mounting inexorably to the flank and then behind him. Only then could Montgomery's dilemma posed by operation 'Pugilist' be foist upon the Axis command: to meet an attack in strength from two directions simultaneously.

The progress of NZ Corps continued. Freyberg observed:

> Enemy elements retired before our advance, first through Bir Soltane and then NW. The only obstacle to progress was the bad going which seemed to be worse than the going maps indicated. 6 Bde were at 'Apple' at 1450. At 1710 8 Armd reported a general enemy movement towards El Hamma. Whole force moved on until about 1900 when we halted for the night. Gave orders for tomorrow as follows: (1) KDGs to move at dawn and recce along whole front at 'Plum' [Tebaga Gap]. (2) 8 Armd to move 0700, gain contact and see if they can turn Eastern [right] flank. (3) GOC, CRA, Harvey and Gentry to carry out recce at 0700. (4) Cav [Divisional Cavalry] to move at first light to guard the East [right] flank of NZ Corps. (5) 5 Bde warned of possible approach of 40 troop carriers full of men reported by Tac R moving South towards Hallouf at 1725. Spent night fwd at Tac... Almost full moon...[19]

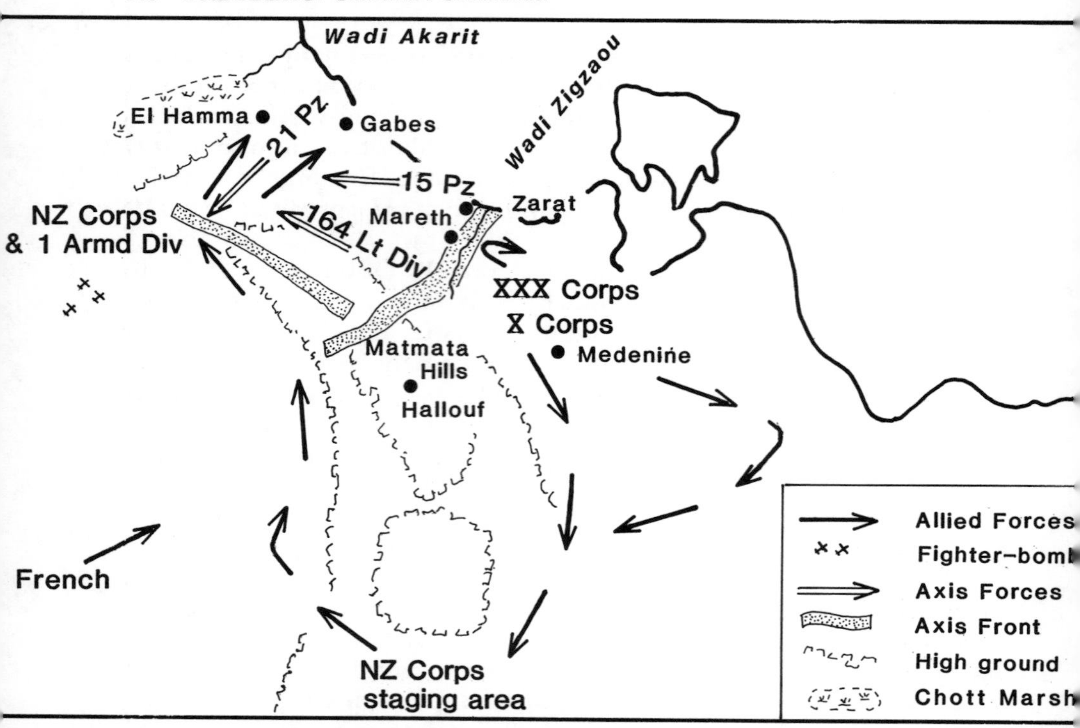

Turning the Mareth Line, 20-27 March 1943, with a 'left hook' operation.

If the soft going had slowed the advance of the whole column, NZ Corps was nevertheless usefully placed on the night of 20/21 March. The Matmata Hills lay between the Corps and the extreme end of the Mareth Line. Wadi el Hallouf and open desert stretched away on the left; only a few miles ahead of the thrust line was Tebaga Gap, an opening between Djebel Melab and Djebel Tebaga, through which they had to pass to get to El Hamma or Gabes, an area right astride the rear of the Mareth position.

The orders for the following morning reflected the caution necessary in approaching the gap code-named 'Plum'. A cavalry screen was to be put out, the King's Dragoon Guards, to probe the gap, and the Divisional Cavalry was to provide security on the Corps' flank. The rear New Zealand infantry brigade group (5 Brigade) was given warning orders about an enemy probe possibly emanating from the direction of Ksar el Hallouf. Armour (8 Armoured Brigade) would move to seek a way through 'Plum' on the short side — the right — although this seems to have been a hopeful probe, rather than a full-scale attack. Significantly, the corps commander, the artillery commander, the commander of the armour, and the commander of 6 Brigade — Freyberg, Weir, Harvey, and Gentry — were going forward themselves to assess the situation on the early morning of the 21 March.

It was a commanders' reconnaissance. There were enough uncertainties in terms of terrain, projected enemy strengths, and the weather for there to be a note of caution. Captain Paddy Costello, the intelligence officer, suggested that:

> Identifications in [the] last few days...confirm our previous information. He appears to be staying in the line waiting for us to take the initiative...Tank strength appears to be up to 200 rather faster than expected. 15 Pz have 50, 21 [Panzer] have 70, and the...10 Pz have 50. The other group of 10 Pz in the North have 40 [?]. 21 Pz is still on the line North of Gabes and 10 Pz is a long way to the North. Centauro has dropped from 90 to 30. There are 1,500 Germans including 15 Pz Div and 22,000 Italians in the Mareth Line. They have 75 88mm guns. A certain amount has been disclosed by air photographs. He is defending the entrance to the wadi at 'Plum'. No evidence of mines.[20]

The air photographs according to Middleton showed that:

> There are new A Tk gun posns [anti-tank gun positions]...which... appear to be occupied. General inference not a lot of additional work except in one area blocking the entrance to the wadi. Trenches and weapon pits along back of wadi appear unoccupied.[21]

For Freyberg, the morning's developments plus the likelihood of three days' bad weather would preclude any decisions on major offensive action until the Sunday afternoon (21 March).

In the evening of 20 March, 8th Army received the summary of a decrypt from the day before; the original was from the Afrika Korps, from General Messe. This disclosed an intention to hold the Mareth position 'to the uttermost', even in the face of an expected attack by 8th Army including a main frontal assault, an outflanking move by mobile armoured forces, and an attack in the Gafsa area. Provision was made for a pull-back to Akarit should stubborn defence seem to be leading to complete annihilation.[22]

After more local intelligence evidence that the Axis command was concerned about the Mareth flank inland, Enigma revealed around midnight on 20/21 March that the Luftwaffe had observed NZ Corps *en route* to Tebaga Gap.[23] What had not been revealed by Enigma was that Messe had ordered the 164 Light Division to Tebaga Gap on 19 March. This would not be reported by Y (wireless traffic) or Enigma till 23 March.

Montgomery had reason to be pleased with the movement of Freyberg's formations. He wrote in his desert diary:

> The daylight move of N.Z. Corps all day on 20 March would direct all eyes to the West; meanwhile I would keep very quiet on the East,

> and the strong attack which was to go in by 30 Corps at 2230 hours on the enemy Eastern flank near the sea would have all the more chance of success. . .[24]

In less than forty-eight hours he would be staring the prospect of defeat for operation 'Pugilist' starkly in the face.

In the early hours of 21 March, NZ Corps now received some disturbing news:

> GS(I) [General Staff Officer, Intelligence] appreciation in from Army at 0130 hrs. Germans appear to be stiffening Trieste and Young Fascists in the Mareth Line. Move of 40 troop carriers in Hallouf area to stiffen Mareth but possibly to operate our L[ine] of C[ommunications]. 15 Pz have not moved through yet. Appreciate 21 Pz Div with 70 tanks, likely to hold the funnel at El Hamma against us. May be joined by 15 Pz Div with 50 tanks if attack at Mareth not considered a draw demanding immediate armd counter-attack.[25]

The prospect of ultimately facing two very experienced Panzer Divisions, with a possible 120 tanks, gave pause for thought. A crop of eighty-eight guns and other heavy weapons would be included in this opposition, and the forcing of the bottle-neck to El Hamma and Gabes might not be an easy, quick operation, especially in that the air support promised while Freyberg forced the gap was to be of only one hour's duration. The enemy had achieved close to parity in armour. In the past the Afrika Korps had tended to get the better of the British armour, and fighting a defensive armoured battle would put the odds in the German's favour.

The more immediate concern on the morning of 21 March was to probe the defences at 'Plum' and decide on what course of action to take. The result of the morning's probes by the King's Dragoon Guards, armoured cars, and 8 Armoured Brigade was a plan for a night attack with 'Plum' as the objective. 'Plum' consisted of the junction of the Roman Wall across the gap with the Tebaga–Kebili road, in front of which was a rise known as Point 201. It was a necessary base from which to launch further assaults through Tebaga Gap itself. The Corps began to deploy, with 6 Brigade starting to move forward at 1315 hours.

Freyberg's diary details a message received from the Army commander:

> Oliver [Leese] attacked last night and got a footing Mareth Position according to plan. Further punch goes in tonight. Enemy clearly intends to stand and fight and Oliver may have a dogfight lasting several days. Make for Peach [El Hamma] and be prepared to operate from Grape [Gabes] towards Mareth with Mobile forces to threaten enemy's rear. . .
>
> Sent reply to Army Commander telling him that we had encountered

> extensive minefield. Intend to attack Plum tonight and exploit as soon as possible. . .[26]

Clearly everything was not going according to plan. This was very different to what had been envisaged in operation 'Pugilist', where XXX Corps was to break through to Gabes. Now Freyberg and NZ Corps were to plough through Tebaga Gap, take El Hamma and head for Gabes. Gabes was then to be the base from which NZ Corps would menace the rear of the Mareth Line. In doing so, and in view of the intelligence received about German tank numbers, this could court disaster. If Leese's XXX Corps was held up attritionally for 'several days' Freyberg would have to lose only one encounter with armour to see NZ Corps isolated and probably cut to pieces. For Freyberg this must have represented an underlining of the dangers of his exposed position. If he was to go further he must have more resources. To do what was asked was to invite the destruction of his command surrounded, piecemeal, at the enemy's leisure. Freyberg's reply to Montgomery was measured — he would attack 'Plum' and exploit when possible.

A further message from the Army commander was received at 2130 hours on 21 March:

> MOST SECRET personal for General Freyberg from Army Comd. Everything points to fact that enemy will be [harassed?] as your movement develops. Situation is as follows you should reach GRAPE as soon as possible. You should then attack GABES and destroy all enemy depots there. Then operate with armoured and mobile forces towards Mareth while holding GABES area securely so as to prevent any withdrawal Northwards. Can you forecast when you might expect to reach GRAPE. 2 U.S. Corps now moving East from GAFSA and this should give enemy further bellyache.[27]

Freyberg's experience warned him not to ride the wings of Montgomery's enthusiasm:

> . . .Consider all this is rather optimistic at present, especially as at same time we got 'I' appreciation which suggested that the position was held by Italians and stated that the enemy armour was not yet committed, but was waiting an indication of which was the main threat. Sent messages to Army Comd saying we would operate against Peach [El Hamma] if Plum was successful, and that in view of the 'I' appreciation, it was difficult to make a forecast, that the posn was undoubtedly being reinforced, and that we would be in a better position to give a forecast tomorrow.[28]

In the meantime, the attack on 'Plum', namely Point 201, was set to go in at 2200 hours. It would be carried out by 6 Brigade with a squadron of Sherman tanks from the 3 Royal Tank Regiment. The infantry battalions were the 25th Battalion on the left, and the 26th Battalion on the right. The attack was to be supported by the whole of the field artillery, plus the medium. The way through the minefield had been cleared by sappers, and the assault began in bright moonlight. It was successful. Over 800 prisoners were taken from the Auto-Saharan Group, the Savona, and the Pistoia units, plus some heavy weapons. Point 201 and the Roman Wall had been secured with only light casualties to the infantry.

Once the attack had clearly succeeded, Brigadier Gentry of 6 Brigade contacted Freyberg and urged that 8 Armoured Brigade should be moved through at once, rather than wait till daylight. Freyberg agreed that Gentry should have a message passed to the Armoured Brigade commander, Brigadier Harvey, to the effect that the latter had permission to pass through and increase the extent of the infantry's success. This message was taken by the commanding officer of the 27th Machine-Gun Battalion to Harvey, who, according to the GSO2 of NZ Corps, was unlikely to have taken much notice of it.[29]

In any event, it was not an order for the armour to move through and the Armoured Brigade's decision not to was perhaps most prudent. Criticism has been levelled at Freyberg for not pushing 8 Armoured Brigade through at this time to crack the Mareth defences. But while 6 Brigade were moving up for their attack, 21 Panzer Division was heading towards Tebaga Gap with increasing momentum, their object being to drive straight through Point 201 and prevent NZ Corps' entrance. 164 Light Division was already on the way. To have driven the 8 Armoured Brigade on at this time would have brought them into an unsought action with the tanks and guns of 21 Panzer Division hours earlier than they encountered them the next morning. It might well have resulted in yet another suicidal British tank action, with tanks separated from the British gun line and picked-off by a wily opponent. The Western Desert campaign is littered with examples of British armour impetuosity, or its concomitant — obstinate reluctance to go forward.

Without armour, NZ Corps would have been vulnerable. There is little doubt that had Freyberg been threatened by the Germans, Montgomery would have had no way of aiding him. XXX Corps had not broken through the Mareth Line. To move the armour of X Corps as far as NZ Corps would have taken three days!

In refusing to be swayed by the Army commander's rather desperate measures for relieving pressure on the Mareth Line, and in refusing to push through armour at the behest of his infantry brigadier, Freyberg demonstrated that he was not about to throw away the advantages already won in an impetuous gesture. He had already gained a successful 200-mile approach march on the Axis rear; the taking of 'Plum'; the drawing off of enemy forces — particularly Deutsche Afrika Korps formations — 21

Panzer Division and 164 Light Division. All had been achieved in difficult terrain.

Ominously, on 21 March, Enigma traffic revealed that 21 Panzer Division had moved from Gabes to 'behind the Mareth front'; that an 88mm battery belonging to 21 Panzers had been sent to Tebaga Gap was disclosed by Army Y (intercepted wireless traffic); and the deduction by 8th Army Intelligence was that 21 Panzer Division would be following this unit. It has been suggested that this information, plus the fact that the main 8th Army thrust through the Mareth Line had been repulsed, had an effect on Freyberg's delay in attacking 'Plum'.[30] The Corps was geared-up for a careful move forward. By 8.14 a.m. on 22 March, 8 Armoured Brigade was reporting heavy artillery fire from its forward position and requested medium artillery support urgently. Freyberg moved forward to assess 8 Armoured Brigade's situation personally. Kippenberger returned from the battlefield and reported little tank movement: the fire was not anti-tank fire but long-range shelling. In his opinion the armour could go on if they were prepared to lose a tank or two.

In his diary, Freyberg stressed the impact of airpower in the battle:

> Later in the morning forward troops reported enemy tanks on the front. Our armour was forward on the small counter feature 9107 with orders to move fwd and get the ridge. . . to the NE of that. The general plan if they get it is [to] bring the guns up and put the 6 Bde in to hold it tonight and then to bring up the rest of the force. No further decision to move 5 Bde or Div HQ until 1500 hours. Div Cav reported tank battle going on. Question of attacking infantry in the hills to the East was discussed between GOC and G1 [Queree] and in the end it was decided that the Free French should be put up in the hills to deal with the situation. Early in the afternoon the RAF reported that they had enemy targets. They are sending 12 tank busters [Hurribombers?], 26 Spitfires and 24 Kittyhawks. At 1405 NZA [artillery] reported tanks firing at one another. Infantry with enemy tanks keeping well off. 8 Armd Bde reported on their right forward front 17 tanks and two knocked out and on the left forward front 14 tanks edging past to the NW. RAF then attacked. It seems clear that some bombs and some strafing was on our own troops but the presence of a force of MEs made the situation obscure. One lot of enemy fighters jettisoned their bombs near Corps HQ and both forces of fighter-bombers disappeared Southwards in a dogfight . . . Although straffed [*sic*] and bombed a bit 8 Armd Bde reported in complimentary terms on efforts of the RAF.[31]

The bombing of NZ Corps by friendly aircraft had been a daily feature of the outflanking march ever since the Corps had moved past Bir Soltane. It was fortunate that at times the bombing was not accurate, and also that it was not prolonged or intensive. It was a dangerous nuisance. Both the United States Army Air Force (USAAF) and the RAF were guilty. It underlined the hazards of desert warfare, and also how far behind the Luftwaffe the Allies were in close support operations. Air support on a massive scale several days later was to prove more effective against the enemy than were Allied ground forces.

The RAF intervention on 22 March was claimed by the RAF to have destroyed five German tanks, hit thirteen others, and destroyed three armoured cars, four trucks, a staff car, and an 88mm gun with its crew.

NZ Corps was making its adjustments on the battlefield and attempting to consolidate its position. This was not without excitement even for the impeturbable Corps commander, as his diary reports:

> GOC returned for dinner. Reported Lt-Col Kellett MP, 2i/c 8 Armd had his head blown off while he was talking to the General. 5 others round about tank wounded. The result of the day's operations was to widen the salient gained by the 6 Bde's night attack and push out on the right. The next step will be to do the same on the left. This is essential to stop the cross observations which the enemy has, enabling him to shell any forward movement and preventing us from bringing up our arty. Gave orders to Div Cav. . . to go across West of the main road — right across and back as far as they can go and just across the minefield to winkle people out. They are to work in close to the Jebel cleaning people out and also the guns which are shooting up the armour, and at night come back close to one of the bns [infantry].[32]

Earlier in the day, NZ Corps had received a report that good progress had been made on the Mareth front on the night of 21/22 March. Heavy enemy movement was reported on the road between Gafsa and Gabes. The armour that NZ Corps had encountered was that of the 21 Panzer Division. Stopping its thrust towards Point 201 in the centre of the gap had been the Corps' main achievement of the day. The enemy's quick use of the gun line exemplified the danger of the action contemplated the previous night, of sending 8 Armoured Brigade right through the gap in the direction of the enemy. Instead, NZ Corps had made its gain in the night infantry assault, consolidated in daylight on 22 March. It was not spectacular, but it was eminently practical.

Freyberg sent a sitrep [situation report] to 8th Army at the end of the day's actions:

> Progress held up by shellfire. 35 to 40 enemy tanks on the front by 1300. Enemy in position on high ground north and east of 'Plum' with cross observation. Results of fighting to date: 1532 PWs; 4-77/28 guns; 4-88mms; 1-75mm; 12-37mms; 20 MMGs; 130 LMGs; 400 rifles captured. 3 Tanks, 5 vehicles KO [knocked out]. Enemy shows every intention of holding present posn as long as possible. Plan is to push

> out the right with the Free French and to the left with the Div Cav and to get the armour on as soon as possible.[33]

Late in the evening of 22 March, 8th Army sent a message to NZ Corps that 10 Panzer Division was believed to be in the Gabes area, and might be available to be used against NZ Corps. For NZ Corps this was unwelcome news. It was in fact in error, but for a few hours it considerably exercised Corps headquarters. The possibility of facing 21 and 15 Panzer Divisions was formidable enough; the sudden possible intervention of the armour of 10 Panzer Division would compound the situation considerably. This information was unnerving, given the Corps' exposed position.

There was worse to come. The attack at Mareth by XXX Corps had not progressed well, and by the night of 22/23 March, only a small bridgehead was in XXX Corps hands, across Wadi Zigzaou. Montgomery's biographer, Nigel Hamilton, later reflected:

> . . . Monty's orders for a renewed assault on the evening of 22 March, to strengthen the bridgehead and extend the crossings across the wadi, were too late. Far from mounting a renewed attack, Beak's 151st Brigade was now attacked itself by a whole German Panzer Division [15th Panzer Division], working hand-in-hand with infantry units of 90th Light Division, Panzer Grenadiers and the Ramcke Brigade. The German counter-attack was both brilliant and merciless: one by one they picked on the Mareth strong-points captured by the Geordies and annihilated the defenders. Casualties mounted; the wadi and trench systems became a devil's cauldron . . . the true fault lay . . . in an operation . . . in which the weight of the assault was too weak and the single channel of reinforcement subject to interdiction by the enemy.[34]

The attack across Wadi Zigzaou was now in tatters. Instead of a clean breakthrough by the infantry, for the armour of X Corps to exploit, XXX Corps were back where they had started. Two battalions of 151 Brigade still remained on the other side of the Wadi with the small number of Valentine tanks sent to support them. Leese still had Tuker's 4 Indian Division to throw in, '. . . but the enemy were now so strong along the Wadi Zigzaou that I felt doubtful of success'.[35]

Montgomery was woken in the early hours of 23 March with news from his Corps commander that XXX Corps had lost the bridgehead. Montgomery lost his iron composure and asked de Guingand 'What am I to do, Freddie?'[36] The important thing, Montgomery decided, was not to throw more troops into a hopeless attritional battle. A new way had to be found:

> Leese was ordered for the moment to hold the bridgehead as best he

> could; de Guingand was told to return to Main Headquarters and to investigate what could be done to reinforce Freyberg's left hook; General Horrocks was asked to appear at 9 am., together with Leese for a conference of the two Corps Commanders [10 Corps and 30 Corps].[37]

Over a week later Montgomery wrote to Brooke, the Chief of Imperial General Staff:

> At 0200 hrs 23 March I had nearly lost all my gains on my right flank. This is not pleasant at any time; but it is particularly unpleasant at 0200 hrs in the early morning![38]

The whole strategy of operation 'Pugilist', of the creation of two pressure points the enemy could not check simultaneously, had well and truly come unstuck. XXX Corps was held fast on the Mareth defences; Freyberg's NZ Corps seemed checked in an isolated valley many miles away. 8th Army had run into serious trouble.

Montgomery took the only course open to him other than a general retreat. On 23 March, the Army commander informed Freyberg that he was shifting the main thrust of 8th Army's attack to the left flank through Tebaga Gap:

> MOST SECRET Personal for General Freyberg from Army Comd. 30 Corps thrust meeting increased resistance and have decided hold tightly there for the present. Instead will reinforce your thrust with 1 Armd Div and this increased strength should enable you to push on and reach Gabes. 15 Pz Div closely engaged on my front. 10 Pz Div engaged in Gafsa area. Troops available to oppose you are 21 Pz Div and have reason to believe certain elements of this div have gone to Gafsa front. Must also expect more of 164 Div to oppose you. For maintenance and other reasons essential to have Corps HQ on your flank and am sending Horrocks to take charge. Am sure you will understand. You and he will work well together and should achieve decisive results. Horrocks and recce parties should reach you tomorrow about 12 noon. 10 Corps to take over when 1 Armd Div have arrived probably afternoon 25 March.[39]

Freyberg and his senior officers of NZ Corps had been preoccupied by the thought of the 10 Panzer Division coming into action against them, and there had been some discussion on how to meet a possible thrust by this formation. The involvement of 15 Panzer Division on the Mareth Line was in a sense welcome news: but until the arrival of Montgomery's promise of reinforcement to the left flank, NZ Corps had been under the impression that the bridgehead at Wadi Zigzaou was still held. Freyberg's diary noted:

> After lunch Sitrep arrived from 30 Corps which caused the G1 [Queree] on first reading to swear. It seems clear that at Mareth a German counter-attack has restored the situation and we are once more across the Wadi Zigzaou. 1600 hrs sent message to Army suggesting another regt of Armd Cs [armoured cars] should be sent round to protect our L of C endangered by large German forces South of Mareth in the Hallouf area.[40]

Freyberg noted the arrival of the Army commander's instruction to transform the left outflanking move into the main effort, with the comment that the arrival of 1 Armoured Division would relieve NZ Corps of responsibility of guarding the army's tail. Horrocks' arrival to take over at Tebaga Gap as Corps commander was less welcome. Freyberg was in fact senior to Brian Horrocks; besides Freyberg was the Corps commander on the spot and he had ably carried out his flank move. Why should Montgomery need a newcomer to take over? In fact, the question of a corps headquarters arose principally because main 8th Army headquarters were sure that the addition of 1 Armoured Division to the formations of NZ Corps would make the forces difficult to control under *ad hoc* arrangements. NZ Corps was run not with a separate corps headquarters, but by simply doubling-up the senior officers of the NZ Division to undertake corps as well as divisional duties. This worked well enough for Freyberg in that he was not separated from his national command as on Crete, and also because the senior officers of the NZ Division were a practised group, familiar with the way each other worked. Unlike Crete, the chain of command of the NZ Division was not to be dislocated greatly: troops in action had commanders who ran their brigades and battalions normally. Officers did not need to get used to someone new while on operations.

This sort of arrangement worked well for Freyberg, but it was not so easily understood by outsiders, who were less appreciative of the fact that the NZ Division in the Middle East was an entire small national army.

Freyberg, in the meantime, had other fish to fry. 6 Brigade were to change position. Leclerc's French forces were probing in the hills and had encountered strong enemy forces. The French had won some very high ground that overlooked German artillery batteries, and arrangements were made to establish wireless observation posts for artillery spotting by dawn of 24 March. 8 Armoured Brigade had put in an attack with the afternoon sun behind them (a portent of things to come) aiming to get round behind the enemy. Again NZ Corps was trying to turn the end of the enemy gun line with tanks and supporting artillery.

The Divisional Cavalry discovered what seemed to be a feasible way across the Jebel, and this led to consideration of another plan. This would be to slip 8 Armoured Brigade through on the night of 24 March to advance quickly to El Hamma, and then to turn on to 21 Panzer Division and fight it out. This was thought possible because it had been confirmed that 10 Panzer Division was engaged at Gafsa, while it was also known that 15 Panzer Division was embroiled on the Mareth Line. When this tank encounter took place, the NZ infantry brigades would advance through Tebaga Gap to Gabes, and be astride the Axis line of retreat:

> ...5 Bde... 6 Bde... will go fwd to Gabes. We will then turn and have a dogfight in the rear of the Mareth Line. Then the war in NA [North Africa] will be over. (PA [John White]: I hope it works out like that. GOC: It will.) Talked over this plan with Harvey on the telephone. Told him to push on in the morning as the enemy will probably stop us on another line and then we would side-slip him at night. If, however, 8 Armd Bde have a big success, they are to go forward and take the cash in hand...[41]

Events elsewhere changed now to Freyberg's advantage. On 23 March, the 10 Panzer Division attacked the US 1 Division at El Guettar and was repulsed with heavy losses. This was reported by Enigma, and, for the following two weeks at intervals, Enigma traffic and Army Y reported that the 10 Panzer Division was held in this area.[42] This allowed the intervention of this armoured division to be estimated as at least an unlikely possibility as time went on. The next day it was discovered that the crossing of the Jebel by 8 Armoured Brigade was not feasible, as it was passable only for jeeps, and perhaps armoured cars. Freyberg:

> ...had a talk to G1 and A/Q. Supply situation OK except for amn which will require watching. Feel enemy may be waiting for us to advance to attack feature ahead, with ATk guns behind it ready to knock us off it. Think we will push on with the right hook tonight a couple of miles and possibly try with the other regt on the other side. Gentry is to go forward another mile and dig in a gun line or we may give Gentry a sqn of tanks and let him push along tonight. It is no use punching forward in the centre. That is playing his game. Push forward on the flanks and hammer hell out of him.[43]

Freyberg was still displeased at the arrival of Horrocks and 1 Armoured Division. He considered that there was no room at present for 1 Armoured Division, and that the 'best thing for Horrocks to do is to face up to Matmata'.[44] Freyberg was aware of the isolation of his situation at 'Plum' — even with 1 Armoured Division, the formations of NZ Corps and 10 Corps did not possess unstoppable strength. In the meantime the commander of NZ Corps was thinking of other options. He considered putting Kippenberger and 5 Brigade through the hills, but, as Queree pointed out, it might not be feasible to get supporting weapons through: little would be gained. Freyberg was aware that the enemy had split his armour and if pressed would eventually crack. He reasoned that 'in the meantime it is no use throwing away troops'.[45]

However, Enigma traffic revealed on 24 March that the 21 Panzer Division and the 164 Light Division had been sent to Tebaga Gap with orders to counter-attack only if they were attacked.

Horrocks' reception at NZ Corps headquarters was decidedly chilly. Freyberg has been described as being 'grim, firm, and not at all forthcoming'.[46] Horrocks had arrived while Freyberg was drafting a reply to a signal from the Army commander, who had asked for Freyberg's agreement in principle to an assault on the enemy forces in Tebaga Gap. In their reply, Freyberg and Horrocks demurred somewhat and proposed the options as follows:

> 1. Carry on as we are going until we can force gap pass 1 Armd Div through. This should be possible in from 5 to 7 days.
> 2. Carry on as at present and pass 1 Armd Div round Kebili to attack Hamma from west, thus stretching enemy. This could probably develop night 27/28.
> 3. Carry out blitz attack by daylight with 8 Armd Bde supported by maximum air and five arty regts. This would be very costly but might break through. In our opinion second course is far the best and is most certain to produce quick results and minimum losses.[47]

What was proposed in the preferred second course was an expansion of what had been considered earlier, using 8 Armoured Brigade. This had the obvious danger of physically dividing 1 Armoured Division from the rest of the forces at Tebaga Gap — if it got into trouble nothing could be done to help. This meant risking a whole armoured division.

Montgomery's reception to the alternatives suggested was straight to the point. As Lieutenant-Colonel Oswald in charge of the Army Commander's Tactical Headquarters later reported:

> Monty was in the Mess. I said. 'That was General Horrocks, he wants to put a proposition to you.' 'Tell me what it is', he replied. So I gave him these three alternatives — including the one to split his forces — Freyberg to go on up the Hamma gap, and Horrocks to take the 1st Armoured Division round the other side. You see, Horrocks was a bit frightened of Freyberg. Freyberg was a well-known character, he was a Commander in his own right, and no man, even Monty couldn't have sacked Freyberg, he'd have had to go through the New Zealand Government to do it. And Freyberg wasn't slow in throwing his weight about. If he didn't like an order from somebody or other, he'd say, 'Well, I'll just have to let my government know about that one' — which

> generally put the stopper on a Corps Commander. Anyway, Horrocks was rather taking over from Freyberg there, and it wasn't easy. So he put forward these alternatives, and Monty quite firmly said: 'Tell that boy Horrocks, tell him to get on with it, the way I told him to do it! Get on with it and stop belly-aching!' That sort of attitude.[48]

The Army commander was quite certain what must be done, and quickly, to get the stalled Mareth moves going again:

> I want to speed up your thrust as much as possible. . . by heavy bombing all night and day. To take full advantage of this you would have to do an afternoon attack with the sun behind you. The plan would be as follows:-
>
> (a) Continuous bombing by Wellingtons and night bombers on night D-1/D.
> (b) Intensive artillery shelling for say one hour before zero. . .
> (c) Air cover and attacks by fighters on any movement to and from the battle area.
>
> I do not believe that any enemy could stand up to such treatment, and you would, after it, burst through the defile quite easily and get to El Hamma and Gabes. . .
>
> The army and air staffs are working it out and we can lay it on if you agree you will accept it. Date: the earlier the better. I would like D day to be tomorrow 25 March, 1 Armoured Division to be up by then, ready to exploit success on 26 March.
>
> I think you would get surprise, as the enemy thinks we always attack at night. . . The RAF will play 100%. Let us call it SUPERCHARGE, and give me a date for D Day.[49]

This was accompanied by a letter from de Guingand with details concerning the proposed air support. Freyberg and Horrocks responded more favourably. Freyberg noted:

> Army Comd's detailed plan reached me by LO who came in Stimson later in the day, and after considering it decided we could carry it out at earliest on 26th. . . Received letter from BGS giving me the air plan which is the greatest air support we have ever had. First conference with Brigs at 0730 [25 March] to get them to consider the various points of preliminary grouping, start line, speed of advance, positioning of tanks, etc. Corps Comd arrived at 0830. Went through with him questions of Command and responsibility for detailed planning.[50]

A conference was planned for 1400 hours. At the conference for 'Supercharge II', the impending assault on the Axis defences at Tebaga

Gap, Freyberg went over the aims and final details of the attack.

The General first presented a situation report. XXX Corps would keep pressure on the Mareth Line; 7 Armoured Division would be aiming to cut the Gabes–Mareth road through an area where 4 Indian Division were opposed by the Pistoia Division, hopefully forcing the 164 Division to be moved back. Those were two of the three thrusts. X Corps and NZ Corps were to combine for the third thrust, and for this 1 Armoured Division would move to the Corps headquarters concentration, namely before the enemy positions at Tebaga Gap. It was this third thrust that was 'Supercharge II':

> We are resuming the offensive here at 1600 hours tomorrow. Our plan is to breach the enemy defences at Plum and get through the bottleneck between Jebel and the high ground. The attack is to be a surprise one. It is a daylight attack which is something we have not attempted in this theatre of war. We hope that by making all the preliminary moves by dark and by lying up cleverly that we shall be able to launch our attack in a few minutes as a complete surprise. He thinks we shall attack about 11 or 12 at night. There must be as little movement in the forward areas as possible. We are making as much use of the light as we can. By attacking at 1600 hours it will be most favourable for the tanks. With the wind blowing... a good number of the positions behind may be blinded... preliminary moves... are to be carried out by dark... there must be no movement around vehicles tomorrow. The enemy will see that the tanks have moved but they won't know where they are... there will be wireless silence... No talk about future operations of any description is to be carried out on the wireless. Another element of surprise in the attack is that it will be a real blitz. We have the biggest air support that we have ever had. The morale effect of this form of attack will be very great. It will develop in a few minutes and will display an enormous depth. There will be a very big artillery bombardment by seven field artillery regiments. The tanks will come forward... behind them the carriers, then the cruisers shepherding the infantry and the infantry on a broad front. That should develop in a few minutes. And behind that again they will see the whole of the tanks of the 1st Armd Div coming through. He will be heavily attacked from the air and by the artillery and will then see this terrific array of something like 300 tanks in front of him.[51]

Here was the linchpin of the plan that was to allow the break through the gap. Aerial and artillery bombardment, followed by tanks, tanks and infantry, and then by a whole concentrated armoured division. It was a very German attack, against a set-piece defence, and the enemy had held a virtual monopoly on this sort of warfare up to this time. Freyberg then assessed the needed artillery bombardment which would be spearheaded by the Desert Air Force's fighter bombers:

> We rely also, on the morale effect and material effect of the bombardment. The success of the operation depends on heavy artillery support, . . . a very heavy bombardment, one 25 pr to 30 yds. It is going to open on an artillery start-line with concentrations on all known enemy positions. There will also be two regiments of mediums shooting on enemy defences behind. It will go to a depth of about 3,000 yards. The whole programme will take somewhere about 100 minutes through to the final objective. This operation is going to be difficult; there is no doubt about that, and you want to make it quite clear it has to go through with great speed and vigour and it is going to be pushed to the extreme limit. It is an all out attack.[52]

Freyberg spelt out the importance of the assault, underlining General Montgomery's intention of transferring the weight of his punch to Tebaga Gap. NZ Corps, now reinforced by X Corps formations, particularly 1 Armoured Division, was to be the instrument to achieve the Army commander's objective: 'If we can make a breach, and I see no reason why we can't, there is no reason why this operation should not collapse the whole of the Mareth position.'

General Freyberg put emphasis on the need for the various formation commanders within NZ Corps and X Corps to exercise the most exact and able military competence:

> The chance of success depends a very great deal on the degree of surprise we can bring off. The number of casualties will be in direct ratio to the skill with [which] Brigadiers and Regimental Officers carry out this attack.

The General turned to the detail of the onslaught:

> The attack is in three phases. First, tonight when the 5th Brigade, operating on our right flank, attack a very important piece of ground with an enemy company on it, we are going to put in a whole battalion with heavy artillery support. We must expect him to resist and counter-attack very heavily as he realises the importance of this high ground. The second phase of this attack is the blitz which we are carrying out at 1600 hrs tomorrow, and the third phase is after the capture of the final objective which we expect to be on three-quarters of an hour before dark. That will enable the 1st Armd Div to see the country and get into position through the gap before dark . . .[53]

Tribute was then paid to General Leclerc's French forces holding ground on the right, and preventing '. . . enemy observation of our right flank'.

He returned to the main attacks:

> I want to go briefly through the outline plan. I have already touched on the artillery programme. Zero hour is timed when the artillery fire opens on the artillery start-line. The attack is being delivered on a two brigade front with our 5th Brigade on the right and 6th Brigade on the left. 5th Brigade will have all three battalions in, one committed to an attack tonight and two committed up to and inclusive of the road. The axis of advance is the main Kebili-Hamma road. The 6th Brigade who are holding the high ground on the left are attacking on a one battalion front. I want to deal with the difficulties of the attack. We are going through a bottleneck which is narrow enough for armour and very narrow for thin-skinned vehicles. Yesterday we took a piece of ground to deny the enemy getting in 88mms which would command the gap. That is a key position just as important as the high ground to be captured tonight. It must be made clear to the 6th Bde battalion how important that piece of ground is. It is a very simple plan. There are two objectives. The axis is at right-angles to our start-line. The start-line of the artillery is at right angles to the axis. It is a simple bombardment plan. The thing is made easier for us by the Roman wall and well-defined road. The wall is surveyed very accurately on the maps and can be recognised. The infantry start-line is a thousand yards ahead of the Roman wall. The 8 Armd Bde is returning to the assembly position for this attack. One regt is already in position on the left. Two regts are moving to an area behind point 201 tonight where they will remain camouflaged. The battalions also will have to find place there for their carriers. The first objective is to capture that ridge which dominates our front and is to the right of the main road. It has a certain amount of defences on it. The second objective is the defensive line in the wadi. The actual artillery concentrations will depend on the data that we get from the air photographs.[54]

Freyberg then turned to the half hour immediately prior to the assault and stressed the importance and function of the air support:

> I want to give you a picture about 15.30 tomorrow. There will be a certain amount of inevitable movement in the forward areas, tanks will be warming up, etc. A certain amount of smoke is going to be fired for an hour before we move. In addition to that the air programme starts at 15.30. There will be two hours air support. An average of 4 Squadrons every quarter of an hour. There are over 20 Squadrons involved of Spitfires, Kittyhawks and tank-busters. The duration of the air support depends on the time the Spitfires can keep over the target. We are having the area, especially this high ground of the gun positions, swept for half an hour before zero and it is at that time that the tank-

> busters are going to work. They will prevent any movement of the 21 Pz Div from the positions it is occupying tomorrow. Tac R will discover where they are. At 1600 the bombardment opens. Half the guns will not have fired before. That will be the signal for everybody to get cracking. The success of this operation depends on how everybody knows his job at zero and how everybody rushes forward as the bombardment starts.[55]

At this point Freyberg was asked a question — was the infantry to move before the tanks got through them? Referring to the 8 Armoured Brigade's armoured fighting vehicles he indicated that:

> We want to try to time the tanks onto the objective not much before the infantry. We know where the start-line is and we know where the tanks are harbouring. The tanks will start at zero; the infantry will start at zero plus 15. The tanks will stay on the first objective until the infantry reach it. They will go forward behind the barrage. The artillery programme will be decided when we have seen the air photographs. A trace will be issued similar to the one at Alamein.[56]

The General turned to the immediate tasks to be undertaken when the final objectives of the breakthrough battle had been achieved:

> On the capture of the final objectives we shall be spread out in an area with a good deal of enemy on our flank and very vigorous action has to be taken to mop up the enemy. We have got to reorganize on the objective and form as firm a base as we can and get our transport ready to go through. The armour has got to rally on a position on this flank and be ready to move out at short notice following the 1st Armd Div.[57]

At this point General Briggs commented that 1 Armoured Division would go three miles past the final objective of NZ Corps, wait till the moon rose, and probably not be under way before midnight. As the situation allowed, transport would be moved up. The purpose was to concentrate in the area. If the enemy resisted heavily it would be necessary 'to face a flank'.

Freyberg went on:

> We have given you an area to which you move and 9 tracks forward [nine columns] and you will then go through according to the progress of the attack. You would be in a position there with the remainder of the Motor Brigade behind. If our advance should be held up, the 1st Armd Div is going on.
>
> Scattered mines are bound to be encountered but minefields are not expected as enemy tanks are moving round all over the area. Vehicles

> blowing up on mines will not stop the advance. I take it that is what is meant by an all-in attack. If the momentum of our attack is finished 1st Armd Div just busts straight through.
> 5th Brigade must watch that right flank. If we were bumped off, that would be very serious.[58]

Ammunition was discussed — 1 Armoured Division tanks might have to advance with 160 rounds apiece, though when NZ Corps was not going forward further, it could assist with re-supply. Freyberg completed his address to the assembled officers:

> We will issue the shortest possible orders with the fullest possible bombardment programme which is the thing you have to go on. We will make it clear what zero hour means.[59]

Remnants of the old fear, about the capabilities of British armour remained. What had befallen the NZ Division at Ruweisat Ridge, and more recently at Alamein, needed to be exorcized. At Alamein, the breakthrough sacrifice of 9 Armoured Brigade on Mityeira Ridge was wasted because the heavy armour that was to follow balked when the time came to move through. Then, 9 Armoured Brigade had been operating as the armoured component of the NZ Division. Now, at Tebaga Gap, 8 Armoured Brigade filled the same role for the NZ Division; the question was, would 1 Armoured Division carry out its role on the day? General Horrocks recalled:

> I remember Freyberg turning to me and saying, 'If we punch the hole will the tanks really go through?' (shades of Alamein!) I said: 'Yes, they will, and I am going through with them myself.'[60]

Freyberg's uncertainty over the willingness of armoured commanders to co-operate with his infantry was accompanied by concern over the likelihood of affecting air support. The letter from de Guingand, of 25 March, spelt out the role and the methods by which the close support proffered by the Desert Air Force was to be obtained:

> My Dear Generals,
> (I feel as if I am writing to the old combination Hindenburg and Ludendorff!) This letter gives you the Army Commander's views as to future operations.
> 1. Supercharge is virtually your course No.1 with stronger and more intimate air support than we have ever tried before.
> 2. The Army Commander wants you to go 100% for Supercharge and produce a simple cut and dried plan and we will give you the maximum air support possible. . .

> 7. We are sending over Darwin... to help you tie up the air support for Supercharge. The RAF have ordered an armoured car to report to NZ HQ and it is proposed that Darwin should be located 'cheek by jowl' with Comd 8 Armd Bde or whoever else is in a position to get the latest information as to how the air support is working. It is important that he should be able to see the battle area from a good OP [observation post], and he will then be able to give the pilots the low-down as to how they are doing. It is important of course that he does keep in the closest touch with one of our commanders as he must have an up-to-the-date picture. Sitting back here it would look as if 8 Armd Bde is the right location.
>
> 8. (a) [omitted list of fighter squadrons].
>
> (b) The length of time they can operate over area continuously depends on the Spitfire Sqns. These can operate continuously for two hours. Therefore you can expect continuous Kittybomber attacks throughout this two-hours period at the density of two squadrons.
>
> (c) The important thing will be to decide on the correct timing. We feel that it might be best to start this intensive air effort about zero minus 30 minutes. This should thoroughly disorganise the defence at the psychological moment and allow the fighter bombers to continue supporting the attack during the most difficult period...
>
> (d) It will be most important to give the air force as soon as possible the maximum information as to your plan of attack and the areas and centre of enemy resistance guns etc that you wish to be attacked...
>
> 9. The Air Force are going flat out on this low strafing... They will not be able to stage such an intensive effort two days running.[61]

This was a considerable commitment to close support by the RAF. This *blitzkrieg* style of operation was a new development for the Allied forces in North Africa. The RAF had adapted tactics regarded as a normal operational procedure by the Germans. In Poland, France, Greece, and Crete, the Germans steadily refined their ground–air co-operation methods. However, the RAF felt that they could not sustain such an effort two days running, despite the German Luftwaffe's previous demonstration of longer capability shown in its close support on Crete, nearly two years earlier, where Richthofen's Fliegerkorps VIII carried on a solid week of interdiction of targets on the island. The Desert Air Force was embarking for the first time on a new policy. The RAF had often attacked ground targets behind enemy lines — it had also attempted some close support. Now it was to combine destruction of airfields, aircraft, ground forces, and lines of communications with a close support blitz in front of an artillery barrage that was itself a prelude for an assault by armour and infantry. Having been so much on the receiving end of such tactics in Crete, it is not hard to see why Freyberg was enthusiastic to apply what was essentially the Germans' methods on the enemy.

Determination.

About the reluctant armour? Perhaps a frank exchange of views between Lumsden, Leese, and the General.

Below: Face of battle: taken on the front of Miteiriya Ridge. The knocked out armour is 9 Armoured Brigade's — an afternoon photo taken by Sir John White.

Out of the line training for operation 'Supercharge' at El Alamein. Freyberg talks with the unreliable Lumsden.

Commander before battle: the General briefs the officers of 2 NZ Division on operation 'Supercharge'

Battle commander: Freyberg on Polly III, sand goggles, binoculars equipped for going forward.

Below: Freyberg's Tactical HQ: GOC in front of left tank. This tank, T37832, was Freyberg's command vehicle. To accommodate and provide some useful work space inside, the gun was removed. Comparison of the two tanks reveals the dummy gun on the left tank.

The light division moves: 2 NZ Division in desert formation.

Sherman tank, the mainstay of the armour. This tank was commanded by McLean the All Black.

The French arrive from Chad, meeting NZ Corps *en route* to Tebaga Gap. From the left: General Leclerc, GOC, Kippenberger, French officer of 'L' Force.

Maps, model, planning: Freyberg talks over tactics with infantry, artillery, and armour commanders.

Hurricane from 8th Army drops a message. Note armoured command vehicle on the left.

Freyberg as passenger in the back leaves by Stimson for Main 8th Army HQ to see General Montgomery.

Dust and smoke as battle rages in Tebaga Gap.

General Messe arrives to surrender to Freyberg.

General Messe of the German-Italian Army surrendering to Freyberg.

Monty and Freyberg.

Snow in Eastern Italy — Sherman tank and Staghound armoured car, the latter probably from NZ Divisional Cavalry.

To Cassino. Freyberg meets the Army Commander, General Mark Clark, as Queree looks on.

Politeness and caution: an experienced commander and his inexperienced and politically ambitious superior.

The role to be undertaken by the Desert Air Force in operation 'Supercharge' shook the higher echelons of air command in the Middle East. Fundamental questions concerning air support for ground forces were debated anew. The Desert Air Force, presided over by Air Marshal Sir Arthur Coningham, had in general terms interpreted level bombing as the best means to deliver explosives to the enemy, involving the maintenance of height (15,000 feet), and including the subordination of fighter aircraft to bomber protection duties. This made for inefficiency and wastage. Accuracy in the support of ground forces was sacrificed. Level bombers at 15,000 feet needed only small margins of error to miss the target. In the absence of large numbers of dive-bombing aircraft, the restriction of fighter aircraft to bomber escort duties eliminated the most likely alternative source of low-altitude close-support, of the kind provided for the Wehrmacht by the Stukas. Moreover, training in such a role was woefully deficient, both in practice and results.

The appointment of Coningham as Air Officer Commanding the Allied Tactical Air Forces in Algiers brought his chief of staff, the thirty-six year old Air Vice-Marshal Harry Broadhurst, to command the Desert Air Force. Broadhurst, an ex-Battle of Britain fighter pilot, decided to improve the air force's close-support tactics, recognizing in part the rather apparent local air superiority of the Allies and the superfluous dictum of fighter escort duties as a limiting factor on fighters' operational employment. He asked Montgomery to 'furnish the typical outfit of enemy vehicles — captured vehicles, tanks, lorries, wireless vehicles. We put them out in the desert and we had a great exercise.' Ordered to 'knock them out', the results were unequivocal!

> Well, they didn't hit very much. They then realised that of course they'd never practised this sort of thing. And even with the vehicles standing still it wasn't all that easy to hit them — never mind going along with flak shooting back![62]

The 8th Army pause around Tripoli gave the Desert Air Force some opportunity to practise close support and air–ground co-operation. The signal from Montgomery to Alexander about the RAF part in operation 'Supercharge' resulted in the dispatch of the AOC's Chief of Staff, Air Commodore Beamish, to inform Broadhurst of Coningham's displeasure. The operation was unsound, Broadhurst was told — '[You] could lose the whole of your Air Force doing this' — 'One kick up the arse and you've had it!'[63] In conjunction with the reminder from Beamish, that Broadhurst's permanent rank was only that of squadron leader, the threat was explicit. On 25 March on attempting to brief fighter-bomber pilots for 'Supercharge', Broadhurst himself was called 'Murderer!'[64]

In the face of such opposition, the arrival of a desert sandstorm at midday on 26 March might well have spelt disaster for the impending attack at Tebaga Gap. General Sir Charles Richardson commented:

> At midday the dust-storm started. I was watching this minute-by-minute, as you can imagine, sitting in our combined RAF/Army vehicle. And then one o'clock, reports coming in from the Air strips: visibility ten yards, impossibility of taking off and so on. And then Harry Broadhurst started moving them around — from airstrips where visibility was impossible to ones where it was better — right up to the last moment. But even so, the scale of the attack was cut considerably. I couldn't help wondering if we wouldn't have to call the whole thing off — because I know the RAF contribution was absolutely vital, not only in the terms of effect, but because of the store which Freyberg put on them. It was a marvellous feat by the Desert Air Force under terribly difficult circumstances.[65]

The innovation was the RAF's use of the NZ Corps' daylight creeping artillery barrage, bombing, and strafing everything beyond the barrage as it moved forward. Guided by the moving barrage, the exploitation of air–ground links refined the Stuka effect.

The role of Broadhurst and the transformation of Desert Air Force close-support tactics in the 8th Army, a role denied by the British official historians, was observed by Broadhurst's senior officer at Advanced Air headquarters, Group Captain F. H. Searl:

> Harry Broadhurst . . . was one of the very few senior officers who had any experience in battle. He very soon altered the attitudes of those who held that a Spitfire wasn't meant to be a fighter-bomber, and sacked anyone who didn't hold with the new role.
>
> With the army we worked out a new technique; we would put into the air perhaps three pairs of fighter-bombers . . . If the army came up with targets, they would be briefed in the air in plain language, no codes at all, by an airman whom they knew and trusted not to fly them into a lot of flak. We first used this at the Hamma gap battle, operating from a converted Sherman . . . It worked like a dream, and thereafter was referred to as the cab-rank system.[66]

All was now ready — as ready as it could be when the two commanders at Tebaga Gap had been given such short notice of the assault. It is a fair measure of the professionalism of both Horrocks and Freyberg that in spite of the latter's coolness towards the former on his arrival at 'Plum', and despite having in mind very different courses of action from that proposed by the Army commander in 'Supercharge II', they were willing to accept Montgomery's new plan. This in itself required a measure of faith in the capabilities of the RAF in the close support role: there could be no trial run. NZ Corps had fallen foul of stray bombs from Allied aircraft during the lead up to Tebaga Gap, unfortunate incidents that made it an act of faith for many soldiers that all would go well. The perennial problem with the armour, this time of the 1 Armoured Division, asked for more faith — it was perhaps Horrocks' assurance that not only would 1 Armoured Division pass through the hole once it had been made, but he would travel with it, that made the possibility of breakthrough a potentially more practicable proposition.

NZ Corps and the reduced X Corps now awaited battle. They were a long way in advance of 8th Army headquarters: nothing could be done quickly by ground forces to assist if they fell into trouble.

The first phase of operation 'Supercharge II' was a necessary preliminary to the main action planned for the afternoon of 26 March. The start line for the blitz attack was overlooked by high ground occupied by German troops. In order to proceed at all, these German forces must be removed. One of the battalions of the NZ Division was assigned the task of taking the heights. The objectives of the attack were two hilltop positions, the first Point 184 (called Objective 'A'), the second another point about 1,000 yards north of Point 184 (called Objective 'B'). Artillery fire was to be concentrated on both hilltops for fifteen minutes, and an extra five minutes for 'B'. This support fire was to come from the 4 and 6 Field Regiments of the NZ Artillery. The infantry companies of the 21st NZ Battalion were on their start lines a little before 12 p.m. 25 March. The artillery barrage opened at 1 a.m. 26 March, and a short time later the infantry companies went into the attack. 'C' Company under Major Laird took Point 184 without difficulty. Some thirty-six Germans from 104 Panzer Grenadier Regiment of 21 Panzer Division were taken prisoner, along with eleven heavy machine-guns, two mortars, and a truck adding to the haul. Only six Germans were killed. 'D' Company, 21st Battalion, under Captain Murray assaulted Hill 'B' where there was more resistance — twelve Germans were killed, eight captured, along with two mortars and one anti-tank gun. The total infantry casualties in the 21st Battalion were four killed and seventeen wounded.

In a short sharp infantry assault with no hitches, 21st Battalion had seized the heights, and proceeded to construct defensive positions on rocky ground. Ominous noises in the night, of tracked vehicles, prompted the Battalion to call for artillery fire on the noise: this was successful in preventing the Germans from starting any counter-attack that they had contemplated. For the next day, 21st Battalion would serve a useful passive function as right flank guard to NZ Corps. This was not as easy as it sounds, because up until the blitz attack mounted in the afternoon, the infantry would have to endure sporadic barrages of enemy artillery fire, without a 'right of reply': the enemy was not to be provoked so that the full weight of the unpleasant surprise should have greater impact.

On the morning of 26 March, NZ Corps signalled 8th Army that the spoiling attack had been successful and that all was ready for the coming engagement: Freyberg's doubts as to whether the coming assault would be as decisive as planned are reflected in the GOC's diary entry for 26 March, prior to the afternoon attack. Worries about the armour and the enemy gun line were now compounded by the weather itself, which threatened to cancel the air support:

> Southerly wind continued and raised the dust, reducing visibility to such an extent that it is doubtful whether the air force will be able to operate. Horrocks came in and had a long talk on the operation and our future movements. Message came in from Army that 15 Pz now on our right front. 10 Corps will still proceed as planned. GOC told Gen Horrocks that he thought 1 Armd Div would be held up, but the latter thinks he will get through all right in the moonlight owing to the surprise we are going to achieve. On Mareth Line 51 Div is making slow progress and Ind Div are in Hallouf. Gen Horrocks was anxious that NZ Div should follow 1st Armd Div as soon as possible to Hamma. GOC said: 'I think it is going to be touch and go with this attack. If he gets a lot of A Tk guns on the ground it is going to be difficult.' Army Comd visualised 'Supercharge' being repeated [at El Hamma]. It all depends on the amount of stuff opposite whether 1st Armd Div will get through. GOC and Gen Horrocks discussed where their respective Tac HQs would be situated.[67]

The worry about the actual air support was in fact crucial to the breakthrough. The possibility that the enemy would be able to have enough anti-tank weapons left to impede the armour was very real, if the air support did not materialize. The revealed presence of the 15 Panzer Division as well as the 21 Panzer Division and the 164 Light Division added to the worries — NZ Corps was to go in to break through against a force that seemed to be most of the formations of the existing Afrika Korps. Some straight talking about the uses of armour was engaged in, with Horrocks being more defensively optimistic than a pessimistic Freyberg. The weather, the extra panzer division, the old doubts about British armour, and the long experience of skilful handling of both tanks and anti-tank weapons by the Germans, presented formidable obstacles. Freyberg was emphatic on the matter of armour:

> . . . The defensive use of tanks. [Freyberg] pointed out that in defence he splits up his force and for attack he concentrates and whatever the Armd Corps people may say it is the right way and the only way. The Armd Corps exists for the Army and not the Army for the Armd Corps.
>
> Corps Comd [Horrocks]: Mines are the one thing I am afraid of.
>
> Comment of GOC [Freyberg]: You have to face the fact you are up against the DAK of 3 Divs, an extremely experienced force in desert fighting. The situation has changed since the Army comd gave his

orders as 15 Pz have now come across.

Comment of Corps Comd: By putting 300 tanks through, even if 8 Armd Bde have been wiped out, they will take on any enemy they find there. We must not let the momentum of your attack die.

GOC: Our infantry will go through if the armour is held up. That is better than armour charging a gunline.

Corps Comd: I do not see the armour charging alone. I see them going from crest to crest.

GOC: Army comd visualises 'Supercharge' being repeated in two days time. We want to have the tanks to manoeuvre with when we get through. Once we get elbow room the enemy is finished. As long as he can hold us in the bottleneck, he has an outside chance of holding the Mareth posn. He will bring the whole of the DAK to hold that posn. Even if the Mareth Line holds and this posn goes, he must be put in the bag. He will hold it, ravine by ravine.

Corps Comd: You have had more experience but what I am hoping is that he is so stretched . . .[68]

Freyberg's concerns about armour charging a gun line and Horrocks' view that 8 Armoured Brigade could be sacrificed to achieve the break in must have sounded a note of warning to Freyberg. If they were sacrificed might not 1 Armoured Division use this as an excuse not to go through? This is exactly what had happened at the outset of El Alamein: 9 Armoured Brigade working for the NZ Division had broken through with very heavy losses: the British 10 Armoured Division was then disinclined to proceed. It is easy to forget that this was only five months (almost to the day) previously. The infantry view of the unreliability of the armour was quite widely held. If the GSO2 of NZ Corps at Mareth could speak of so many disappointments[69], a respected corps commander like Sidney Kirkman was more forthright:

> . . . the armour was never very good in the desert . . . They didn't understand the gunners — they used to charge about by themselves, whilst the Boche was much more cunning, would have his anti-tank guns put out, and would then retire and our people would then charge in on the anti-tank guns . . .[70]

Added to the problem of tactics was the mathematics of armour versus anti-tank weapons. The best battle tank that the British could field was the US M4 Sherman. The thickest armour on the Sherman was 55mm. The German 88mm flak gun used as a formidable anti-tank weapon fired shells that could penetrate over 110mm of 30^0 armour plate at 450 metres (500 yards)[71]; at 960 metres (1,000 yards) just over 100mm of armour; at 1,350 metres (1,500 yards) over 90mm of armour; and 83mm at 1,800 metres (2,000 yards). The British tanks were out-ranged by the German

88mm guns and were therefore prevented from coming close enough to engage targets. It was only hidebound prejudice that prevented the British from having an anti-tank weapon at least the equal in hitting power to the 88mm flak gun. The British 3.7 inch anti-aircraft gun was designed for the same role as the German 88: to engage aircraft. Unlike the Germans, British Army authorities failed to perceive that an anti-aircraft gun might attack ground targets. At Fort Solaro on 20 June 1942, three 3.7s held off tanks of the 15 and 21 Panzer Divisions *en route* to Tobruk: five tanks were stopped and considerable casualties caused among the crews. The situation was only restored by a German infantry attack which was successful because the Fort Solaro gunners had no infantry support. A trial of the 3.7 as an anti-tank gun in the Knightsbridge box was regarded as a failure because of the inadequate sights, the fact the gun stood high off the ground and because it blew sand into the air when it was fired.[72]

Freyberg was worried. He had seen a feinting flank movement with some inherent possibilities transformed into the main attack through the failure of the abortive assault on the Mareth defences. Montgomery's chief of staff was disturbed for the other reasons: the apparent delay to the opening of the assault might lead to fighting greater German forces that might be difficult to cope with. He wrote to McCreery, Alexander's chief of staff, on 25 March:

> NZ Corps are going hammer and tongs, and their main problem is to get through the narrow bottleneck overlooked by the Tebaga and Matmata hills. We felt the best way to get them through was to stage a real blitz attack, using all possible air support and thrust our way through. We had hoped to stage this attack today, but Generals Freyberg and Horrocks say the 26th is the earliest. My own view is that today might prove easier than tomorrow in view of the fact that the enemy is reinforcing with 15 Panzer Div, and also we must sooner or later expect more attention by enemy air on our front. We are now going all out to deal with air support for tomorrow; the air are co-operating in the most whole-hearted way and are prepared to run considerable risks to give the very closest type of support. We have never tried out this blitz method before, of trying to demoralise the enemy's defences by very strong strafing attacks. I have great hopes that success will result provided the main drive by the tanks is pressed resolutely.[73]

Freyberg had kept his misgivings and doubts largely to himself: there was no point in weakening the resolution of his brigadiers and battalion commanders. He consulted with his brigadiers:

> Everything seems set for the attack and spirits are high. Feel that we are certain to achieve surprise, but must not under-estimate the strength of the enemy. Although the dust was very bad the Air Force decided

> to play. In any case the dust blowing from South to North is going to be a decided advantage for our infantry and tanks . . . On talking to Gentry ascertained that Morton's bn [25th Battalion] also Div Cav, is already on the left of the first objective and will assist in the defence. News through that Americans are doing very well and will thrust on Gabes tomorrow with an armd div and two inf divs. Told Kip I thought it was going to be tough. Reply: It will be tougher for him. 1530 hrs to the minute escorted medium bombers flew overhead. The stage is set as perfectly as it could be for a daylight attack. The dust is blowing straight into the eyes of the enemy.[74]

On the previous two nights the entire bomber strength of the Desert Air Force had attacked the rear areas of the Axis forces, aiming at cutting telecommunications and disrupting and destroying road transport. It was an adaptation of what the Luftwaffe had done in France in 1940. Now on the afternoon, in spite of the sandstorm raging, the main air attacks went in:

> At 15.30 hours on 26 March, three formations of light and medium bombers launched a simultaneous pattern-bombing attack on the main enemy positions. The intention was to create disorganisation and particularly to disrupt telephone communications. This attack made a low and evasive approach and met no air opposition. Immediately afterwards, the first relay of fighter-bombers entered the area and began to bomb and machine gun from the lowest possible heights. A strength of two and a half squadrons was maintained in the area, fresh relays arriving at quarter-hour intervals. Pilots were briefed to bomb specific targets and then to attack gun positions with the object of killing the crews, particularly of those guns which were in a position to hold up our armour. Hurricane 'Tank Busters' also attacked and broke up enemy tank concentrations. A Spitfire patrol of one squadron strength was maintained over the area to protect the fighter-bombers, while at the same time light bombers under the control of NATAF [North African Tactical Air Force] attacked enemy air forces as a diversion. The enemy were surprised and no air opposition was encountered over the battle area . . . Half an hour after the air offensive opened, infantry attacked under cover of a heavy barrage creeping forward at the rate of 100 feet a minute, thus automatically defining the bomb line. [75]

The infantry of the 5 and 6 NZ Brigades were on the start lines with units of 8 Armoured Brigade. To the right of the Kebili–Hamma road, the 23rd Battalion was with the Staffordshire Yeomanry, and to the right of them the 28th Maori Battalion and the Nottinghamshire Yeomanry. On the left of the Kebili–Hamma road was the 24th Battalion, behind the 3 Royal Tank Regiment. On their left was the flanking force of the

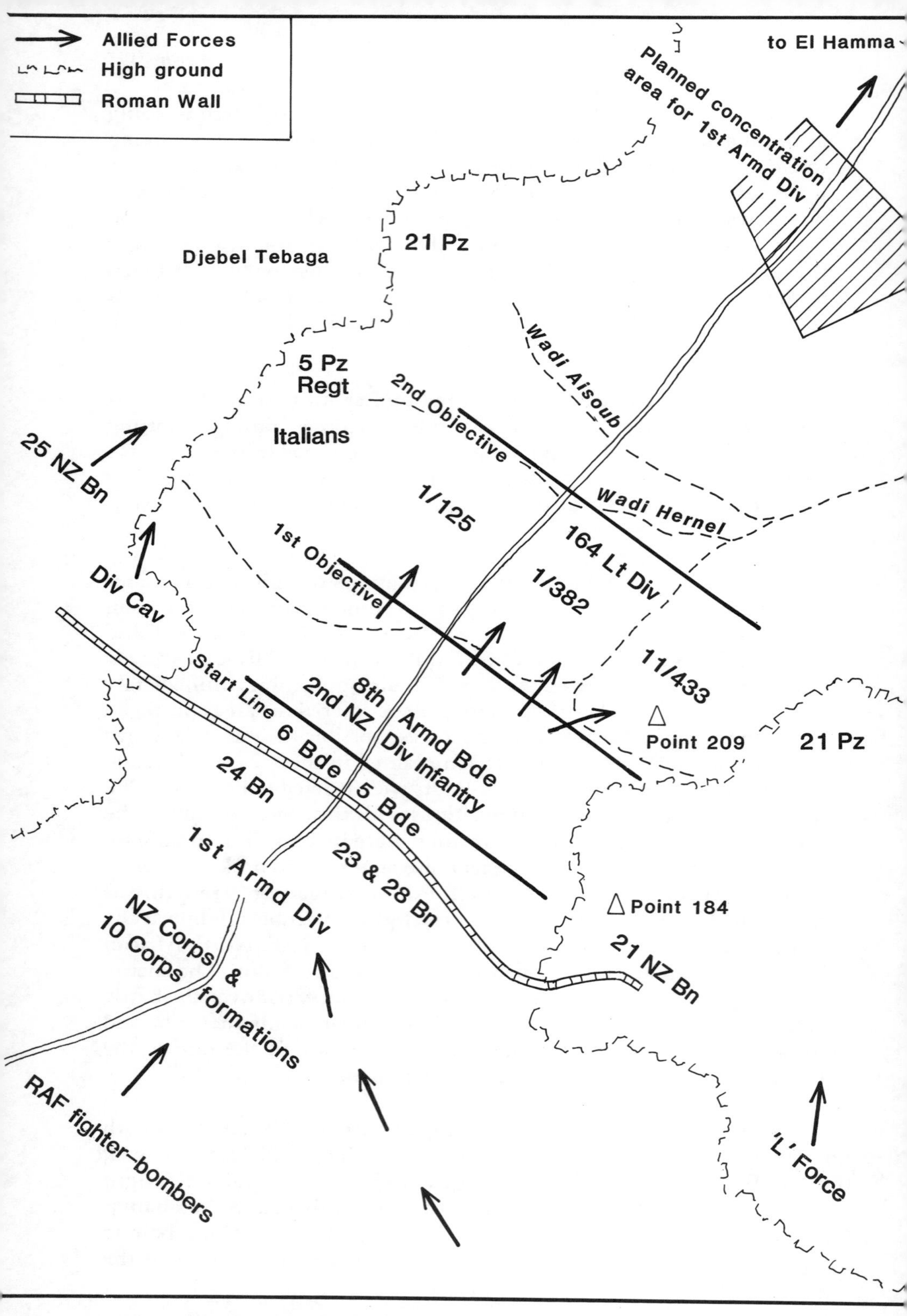

The Battle of Tebaga Gap, 26 March 1943.

NZ Divisional Cavalry. On the extreme right as a flank guard lay the 21st Battalion around Point 184.

If the dust of the sandstorm had threatened to close down Freyberg's air support, it now came to NZ Corps' aid. The sun, the smoke of bombardment, and the swirling sand drove straight into the eyes of the enemy. Freyberg noted in his battle diary:

> At 1600 the guns opened; at 1615 the infantry were going forward to the start-line. Dust storm prevented observation results [of] air bombing and strafing and tank busting but some fires were seen.[76]

A little more colourfully, the General later described the scene in his account to Prime Minister Fraser:

> At three o'clock on 26 March, as I drove up the valley in my tank, all was quiet except for the occasional shellfire. There was no unusual movement or sign of a coming attack. Exactly half an hour later, the first squadrons of the RAF roared overhead and relays of Spitfires, Kitty-bombers, and tank-busters swept over the enemy positions giving the greatest measure of air support ever seen by our army. At four o'clock 200 field and medium guns opened their bombardment on a front of 5,000 yards. In an instant the attack developed and 150 tanks and three battalions of infantry appeared as from nowhere, advancing in the smokescreen provided by the dust-storm. It was a most awe-inspiring spectacle of modern warfare. The roar of the bombers and fighters ahead of our advance merged with our barrage of bursting shells. Following close behind this intense barrage as it advanced came waves of Sherman tanks, carriers, and infantry and sappers on foot, preceded by three squadrons of Crusader tanks. Behind New Zealand Corps, coming down the foward slopes just in the rear of our front line, were 150 tanks of 1st Armoured Division, followed by their Motor Brigade in lorries, advancing in nine columns.[77]

At 1636 hours, 8 Armoured Brigade, followed by infantry, reached its objective. Progress was rapid. It was just over 1,000 yards to the first objective from the start line. The second objective lay over 1,600 yards beyond the first objective. Matters were more complicated here because a number of enemy formations were deployed within this second area, right across Tebaga Gap.

The 21st Battalion was disposed as flank guard about the ground on the right centred on Point 184. Further to their right was Leclerc's 'L' Force. In the hilly country in front of 21st Battalion and 'L' Force were elements of the 21 Panzer Division, in particular a battalion of 104 Panzer Grenadier Regiment.

On the eastern side of the gap in front of the Nottinghamshire

Yeomanry of 8 Armoured Brigade and the 28th Maori Battalion was higher ground overlooked by a feature known as Point 209. On and around Point 209 was II Battalion of 433 Panzer Grenadier Regiment of 164 Light Division. In the centre of the gap with the road at their right lay I Battalion of 382 Panzer Grenadier Regiment, also of 164 Light Division. Heading towards them behind the barrage were the Staffordshire Yeomanry and 23rd Battalion. Across the Kebili–Hamma road was another formation of 164 Light Division, I Battalion of 125 Panzer Grenadier Regiment. The 3 Royal Tank Regiment and the 24th NZ Battalion bore down on them.

To the west of the troops of 125 Panzer Grenadier Regiment, covering the other side of the gap, up into the lower slopes of Jebel Tebaga itself were three other formations — some Italian troops, 5 Panzer Regiment of the 21 Panzer Division, and I Battalion of 433 Panzer Grenadier Regiment of 164 Light Division. In front of these forces on the west flank of Tebaga Gap were the light armoured car forces of the NZ Division: the Divisional Cavalry.

Behind these mainly Deutsche Afrika Korps formations across the gap was the second objective — the western end of Wadi Hernel. Once this entry area was secure enough for the passage of armour then the 1 Armoured Division of X Corps would be passed through.

The effectiveness of the sudden assault out of the sun and the sand may be gauged by the persistent pace. As the fighter-bombers and the shellfire continued to blast away at 30 metres (100 feet) a minute, 8 Armoured Brigade reported its forward drive. Freyberg noted:

> By 1730 8 Armd Bde had claimed knocked out 1 Mk IV Special, 1 Mk III Special, and 3 A Tk guns . . . destroyed. Div Cav made good progress on high ground on left. At 1745 8 Armd Bde reported being on final objective and were engaging enemy tanks on the left [probably of 5 Panzer Regiment of 21st Panzer Division].
>
> The infantry advance encountered heavy fire and was held up between the first and final objectives by tanks on the left, and strong points on the high ground on the right. 28 Maori Bn captured feature to West of point 209 with the bayonet and put in attack on point 209 which, however, enemy held. First Armd Div were ordered through. Meanwhile mopping up proceeded between objectives and several tank actions took place before darkness fell. For a while it was quite a 'sticky spot' on the left, but at the end of the day 8 Armd Bde were able to report a total of 18 enemy tanks knocked out, together with number of guns including 2 88mm. At 1939 2 Armd Bde [of 1st Armoured Division] had reached our FDLs ready to go forward at moonrise. Prisoners began to come in, high proportion being German. At 2050 8 Armd Bde reported that the enemy tanks were advancing in a Northerly direction! G1 [Queree] told them there seemed to be a tendency of everything [to go] in that direction. Comd 6 Bde [Gentry]

> reported that 25 Bn ran into a good bit of MG fire and had a number of casualties, probably over 100. Prisoners taken about 150 Germans and some Italians. At 2100 hours there was still a considerable amount of mopping up to be done on the front.[78]

The breakthrough at Tebaga Gap had been achieved, and the prospect of forcing the enemy to a wholesale retreat was imminent. Freyberg sent a message to Montgomery:

> Attack has gone according to plan. Tanks reached final objective [of the breakthrough] and 1st Armd Div went through. Still confused fighting on front and on foothills on east and west. Some tanks and infantry pockets between objectives. Point 209 not yet captured. Some casualties. Force to be made mobile ready to go forward on success of 1st Armd Div. Identifications confirm that whole of 164 Div is in front of us.[79]

The further advance of 1 Armoured Division was now to complicate matters drastically for the Germans. The Axis defences were penetrated. Freyberg was jubilant:

> At moonrise 1st Armd Div pushed on. Flares of RAF night bombers to be seen to the NE. Some slight enemy bombing. Bombs in Divisional HQ area. . . During the night 1st Armd Div made good progress and by first light were 5 kms South of Hamma. They knocked out various MET [motorized enemy transport] on the way and overran some guns. They were held up short of Hamma by infantry and an A Tk gun line.[80]

A group of anti-tank guns had been placed by the commander of the Tebaga Gap forces, von Lieberstein, across the road to El Hamma. These gunners did not expect the British armour to push on in the dark and mistook the approaching tanks for Panzers. Instead of stopping 1 Armoured Division in its tracks, the Germans were now overrun, or in retreat. The 21 Panzer Division's *War Diary* gives evidences of utmost confusion:

> 0001 hrs [i.e. midnight 26/27 March]: Report received that enemy tanks [1st Armoured Division] were advancing 2 kms south of Div Battle HQ.
>
> 0015 hrs: The G1 decided to move battle HQ. The move had to be made in a hurry, and the enemy tanks had advanced to a point level with Div Battle HQ and were spraying the area right and left of the track with fire. The Ops staff like many other German units, took advantage of the heavy sand-storm and disengaged from the enemy unseen, moving parallel to the enemy advance.[81]

The armoured phalanx that had borne down on the headquarters of 21 Panzer Division was sizeable. The tank strength of the main offensive component — the 2 Armoured Brigade — consisted of 140 runners: sixty-seven Shermans, thirteen Grants, twenty-two Crusader IIIs, and thirty-eight Crusader IIs in three regiments: the Bays, the 9 Lancers, and the 10 Hussars.

The parallel race that followed, with German vehicles screened in part by the swirling dust out of which the armoured thrust had come, was won by the Germans. A few miles south of El Hamma, three 88 guns, four 5cm anti-tank and four 10cm field guns formed an improvised anti-tank screen. This posed the usual problem for 1st Armoured Division. All of the tanks were outgunned by the 88 guns of the German gun line, and their armour, as mentioned earlier, was not adequate to withstand the 88 shells. 1 Armoured Division was stalled in front of El Hamma, and General Horrocks decided to wait for NZ Corps' support. An attempted intervention by the newly arrived 15 Panzer Division came to nought: the Germans ran into the artillery formations of 1 Armoured Division and the ubiquitous hard-working 8 Armoured Brigade of NZ Corps. Freyberg wrote in his diary:

> 1 Armd Div reported tanks attacking them in the rear and application was made to us that 8 Armd Bde should be sent fwd. Presumably large number of tanks, as many as 40 being reported, came from 15Pz Div. Policy was to clear up situation and push on to join 1st Armd Div. Orders were given for force to be reconstituted with this end in view. Tanks were still on our front being engaged by 8 Armd Bde. . .
>
> Tac R shows no movement seen on Gabes–Mareth road, but most secret 'I' says slight indication of move from Spezia Sector. No sign that 90 Lt [90th Light Division] key to the [Mareth] posn has moved. Air photos show many guns moved from the South and 88mms are on either side of the [Gabes–Mareth] road, indicating that Mareth withdrawal is prepared for even if not begun. 15 Pz Div is on left of 21 [Panzer Division]. Americans still containing 10 Pz Div and 501 Tiger Bn North of Chotts. Motor Bn of the 1st Armd Div reported to be on the high ground, the key to Hamma. 21 Pz Div reported to be moving NE with 20 tanks. General tendency seems to be for enemy to move into the hills.[82]

In fact, the RAF had noted signs of a general withdrawal from Mareth on 26 March, when Freyberg was busy with Horrocks on the 'Supercharge II' assault. Also on the afternoon of 26 March, Enigma traffic had disclosed that von Arnim had come to this decision to withdraw two days earlier, against Messe's and Kesselring's opposition.[83] Von Arnim's purpose was then that of holding 'Plum' long enough for the infantry from Mareth to get clear. The retreat was under way. Neither Horrocks nor Freyberg were aware of the Enigma revelations and they still laboured under the common illusion that the Deutsche Afrika Korps was still commanded by Rommel himself.

At mid-morning on 27 March the NZ Corps GSO1 sent a situation report to 8th Army by air. This read:

> The situation at 1030 hrs is that on the left between the Road and Jebel Tebaga the front is clear of enemy and all enemy tanks have withdrawn. 6 NZ Bde are holding a line but have all transport fwd and ready to exploit. On the eastern side of the road there is an A Tk gun-line and inf posn established at Pt 209 in Y 9308 along the spur running West. The line of enemy resistance is the Pt 209 feature and East of Pt 227 in Y 9507 which is held by inf with guns and there is a large concentration of guns and tanks in wadis between these points and to the North. There is considerable shelling by both sides. During the night mopping up proceeded and is still continuing. 8 Armd Bde is engaging enemy tank concentration, the enemy tanks having now withdrawn into the wadis previously mentioned. 8 Armd Bde has been instructed to move to the North and East with the object of engaging and clearing up this concentration. KDGs have been passed through the objective and are exploiting to the NE. 18 enemy tanks claimed knocked out on 26th, 10 to date on 27th. Count of P[O]Ws to date Germans 400 Italians 350 others coming in. Many guns and A Tk guns overrun and being destroyed. Preparations are being made to move fwd to 1 Armd Div as soon as possible when situation permits.[84]

The previous night the army commander had been very enthusiastic about the attack at Tebaga Gap. After Freyberg had signalled to him, Montgomery communicated with Alexander:

> My attack on the left went in at 1600 hours today with the sun behind the attacking troops. Attack preceded by heavy air bombing and supported by some twenty squadrons of Spitfires, Kittybombers, and Tank busters. Attack was a complete success and broke through enemy defences. First armoured Division passed through and is now in good position to exploit success in moonlight tonight and at dawn tomorrow toward El Hamma and Gabes and this thrust will be pressed all day tomorrow. Enemy certain to resist desperately and he will be fought relentlessly. Enemy about Mareth and Zarat will soon I hope, be in a very awkward situation.[85]

With the stiffening of German resistance given them by the gun line in front of El Hamma, and the pockets of tanks and infantry still in the rear, the dispersal of the formations of X Corps and NZ Corps determined that consolidation was a priority.

The breakthrough by NZ Corps, and the drive for El Hamma by 1 Armoured Division, had strung out the attacking formations between Tebaga Gap and El Hamma. To ensure that the line of communication to the rear was not endangered, NZ Corps had to mop up before exploiting further, and might cope with the arrival of 15 Panzer Division which attempted to threaten 1 Armoured Division's rear. The German defensive position had been shattered. It was now a matter of how to wreck it further. Freyberg's diary observed:

> Corps Comd [Horrocks] was anxious NZ Corps should follow 1st Armd Div through to Hamma. Should represent that this was exactly what enemy was expecting and it would stretch him more if NZ Corps moved to the East. By the evening KDG patrols were more or less in contact with 1st Armd Div so we had a somewhat doubtful L of C through. Division began to move forward in the evening and by night. Dust and late rising of the moon made movement extremely difficult . . . GOC [Freyberg commented]: . . . It is going very well. He has taken a real knock. He has been surrendering all over the shop.[86]

NZ Corps had been prevented from following the 1 Armoured Division. It was busy tidying the remaining opposition at the gap, and engaged in preventive operations against elements of 15 Panzer Division. It was supported by artillery from the tail of 1 Armoured Division. As Horrocks' armoured division was now stopped before El Hamma, Freyberg decided that to take NZ Corps there might not make further leverage for shifting the enemy. X Corps' *War Diary* records that in the early hours of 28 March:'0200 Gen Freyberg arrived and had conference with GOC [X Corps, meaning Horrocks]; decided that NZ Corps should turn NE and advance between GABES and HAMMA.'[87] This was a switch from Montgomery's plan to repeat 'Supercharge II' at El Hamma in the manner that Tebaga Gap had been blown open. It was probably just as well. Air support may not have been available to the extent it had been at Tebaga Gap, and the Germans would not have been caught by surprise in the same way. Nor had there been adequate reconnaissance beyond El Hamma. Gabes stood further across the enemy rear than El Hamma: any occupation of Gabes would stop the passage of enemy forces to the east from Mareth, unless they were in overwhelming numbers.

At this point Horrocks and Freyberg were not aware that the enemy withdrawal from Mareth was well under way, although as we have seen, Freyberg suspected something was up. While there was agreement in principle to the new move, the change was one that Horrocks thought should be referred to the Army commander.

Within three or so hours of the short conference, Freyberg had NZ Corps back on the move:

> Div HQ up at 0530 and moved fwd few miles. Div Cav swung to the East and patrols from Div Cav and KDGs proceeded to investigate approaches to Merterba Wadi, mopping up as they went. Two bns of Spezia Div were captured intact with all their equipment. By 0945 a thousand prisoners had been taken. KDGs reported going in the plain OK. Ditto Div Cav. Wadis would require bulldozing. Div moving in NE and Easterly direction. 5 Bde Group conforming but on a different axis. Main road Div Axis — 5 Bde by more Southerly road.[88]

Although the thrust through Tebaga Gap had been utterly successful, the German and Italian forces from the Mareth Line had adroitly made their way rearwards beyond Gabes, mainly because they had begun to do so before the assault on the gap had broken through. The halt before El Hamma, the reduction of the remaining Axis troops in the gap, and the actions against 15 Panzer Division had taken long enough for the enemy to withdraw most of the Mareth Line infantry. The NZ Corps and X Corps had not failed to outflank. To the contrary: the great march to Tebaga Gap and the subsequent attack on 26/27 March had ensured further flight westwards by the Axis forces. The real benefit was reaped early on 28 March. In his diary, Montgomery wrote:

> By dawn it was clear that the enemy had pulled out from the MARETH position . . . By 0900 hours the whole of the famous MARETH position was in my hands and Divisions of 30 Corps were pushing ahead towards GABES.[89]

Where XXX Corps had failed to breach the Mareth defences, the solid work of a motorized infantry division, an armoured division, and sundry augmenting forces cobbled together for the task had made the Mareth position untenable. The Axis formations were hustled back, in retreat, further into Tunisia. The evacuation of the Mareth Line was not clear to Horrocks and Freyberg until 28 March. The movements of 1 Armoured Division and the movements of the formations of NZ Corps have to be seen with that in mind. Blocked at El Hamma, agreeing to Freyberg's suggestion of a move on Gabes by at least NZ Corps, Horrocks insisted he had to clear the change in plans with the Army commander. Freyberg's diary noted:

> Message in from Corps Comd [Horrocks]: Hamma gun line hard nut to crack. He agrees with GOC [Freyberg] to our Easterly move and suggests that after we have turned and gone for Gabes, 1 Armd Div should follow South as in the original plan. This was not Army Comd's intention and he [Horrocks] wants matter referred to Army Comd for approval.[90]

X Corps *War Diary* has evidence that to sort out the situation with the Army commander, Horrocks flew to Montgomery's Tactical Army Headquarters at 1300 hours. At 1350 hours, X Corps issued an Operation Order which summarized the situation, and the next moves. This was presumably made ready by Horrocks for issue once he had Montgomery's permission. X Corps Operation Order No. 15 at first takes into account an appreciation of the enemy and the Allied position:

> 1. . . . There is now no doubt that the enemy are withdrawing from the MARETH LINE and that he is trying to hold a flank from the mountains about Z.0003 — WADI EL MERTEBA — incl HAMMA, behind which he can withdraw 90 Lt Div and the remaining garrison of the MARETH LINE.
>
> The enemy is off his balance and has had serious losses both in men, guns and AFV's, and it is believed that 15 and 21 Pz Dvs muster not more than 50 runners maximum this morning.
>
> . . . it is unlikely that he has had either the time or the resources to defend GABES Gap EAST of HAMMA. It is important to get a bridgehead on the GABES Gap before the enemy can settle in, and also to cut off troops SOUTH of that Line.
>
> . . . 30 CORPS are advancing today to clear the MARETH LINE.
>
> 4. Ind Div have now got two Inf Bdes WEST . . . on and NORTH of the road HALLOUF — DIR SULTANE [*sic*]. 2 US Corps are today attacking . . . on the axes of the roads GAFSA-GABES and GAFSA-MAHARES [*sic*] . . .[91]

The movements envisaged were to result in the occupation of the Gabes Gap area. There were two phases:

> *Phase 1.* Advance of NZ Corps to the line of the track BIR ZELTEN E. 3696 — EL HAMMA, code name 'FROG', while 1 Armd Div contains and bluffs the enemy at EL HAMMA . . .
>
> 2 NZ Corps will move with centre line track OGLAT MERTEBA Z.0315 — GABES. For this operation, 12 L[ancers] less one Sqn will be in support of 2 NZ Corps and will be positioned by 2 NZ Corps on their Northern flank . . .
>
> NZ Corps will be responsible for containing the enemy in the DJEBEL MELAB . . . During this Phase, 1 Armd Div will demonstrate and stage a mock attack against EL HAMMA in order to divert the enemy's attention from the NZ Corps move . . .
>
> *Phase 2.* 2 NZ Corps will occupy the GABES OASIS, code name 'NEWT', while 1 Armd Div moves up to occupy the GABES gap between excl GABES and excl EL HAMMA . . .
>
> 1 Armd Div will move, on receipt of orders from this HQ . . . and pass behind the WESTERN rearward flank of 2 NZ Corps . . .

> ...principle will be that 1 Armd Div will conform to Western flank of 2 NZ Corps...
>
> In the initial stages of the Phase, 1 Armd Div will leave a force in their present posn sufficient to contain the enemy in EL HAMMA between the DJEBEL HALLOUGA and DJEBEL EL AZIZIA, Y.92. This force will be relieved by other troops under arrangements 10 Corps as early as possible, as will the 2 NZ Corps troops in the DJEBEL MELAB.
>
> The movement of 1 Armd Div, less holding force in the EL HAMMA area is NOT likely to be ordered to commence before 0100 hrs 29 Mar 43, and the Div will be prepared to move by moonlight.[92]

Horrocks did not return to X Corps until 1600 hours. At 1550, XXX Corps reported to X Corps that the enemy had gone from the Mareth Line. In the meantime NZ Corps was already on the move, although the main forces found the ground more difficult than did the lighter vehicles of the screen:

> 5 Bde proceeded on a Southerly axis while 6 Bde and 8 Armd advanced in general direction of Jebel Halouga [*sic*], cleaning up the opposition as they went. KDGs who were out in front had a field day with enemy pockets and taking prisoners. Going was generally difficult and not much progress was made by main force. Heavy dust storms continued. 6 Bde were bombed and suffered some casualties on the move up. General impression is that Mareth Line will be evacuated and that he will be back behind Hamma and Gabes by tomorrow.[93]

On 28 March, Enigma revealed that the 15 and 21 Panzer Divisions would withdraw as the German and Italian infantry had completed their retreat to Wadi Akarit over the last two days.[94] These forces had been covered by the two armoured divisions and their anti-tank screen. It was also revealed by Army Y that the tank losses of 15 Panzer Division had been considerable in its encounters with the formations of NZ Corps: 15 Panzer Division had, by persisting in its covering role, been severely mauled.[95]

After Horrocks' return from Tactical Army Headquarters, an amendment to X Corps Operation Order No. 15 was issued, with a time of signature of 1815 hours, 28 March. It noted that the situation had altered:

> ... The enemy has failed to hold the flank line along the Wadi MERTEBA, and has definitely evacuated the MARETH Line ...
>
> 51 (H) Div [51st Highland Division of 30 Corps] are now moving along the Main Road toward GABES from North of MARETH.
>
> 4. Ind Div are concentrating at ZELTENE ... preparatory to advancing North up the Main Road from that place to GABES ... 10 Corps will occupy the line excl GABES to incl HAMMA ...

> No major action or attack will be undertaken as the policy now is for us to conserve our resources of men and material. The enemy will be dislodged by maneouvre and fire . . .[96]

The Axis forces having retired, 8th Army now concentrated and re-formed before attempting to push the enemy from Wadi Akarit. Montgomery did not intend to make the mistake that had cost heavily at Wadi Zigzaou on the Mareth Line: sending an inadequate assault force against enemy positions with inadequate support on a too narrow front. Instead of a lone infantry brigade, three infantry divisions would attack in one night.

The occupation of Gabes by NZ Corps can be seen as part of the tidying up — following the Axis defeat at Tebaga Gap and the simultaneous flight from the Mareth positions. While the NZ 6 Brigade had been advancing steadily, the troops of 5 NZ Brigade had been sent towards Gabes on a different axis, along with the Free French. This meant in effect that on the morning of 29 March, NZ Corps was moving on a two brigade front. At about 11 a.m., armoured cars of the King's Dragoon Guards and bren-gun carriers of the 23rd NZ Battalion arrived at Gabes at the same time as the last elements of 15 Panzer Division detonated charges destroying the bridge on the other side of the town. Brigadier Kippenberger, of 5 Brigade, arrived soon afterwards. By this stage XXX Corps had moved close to Gabes, and its commander, Lieutenant-General Oliver Leese, met Kippenberger at the bridge. Freyberg's Tactical Headquarters — the three Honey tanks — entered not long after this. The two corps commanders of operation 'Pugilist' were in the same locality after the highly eventful and very different journeys of their disparate corps.

Montgomery's message to Freyberg and Horrocks was apposite:

> Personal for Gen Freyberg and Gen Horrocks from Army comd. My very best congratulations to NZ Corps and 10 Corps on splendid results achieved by the left hook. These results have led to the complete disintegration of the enemy resistance and the whole Mareth posn is now in our hands. Give my congratulations to all your officers and men and tell them how pleased I am with what they have done.[97]

CHAPTER 7

The Immovable Object

With their Mareth Line broken the Axis forces in Tunisia began their hotly pursued retreat. It was a fighting retreat and on the heights above Tunis, dominated by Takrouna, 2 NZ Division took heavy casualties. This final and desperate attempt by the Axis commanders to stem the Allied advance failed. The Enfidaville Line was broken in hard fighting over 19-21 April 1943. On 13 May Field-Marshal Messe, commander of 1st Italian Army, the Major-General von Liebenstein, commander of the German 164 Light Division, surrendered to Lieutenant-General Freyberg, then acting commander of X Corps (a short term appointment, with Inglis deputing as commander of 2 NZ Division).

Since the battle of El Alamein the NZ Division had taken 1,024 casualties, with 413 of these killed in action. After such hard fighting, and with reinforcements, sparse as they were, no compensation for the veterans lost, it is hardly surprising that within a few days of the Axis surrender the Division turned its back on the purple hills of Tunisia. The New Zealanders returned to Maadi Camp, in Egypt, 3,000 kilometres in distance, in seventeen days.

Back in Egypt they rested, re-formed, incorporated reinforcements, and waited for their next assignment. On 6 June Freyberg flew back to New Zealand, to discuss reinforcement shortcomings and the probable next role for his Division with Prime Minister Fraser. Twelve days after Freyberg returned, the first of the furlough drafts (*Ruapehu*) arrived in New Zealand, with its tired veterans. Fraser had refused to commit 2 NZ Division to the invasion of Sicily and had briefed Freyberg on the immense difficulties of reinforcing the Division whilst New Zealand maintained the food and wool production demanded by the Allies.

But there was a new campaign in store for Freyberg's soldiers — in Italy. On 3 September the first Allied troops landed on the toe of the Italian peninsula, and on 8 September Italy surrendered. Italy's former ally, Germany, responded by seizing control of Italy's government and military strongholds. A hard German defence followed, in a rugged and narrow peninsula, favourable to defence tactics. On 9 October the first New Zealand troops landed at Taranto, Italy.

In Italy, Freyberg found no wide spaces to employ his celebrated juncture of armour, infantry, and air. He had remarked to New Zealand's Minister of Defence, Fred Jones, in August 1943, that 'There are now many divisions trained to carry out initial landings, but we are the only British division equipped, trained and experienced for flanking operations'.[1] The narrow Italian tracks, the steep hillsides, mud, snow, and slush put an end to that luxury. In Italy Freyberg's division fought at mule pace — and mules were their most used beast of burden. In the Sangro battle, 2 NZ Division was lucky: there was limited opposition, but at Orsogna, in a prelude to the battle of attrition ahead, a German paratroop unit stopped every attack. Losses in Italy were heavy. In three months (October/mid-January) 2 NZ Division suffered 1,246 casualties — 413 killed in action.

To the alarm of Allied strategists, the Italian campaign no longer served its purpose as a secondary enterprise pinning down German divisions at little cost to the Allies. It had become a vortex into which Allied divisions and supplies, needed for the Second Front in Europe, were sucked to ungainly death.

Advance along the Adriatic coast was as costly as it was slow. It was decided to attempt to break through across the Apennines, and the NZ Division was moved in secret to join General Mark Clark's 5th Army, facing the German Gustav Line. The goal was Rome, but guarding the valley through which passed the Naples to Rome highway stood the barrier of the German controlled town, hill, and ancient Benedictine abbey, of Cassino.

The initial moves for Freyberg and the NZ Division were straightforward enough. The Division received a warning order on 9 January 1944, and the movement from the Adriatic coast took about a week from 13 January, the positions being relieved by 4 Indian Division.[2] Alexander instructed the 8th Army to release 4 Indian Division immediately to join 2 NZ Division to form a temporary NZ Corps under Freyberg's command.[3] To these two divisions would later be added the British 78 Division, but this unit would not arrive in the Cassino sector until 18 February, at the conclusion of NZ Corps' opening battle.

At 10 a.m. 3 February, NZ Corps came into being, within General Mark Clark's 5th Army. Freyberg was immediately faced with the need to form a corps staff. As at Mareth, he improvised, making the NZ Division's senior officers assume dual roles, in the Division and at Corps level. Colonel Queree became BGS of NZ Corps, and Lieutenant-Colonel Thornton was brought in from the artillery to be the GSO1 of the Division.

To disguise the movement of two of 8th Army's most experienced divisions to 5th Army's front, NZ Corps was given the cover name of 'Spadger Force'. Freyberg set about organizing his priorities, in terms of role, striking power, and significantly, the availability of air support.[4]

Freyberg was under no illusion as to the difficulties ahead. On 20 and 21 January, the 36 Division of US 2 Corps had attempted to cross the Rapido River at St Angelo and had been bloodily repulsed. The first failure at Cassino had taken place. On 22 January, Allied forces carried out landings to the north of the German Gustav Line at Anzio, the intention being that a US 6 Corps, under General Lucas, would outflank the Gustav

Line, and drive for Rome. Any hope that Lucas would seize the initiative and take advantage of a surprise attack was doomed when Clark instructed Lucas to be cautious.[5]

On 22 January Freyberg addressed the officers of the NZ Division on the likely role of the Corps:

> No doubt we shall be faced with either of two operations. 1. Breaking a gun line or 2. Crossing a river. We want to know why both 56 Division and the Americans failed. I have never known a river to really block an attack. Either there was something wrong with the recce, or there was something wrong with the plan. The sooner we can find out the better and learn a lesson from it.[6]

The British X Corps had failed to cross the Garigliano River nearer the coast, also a part of the Gustav Line. Two river attacks had not succeeded and the progress at Anzio was stalled, and would in all likelhood come under threat from German counter-attacks. The operations of NZ Corps at Cassino were essential to relieve pressure on the Anzio beach-head.

What importance had the Germans placed on Cassino as part of the Gustav Line? The great hill above the town of Cassino with the famous Benedictine monastery on its summit bulged over the Rapido and Liri Valleys, commanding the road and rail communications through the Liri Valley to Rome. A great sweep of climbing ridges rose, connected to Monastery Hill, proceeding like a clothed giant arm inland to Monte Cairo. Inside the arm, behind the town, the ground rose and was fractured irregularly with various ridges and outcrops, and sudden ravines. From a distance, this clothed arm looked smooth, broken only in parts. This was a complete deception, for the actual terrain in these ridges and hills was very different.

To the Germans, Cassino was the decisive key to the Gustav Line. Its natural attributes made it potentially the strongest part of the line. On 13 December 1943, the German High Command talked about the Monte Cassino–Monte Cairo massif as 'decisive', and Hitler himself decreed that the defences of Monte Cassino were to be raised to 'fortress strength'. On 27 December Jodl told Kesselring that Hitler wished him to concentrate his best reserves for the defence of the massif, placing them under a single commander, for this position 'must on no account be lost'.[7]

The deceptive topography at Cassino, on the complex of hills and slopes about Monastery Hill, was to exact a fearful price in the hands of the defenders:

> As is usual in mountainous country the ridges, when seen from a distance, look like smooth, bare slopes running up or down. At Cassino this appearance concealed the horrible nature of the ground. This was unspeakably rough and broken with minor ridges, knolls, and hollows

> jumbled all together. At one point deep clefts might be the obstacle, at another sheer rock faces or steep slabs, or all three might be found in a few acres. Huge boulders were scattered about, here and there were patches of scrub, while the gorges were often choked with innocent-looking savage thorn. To attacking troops the ground set vile tactical puzzles one after another. This or that knoll or ridge might seem to be promising objectives but would turn out to be commanded from an unlikely direction by another knoll or ridge or several. A line of approach might look as if it would 'go' and would turn out to be blocked by some impassable obstacle. The advantages of the ground lay wholly with defending troops.[8]

Defensive works at Cassino were constructed late in 1943. On the Gustav Line divisions were allotted labour for their sectors, and Corps 'liberally supplied' engineer units. Some 44,000 Todt workers (impressed from Germany's conquered territories) were sent to work at Cassino. In November, the German High Command provided 100 steel *Stahlunterstande* (shelters) with more to come; seventy-six armoured *Panzerstande* (casements), and a number of armoured machine-gun nests. The German 'Armoured Portable Pill Box' was dome-shaped, 6 feet (nearly 2 metres) high with 3 feet (90 cm) exposed above ground. The armour on the front varied from over 3.5 inches to over 5.25 inches. One MG (machine-gun) 42 or MG 34 went inside it.[9]

Defensive areas included Monte Cassino, St Angelo Hill, Majola Hill, Monte Castellone, and Cassino town itself. They combined high and low ground, a large hill mass, the river line of the upper Rapido, and a fortified town. Defensive work went on from November 1943 into January 1944. Most engineer resources were given over to the Liri Valley, Cassino town, and the west bank of the Rapido between Cassino itself and Cairo village. By the close of December 1943, the defences of the town of Cassino and Castle Hill, Point 193, were well developed. Bunkers and emplacements for soldiers and weapons were ready, sometimes improved by girders, railway sleepers, rails, and concrete. The demolition of houses to improve fields of fire continued, as well as the construction of wire obstacles, up to six yards deep.[10]

If the defences of Cassino amounted to strong natural positions extended by skilled military engineering, it is important to realize that the New Zealand infantry commanders had already drawn some very apposite conclusions about the nature of the fighting in Italy. The battalion and company commanders of the 5 NZ Brigade, in particular, had pooled their experiences from the Sangro battles of 28-29 November and 24 December 1943. They give and interesting picture:

> 1. *GERMAN minor tactics . . .*
>
> Posns in great depth are cushioned by outpost lines held by

> comparatively few troops having a high proportion of automatic weapons and strong mortar support . . .
>
> As a general rule posts are sited on reverse slopes, but there is also a greater tendency to hold the top of ridges than . . . in AFRICA. Assaulting tps should be directed to the high ground. The capture of this almost invariably loosens the enemy def[ensive] posns in the area.
>
> Wadis are seldom held by tps but are covered by both mortar and MG fire.
>
> Positions are sited in the main to meet an attack from the expected direction. All round defence on the top of ridges. Considerable use is made of houses for MG fire and mortar posts.
>
> Section posts are the rule. These are well sited and concealed and each has a deep dug-out. Approaches are covered by heavy MG fire on fixed lines. DF task comes down quickly and is predominantly mortar.
>
> Wire . . . encountered only once . . . not a substantial obstacle. Mines . . . have not been used extensively, but may be expected on and near roads and tracks.
>
> Early counter-attacks are the rule . . . any plan of attack must include provision against counter-attack. Tanks and flamethrowers are used extensively but the attack is rarely supported by artillery.
>
> The German . . . fight[s] skilfully . . . stubbornly. Isolated posts will fight it out although surrounded . . .[11]

Small numbers of troops, plenty of automatic weapons, positions in great depth, strong mortar support, quick counter-attacks, skilful, stubborn all-round defence: at Cassino the attackers would meet all these repeatedly.

The battalion and company commanders of 5 Brigade agreed that night attacks were preferred, the depth of infantry objectives should be a maximum of 2,000 yards (about 1,800 metres), and advance should not include the passing of more than one natural feature. For platoons, companies, and battalions, two-thirds of the formation should be forward, and one-third in reserve. A good rate of advance 'in fair going' would be 100 yards in three minutes by day, 100 yards in five minutes by night, with company frontages of 300 to 400 yards. In defence, company frontages would be about 500 yards, battalion frontages around 1,500 yards. Any exploitation of attack should only be to a 'clearly defined objective' and the force commander should have complete discretion over the action to be taken. Troops in the assault could not take part in exploitation movements, nor exploitation troops in the assault. It was noted that artillery barrages were often only partly useful, for infantry could not always maintain the rate of advance specified. It was agreed that 25 pounders 'will NOT destroy field defences of the type encountered', and that the German troops simply remained under cover until the barrage moved on. There was more scope for the use of smoke for screening than in Africa. Tanks were seen as useful in support of infantry in attack and defence, particularly in stopping counter-attacks. Some improvements in the mortars of the Allied forces pleased the commanders, 'an arm in which the GERMANS have been consistently superior to us . . .'[12] Mules were now accepted as indispensable to progress. The scale recommended was seventy per battalion.

These issues concerned the officers of 5 Brigade as they contemplated the future, not simply because Brigadier H. Kippenberger was to become acting commander of the NZ Division, while Colonel Hartnell took over 5 Brigade.

2 NZ Division possessed the dynamic for the task, but geography favoured the defenders. The depth of German defences at Cassino commonly stretched back 4,000 yards. On the interlocking slopes of the Cassino massif, these must have appeared to the attackers as an endless maze. The dominating brooding feature of Monastery Hill jutting over the battlefield made the capture of high ground both necessary and yet precarious. With the exception of the top of Monastery Hill, every other close feature including Castle Hill and the multiplicity of numerous hillocks — Point 593 et al. — could be enfiladed by the German defenders from yet further higher ground. Herein lay the central infantry problem at Cassino made worse by the supplementary strength of the well-sited and well dug-in German positions. To break through the Gustav Line, through the Cassino position, the capture of Monastery Hill was necessary. To reach the top of Monastery Hill meant — unless one chanced the fortified town with its artificially narrowed approaches — taking the lesser heights first. Each of these was dominated by carefully planned interlocking fire from yet higher positions. The lesser heights had to be seized, and counter-attacks repulsed. It was a gruelling prospect and, worst of all, not immediately recognizable until the troops were on the ground.

In such unenviable circumstances it is easy to see the likely development of a costly and protracted attritional encounter where, even if the Germans lacked numbers, their troops might hold against numerically superior Allied forces, provided the defenders were hidden, and had enough mortar support, automatic weapons, food, and water to sustain the defence.

The infantry tasks that must be set for an assault on the Cassino positions were high-risk for the attackers. Any unnecessary exposure, lack of depth in attack, or lack of co-ordination were all likely to be paid for in bloody failure. The terrain-imposed obstacles and the German defences ran beyond 2,000 yards. If thrusts into the enemy positions were limited to around 2,000 yards, then even a successful assault to this distance brought the attackers into the German positions, but not through them.

The German defensive model in Italy, copied at Cassino, was well described by Kesselring:

> e. Depending on the importance of the position and the natural

defensive features of the terrain, the improvements varied from a simple field type of improvement all the way through to permanent style concrete and armoured projects and mine fields. Observations of the following principles was considered to be of decisive importance:

e1. Camouflage, and a field of fire from flanking installations as far as possible.

e2. Natural antitank obstacles, supplemented by artificial obstacles (antitank ditches, steep walls, swamping, etc.) throughout the depth of the fortified zone.

e3. Building separately protected shelters and firing positions ...

e4. Camouflaged and if possible covered communication trenches (approach trenches) from the rear to the advanced and lateral positions.

e5. Mining operations ...[13]

The combination of this utilization of the ground and construction of interlocking defences resulted in a concealed nightmare for attacking infantry.

On Colle Sant'Angelo, Points 444 and 593/569 were armoured machine-gun nests, snipers' posts and a whole series of mortar emplacements. These latter, camouflaged and protected by thick logs, were normally placed in deep gullies or behind shelves of rock and could lay down their high trajectory fire without ever having to be moved from this deep cover.[14]

Weapon pits blasted out of rock ... camouflaged with skill ... remained invisible to the unsuspecting attackers. A sudden burst of fire was invariably the first indication that the innocent looking scrub and rock contained hidden and resolute defenders.[15]

The role Freyberg envisaged for NZ Corps in the Cassino sector was not one of direct assault, but one of exploitation and movement. The NZ Division was designed for that role, and the attachments of British armoured brigades in the desert, while the third infantry brigade was redeployed as an armoured unit, were to enhance its effectiveness. Now in Italy, with its own armour, the Division looked foward to undertaking such tasks. Addressing officers and non-commissioned officers of the new 4 NZ Armoured Brigade on 27 January 1944, Freyberg returned to this theme:

... We are what is known as a light division ... exploiting ... a gap, ... also capable of carrying out the functions of an infantry division. It must be noted that we have not the same power of endurance as the infantry division because of our lack of one infantry brigade. That applies particularly to attack. In defence our endurance is longer ... The light division is able to go long distances behind the enemy line

> ... We are faced here with a continuous line which has no flanks and we are faced with bad-ish going ... We can deal with the going ahead as long as it is not mud.[16]

It follows that the best use of such a division was in an exploiting role, going through a gap made by someone else. The inclusion of 4 Indian Division in NZ Corps gave Freyberg additional infantry for the endurance the light division lacked in attack. There is no doubt that the commander of 15th Army Group had this role in mind for NZ Corps when he constructed the formation. It was the exploitive role, a quick rush to Rome, that Montgomery sought when he began the Sangro campaign. The NZ Division would sweep to Rome, behind enemy lines, after a breakthrough. When Alexander's Chief of Staff, Harding, informed 5th Army by signal of the formation of NZ Corps, the message stressed elements of this plan:

> MOST SECRET(.) C-inC has decided ... to form a N.Z. Corps under General FREYBERG's comd (.) this Corps will remain in reserve for the present but C-in-C has instructed Gen FREYBERG to prepare for his consideration an outline plan for N.Z. Corps to be ready to carry on the momentum of the attacks now being carried out by F.E.C. [the French Corps] and 2 U.S. Corps should that be necessary (.) this attack cannot take place before 8 Feb (.) meantime please instruct 2 U.S. Corps and F.E.C., to give Gen FREYBERG every facility to obtain information and carry out recces (.) when Gen FREYBERG has prepared his plans C-in-C will discuss them with Gen CLARK and decide if and when they are to be put into effect (.) ...[17]

The role envisaged was one of exploitation, breaking through to the forces at Anzio, and moving on Rome. At the same time, as an experienced battle commander, Freyberg was by now well aware of the formidable nature of the terrain facing the Allies at Cassino, at least in general terms. He expected casualties. However, it was not just NZ Corps that was to undertake the breakthrough. The Americans, and further inland, the French, were already in the midst of assaults to wrest the enemy from their defences. A sizeable and moveable force could be thrown against Cassino.

But how well had Freyberg's new allies previously performed? The 36 Texas Division under General Fred L. Walker had been crushingly repulsed in its efforts to cross the Rapido. Two of the 36 Division's three regiments, mauled in the abortive exposed assault, had assaulted strong defences, graphically outlined in the NZ Division's Intelligence Summary of 19 January. This operation was ordered by the US 2 Corps Commander, General Keyes, at the behest of the Army Commander, General Mark Clark. Walker, during the First World War, had commanded an American battalion that had slaughtered a German division when it attempted to cross the Marne under his unit's guns. He knew what would happen in the much less auspicious circumstances prevailing at Cassino, but Keyes and Clark insisted on the assault. In the resulting débâcle, Keyes intervened after the first repulse and compelled Walker to send in a second attack which also came to nought. Key features of these attacks were the rushed nature of the assaults in terms of preparation, the ignoring of the exposed areas over which approaches were made, and the mistaken belief that by throwing in more men when reverses occurred, the enemy defences could be overcome. Nothing was further from the truth. Clark himself had ignored a warning nearly a month earlier from one of his divisional commanders, Lucian Truscott, that an attack over the Rapido at this point would come to disaster: this was at a time when it was contemplated that Truscott would undertake such an assault.[18]

The next stage of 5th Army's attack on the Cassino position was to mount two prolonged assaults. The French Expeditionary Corps (FEC) attacked through the mountainous region of Monte Cairo, while the other US division in 2 Corps, the 34 Division under General Ryder, assaulted the main Cassino defences. The latter crossed the Rapido north (or to the observer on the Allied side of the Gustav Line, the right) of Cassino town, began the long process of scaling heights, and worked up and around towards the monastery. Short of a frontal attack through the town and straight up Monastery Hill, which was impossible, this was the way ground contours led the attackers.

The French, under General Juin, had been engaged in mounting a thrust deep into the mountainous interior in the direction of Atina, where the Germans were thin on the ground. On 23 January, Clark asked Juin to give up the deep move and instead attack the Belvedere/Abate massif, to the north of Cassino. This, it was argued, would stop German reserves being used against the 34 Division's attack. Shifting Juin's thrust line to the south of Monte Cairo was more convenient for the Americans; but for the French, the terrain would be more difficult. The Algerian Division was to assault a difficult part of the Gustav Line, then via Terrelle push far into the enemy rear. Monsabert, of the Algerian Division, expostulated to Juin:

> Storm Belvedere? Who's dreamed up that one? Have they even looked at it? You'd first have to cross two rivers, the Rapido and the Secco, then smash through the Gustav Line in the valley, and finally, all the time attacking the Boche, climb more than 2000 feet over a bare rock-pile, itself heavily fortified, that can be fired on from . . . Cifalco and the rest of the summits round about. It's pure wishful thinking! A crazy gamble, mon général![19]

The Americans needed support in their plan for the US 34 Division's attack. Juin finally insisted to Monsabert: 'It is a matter of honour.' The

French did not break through to the German rear, and the Americans were tardy in making progress on their front.

The 34 Division launched its attack across the Rapido at the barracks area to the north of the town. There the 133 Regiment of the 34 Division was held for nearly nine days; the 168 Regiment finally took the village of Cairo further north on 30 January. The 135 and 142 Regiments were pushed through Cairo village to attack high ground further in. When the 133 Regiment finally cleared the barracks area on 1 and 2 February, they turned in the direction of Cassino but were held up by machine-gun and anti-tank fire.

The arrival of NZ Corps in the region of Cassino was not greeted with unbounded enthusiasm by the Army Commander, Mark Clark. It might have been expected that he would have been pleased to receive two battle-hardened divisions from 8th Army, particularly in view of the losses that 5th Army was sustaining in carrying his offensive operations on both the Anzio and Cassino fronts. Clark's reaction to Alexander's proposal that 8th Army divisions were to be used by 5th Army was succinct: 'Hell, I don't want any troops from the Eighth Army. No use giving me, an American, British troops.'[20] He regarded Freyberg as a 'prima donna', who he believed he would have to handle with 'kid gloves'.[21]

In Clark's memoirs, *Calculated Risk,* he wrote:

> Freyberg had been directed by Alexander to prepare recommendations for employment of his reinforced New Zealanders on the Fifth Army front. I had not been consulted about such recommendations. I got a definite impression that 15th Army Group and Freyberg were going to tell me what to do. I objected as diplomatically as possible, pointing out that their plans for using the New Zealanders and Indian troops in the Cassino–Monte Cairo mountain sector would not fit in well . . .[22]

Clark realized that these troops would not be just putty in his hands — he resented their coming:

> These are Dominion troops who are very jealous of their prerogatives. The British have found them difficult to handle. They have always been given special considerations which we would not give to our own troops.[23]

Clark's reactions to the prospect of the New Zealand and Indian troops were hardly appropriate for an Allied Army commander. Although in public he put a good face on it, there is little doubt that he allowed his resentments of the British and the New Zealand forces to cloud his judgement, which was translated into ensuring battlefield defeat for the long-suffering 34 Division.

For Freyberg who had been ordered by Alexander to go to Cassino, the prospect facing NZ Corps was daunting. NZ Corps' outline plan of 2 February is not so revealing in itself. Rather it demonstrates the limitations placed upon General Freyberg by both circumstances and current battle conditions.

> . . . I do not know the GS(I) Appreciation regarding the resistance likely to be met on our immediate front. Neither do I know the extent to which the various rivers on the line of advance have been put into a state of defence. If, for instance, the line of the River LIRI is fortified the advance along Route 6 will be delayed. . .The general policy which I propose is:
> (i) Clear the CAIRO massif thus enabling the RAPIDO River to be crossed and operations in the valley along Route 6 to take place.
> (ii) Square up on a two Div front operating on one thrust line along Route 6 and employ the full power of the arty and air to blast through in a series of operations. In order to implement this policy full support of available air forces is required, together with an ample amn supply.
> . . . In considering the outline plan for the NZ Corps to advance and join up with 6 Corps two sets of circumstances have been considered:
> (i) If the high ground west of CASSINO is still in enemy hands.
> (ii) If 2 US Corps has captured the CASSINO spur . . . assistance will be required:
>   (i) A small organisation, to include a senior Air Force officer to work with us during operations in order that full air support can be expeditiously arranged.[24]

What Freyberg had in mind was clearly the task that Alexander had suggested for the new corps: one of exploiting the progress of the Americans and driving through into the Liri Valley. It did of course have the rider — whatever was contemplated would depend on whether US 2 Corps had taken the high ground (the Cassino spur), commanding the opening to the Liri Valley. The matter of air support was important and would need to be sorted out. The General needed the quality of close support provided by the Desert Air Force at the turning of the Mareth Line.

At a conference at NZ Division headquarters at 9 a.m. on 3 February 1944, the role of air support linked with artillery bombardment was discussed as a prerequisite of any break into the Liri Valley. Attended by the brigade commanders and other senior officers of the NZ Division, in company with the commander of 4 Indian Division, General Tuker, and members of his staff, it was decided that:

> The bombardment would go to a depth of 1000 yards and the fighter bombers would shoot up everything within two or three miles of the

> bombardment — that is similar to the air force support in the battle of Tebaga Gap. We have had some disappointment in the past regarding air.[25]

But the lessons of the desert had not been absorbed by the air forces in Italy; not the least factor in this being the unfamiliarity of the Americans in this role. But Freyberg was not to know this yet.

An outline plan for NZ Corps, considered on 4 February, involved the co-operation of the French Corps. It was basically an attempt to turn the Cassino position widely. The French would move through on Terelle, while 4 Indian Division went through the mountains to the north of Monte Castellone. A brigade of the NZ Division would start with its infantry on Majola Hill and head to take Albaneta Farm and Point 593. The other NZ infantry brigade and the NZ armoured brigade would be ready in the Rapido Valley to go through into the Liri Valley, once the thrust through the mountains had come to a favourable decision.[26] This plan was said to have been influenced by General Tuker who wanted to avoid an attritional conflict against the Cassino position.

There were some drawbacks in this plan which would quickly have become apparent to NZ Corps had it been tried. It was winter time, and the roads into the mountainous interior were not good. Supplies would have to be taken for the 4 Indian Division by mule, over lengthening lines of communications as the division advanced. The NZ Infantry Brigade would also have required supply by mule, as it began its advance over the broken ground from Majola Hill towards Point 593 and Albaneta Farm. NZ Corps had been supplied with 1,500 mules in five animal transport companies.[27] These, given casualties and the necessity to carry food for the mules, were estimated as only sufficient to maintain just over one brigade about six or seven miles in advance of the supply base. Obviously this was insufficient to keep one brigade in action in the hills above Cassino, and supply the other three brigades of 4 Indian Division, in the mountains.

An additional drawback in the plan was the spread-out nature of the assault. The French had not been able to break through to Terrelle by the time the plan was due for implementation on 4 February, though that had been what US 2 Corps had asked. The lone NZ Infantry Brigade would have a solid fight on its hands to take Albaneta Farm and Point 593. This is itself was no simple task. The defences in the fortified town area of Cassino and the defences on Castle Hill and Monastery Hill — tanks, concealed machine-gun posts, mortar positions, infantry and mines — would be untouched, and it is difficult to see how the remaining New Zealand infantry and armoured brigades would be able successfully to break through into the Liri Valley from the Rapido Valley, even if the mountain attacks were successful. Given the German capacity to fight tenaciously when cut off, these brigades might well have been unable simply to achieve their tasks, especially if they lacked the necessary strength to break through.

The abandonment of this plan by NZ Corps had little to do with their lack of formal staff, or the so-called inexperience of the New Zealand staff in mountain warfare. The insufficiency of animal transport was a factor.[28] In any case, 5th Army issued orders the next day that insisted the NZ Corps perform a different role — and NZ Corps was under the command of 5th Army; it could not just go off and strike where it liked. The abandonment of the inland turning movement had nothing to do with the merits of demerits of the plan.

On 5 February, 5th Army issued an Operations Instruction which read:

> . . . upon the capture of the Cassino heights . . . FEC . . . will attack to the west . . . making its main effort along the Terelle-Roccasecca trail, seize Roccasecca and the high ground east of the Melfa River . . .
>
> . . . II Corps. . . will seize Piedimonte and the high ground north-west thereof . . .
>
> NZ Corps . . . will assemble in the Monte Trocchio area . . . [and] be prepared, on Army Order, to debouch into the Liri Valley, pass through elements of II Corps and, making its main effort along Highway Six, attack to the north-west within its zone of action.
>
> 10 Corps . . . will attack . . . to the north in the direction of San Giorgio a Liri.[29]

This was the original exploitation role envisaged by Alexander in the employment of NZ Corps. Essentially, it was based on the premise that US 2 Corps could subdue the defences of the Cassino position sufficiently for NZ Corps to go through and operate beyond the Gustav Line. The plans envisaged by Freyberg and Tuker over the last few days were not so much 'abandoned' as put aside because the circumstances for their application did not obtain. It was the orders of 5th Army that set the parameters for future operations.

The changes involved in the Cassino sector now had to do with the adjustment of 5th Army formations, to fit NZ Corps into the line, and with preparations for forthcoming operations. As what was now contemplated involved a passing through of the entire corps to the Liri Valley, the matter of close air support became important to resolve. A conference on air support was held at NZ Corps headquarters at 10 a.m. on 6 February. It was decided:

> *THE 'SET PIECE' ATTACK*
>
> 1. *Targets* will be pre-arranged and on a time programme.
>   Infm required on:
>   (a) areas that can be most effectively bombed, i.e. gun areas.
>   (b) localities that can be most effectively strafed, i.e. roads.

2. *Landmarks for Aircraft*
In addition to town of CASSINO is there any further aid that would assist a/c to locate targets, i.e. red and blue smoke at any particular point?

CLOSE AIR SUPPORT DURING THE ADVANCE

3. *Targets* will be mostly impromptu and could be called for
   (a) by usual method on Support Demand Form RAF Form 1871.
   (b) likely areas could be gridded into squares 1000 x 500 yds and numbered.
4. *Air Force Controller*
If available, could one be supplied to direct [*sic*] a/c in the air from one target (perhaps one already occupied by our tps) to an alternative target further back.

GROUND TO AIR RECOGNITION

5. What is considered by Air Support Comd method of ground to air recognition.
i.e., red and blue smoke
Nairn beacon
ground strips[30]

It is clear that Freyberg intended to repeat the tactic of the thrust into the Liri Valley in terms of air support and of the breakthrough at Tebaga Gap. He wanted a forward air controller to operate in the same manner as in the desert battle: to direct the fighter bombers on to targets. It was the 'cab rank' system again.

The next day, 7 February, a conference at New Zealand headquarters looked at the prospective assault. Two or three brigades of infantry, around 160 tanks, and a great deal of military transport were to go forward. Five regiments of field artillery were to be used behind the river; another nine regiments of artillery would be used forward of the Rapido. This mass of artillery plus air support was to cover and assist the attack:

> . . . we shall follow the whole Alamein technique sweeping the routes forward for supporting arms and tanks. The object is to get tanks through . . . At daylight (air force daylight) we are bringing across as in the battle of Hamma the whole of the air force in Italy. The amount of air we shall have will be 50 per cent greater than at Hamma. Not less than 250 operational Kittybombers and mediums and lights as well. We will have a terrific weight of air.[31]

The air support in the first instance was to be brought to bear in the road areas and hillsides of Cassino and St Angelo.

Freyberg did not understand that the Allied air forces in Italy applied air support generally in a way that was in doctrine totally different to that provided by the Desert Air Force at Tebaga Gap. Both the RAF and

USAAF in Italy believed air support meant bombing, and bombing meant flattening an area. This was not the tactical application adapted from the Luftwaffe, where the air force was used for tasks with the army, as the attack went forward. Static area bombardment, of a prescribed zone in front of an assault, was the *modus operandi* in Italy. The air force did its job. When the air force had finished, then the army went in. The really crucial difference was that the air forces in Italy would not, except on a very small scale, engage in a moving, changing, ground-determined, target-attack role, in the German manner of mobile aerial artillery. This was a fundamental lack of adaptability. For Freyberg and NZ Corps this was an Achilles' heel that would impede battlefield progress.

On 5 February, General Marshall and the American chiefs of staff expressed concern on the subject of the Italian campaign to Churchill:

> US Chiefs of Staff feel some concern over progress of operations in Italy. Chiefs of Staff fear that present situation may be developing into an attrition battle with steadily mounting losses without decisive gains. Also it would appear . . . that there has been *no* heavily mounted aggressive offensive on Main Front. Reports seem to indicate that action on Main Fifth Army Front has been more in the nature of attacks by comparatively small units.[32]

The attacks by British X Corps (on the Garigliano), by US 2 Corps, and by the French Corps were judged as insufficiently aggressive. The lack of progress at Anzio was of concern. What was not appreciated was that, having sunk into an awkward position because of the Anzio operation, 5th Army might only sink deeper if it was forced to respond operationally to political pressure. This was particularly so at the strongest point of the Gustav Line, the Cassino position.

On 6 February, Churchill questioned General Maitland Wilson, the overall commander in Italy, about progress. This led to a response from the commander of 15th Army Group, Alexander. He signalled to the British Prime Minister on 8 February on forthcoming operations on the 'Main Front': 'I have high hopes of a breakthrough in this sector and if it looks promising I shall reinforce Freyberg with the 78th Division . . . and thus exploit success gained . . .'[33] This showed a willingness to offer something, while actually holding back on committing anything extra. The use of 78 Division was conditional on success. Extra troops to exploit a breakthrough are usually needed then and there, rather than be started on their way during the battle. The corps commander, in this case Freyberg, now had to consider his command arrangements to be able to cover three divisions, not two. He might go into battle *without* a new third division. This did happen: 78 Division did not arrive in time for Freyberg's opening operations at Cassino. While on paper NZ Corps had three divisions, in the first battle there would only be two.

Freyberg's reaction to the possible addition of 78 Division to NZ Corps was not optimistic. He told General Harding, Alexander's chief of staff on 8 February:

> The thing now becomes a much bigger job and one has to consider whether one has a whole HQ or not. I don't think one can improvise. As the thing went on we might want help. I will try and go on. I will put in a deputy commander and use the original HQ for both of us, and if it is too much will have to ask for a HQ.[34]

Freyberg had tried to run his temporary NZ Corps without disrupting his own chain of command. Now, faced with the prospect of a three division corps in the near future, changes would have to made. He decided as an interim measure to make his most talented brigade commander, Brigadier Kippenberger, the acting commander of the NZ Division, promoting him to the rank of Major-General. These changes were signalled to Wellington on 14 February. A swift and warm response came back from the New Zealand War Cabinet on both counts — the possible inclusion of 78 Division as part of NZ Corps, and Kippenberger's promotion — confirming Freyberg's decisions.[35]

To replace Kippenberger, as has been mentioned earlier, Colonel Hartnell was brought in to command the 5 NZ Infantry Brigade. This was not the only change in command in NZ Corps. General Tuker, the regular commander of 4 Indian Division, became ill, and took no further part in the battles. Command of 4 Indian Division now devolved on the Division's Commander Royal Artillery (CRA), Brigadier Dimoline.

A change of plan followed. In the 5th Army Operations Instruction of 5 February, NZ Corps was to be the exploiting force, driving through after a successful American assault on Cassino. The days of 6-8 February had brought NZ Corps into the line, with the 5 NZ Brigade taking over the US 36 Division's positions opposite St Angelo, while the rest of the NZ Division and 4 Indian Division moved in and concentrated in the rear, to be ready for the breakout. Now with political pressure on Wilson and Alexander to achieve results, the Army commander and Alexander decided that 4 Indian Division would relieve the US 34 Division at a date yet to be specified.[36]

This altered the direction of any operation by NZ Corps. The original plan for a breakthrough still stood, provided that the US 34 Division could take Cassino massif. If this did not occur, then NZ Corps would have to complete the work that the 34 Division was engaged in: taking the massif. This was unsatisfactory. More planning would be needed to have ready a projected thrust in a completely different area to that already contemplated by Freyberg: speed would be the key, as Alexander had prescribed a contingency date for NZ Corps. As well, a large amount of readjustment would need to be done by the troops of NZ Corps, if

4 Indian Division was to be ready at the right place and the projected time. This was not so easy in an area already quite congested with Allied formations.

On 9 February, NZ Corps issued a new Operation Instruction No. 4:

> *INFORMATION*
> 1. Enemy in front of 2 US Corps have been reinforced and resistance has hardened . . .
>
> *INTENTION*
> 2. NZ Corps will be prepared to attack and capture MONASTERY HILL and CASSINO in the event of 2 US Corps being unable to complete this task by dark 12 Feb 44.[37]

It might now seem that Freyberg planned an assault that followed a similar pattern to that of the US 34 Division. This is to misunderstand the situation. Clark had felt that one more push would take the Cassino position — the heights in particular. The idea was that if US 2 Corps could not finish the job, then the fresh troops of NZ Corps would. Thus, to plan for this, Freyberg was tied in to the area of the American thrust. If US 2 Corps failed, then 4 Indian Division would move into the positions of the 34 Division. The situation must have been barely tolerable. The fresh corps was to be poised to strike as an exploitation force into the Liri Valley. It was also to be prepared to fight a completely different battle by 12 February, *if* US 2 Corps failed. No other corps at Cassino would face this kind of alternative in the space of so short a time: one of the two options would materialize in three days' time. Already, Freyberg had been trapped by the vacillations of Clark and Alexander.

Freyberg's diary noted wet conditions on Wednesday 9 February.[38] At 8 a.m., the General met with the new acting commander of the NZ Division, Major-General Kippenberger. The organization of the Corps was discussed, along with the plan of operations. This was followed by a meeting with the commander of 4 Indian Division; at 10 a.m., Freyberg left with his BGS, Colonel Queree, and the Deputy Assistant Quartermaster-General (DAQMG), to proceed to 5th Army headquarters for orders. The General saw Clark, and talked to Gruenther, the chief of staff. Freyberg and his officers then returned to NZ Corps headquarters in the early afternoon. The prospects for the projected American attack by 34 Division on the Cassino massif were held to be good. The NZ Corps commander advised US 2 Corps that NZ Corps would be ready to take over on 12 February, if the 34 Division attack on the 11 February had not succeeded. A message was sent to the acting commander of 4 Indian Division, Brigadier Dimoline, advising them to be prepared for operations on 12 February. The evening was spent working on the plan of operations.[39]

The next day, 10 February, 7 Brigade of 4 Indian Division began to move from its concentration area to the new one near Cairo village, where the Brigade would need to be if they were to take over from the Americans in the hills on 12 February. Part of the move was by road, by now deep in mud. The four-wheel drive trucks of the Division stuck or skidded, and a number of accidents took place before the lorries were replaced by borrowed light jeeps and trailers from the Americans. One accident was significant. Two trucks went over a steep bank, and their loads were not recoverable. This accident lost the entire reserve of mortar bombs and grenades of the 1 Royal Sussex Regiment, and these had not been replaced by the time the attack opened, days later. As this formation was the spearhead of 4 Indian Division's projected thrust in the hills, it was a loss of some moment.

The NZ Corps' Intelligence Summary No. 20 gave an optimistic picture of the position in the hills. This appreciation was based on what US 2 Corps reported of the progress by 34 Division. As future moves by formations of NZ Corps were based upon American intelligence about the front, erroneous impressions could have dangerous consequences. Just how wrong the Americans were will soon be seen. The NZ Corps' Intelligence Summary for 10 February reported that Allied troops held Point 593, while the Germans held Abbey Hill. The Germans were declared to have made three attacks to retake Point 593, and all were repulsed with losses. At the same time, it was noted that the Germans had not made substantial progress at the beach-head at Anzio.[40]

Freyberg, in a diary entry of 10 February, noted that Keyes, the commander of US 2 Corps, had called at 10 a.m. to say that a counter-attack against the 34 Division had been held. Freyberg discussed with Keyes the prospects for the latter's attack for the next day. The commander of NZ Corps discussed NZ Corps' attack plan with Kippenberger, Weir, and Hartnell, the new commanding officer of 5 NZ Brigade. Later, General Keightley, the commander of the British 78 Division visited NZ Corps headquarters. Freyberg discussed plans with him, for it was known that 78 Division might come under the command of NZ Corps in the days ahead.

11 February was the day of the American attack. NZ Corps' Intelligence Summary No. 21 noted that although the Germans still held Cassino town and Abbey Hill, the fighting had gone against them. It was said that two German counter-attacks had failed the previous afternoon. The Germans had had to defend Point 468 itself, and had halted Allied forces 100 yards away. Abbey Hill still commanded Points 165 and 445, but the German strongpoints in the northern half of Cassino itself had been reduced.[41]

The morning of 11 February was cold and wet. Freyberg had a long session with Keightley of 78 Division. Gruenther, 5 Army's chief of staff rang at 11.30 a.m., and arranged a meeting with Freyberg at 5th Army headquarters, between 3.30 and 4 p.m. Freyberg told Gruenther that NZ Corps was slightly behind its schedule in its moves, but most of the preliminaries were complete. The chief of staff commented that Anzio had quietened down. According to him, the attack by 34 Division was reported to be going well at 8.30 a.m., but was coming under heavy fire: 'He was not worried but there was a lot of agitation for more force up there.'[42] Gruenther asked Freyberg if he thought the Americans should attack when NZ Corps did. Freyberg commented that he did not think the Americans would be able to, and the chief of staff agreed. Freyberg told Gruenther that NZ Corps' plans had been made without the expectation of American ground support. Gruenther said that although the 34 Division's attack was full of hope, he would not bet on it succeeding.[43]

After this, Freyberg talked with his BGS and Dimoline of 4 Indian Division about NZ Corps' plan of operations. At 3 p.m., Freyberg went off to see Gruenther at 5th Army headquarters, then returned and rang 4 Indian Division.

Freyberg and Queree, the BGS, now discussed the situation as it was definite that NZ Corps would be committed in the 34 Division's area. It was suggested that Weir, the CRA, should go and see the US 2 Corps artillery about an artillery attack on the monastery. Queree noted that this would need to be cleared by Clark himself. Freyberg said, 'We are going on with our bombardment and if the monastery is hit, it cannot be helped. Same thing applies to dive bombing.'[44] It was decided that all relevant officers would meet at NZ Corps headquarters at 8 a.m. on 12 February. There was concern that air support would not be available then, as it was needed at Anzio.[45]

Freyberg then received bad news. US 2 Corps had failed in its attack to dislodge the Germans off the heights of the Cassino position:

> Gen Gruenther rang in the evening to say that Gen Clark had phoned Gen Keyes and that the torch was now thrown to NZ Corps, which will include the direction of the artillery from tomorrow. GOC said we would get ahead with it. Gen G[ruenther] said 'If you think of anything we should be doing, please let us know . . . We may be making mistakes.' GOC: 'You are helping 100 per cent in a way we have never been helped before.' Told Gen G we wanted Allen [US liaison officer, 5th Army] transferred to us.[46]

At 11.30 p.m., Freyberg contacted Dimoline. He emphasized there must be no delay. Freyberg suggested that Dimoline use three battalions for the attack rather than four. Afterwards Freyberg said to Queree that 'we have had many torches thrown to us. This was a tough one but it would be alright.'[47]

Carrying a torch, at speed, over wet ground is hazardous. General Alexander perhaps had this in mind in his Operation Instruction of 11 February:

> The C-in-C is naturally anxious that the advance of the NZ Corps up the Liri Valley astride Highway 6 should take place as early as possible. At the same time, he considers it essential to the success of that operation that the ground should be dry enough to permit the operation of armour off the roads, and that the weather, during any large scale daylight operations should be suitable for effective air support. The C-in-C therefore orders that any major operation by NZ Corps in the Liri Valley will not take place unless and until the physical conditions mentioned above obtain. This does not apply to the attack of 4 Ind. Div. to clear the high ground West of Cassino of the enemy, or to the establishment of a bridgehead over the Rapido in the Cassino area, both of which operations will be carried out as quickly as possible, so that NZ Corps can begin to advance Westward from the Cassino Bridgehead as soon as the physical conditions laid down above are fulfilled . . .[48]

In view of the prevailing wet ground conditions Alexander regarded the renewal or continuance of offensive operations by NZ Corps as preliminary. The 'New Zealanders' were to gain objectives that were prerequisites to a thrust into the Liri Valley. Even the winning of the goals need not ensure that such an offensive would follow immediately. Because of Alexander's rider, that the armour should be able to operate off roads, any thrust towards Anzio or Rome relied on good weather.

According to the NZ Corps' Intelligence Summary No. 22 of 12 February, it had become clear that the Germans still held the town, and that the fighting was still for 'possession of the dominant hills'. The Germans were on Points 444 and 569 but not on 593. The Germans had lost 468 yesterday, and their loss of 468 and 593 were described as serious.[49] Away at Anzio, 'the enemy has not so far been able to make much progress'. In fact, because of German counter-attacks and American optimism, the situation in the hills above Cassino was rather different, as 4 Indian Division was soon unpleasantly to find out.

It was a busy day for NZ Corps in its new forward role. Freyberg met with his staff and the commander of the NZ Division at about 8 a.m. It was reported that air support was not available for the day, and there were some doubts raised about striking the Abbey of Monte Cassino. The reservation was expressed that: '. . . in any case [the] wall of [the] Abbey is so thick (12ft at the bottom and 5ft at the top) that bombing of it is not looked upon as much use. The wall is really the only military objective.'[50]

The monastery, on the top of Monastery Hill, gave the troops below a feeling that they were under continual observation. It is now generally accepted that the Germans had not occupied the monastery, nor were they using it as an artillery observation post. This is probably correct, for the view from most German positions on Monastery Hill was spectacular, and there may have been no need for using it. Two senior United States officers overflew the monastery on 13 February and reported seeing a few German personnel and radio masts, thus proving occupation. This was not confirmed. Nonetheless, even a couple of officers with binoculars and a radio would have been enough for an artillery observation post. While the Germans later made much of the destruction of the building for propaganda purposes, the commander of XIV Panzer Corps was explicit in his opinion on its use:

> . . . even under the normal conditions Monte Cassino would never have been occupied by artillery spotters. True, it commanded a view of the entire district . . . but on our side it was considered tactical opinion that so conspicuous a landmark would be quite unsuitable as an observation post, since we could expect it to be put out of action by heavy fire very soon after the big battle had started.[51]

Von Senger, the German commander, expected the monastery to be fired on in the normal course of battle for the Cassino position, simply because the Germans had tied the monastery and the hill into their defence line. Von Senger himself had lifted a 330 yard prohibition over the positioning of German troops near the monastery, in December 1943.[52] The alacrity with which German mortar teams occupied the useful ruins after the bombing did not exemplify a hands-off position.

The weather did not favour NZ Corps. At the early morning meeting, Hanson, the CRE, arrived with the news that the ground to the left of the railway was flooded, and would be impassable to infantry for the next four or five days. As there had been demolitions on the railway embankment, bridging would be required.[53] This was a blow because the embankment was to be used for an alternative to Route 6 through the town for the armour. The line of the railway bypassed the town and not all the bridging could be done in one night.[54] This flooding narrowed the front on which the infantry, in support of engineers intent on bridging, could operate.

At 9.30 a.m., Freyberg attended a handing-over conference at US 2 Corps' headquarters at which 2 Corps' commander, General Keyes, optimistic as usual, summed-up a situation that, to others, looked ominous:

> Briefly we have reached about the extent of our efforts on this hill. We feel that it as a matter of fresh troops, more troops rather than the difficulties that are found up there . . . We have had a greater reaction in the last 12 to 14 hours than we have ever had up there before.[55]

The arrangements for the afternoon were broken by the late return to 4 Indian Division headquarters of the commander of 7 Indian Brigade after an inspection of the front. The 7 Indian Brigade had run into trouble. Two battalions had reinforced troops of the US 36 Division in holding-off German counter-attacks around Monte Castellone, on the flank, *en route* to the dominating heights. Reconnaissance parties were sent out to make contact with the Americans and monitor the situation. On reaching headquarters Lovett reported that the American position seemed insecure, and that 'On 593 they have called on all cooks etc. to hold the line.'[56]

The forward situation, still not clear to the commanders and the staff back at the various headquarters, was much worse as Lieutenant-Colonel Glennie, the commander of 1 Royal Sussex, found on the evening of 12 February: 'On arrival it was found that the sector was held by four US battalions (now each only 100 strong) from three different regiments of two divisions.'[57] Down at 2 Corps headquarters it was thought that Point 593 and the ridge between Points 450 to 455 were occupied by the 168 and 141 US Infantry Regiments. In fact the Americans had been driven off the crest and were positioned in gullies some 200 yards below.[58] On 10 February, Point 593 itself had fallen to a German counter-attack. Communications to the rear were so bad that the news had not got back.

Freyberg was unaware of this. He gave orders by phone to Dimoline to shore up the Castellone area and Point 593, and, via 5th Army headquarters, requested French help in suppressing fire from the Terelle area.[59] He also rang Keyes of US 2 Corps who, still optimistic, told Freyberg that he (Keyes) thought everything on the front was under control.[60]

At 4.30 p.m. there was a divisional commanders' conference. Dimoline was not present. This conference mostly concerned itself with plans for an armoured break out into the Liri Valley. NZ Corps was now strengthened by an American Armoured Combat Group of 175 tanks and tank-destroyers (a 75mm gun with a Sherman chassis), which doubled NZ Corps' armoured strength to the size of the armoured force at Tebaga Gap.

Some time during 12 February, the ailing General Tuker, commander of 4 Indian Division, saw Freyberg and delivered two letters concerning the forthcoming assault on the Cassino position by his troops. They provided details of the construction of the abbey itself, and urged that Monastery Hill be subjected to aerial bombardment to soften the defences. There was also a plea for a turning operation to be used rather than an assault on the heights.

The letter describing the strength of the monastery gave Freyberg his most precise assessment of its capacity to withstand bombardment:

SUBJECT: *OPERATIONS* *SECRET*

Main 4 Ind Div,
No. 433/1/G
12 Feb 44.

Main NZ Corps

1. After considerable trouble and investigating many bookshops in NAPLES, I have at last found a book, dated 1879, which gives certain details of the construction of the MONTE CASSINO Monastery.

2. The Monastery was converted into a fortress in the 19th Century. The Main Gate has massive timber branches in a low archway consisting of large stone blocks 9 to 10 metres long. The gate is the *only* means of entrance to the Monastery.

3. The walls are about 15ft high, or more where there are Monk's cells against the walls. The walls are of solid masonry and at least 10ft thick at the base.

4. Since the place was constructed as a fortress as late as the 19th Century it stands to reason that the walls will be suitably pierced for loopholes and will be battlemented.

5. MONTE CASSINO is therefore a modern fortress and must be dealt with by modern means. No practicable means available within the capacity of field engineers can possibly cope with this place.

It can only be directly dealt with by applying 'block buster' bombs from the air, hoping thereby to render the garrison incapable of resistance. The 1,000 lbs bomb would be next to useless to effect this.

6. Whether the Monastery is now occupied by a German Garrison or not, it is certain that it will be held as a keep by the last remnants of the Garrison of the position. It is therefore also essential that the building should be so demolished as to prevent its effective occupation at that time.

7. I would ask that you would give me definite information *at once* as to how this fortress will be dealt with as the means are not within the capacity of this Division.

8. I would point out that it has only been by investigation on the part of this Div, with no help whatsoever from 'I' sources outside, that we have got any idea as to what this fortress comprises although the fortress has been a thorn in our side for many weeks.

When a formation is called upon to reduce such a place, it should be apparent that the place is reducible by the means at the disposal of that Div or that the means are ready for it, without having to go to the bookstalls of NAPLES to find out what should have been fully considered many weeks ago.

(Sgd) TUKER
Maj-Gen
Comd.[61]

Did Tuker's assessment make the bombing of the abbey less of an option? Freyberg regarded the walls of the monastery the real target when he considered the abbey. He needed fighter bombers to breach the walls so that the following Indian infantry could move in to the ruins after the attack. Freyberg, Tuker, Kippenberger, and Dimoline were all under the impression that the monastery was being used by the enemy, at the very least as an artillery observation post. So were many of the American troops who had borne the brunt of the earlier action. At 9.30 p.m. on 12 February, Freyberg rang Gruenther:

> Air mission to bomb the monastery is laid on. He [Gruenther] discussed matter with Army Comd [Clark] who said that if it was the GOCs considered opinion that it was a military objective then he concurs. GOC [Freyberg] said that the General who had to do the attack [Dimoline] considered that if the place was not softened the most difficult feature in the attack would be an obstacle which might cause the attack to fail. Gen G. said that the Army Comd had pointed out that the fact that it was demolished would not necessarily lessen its value as an obstacle. The GOC said he did not think the bombing and shelling would demolish it. That would damage it. The thing was they would soften the people who are there. Gen G. mentioned reports that there are possibly civilians there and said 'But if your judgement is that you think it should be done it shall be done.' Finally he asked that 2 Corps be advised and that a time be fixed. Gen G. did not know exactly where troops of 2 Corps might be. This was passed to G2 (Air) [Robin Bell] NZ Corps.[62]

The fighter-bomber attack was to breach the walls, hence Freyberg's conclusion that the abbey would not be entirely destroyed. The level of destruction would depend on how precise the attack was. Clark had given his conditional permission for the attack, and if Clark was unhappy about the bombing (as he declared he was after the war, and contrived to blame Freyberg), then as Army commander he could simply have refused permission for the attack.

The Germans were handed a propaganda coup: the barbaric destruction of a historic building. Clark blamed Freyberg and Alexander for the results of the air attack. Yet the Germans had built their defences around the monastery and had facilitated the removal of works of art and religious relics before the bombing.[63] And Clark, for all his protestations, had concurred in the attack, albeit reluctantly. A detailed examination of the destruction of the monastery is beyond the scope of this study. The most likely explanation is that by Graham and Bidwell.[64] It is suggested that Gruenther himself was to cancel the fighter-bomber mission requested by Freyberg for around 10 a.m. on 13 February, at the behest of 2 Corps who needed to be back behind a bomb safety line.[65] Certainly the eventual translation of the air attack into an assault by heavy and medium bombing aircraft was the decision of the USAAF commander, General Eaker, who decided to use maximum blasting power simply because his superior,

General Arnold, had chided Eaker for not adequately supporting the ground forces in Italy. The resultant devastation not only served no useful purpose, and in fact aided the enemy; the method of attack was wrong, the types of aircraft used were wrong, and the doctrine of carpet-bombing was wrong.

At around 10 p.m. on 12 February, Freyberg discussed with his BGS, Queree, the take-over by 4 Indian Division of 2 Corps positions in the hills. Freyberg said:

> I am not concerned about the date of his attack but must get front taken over so that he knows it. He [Dimoline] must get his troops positioned so that he can do the thing without muddle. The situation is too difficult if they do not start on a known point. They should take that over and go in on a two bde front and have two bns as a firm base one on one side and one on the other.[66]

Freyberg now realized that 4 Indian Division would not be ready to mount their attack towards the monastery till 15/16 February.

NZ Corps spent 13 February in further preparations for an impending ground assault and awaited the air attack on the monastery. Freyberg visited 4 Indian Division at around 9 a.m. and discussed the plan for taking over from the Americans, which was by no means near completion. On his return he saw Kippenberger and Queree. At 1.50 p.m., the commander of NZ Corps went to 5th Army headquarters with his GSO2 (Air) to see Gruenther about the abbey bombing. He was informed that the air force had decided to smash the monastery with 700 tons of bombs, using mainly 1,000 and 2,000 pounders.[67]

Queree, the BGS, had in the meantime been to 4 Indian Division. He told Freyberg that their attack had been put back to the night of 16/17 February because of delays in taking over from the Americans. Lovett, still confident, had opined that the American infantry were in terrible shape but the Germans were in a much worse state. The General rang Dimoline and told him he would have to work to the projected date. The NZ Corps commander then rang Gruenther to ask if the attack could be put back twenty-four hours on to the previously agreed date. Gruenther thought this would be all right provided the weather held and nothing untoward occurred at Anzio. The chief of staff asked Freyberg for permission to warn the abbey of the bombing, by leaflet, and the General agreed.[68]

Late in the afternoon of 14 February, Freyberg met with Dimoline. 4 Indian Division was now in trouble with its attack plan. A reconnaissance from the night of 13/14 revealed that the selected assault front was too narrow, and that the enemy could bring down direct fire on it. The same plan could be used but the attack would have to go in higher up. Dimoline sought a postponement to detail the use of the new ground but Freyberg said he must stick to the date if possible.[69] Dimoline rang back in the evening and the situation became even more awkward:

> He [Dimoline] did not realise bombing was on tomorrow. Said he could not withdraw his troops as they were carrying out relief tonight and said further that as they were less than 50 per cent in possession of 593 attack to take it was necessary. He proposed to attack it tomorrow night, wait another day and do his main attack on the 17/18. GOC [Freyberg] . . . tried to shake Dimoline but without success . . . GOC . . . had long conversation pointing out that the bombing had been put on at their request, that if we cancelled the programme now we would never get the air again and that this delay from day to day was making us look ridiculous. Dimoline said that he realised all that but that he had to take the opinion of the Brigadier on the ground and that he would not be prepared to order the Division to attack until firm base was secured. Someone else might do it, but he would not. GOC told him that there were two things to consider. One, the Air, he must remember that he was a Divisional Commander and it was his decision to make. Could he withdraw troops to the 1000 yard limit so that the bombing could go on tomorrow. He was given half an hour to make a decision. Second was whether the attack could not be put in on the night 16/17 as arranged. GOC said it was impossible to go on putting it off from day to day.[70]

A crisis had arisen that was not of Freyberg's making. 4 Indian Division had not been able even to get to its start line for its ground assault on the heights. That start line on Point 593 would have to be fought for first. The assumption of 593 as a starting point was based on the 2 Corps' claim that 593 was in American hands. This was not the case. Misinformation from the battered 2 Corps troops in the hill positions had involved units of 4 Indian Division in necessary but time-consuming actions before reaching anywhere near the start lines. The supply situation had quickly become critical — the long tenuous supply route, the mule casualties, the compulsion to use infantry on portering tasks, the clogging of the routes as 2 Corps extricated itself often with difficulty — all these made a quick adjustment by 4 Indian Division impossible. As the protracted impediments to 4 Indian Division's occupation of the high ground unravelled, a new problem emerged. The air support was not what Freyberg really wanted, and he had no control over the timing of it. He was at the whim of the air forces, the higher commanders, the weather, and Anzio. No doubt he felt that whatever he got in terms of air support was better than going into the attack with nothing at all, but the timetable forced upon him did not marry with the continually postponing readiness of 4 Indian Division.

It was a bad day for Freyberg. Keightley had come to him in the morning with the news that his [Freyberg's] son was missing. In the evening came news that Paul Freyberg was a prisoner of war. The problems of the whole Cassino front which faced the NZ Corps must have weighed heavily on the General. Around this time, Stevens, commanding 2NZEF rear headquarters noted:

> ... [O]ne occasion when I think that his normal optimism and confidence temporarily left him, and that was at Cassino. It was the only time in the war when I saw him looking depressed, and walking along slowly with shoulders hunched and his hands in his pockets. (I have never forgotten this unusual picture.) At the time he was ... having trouble with higher authority over his insistence on limiting casualties ... and in addition was much involved in the argument about whether or not the monastery was to be bombed.[71]

Major John White noted in the GOC's diary that it was 'Altogether a rather difficult day for the GOC.'[72]

If the commander of NZ Corps was depressed by the prospect before him, his opponent General Frido von Senger und Etterlin of XIV Panzer Corps was resigned to a long contest, as he struggled to hold the line against all comers. Anzio, the pressure down the Gustav Line, and the assaults on the heights by US 2 Corps had been a drain on German resources. XIV Panzer Corps' defence of the Gustav Line had held, but it had been:

> ... necessary to weaken quiet sectors to danger point ... The heavy demand for troops to contain the Anzio beachhead has denuded the Corps of almost all reserves. Even the divisions have almost no local reserves. Sectors where there is no immediate threat have been weakened to such an extent that any enemy pressure there ... must bring about new crises.[73]

To von Senger, the forces in the Cassino position:

> ... cannot be guaranteed adequate to hold out against another major attack ... Exhaustion among the troops (who have been exposed for weeks to the worst rigours of mountain warfare with inadequate equipment ... supplies, and no hope of relief) increases daily ... The continuous decrease in manpower in this sector makes it impossible to defend the line in depth, and compels us to adopt a policy of linear defence in exposed positions ... If the enemy decides to concentrate his artillery, air and infantry in co-operation on a few deciding points (Cassino, Monte Cassino, Albaneta, Colle Sant'Angelo) he will probably succeed in his aims.[74]

The German losses were high. However, their tactical defence and a good deal of foresight lessened the odds considerably.

Broadly speaking, the German defences at Cassino were based on natural strength and were improved by their flooding of flat areas in front of the town, and by fortifications by wire, mines, well-concealed automatic weapons posts, and mortar and gun positions. The defenders' strategy was to limit the attackers' options at any particular place, so that only small numbers of the assaulting forces could be funnelled towards the defences at one particular time. It was a defence which waited upon the enemy, allowed him to choose where to attack, and then by the strength of the defences and the narrowness of attacking frontage led the attackers into a funnel and defeated them piecemeal. Freyberg, like US 2 Corps, did not have the resources to apply pressure on several areas at once, and close air support was not available as of right, nor was it particularly reliable. The prospects of NZ Corps were dim. Freyberg had great difficulty in getting NZ Corps into a position for his operation 'Avenger' attack.

Thursday 15 February began fine, windy, and cold. Freyberg rang Dimoline, talked about the bombing, and said he wanted 4 Indian Division to attack on 16 February: 'If not he had to go cap in hand to the Army Comd. Brig Dimoline said "It is a bit worrying but I think it will be alright".'[75]

Dimoline's difficulty in correctly placing 4 Indian Division led him to take an extraordinary step. Kippenberger relates:

> Poor Dimoline was having a really dreadful time getting his Division into position. I never really appreciated the difficulties until I went over the ground after the war. He got me to make an appointment for us both with General Freyberg, as he thought his task was impossible and his difficulties not fully realised. The General refused to see us together: he told me he was not going to have any sort of soviet of divisional commanders.[76]

Freyberg too was under pressure to finish 2 Corps' offensive and take the heights as a preliminary to breaking into the Liri Valley. That pressure came from above: from an Army commander who disliked British and the Dominion troops, and from Alexander himself, concerned by the Anzio situation. It is possible that Freyberg did not fully appreciate the excessive difficulties the hills posed to attackers. Even as prescient an observer as Kippenberger was unaware of the extent of the problem until after the war. The on-again/off-again statements by Dimoline unfairly suggested that the temporary commander of 4 Indian Division was dithering in the face of strong-minded opposition from his brigadiers. It was not Dimoline's fault at all. The intelligence assessment at the point of take-over from the Americans had been clearly wrong. But the forward area in the hills was remote given the long route imposed by the alert German defences, and there was no quick way of checking. Ultra intercepts revealed nothing of much value in the hill area of Cassino.[77] It was physically impossible for Dimoline or Freyberg to go to the forward 7 Brigade positions in front of Point 593. Wheeled transport could not get all the way up. To go there would have taken the commanders away from their headquarters for too long a period of time. Freyberg's record in terms of exposure to danger is formidable — it would not have been danger that inhibited him.

Shortly after talking to Dimoline on the morning of 15 February, Freyberg went to 4 Indian Division headquarters, and from there he witnessed the raid on the monastery:

> It was most impressive. Some Forts went astray but generally speaking bombing was accurate. Medium bombing was extremely so. Returned HQ for lunch. Rang COS [Gruenther] to say thank you for the air effort and asked him not to send any more Forts [B-17 Fortresses].[78]

The bombing of the abbey went on, with pauses, for three hours, from 9.30 a.m. 135 B-17s dropped 257 tons of 500lb bombs and 59 tons of incendiaries; the mediums, forty-seven Mitchells and forty Marauders dropped 283 1000lb bombs.[79] These smashed the roofs and upper floors of the abbey, but did not break down the walls. The specific task of breaching the walls to allow infantry entrance had not been done.

The aerial bombardment was no longer vital: 4 Indian Division was in no position to take advantage of the bombing and occupy the ruins. The Germans swiftly placed mortar teams in the ruins, rendering useful assistance to troops on the nearby heights. The attack had been a failure. The air force had not breached the walls; they had insisted that their timetable be adhered to, despite the knowledge that the ground forces could not be ready on time.

It had been a spectacular diversion and at its conclusion Ultra cast a black cloud over the fate of operation 'Avenger'. Troop movements, disclosed by intercepts on and inclusive of 10-15 February, indicated that the Germans were about to launch a determined counter-offensive at Anzio.[80] This made a NZ Corps attack more urgent: it could take the pressure off the beach-head.

NZ Corps, albeit somewhat disorganized, was now poised to attack the Cassino position. 4 Indian Division would gain the heights. The NZ Division and the attached armour would thrust along the railway embankment and construct an alternative road to Route 6, which would have taken them through into the Liri. The defenders were ready for the attack. The commander of XIV Panzer Corps was dubious of the defenders' chances. In the Cassino sector, 90 Panzer Grenadier Division was deployed, under Lieutenant-General Ernst-Guenther Baade. Artillery was in short supply: the defenders possessed only one-quarter of the guns brought up by their attackers. 90 Panzer Grenadier Division would only have two hours worth of shells for full-scale fighting on 16 February.[81]

The troops in the Cassino sector included fourteen infantry battalions, two companies of tanks, part of two Nebelwerfer (multi-barrelled mortar) regiments, one assault gun battalion, six artillery batteries, and just over one battalion of anti-tank guns.[82] The Allies' superiority in guns and tanks was negated by the terrain and the defences. The NZ Division section, the railway station, and the town were held by 211 Regiment of 90 Panzer Grenadier Division under Major Knuth, consisting of two of its own battalions, and one from 361 Panzer Grenadier Regiment.

The heights — Monastery Hill to Albaneta Farm and 445, 593, et al, — were held by 1 Parachute Regiment under Colonel Schulz, composed of two battalions of 1 Parachute Regiment, one from 3 Parachute Regiment, and the Parachute Machine-Gun Battalion, some four battalions in all.[83] These were excellent troops in strong positions. The huge disparity in infantry numbers between NZ Corps and the Germans in favour of the Allies was to be entirely negated by the nature of the defences: only a few troops would be able to be used by the Allies at once.

Lieutenant-Colonel Glennie of 1 Royal Sussex had decided to attack Point 593 with just one company, because of the lack of room and because of uncertainty as to the Germans' numbers. The idea was that it was better to present a smaller target with more space to fight in.[84] Under 500 yards from 'C' Company, 1 Royal Sussex:

> . . . [there] loomed the rocky crest of Pt 593, with the ruins of a small fort upon its summit. The slopes were shaggy with great boulders, sharp ledges and patches of scrub. These natural hideouts sheltered German spandau teams and bomb squads. Enemy outposts were less than 70 yards distant. The slightest movement drew retaliatory fire . . . There was no elbow room for deployment, no cover behind which to concentrate effectively, no opportunity to withdraw in order to obtain space for manoeuvre.[85]

With two platoons in advance, the attack was opened fire on only 50 yards from the start line. 'C' Company, sixty-three men and three officers, quickly used up their own grenades and those of other companies sent forward. The loss of the grenade reserves was now felt. Support fire could not be given, for the space was too small to avoid hitting the forward company. Three officers and thirty-two men became casualties. The Germans had few casualties.

This became an all-too familiar pattern. In order to attack, the assault troops had to expose themselves. The amount of room to move was limited by terrain or defences, or both. The defenders remained under cover, and used considerable numbers of automatic weapons. Mortar fire could be

Senior officers of NZ Corps for the February battle: Dimoline of 4 Indian Division, Kippenberger of 2 NZ Division, and the Corps Commander, Freyberg.

GOC NZ Corps, Dimoline, Kippenberger.

. . . the bombs explode close by New Zealand HQ: the Americans have missed the target again, a not unusual occurrence!

What was left of the Round House — the engine sheds — with the Hummock behind on the left.

Looking at the Station ruin, and upwards: the massif of Monastery Hill. Hangman's Hill is the nob on the left, while the white ruin, top centre, is the monastery.

Monastery Hill with the abbey on top, the town at the base.

Road approach. The monastery top centre, Hangman's Hill on the left, Castle Hill in front of Monastery Hill.

Closer: Castle Hill in the foreground. Ravine to the right up to Monastery Hill (Point 516) and Point 445. Hangman's Hill on the left.

Closer still. Note the accumulation of ruins at the base of Castle Hill. In the background, Monastery Hill on the left, 445 on the right.

Closer: right under Castle Hill. A rugged climb for infantry. The monastery behind Castle Hill; Point 445 on the right.

Right under Castle Hill in the town. A sniper's paradise. Castle Hill rises on the right; Monastery Hill rises in the left background.

The town: one of the less damaged streets: still impassable for tanks.

The reality of war. In the rubbish of battle, a decomposing solider lies unburied.

Below: the town: the heart of the problem. No armour could get in, and infantry advancing would be exposed while defenders could be ideally concealed. For scale, see the tiny soldier in the right shadow!

The front of the Continental Hotel: the holes were fire positions for Neuhoff's paratroopers. No infantry could live where the cameraman is standing. Note the road in front.

The jaws of death: the impregnable Continental Hotel. The following shot is taken from here.

Paratroopers' view from the Continental Hotel, looking straight down a now cleared Route 6. The New Zealand infantry had to attack towards the camera, into the mincer.

From the same position, looking hard right, along Route 6 from the corner, foreground. The road runs along the base of Monastery Hill in the direction of the Baron's Palace and the Liri Valley. The Hotel Des Roses is along on the right of the road. These photos represent the tactical prize NZ Corps wanted: a road to run tanks through to the Liri.

The GOC takes Fraser on a tour of the ruins. Puttick is the officer after Freyberg.

Beyond Cassino. Freyberg and his officers look out over open country.

easily called in: the German mortar teams knew where their defensive positions were because they had carefully measured their exact locations.

Freyberg reacted to the failure of the Indian Brigade attack by trying to persuade Dimoline to move to a two-brigade front on a more direct route, via 445, and bypass 593. Dimoline said that his brigade commander was convinced that 593 was the key to getting on to the monastery position.[86] He said that 593 would be taken that night, and that the main attack would go in the next night, 17/18 February. Freyberg reminded Dimoline that the main attack would have to go in the next night, come what may.

Clark rang NZ Corps headquarters to say that the promised air support would have to be used over the beach-head. He later told Freyberg that he would approach the Desert Air Force for some air support. Freyberg retorted that the main attack by NZ Corps would still go in on the next night.

The afternoon conversation with Clark must have borne some fruit, because when Dimoline rang Freyberg at 7.30 p.m., he said that bombing and strafing by 'three lots of about 16' aircraft on the north-east spur had been 'very good indeed'.[87] It was the Army commander who had prevailed upon the air force: Freyberg was at their whim in terms of when they decided to assist. This lack of direct Corps–Army co-operation meant that the air attack took place many hours before the infantry assault. Infantry could not live on the open ground in the hills in daylight.

On the night of Wednesday 16 February, 1 Royal Sussex were once more to attack Point 593. The shortage of mortar bombs was solved by using salvaged American bombs in German and Italian mortars brought back from North Africa. The American bombs would not fit British mortars. A request for grenades resulted in a half-hour delay, until more arrived by mule. The mules had been shelled, however, and less than half the numbers of grenades arrived.[88] Finally, at around 11.30 p.m., the attack was ready to go forward. This time the whole battalion was to be used.

Here the Allied artillery intervened to assist the German defenders. To lessen enfilading fire on the attacking force from Point 575, some 800 yards distant from 593, the guns firing from the valley west of Cassino had to put their shells low over the heads of the attacking force in order to be able to reach Point 575. Majdalany insisted that the shells:

> ... had to skim the top of the Snakeshead by a few feet, and gunnery as precise as this allowed no margin for error. The tiniest fraction of a variation in elevation and the shells would hit the [ridge] top ... This is precisely what happened. As the two leading companies ... formed up on the start-line of the attack, the artillery opened up on Pt. 575. But several shells failed to clear the Snakeshead, and burst among the leading companies and Battalion HQ. It is axiomatic that the most demoralising beginning to any operation is for the attacking force to

> be shelled on its own start-line. It is not less disturbing if the shells happen to be from its own guns.[89]

Despite having been assaulted by their own artillery, 1 Royal Sussex proceeded to attack. The sour failure of the attack is representative of the host of minor tactical dangers that awaited such a foray in the hills that were the natural outer bastions of Monastery Hill. 'B' Company, making initial headway against the lower positions, ran into heavy fire from the crest positions on Point 593. The few that made it to the top and over were taken prisoner, or fell over the small concealed cliffs beyond. 'A' Company was blocked off by unmarked ravines to the front and left. As a few of 'D' Company made it to the crest of 593, a German fortuitously fired three green Very lights, the signal for the Royal Sussex to withdraw. The crest men, the rest of 'D' Company hemmed in by a ravine, and the remnants of 'B' Company, retired. A final effort by 'B' Company got nowhere in the face of heavy machine-gun fire and numerous grenades. The battalion retreated with ten officers and 130 others as casualties. The two attacks had taken their toll on 1 Royal Sussex: in two nights twelve out of fifteen officers and 162 out of 313 men had become casualties.

Early on 17 February, 4 Indian Division reported that the attack on Point 593 had failed with casualties. At around 7 a.m., Freyberg spoke to Dimoline:

> GOC said 'It is a tough nut. It looks formidable to me. DAF [Desert Air Force] coming over today. The other show looks easier than 593.' Brig Dimoline 'I am beginning to think you are right, sir.' GOC continued 'I want to go on a broad front. You want to get your assembly right and your artillery . . .'[90]

The failure to take Point 593 could not be helped. The attack must now go in without holding the start line planned for the Royal Sussex. The direction of the attack was now altered to the thrust through the area of Point 445, to the left of the Snakeshead Ridge, topped by 593 still blocking the route to the rear of the ruined monastery. Freyberg hoped the Indian Division would do better by leaving 593, and would be able to reach the top of Monastery Hill and take the ruin and the eastern slopes. They would then link with the NZ Division who were to push along the railway embankment followed by the tanks of the American Combat Group. The embankment there bridged, would become a tank road beyond the town, running parallel to Route 6, round the base of Monastery Hill, into the Liri. If the Indian Division could take the forward slopes of Monastery Hill the two divisions should be able to link up.

At 10.50 a.m., Freyberg spoke to the GSO1 of 4 Indian Division who commented that the brigade commander of 7 Brigade was happy about the projected plan for 'tonight'. Freyberg affirmed that the NZ Division was going for the railway station. It was noted that the Desert Air Force had been grounded.[91]

The chief of staff of 5th Army rang Freyberg and informed him that an enemy offensive at the Anzio beach-head had made some progress, but there were serious developments. Freyberg told Gruenther that NZ Corps' attack was set up and ready for that night. At 3 p.m., Freyberg left for 5th Army headquarters. Major John White noted that 'GOC is clearly anxious over tonight's attack. Calm but preoccupied.'[92]

Freyberg talked over the plans with Weir, the CRA, at 7.45 p.m. He said he would have preferred to have the high ground already in their hands. He judged that Point 593 was of minor importance now, and that Indian Division would do themselves little good by persisting in that goal. Weir disagreed — he thought that for the Indian infantry to hold Monastery Hill they must have 593. He rang the CRA again after dinner, and checked the artillery support: 150 rounds per gun for 5 NZ Brigade, and 450 rounds per gun for 4 Indian Division. Weir said that the attack would need it all. There was also to be a large counter-battery programme. In all, there were around 500 guns, including those from the British X Corps and the French Expeditionary Corps, that could reach.[93]

A realization that the Cassino defences were formidable grew in NZ Corps. NZ Corps Intelligence Summary No. 27, of 1800 hours, 17 February, detailed information from a prisoner of war taken by US 36 Division and identified as belonging to 200 Grenadier Regiment:

> [He] says there is another defensive position running from [numbered map references]. He states that he was in bunkers in this area for several days and that they are from 50 to 80 metres apart. He says the roof is composed of steel 3cm thick, concrete 50cm thick, and enough dirt to make the roof . . . 2½ metres thick. MG positions are in special built positions . . . and from his description the pill-boxes may be the portable 'crab' discussed in a previous report.[94]

NZ Corps attacked on two geographically disconnected fronts. 4 Indian Division attacked in the hills, with the object of seizing Monastery Hill. NZ Division thrust in south of the town to gain the railway embankment and an alternative route into the Liri Valley.

In the Indian attack, five battalions were used: the 4/6 Rajputana Rifles, the remnants of 1 Royal Sussex, 1/9 Gurkha Rifles, and 4/16 Punjab Regiment. These battalions were intended to take a series of Points — 445, 444, 593, 569 — almost at the same time; once these were held, the way would be open to the monastery.

The 4/6 Rajputanas began at midnight, 17/18 February, and at 3.30 a.m. reported that Point 593 was in their hands, though still bitterly contested by the enemy. The attack on Point 593 began two hours before the other action. It was believed to be urgent to subdue 593 first.

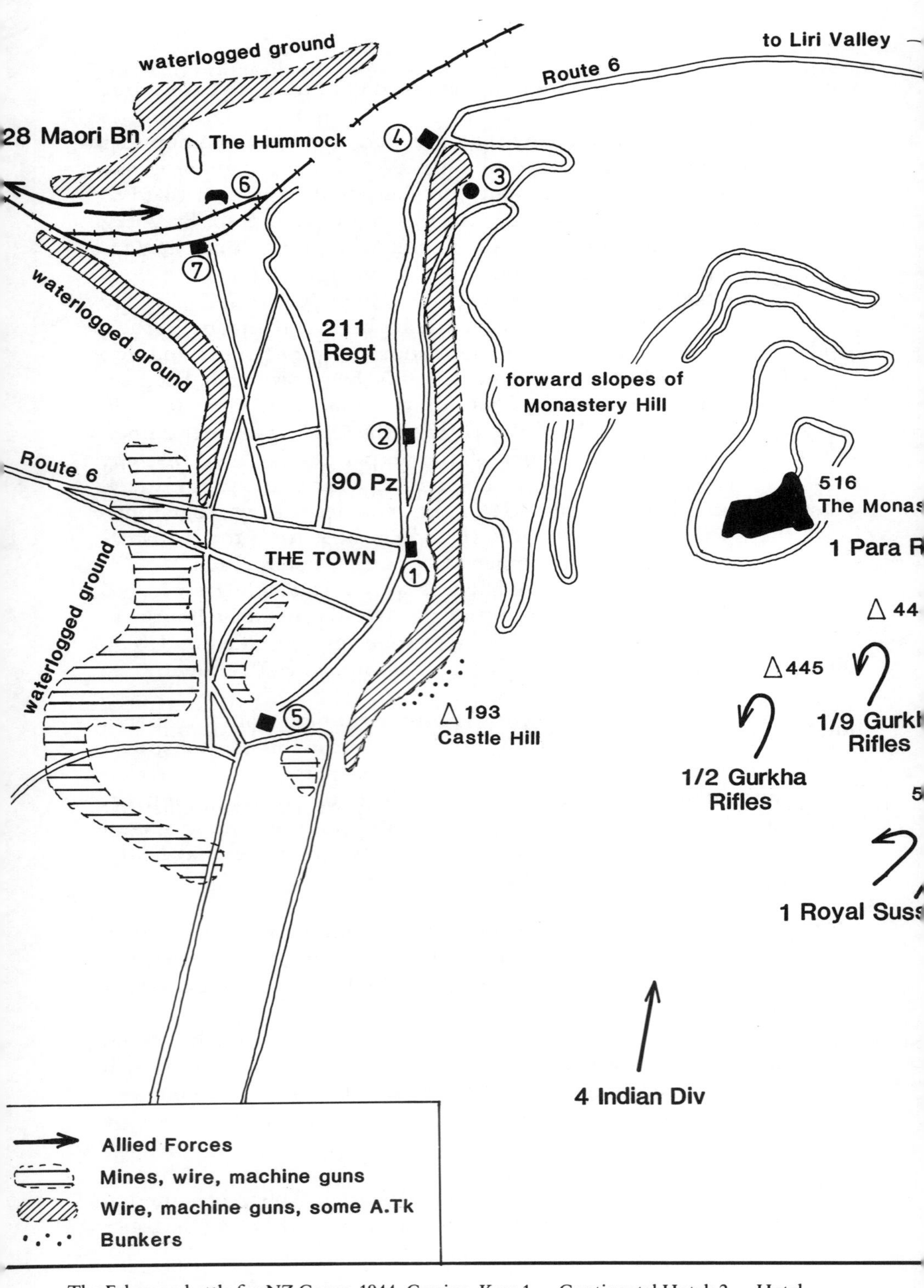

The February battle for NZ Corps, 1944, Cassino. Key: 1 — Continental Hotel; 2 — Hotel Des Roses; 3 — Colosseum; 4 — Baron's Palace; 5 — jail; 6 — Round House (engine sheds); 7 — railway station.

Around 2 a.m., 1/9 Gurkhas started to drive in the direction of Point 444 and the monastery. 'A' Company was caught in heavy machine-gun fire, sending them off in the direction of Point 450. 'B' Company mounted an assault on 593 and 569, but failed to make ground. 'C' Company was sent into the gap, and 'D' Company followed later towards 'A' Company. The attack of 1/9 Gurkhas was diffused.

Even worse, 1/2 Gurkhas were to take 445 and move on to the monastery, but suffered disaster immediately. There was scrub in front of them. Their commanding officer's orders had said 'Reach . . . [scrub] as quickly as possible. Do not pause for a fire-fight or mop up. If enemy throws grenades, rush him.'[95] The Gurkhas charged. The scrub was actually thick thorn bushes full of mines and tripwires leading to booby-traps. Within the thorn:

> German emplacements [were] so close that they were within a grenade's throw of the start line and yet completely hidden in the darkness. The German defences were based on machine gun posts, fifty yards apart, between . . . [which] were weapon pits, each containing one man with a machine pistol and a large number of grenades.[96]

In ten minutes the two forward companies lost two-thirds of their men. The other companies got no further. By 5 a.m. 1/2 Gurkhas were back where they had begun, having lost eleven officers and 138 men.[97] The forward battalions of 7 Brigade had suffered 530 casualties.[98] Optimistic reports reached NZ Corps headquarters in the course of the morning, but, by the early afternoon, it was clear 4 Indian Division's attempt had failed:

> 1330 [hours] G1 4 Ind Div rang to pass on report from Dimoline that Boche has a very strong position in horseshoe from 575 (west of 569) to 569 right round to the monastery, with MGs positions with steel and concrete pill boxes. It was as a result of that, last nights party was expensive. . . It is considered a waste of time to batter at that position from our present line. . .[99]

In the Rapido Valley, south of the town, 28th Maori Battalion and the NZ Division Engineers, set out along the railway embankment in the direction of the station.

The German defences in this area were centred on the station, its engine sheds, and a small but significant hillock of rising ground to the south of the station, known as the 'Hummock'. The ground either side of the embankment before the station was wired, with machine-gun posts behind. Had the ground been dry, there would have been two extensive areas of flat land on which to deploy infantry. The weather had been kind to the Germans. It was wet and they had aided this advantage by flooding these flat areas so that they were waterlogged — too soft for tanks, and too much under water for infantry to be easily deployed. Wire and mines increased the defenders' advantage and the result was that only one New Zealand battalion could be sent forward, and this could be only on a two company frontage.

The attack began at around 11.30 p.m., with darkness masking the advance of the Maori infantry, who rolled forward with the energy and panache that the 28th Battalion displayed in its assault roles. Despite machine-gun posts, wire, the mines, and the narrowness of the frontage, the leading companies had reached the station yards by midnight. At the crucial moment two men flung themselves on the wire and the Maori attacked with bayonets and grenades. The enemy posts were eliminated, the wire removed, and the rest of 'B' Company drove into the yards to attack the defenders of the engine sheds.

In the meantime, 'A' Company had advanced on the left, but had been held up in front of the Hummock. On the Hummock were well-emplaced German machine-gunners covering the flooded creek at the bottom which had been laced with wire and mines. 'A' Company could do nothing but keep the enemy under fire. They tried to find a flank, but none could be found.[100]

The Germans had blown up the embankment in several places and the engineers had begun work on these, covered by the forward infantry. By 2 a.m., the engineers were working on three of the demolitions at once, with one untouched. At 3 a.m., however, the moon came up and the Germans gained a clearer knowledge of the intentions of the New Zealand troops. Mortar and machine-gun fire swept the demolition areas, and on occasion the engineers had been compelled to stop. The Rapido River had been crossed but the demolitions were not completed and, shortly before daylight, the engineers were withdrawn, after heavier enemy fire, to await an artillery smoke-screen.

After dawn at 7 a.m. the Germans began their counter-attack. Covered by fire from a concealed tank, a scratch force of 211 Regiment set out from the town for the station. The Maori companies who observed them called down a heavy concentration of artillery fire and broke up the attack. Several sections of enemy tried to make it to the station. More support fire — smoke and high explosive — were called for. The 28th's companies were cut off from the Division, and the wind dispersed the smoke. To maintain the screen the 4 Field Regiment fired more than 9000 rounds of smoke shell. It was necessary for the Maori to hold out to allow the engineers to complete their work during the night.

This was not to be. Using the NZ Corps' smoke-screen as cover, the Germans sent more infantry and two tanks into the station area, under heavy covering fire of mortars, machine-guns, and German artillery. German infantry and tanks were now too close to be engaged by New Zealand artillery. The Maori possessed no anti-tank guns to answer the tanks' close-range fire. 'B' Company's radio had ceased to function during the fighting, and the first warning of diaster came when the remnants of the two companies arrived from over the Rapido part of the embankment at around 4 p.m. With them were the remnant of 'A' Company. Of the 200 soldiers that had set out, only sixty-six returned: forty from 'A' Company and a bare twenty-six from 'B' Company. Some stragglers made it back later, some greviously wounded.[101]

The February attack, operation Avenger, had gained little. Freyberg had been forced to use the Americans' positions as his starting place, in the high ground above the Rapido. Unless the hillocks were taken, the top of Monastery Hill could not be taken. The 4 Indian Division had been served badly by US 2 Corps. The forward positions were not as the Americans they relieved had described. This meant that the Division had to battle for a start line which it never really gained. This in turn led to postponement after postponement of the opening of the attack, to Freyberg's frustration and annoyance. Dimoline had the worst of all worlds: he required the bombing of the monastery to neutralize the defence. When it came, it came at a time when he could not even take advantage of the misapplication of air power.

The air support that came was not what Freyberg had asked for. It came conditional on an air force timetable, and applied an inappropriate solution to the infantry's problem. Clark's concern was to persuade Freyberg to assault the enemy positions as quickly as possible, not with concern for a NZ Corps success but because this attack would take pressure off the counter-attacked Allied forces at Anzio. Clark showed little interest in the NZ Corps' problems or in their attacks.

The natural defences in the Cassino position had been made virtually impregnable by the Germans. The Indian Division ran into the troops of the veteran 1st Parachute Division on the heights. With failure in the hills, even success by the NZ Division at the station would have been very conditional. Neither the high ground above, nor the town, had been neutralized, and it is not likely that an armoured push would have moved far.

CHAPTER 8

The Impossible Dream

The NZ Corps' second battle of Cassino took place nearly a month after the February repulses, though it was never intended that such a lengthy period of delay should ensue. The battle plan had its origins in a conversation between the commander of NZ Corps, and his CRA, soon after news had been received of the Maori Battalion companies' eviction from the railway station. They had been lamenting the lack of an anti-tank gun which might have prevented the withdrawal of the 28th Battalion's companies:

> 1715 [hours, 18 February] Spoke to CRA who felt they should have got the 17 pr [pounder] up. Tanks apparently came from the north, infantry from the west, crossing the old railway bridge. GOC commented 'A well executed operation'. CRA agreed that this setback prejudices the whole plan because of the bridges near by. GOC said he did not think the attack on the convent [the monastery] was on — too costly. He asked CRA whether he thought turning the enemy out of the village [Cassino town] would turn the position. CRA thought not. Had to get a considerable way beyond that. They agreed it might be a first step but it would also be a tough nut. House to house fighting. GOC commented that a river crossing is not a very attractive proposition and cannot be done silently. [He was thinking of the Rapido at St Angelo.] GOC 'I think the only thing is to clear them out of the village.' CRA 'It looks a bit like that.' If so, a carefully laid on plan to demolish with heavy bombing co-ordinating with withdrawal of our troops and followed by assault, would be necessary.[1]

Already, on 18 February, the General was thinking of another way to attack and break through the Cassino deadlock. Despite the losses to both 7 Brigade of 4 Indian Division and two of the Maori Battalion's companies, NZ Corps still possessed enough infantry for another attack. Besides, on 18 February the British 78 Division, under General Keightley, had come under Freyberg's command as part of NZ Corps. This brought NZ Corps' infantry strength to at least twenty battalions, not including the four battalions mauled in the February attacks. As well there were over three hundred tanks in the two armoured formations, and the reconnaissance units of the NZ, 4 Indian, and 78 Divisions all possessed armoured vehicles of some sort. Artillery strength was now greatly increased, both in the numbers and calibre of guns that could be used against the Cassino position. At the battle's height, over 900 guns could and would be called on. In open country, NZ Corps with these resources would have seemed unstoppable. But this was not open country.

On 19 February the General discussed the possibilities of further operations with the commander of the NZ Division, Major-General H. Kippenberger:

> . . . rang Kip. GOC said it was either the assault or the river crossing. Kip said he was inclined to give the latter a go but thought it would fail — fail disastrously. GOC 'I think it gives the best chance for attacking the village [Cassino town]. It would open up a new situation. Would give a chance of getting tanks over river.' Kip: 'It is the only plan I can see.'[2]

The choices facing Freyberg were daunting. NZ Corps could not make a deep outflanking movement in the mountains because of the lack of mule transport, and the attendant possibility that a move in this direction might not achieve the turning of the Cassino position. If troops got through to the Liri after such a move, they would lack artillery and armour, which could not follow over the mountainous terrain. A large body of infantry would then have to await a breakthrough by the armour into the Liri. It was just possible that the Germans would not obligingly vacate the Cassino defences just because some more troops were in the rear. The grounds for such considerations rested in part upon the fact that the Germans had simply stayed put with the invasion in the rear at Anzio. They had scratched together bits of units that proved to be enough to discourage an Allied break out from the beach-head. This may also have been later borne out when operation 'Diadem' took place in May 1944. A large number of divisions broke through on a wide front. The Polish Corps was to take the Cassino position. The defence was just as stubborn, in spite of the Allies pouring past into the rear areas. The point is that a smaller scale movement round the flank did not solve the problem — how to get the armour into the Liri Valley and drive for Rome.

The idea of a river crossing at St Angelo to reach the Liri was as fraught with difficulties: a repeat of the US 36 Division's débâcle would be the most likely result. The only other way was to find a route through the Cassino position, one that would negate the hilltops and reach Route 6 and the Liri. It would be suicidal to go straight up Route 6: the approach was under the enemy guns all the way. The only other option, apart from not attacking at all, was to take the town of Cassino, coming from an oblique angle from the north, close in beside Castle Hill (Point 193). This had the advantage that the hillocks higher up were masked to some extent by the Castle ridge, and provided that position could be taken as a flank drive, the attackers would get into the town. The approach was on a narrow front, but because of the nature of the German preparations, all approaches were designed to be narrow.

The other option, of doing nothing, was not permitted to the NZ Corps commander. Clark required action that would take the pressure from Anzio. Allied subordinates could not pick and choose their battles, especially when Clark insisted that the New Zealand commander assumed too many privileges. It has been established that the town of Cassino was fortified well before the battles began. Air support was needed to take the town and Freyberg envisaged a heavy air attack to neutralize the defences, or at least to make them more vulnerable to an infantry assault. Freyberg planned an attack immediately to follow the aerial bombardment, to go in before the garrison of Cassino had time to recover.

On the night of 19 February, Freyberg visited 5th Army headquarters and obtained approval from the Army commander, and also from Alexander and Wilson who were then visiting 5th Army. On 20 February Wilson warned the chiefs of staff of the risks entailed:

> ...based upon a personal visit to V Army on 19 February ... The situation at Cassino is one of considerable difficulty. In addition to the exhaustion of II US Corps and French Corps, there is a risk of using up the NZ Corps prematurely ... The situation at Anzio must NOT be allowed to cause plans to be rushed or attacks launched until everything is ready. We CANNOT afford a failure.[3]

The preparations were, nonetheless, hurried along. Clark, the Army Commander who seemed to consider the NZ Corps to be expendable, wanted exactly what Wilson did not: another diversion for Anzio. The situation at the beach-head quietened and the urgency of a Cassino victory lessened, yet neither Clark nor Alexander cancelled the operation. Freyberg had been ordered to take the Cassino position and break through to the Liri — until they said otherwise he was to find a way to do it. The preparations went ahead.

As far as the air attack was concerned, the senior airmen were somewhat divided as to the likely effects of bombing the town. Major-General Cannon, commander of the Mediterranean Allied Tactical Air Force thought that it was possible to 'whip out Cassino like an old tooth'.[4] General Eaker, on the other hand, wrote to the US Air chief of staff that:

> Little useful purpose is served by our blasting the opposition unless the Army does follow through ... Personally, I do not feel it will throw the German out of his present position completely or entirely ... if he decides to hold to the last man ..[5]

Eaker's last line, in view of the change in the town's garrison prior to the attack, was an omen. Freyberg was not privy to the doubts felt by Eaker and the air preparations went on with speed.

A meeting took place at 1100 hours on 21 February 1944 at NZ Corps headquarters to work out air and artillery policy for the forthcoming NZ Corps attack. The minutes recorded:

1. *POLICY*
   (a) The weight of air effort available was estimated at
      (i) *Strategical Air Force*
      12 gps of heavy bombers, approx 360 aircraft.
      Bomb load approx 900 tons.
      (ii) *Medium Bombers*
      5 gps, approx 200 aircraft
      Bomb load approx 180 tons.
      (iii) *Fighter-Bombers*
      This effort would probably be required at the beachhead and could NOT BE considered in the estimate.
      Fighter bombers might be available after 1600 hours, see para 3(c)(ii).
   Total weight of air effort available approx 1080 tons.
   (b) *Target area*
   It was decided that in order to get the maximum effect from bombing the size of the target must be kept as small as possible. In order to cover the town and defences around the town it was considered that two aiming points would be necessary. These to be decided later.
   (c) *Possibility of 'turn around' for aircraft*
      (i) It would NOT be possible for medium bombers to effect a 'turn around' under four hours.
      (ii) Fighter bombers might become available after an initial sortie on the beachhead.
2. *TIMINGS*
   (a) To obtain full scale air attack, the Air Support Command must decide on D day. GOC [Freyberg] stated that 24 Feb would be the earliest possible day for the ground forces. Decision for D day would be made on the previous night in accordance with weather forecast and availability of aircraft for the next day.
   (b) It would take 3½–4 hours to deliver the air attack.
   (c) Zero hour for the ground attack would be at the conclusion of the bombing, and approx timings were decided upon as follows:

   Air attack from earliest after 0900 hrs up to 1300 hrs. Zero hour 1300 hrs approx.

   These timings are subject to alteration during detailed planning.
   (d) The order in which groups of aircraft attack would be left to the Air Support Command, the general policy being a gradual

increase in tempo with maximum weight of bombs at the end.

(e) During exploitation by armour medium and if available fighter bombers, would give 30 mins air support between 1600 and 1700 hrs on targets to be decided later.

3. *CONTROL*
It was decided that a fwd controller would be established on TROCCHIO, Zero hour would mean 'no more bombs on CASSINO' and any aircraft that came over after zero hour would come under control of the 'fwd controller' would direct them on to previously selected targets outside CASSINO.

4. *ARTY*
(a) The arty bombardment would NOT commence before the air attack.
(b) No smoke would be used until the air attack was over in order to prevent the target being obscured.
(c) Arty of the French Corps would be asked to smoke enemy OPs on the high ground near TERELLE. This is being arranged between Gen LEWIS and Brig. WEIR.
(d) In addition Gen LEWIS is arranging for both 10 Corps and French Corps to carry out counter bty fire on all hostile btys which could bring fire to bear on the attacking infantry.

(Sgd) R. C. QUEREE
Brigadier,
BGS, New Zealand Corps.[6]

Fighter bombers were unlikely to be available because of Anzio. From a tactical viewpoint, these aircraft were desirable for continuing close support. The timing of the attack would be determined by the Air Support Command. Freyberg, a corps commander, was ordered to assault perhaps the most difficult defensive position in Europe, with his attack timed to suit the air force. This is in contrast to Tebaga Gap, where the RAF worked to the Army's timetable, in spite of raging dust storms. At Cassino, the weather was another variable that needed consideration but only an extra 30 minutes was given for air support when the armour attacked with no assurance of fighter-bombers.

Freyberg was not privileged to time his air support but must take the support the air forces gave. Besides this, a number of warnings were given by air force officers. There might be misdirected bombs and the rubble and craters might stop the armour. Freyberg made the point that if his armour was stopped then neither could German armour operate, and obstacles created could be cleared by bulldozers. It was later found that the surviving enemy tanks in Cassino were in fixed positions, and had close air support been available for the infantry, these strong points might have been eliminated. Despite dissatisfaction over air–ground support the concensus view by all at the conference was that if the infantry got in fast, supported by artillery, then there was a good chance of the attack being successful.[7]

The operational instructions for NZ Corps were compiled quickly. Freyberg had informed Air Support Command that the Corps would be ready to attack by 24 February and NZ Division received its orders the day before. Operation 'Dickens', as the attack was code-named, involved considerable readjustments of dispositions, and the weather worsened to delay its implementation. The February battle had suffered from delay after delay and now the new assault became a litany of postponements. As a preliminary for 'Dickens' it was necessary for the airfields in Italy and Sardinia to be dry enough for the bombers to take off to bomb the town. The Liri Valley needed to be dry enough for tanks to operate on roads — one of Alexander's original conditions of 11 February, for without firm ground, exploitation by the armour would be too hazardous. To be sure, there was a precondition of three fine days before the operation, with the likelihood of two more to follow.[8] The weather broke on 23 February, and the operation was postponed for twenty-four hours.

Postponement followed, day after day, for three weeks. The real problem was that the troops, on twenty-four hours notice of readiness, must stay in forward positions in the cold, rain, sleet, and with snow on the higher ground. Morale plummeted, with the weather's impact added to by the sounds of Germans improving their strongholds. Even the General was affected: his GSO1 felt that with the rest of the NZ Division, his heart was no longer in the dangerous and unpleasant task ahead.[9]

With morale low, it plummeted further as a number of necessary changes in command disrupted the familiar organizational patterns. Brigadier Galloway replaced Dimoline as commander of 4 Indian Division, Tuker still being ill. Of all of his subordinates, the man Freyberg could ill afford to lose, Major-General Kippenberger, now became a casualty on 2 March. He stepped on a Schu mine, and lost one foot and badly mangled the other. Freyberg brought Brigadier Parkinson from 6 NZ Brigade to command the NZ Division; Lieutenant-Colonel Bonifant of the Divisional Cavalry took over 6 Brigade, and Major Stace was given command of the Divisional Cavalry. There had already been a change of command in 5 Brigade: Brigadier Hartnell went home on the furlough scheme on 28 February, and Colonel Burrows replaced him. The main senior infantry formation commands, along with the command of the NZ Division, were now with new men. As NZ Corps commands were tied to the senior positions within the division, a particular adaptability was demanded from senior officers to cope with these changing circumstances. Fortunately for the Corps, there was some continuity, for Freyberg still possessed a dependable core, of Queree as BGS, Thornton as GSO1, and Weir as CRA. Weir's task was especially formidable given that the CRA had nearly 1,000 guns at his disposal.

As NZ Corps waited for the elusive code-name 'Bradman' that would signify the beginnings of attack on Cassino, the Germans used the interlude to readjust their deployment and improve their formidable defences. On 25 February the 90 Panzer Grenadier Division, under Baade, turned over its responsibility for the main Cassino position to the élite 1 Parachute Division, under Lieutenant-General Heidrich, the same Heidrich who commanded the 3 Parachute Regiment when it dropped on Crete in 1941. A battle-hardened Parachute Division with a ration strength of around 13,000 and a fighting strength of about 6,000, they were troops who would contest their defences fiercely against an opponent.[10] Some of their number had already proved their metal in the hammering meted out to the 7 Brigade of 4 Indian Division in the February battle.

Heidrich deployed the 1 Parachute Division well. The 3 Parachute Regiment took centre stage, with its II Battalion located in the town of Cassino, I and III Battalions were placed on Monastery Hill, and the Parachute Machine-Gun Battalion south of the town. The 4 Parachute Regiment had II Battalion at Albaneta Farm and I and III Battalions on Colle St Angelo. I and II Battalions of 1 Parachute Regiment faced Castellone, and IV Alpine Battalion was on distant Monte Cairo. The 3 Parachute Regiment on which the main blows would fall was commanded by Colonel Heilmann who also commanded II Battalion, 8 Panzer Grenadier Regiment from 3 Panzer Grenadier Division. To the south of the 1 Parachute Division was the 15 Panzer Grenadier Division, while to the north centred on Terelle was the 44 Hoch und Deutschland Infantry Division.[11]

The zeal with which the paratroops set about their tasks may be seen in one of the minor problems the commander of XIV Panzer Corps experienced with them. Von Senger wrote in his diary:

> . . . it was never possible to obtain a clear picture of the course of the battle from the Command Post of Regiment 3 [Heilmann]. The Paratroops were in the habit of not reporting the smaller losses of ground, because they hoped soon to recover it. Often reports from the Corps artillery, which I had allocated in good measure to this division, were more accurate.[12]

The parachutists set about with haste to improve their defences and add to their supplies of food and ammunition. They were determined to hold the Cassino position.

Freyberg's Corps also prepared with exactitude and with attention to the need to form huge artillery shell reserves. The artillery of NZ Corps used great numbers of shells, so much so that on 8 March, the field artillery had to restrict firing during the lull to twenty-five rounds per gun per day, and the mediums to twenty rounds. The power of the concentrations of guns may be seen in the comments of the CRA, NZ Corps:

> . . . Another time I plainly saw a three-gun self-propelled battery emerge from Santa Lucia and go into action north of Route 6. I gave no orders but merely watched. In a matter of a few minutes hundreds of shells arrived and smothered the three guns, leaving them blackened skeletons.[13]

An attempt to win close air support from fighter-bombers is evidenced in Air Support Instruction for the NZ Division, issued on 11 March. The instruction ordered:

> An Air Controller will accompany Tac 2 NZ Div who is capable of speaking to fighter-bomber aircraft while they are in the air approaching their targets. He has no direct contact with aerodromes or air sp control.
>
> 5. *AIR PROGRAMME ON 'D' DAY*
>   (a) Lt, med and hy bombers will be exclusively engaged on concentrated attacks on CASSINO area up to zero hr.
>   (b) Fighter-bombers will attack the targets set out hereunder at frequent intervals from 1300 hrs until approx 1700 hrs, depending upon the turn-around of aircraft:—
>   (i) CASSINO rly sta until directed by controller at Tac 2 Div on to rd junc [map reference]:
>   (ii) Area [same] rd junc [map ref.] until directed on to pt 435 [map ref.]:
>   (iii) Area of pt 435 as long as required.
>   (c) In the event of last target being no longer required, fighter-bombers can be directed on to enemy areas along Highway 6 by the controller.
>   (d) Pinpoint targets within the areas given in (b) above can be heavily attacked if a request is passed to controller.
>   (e) Other than the variations quoted in (c) and (d) above, NO direct air sp on to outside targets is available on this day.
> 6. *AIR PROGRAMME FOR D PLUS 1 DAY*
>   (a) Up to 1100 hrs lt and med bombers attack the following five points in the order of priority . . . [map references follow, numbered i to v]
>   (b) These targets may be attacked again . . . if required . . .
>   (c) All fighter-bombers during this day are allotted to answer impromptu calls for direct air sp. Those calls may be done either through tcls in the normal manner or through HQ 2 NZ Div. The estimated time for answers to calls is two hours.[14]

By this order fighter-bombers could be tasked by the controller at Tactical

2 NZ Division, but not much variation on flight plans was permitted. The controller's main problem was that if bombing by the main force of bombers transformed the terrain of the town, the areas that the fighter-bombers were restricted to might be unrecognizable. For the second day there was a provision for impromptu calls for fighter-bombers to address targets. But the estimated response time was two hours. A target in one place might not be there two hours later.

The relatively small area of flying space over Cassino town called for an improved variant on the Desert Air Force's provision at Tebaga Gap. Very precise flying and bombing, on a cab-rank basis, was needed so that aircraft were called down from overhead when needed. The air forces did not provide that. It came down to the same old trouble — air doctrine's precedence over the needs of ground support.

The Ides of March proved to be the opening day of the March battle. At 8.30 a.m. the first of 455 aircraft arrived over the town of Cassino. These consisted of 164 Liberators and 114 Fortresses — the heavies; 105 Marauders and 72 Mitchells — the mediums. In the course of three and a half hours, over 990 tons of high explosive were dropped — some 2,223 one thousand pound bombs. Not all the bombs hit the target, a number of aircraft lost their way and nearly half the bombs fell in a mile radius of the centre of the town.[15] The town itself was abruptly transformed into an almost unrecognizable landscape of white-grey ruins, and heaps of rubble and deep bomb craters lay across roads and where buildings had been. Some walls and shells of buildings survived, and the bottom floors of multi-storey buildings sometimes remained sufficiently intact to shelter built-in tanks and gun positions. The Continental Hotel was the best example of this. For the paratroopers in the town, it was an endless nightmare. Lieutenant Schuster of No. 7 Company, 3 Parachute Regiment recounted:

> Tensely we waited in our holes for the bombs to drop. Then they came . . . The whole earth quaked and shuddered under the impact. Then a sudden silence. Hardly had the dust settled a little than I dashed out to visit the other two strongpoints. I stumbled blindly about in a welter of craters . . . and then the next great wave . . . I could not go back. I remained where I was . . . We could no longer see each other; all we could do was to touch and feel the next man. The blackness of the night enveloped us, and on our tongues was the taste of burnt earth. 'I'll come again,' I said, felt my way towards the exit and rolled out into a crater. I had to grope my way forward as though in a dense fog, crawling, falling, leaping; as I reached my post, another wave was on the way in. The men pulled me head over heels into our hole. Then down came the bombs again. A pause, and once more I groped my way across the tortured earth. Direct hits — here, here and here; a hand sticking out of the debris told me what had happened. When I got back,

> the men read in my eyes what I had seen . . . The crash of bursting bombs increased in intensity. We clung to each other, instinctively keeping our mouths open. It went on and on. Time no longer existed, everything was unreal. We shifted our positions and, well, we thought, if we can move, we're still alive — sixteen of us.
> Rubble and dust came pouring down into our hole. Breathing became a desperate and urgent business. At all costs we had to avoid being suffocated, buried alive. Crouching in silence, we waited for the pitiless hail to end.[16]

The 3 Parachute Regiment was less than full strength at Cassino, having not made up the losses of Ortona. Now with just over 300 men, they lost over half their strength in the bombing. No. 7 Company was nearly wiped out and No. 5 and No. 8 were reduced to twenty to thirty paratroops each. Only No. 6 Company had managed to survive untouched: its troopers had gone into a rocky cave with II Battalion headquarters, below Monastery Hill.[17]

Despite the intensity of the bombing, these losses did not deter the paratroops from defending Cassino. The bombing had actually given them something of an advantage, even if it had cost them sorely. Outside the town were 890 NZ Corps guns, nearly 400 tanks, and twenty battalions of infantry. But to enter they must move throught the rubble heaps and craters into a landscape that no longer corresponded with anything on a map, or to the remembered layout of the town.

In the afternoon, when the bombing ceased, the 890 guns of the Allied artillery opened a bombardment equivalent to about 36 per cent of the entire artillery support for the March battle.[18] Some 195,969 rounds were fired to support the attack. The artillery churned up the rubble and made even more craters in the town area. Cassino became a giant rubbish heap, in which an increasingly bitter tangled battle would develop, fought in each corner, each wall, each cellar, room, hole — at times by troops separated only by the thickness of a wall. The Germans in Cassino had suffered grevious losses, and numerically their hold on the devastated town was slender. Yet numbers were not all important. The air attack provided even more of a chance of keeping the Allied armour at bay, and had ensured that the attacking infantry could enter only in driblets, with little elbow room to admit more without a congestion that would simply provide the defenders with more targets. Moreover, the damage to the town had not been even in its spread. Although the buildings overall had been blasted into ruins, those in the southern area of the town had suffered less. Thus the Continental Hotel was a ruin in terms of its peacetime role, but enough of the bottom floor had survived intact for the guns and defenders to be ready to repel all comers. As the Continental Hotel sat squarely on the right-angled corner of Route 6 inside the town, its continued possession by the paratroopers would prevent any armour going through to the Liri Valley. And this, along with the Hotel Des Roses, was not the only position in the southern part of Cassino over which the Allied infantry would have to struggle. Where the heaviest damage from the bombing lay was in the congested built-up area north of the Continental, between it and the base of Castle Hill. Here, bomb damage had simply created an impassable wilderness for vehicles.

To the Allied troops waiting for the bombing to cease, it had seemed that nothing could survive the explosive maelstrom. It was now time to attack. The NZ 6 Brigade was to advance on the town from the north supported by tanks from 19 Armoured Regiment. The first objective was the Quisling Line, the stretch of Route 6 running into the town area to the Continental Hotel, to be reached by 2 p.m. at the rate of 100 yards every ten minutes. The 25 Battalion was to do this, and also to take Castle Hill — Point 193 — which dominated 4 Indian Division's approach to the town. Following the 25th Battalion would be the 24th and 26th Battalions. After reaching Route 6, these two would go further through to the railway station and the Baron's Palace, known as the Jockey Line. This would be reached by dusk on the first day, to allow the American armour to slip through and make the penetration of the Liri Valley. The 5 Brigade of 4 Indian Division would in the meantime have taken over Castle Hill from the New Zealand infantry, and by leap-frogging along the face of Monastery Hill, secure one of the high points, Hangman's Hill.[19] This done, a build-up on Hangman's Hill would take place, and the monastery itself assaulted. At that stage, the highest point in the local enemy defences would be in Allied hands, and the flank of the thrust into the Liri secured.

Getting through to the Liri with secure flanks was the aim for NZ Corps. By contrast, Colonel Heilmann's task, in spite of his straightened numbers, was simpler. He had to keep the Allies out, and their hands off Route 6. For Freyberg a draw would mean defeat and another repulse. For Heidrich and Heilmann in the town, a win was impossible: the numerical supremacy of the NZ Corps alone was too great. A draw in which NZ Corps was denied its breakthrough to the Liri would, however, be as good as a win. For the Germans, concealment, effective fire, and counter-attack when necessary would be the methods needed for holding on. For NZ Corps' infantry to advance would mean leaving cover and exposure to fire, a procedure all the more desperate if the tanks could not accompany them into the ruins of the town.

As an omen of the difficulties to come, one of the two roads into the town from the north had been made completely unusable to tanks and infantry. The attacking force came down the Caruso Road. At this point a large bomb crater held up the tanks for half an hour behind the infantry. The tanks of 19 Armoured Regiment became progressively stalled by other obstacles in the way. Some stopped at the foot of Castle Hill and others could not get through to the Botanic Gardens area, not far before Route

6. Help from the bulldozers of the engineers was asked for, but these vehicles were vulnerable to enemy fire, and they could not be brought in to work effectively on the rubble heaps. Attempts by the tanks to rush the rubble heaps came to nothing, and some tanks became stuck. The infantry went on without tank support.

25th Battalion, under Lieutenant-Colonel MacDuff, led the way into the ruins of the northern area of the town. They looked: '. . . as if it had been raked over by some monster comb and then pounded all over the place by a giant hammer.'[20] The rifle and machine-gun fire that awaited them was fierce, coming from the ruins of closely packed houses in front, and from Castle Hill. This broke down any cohesion in the attacking companies, and it was soon a matter of platoons and sections fighting it out. Craters and debris slowed progress further. Instead of 100 yards in ten minutes, the rate of advance had slowed to near 100 yards an hour — if and when troops could make their way forward. The failure of the radios compounded the situation — runners who were sent back became casualties, and 'C' Company left at the gaol, in reserve, could not establish what was going on forward. 'B' Company could not clear the enemy from the houses at the base of Castle Hill, and 'A' Company moved very slowly in the general direction of Route 6. The one 25th Battalion success was that of 'D' Company. Assigned to take Point 193, the Castle, most of the Company managed to move up a steep ridge running from a ravine. Attacked in the Castle, the paratroopers were driven into the keep, and after some exchanges of fire and grenades, the Germans from I Battalion, 3 Parachute Regiment, surrendered.[21]

In the afternoon:

> From 1300 hrs onwards fighter bombers came over at intervals of approx 8 aircraft every 10 minutes . . . for bombing and strafing . . . a total of 250 . . . sorties were flown and 112 tons of bombs dropped . . .[22]

These aircraft were detailed for three targets: the railway station, the ampitheatre, and Hangman's Hill (Point 435):

> A forward fighter controller was established at NZ Div HQ and was able to switch aircraft to any of these three targets and to any point in relation to them. This controller produced excellent results. Communications worked well and he was able to take on definite pinpoints of mortar positions and machine-gun posts, which appeared in the course of the afternoon to be holding up the advance.[23]

This was the close support that NZ Corps required. However, the targets attacked were not those giving immediate trouble to the attacking NZ infantry; and more acceptable targets could not be identified because the radios had become inoperable and the 'map' face of the town had altered because of the bomb damage. Also fighting had now become so close that only by moving away from the opposition might enough space have been created for the fighter-bombers to operate without hitting their own troops. The artillery barrage in front of the 25th Battalion's original direction of advance also complicated the matter. No forward air controller could have gone forward in a converted tank had one been available: the bomb damage in the town had stopped all armoured movement.

A situation report from NZ Corps at 1900 hours on 15 March reviewed the infantry's progress:

> 6 NZ INF BDE moved off . . . rds leading SOUTH into town badly damaged by bombing and made going for own tks impossible without engr work (.) enemy in some str on 193 feature [map ref] engaged own tps advancing through town below by sniping and MG fire (.) after very hard fighting pt 193 captured at 1630 hrs following inf assault from SOUTH side (.) inf adv SOUTH through town slow in face of strong enemy resistance (.) fwd tps . . . now . . . in house to house fighting (.) . . . tks . . . are unable to get up to fwd inf due to condition of rds through and round town (.) engrs work in town seriously interfered with by accurate enemy SA fire (.) . . . 4 IND DIV . . . 5 IND INF BDE will take over pt 193 [map ref] 1930 hrs and are to continue adv along eastern slopes of MONASTERY HILL (.)[24]

Instead of being well through the main built-up area of the town, the infantry were now caught in the ruins created by the Allied air forces in the morning. Instead of a sound plan operating, where the infantry accompanied by the tanks of 19 Armoured Regiment moved steadily through systematically clearing out the enemy's posts, the attacking elements of infantry and armour had separated. It was a separation that would not be repaired for some time to come.

The movement of the 26th Battalion was held back because of the slow progress of the 25th Battalion. Near dusk, the companies carefully moved into the trackless ruins. It took nearly three hours to reach Route 6, a process hampered by the continued failure of the radios. Two companies were left along the northern fork of Route 6; the other two moved into the area of the Municipal buildings, where the mud of the open Botanical Gardens separated them from the Germans. The General's diary recorded the problem brought by rain:

> Rain is a bit of a nuisance . . . Great difficulty in Cassino is caused by the rubble and sizes of the bomb craters which are also filling with water either from the surface of from under-soil water.[25]

The rain and flooding and emergence of water from a waterlogged water table not only increased the impassibility of Cassino's former streets; it

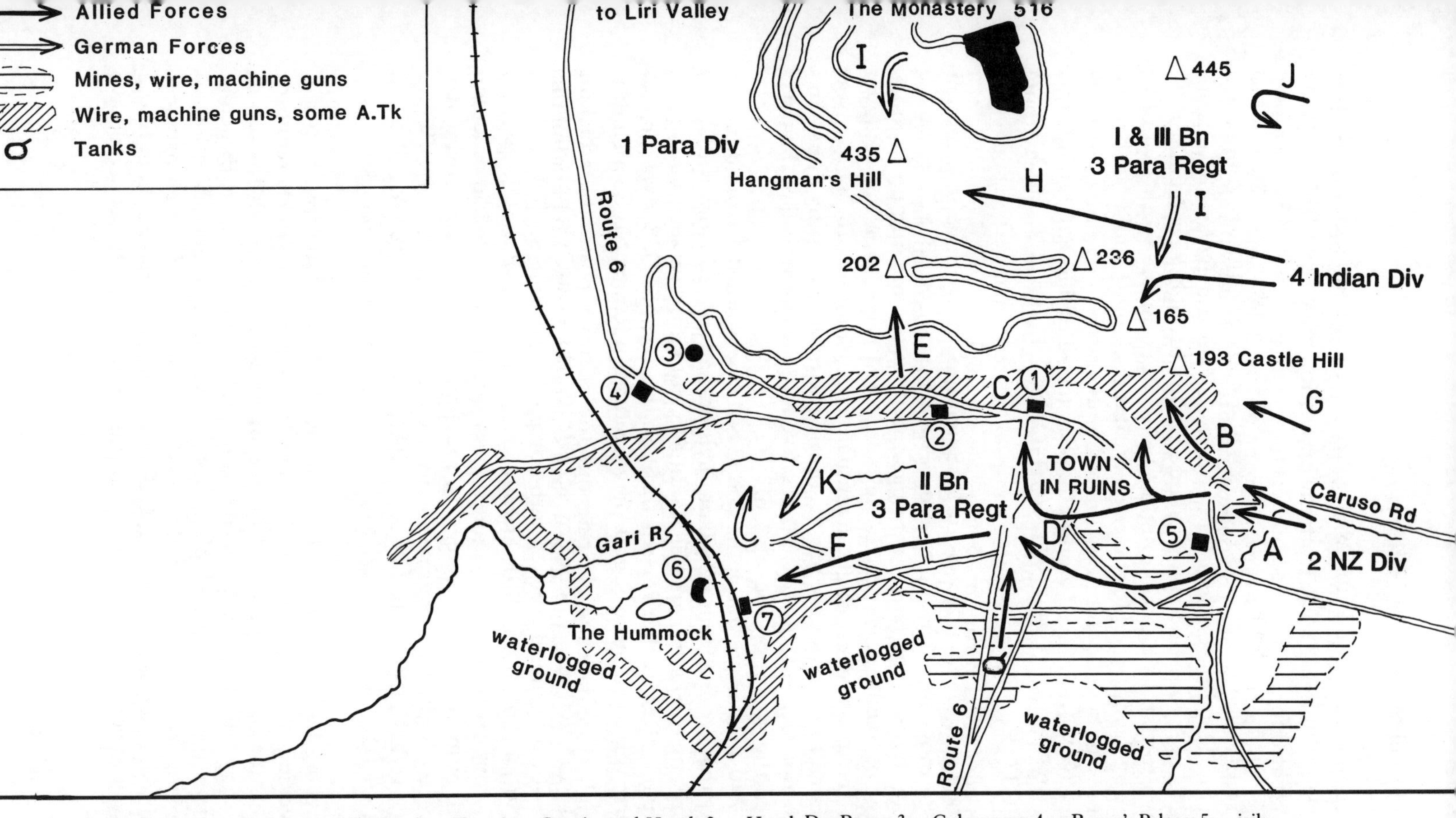

The March battle for NZ Corps, 1944, Cassino. Key: 1 — Continental Hotel; 2 — Hotel Des Roses; 3 — Colosseum; 4 — Baron's Palace; 5 — jail; 6 — Round House (engine sheds); 7 — railway station; A — NZ Infantry enter town; B — 25th NZ Battalion take Castle Hill; C — area of unsuccessful assaults on the Continental Hotel by 25th, 23rd, 28th NZ Battalion, includes face of Castle Hill; D — 24th NZ Battalion fails to drive through town; E — elements of 24th NZ Battalion get Point 202; F — 26th NZ Battalion and 19 Armoured Regiment take the railway station; G — 1/4 Essex and later 6 Royal West Kents hold Castle Hill; H — Hangman's Hill taken by 1/9 Gurkhas; I — German counter-attacks from the monastery, and down on to 165, to 193, and to 435; J — 2/7 Gurkhas fail to take Point 445; K — abortive German attempt to retake railway station is repulsed.

also bound rubble and ruin with mud, giving a consistency of dough. The Situation Report No. 46 from NZ Corps the next morning was not encouraging:

> SITREP 0900 hrs . . . 1/4 ESSEX relieved 25 NZ INF BN on pt 193 . . . by 2230 hrs 15 mar[*sic*](.) . . . h[eav]y rain and extremely difficult going over ruins and craters in nil visibility brought ops in CASSINO town to standstill during night (.) . . . engrs unable work fwd of rd fork by daylight and foot recce indicates tks [tanks] could NOT move at present beyond this pt owing to bomb craters and mines(.) own tks have NOT yet moved along Highway 6 fwd of TROCCHIO(.) total P[O]W . . . 20(.) IDENTIFICATIONS(.) 1 and 2 BNS 3 PARA REGT(.)[26]

The tanks of 1 and 4 Troops of 'A' Squadron, 19 Armoured Regiment were to move into Cassino to support a drive by 26th Battalion for the railway station. The tanks were painfully slow in moving up Route 6, because of bomb craters and the delay imposed as engineers and bridging tanks fixed a way through. Eventually they moved off. Smoke was generated throughout the day to shroud the town area — by guns, tank shells, mortars, and smoke canisters. Even so, the late arrival of the tanks delayed the attack on the station.[27]

At 7.40 a.m. on 16 March the GSO2 NZ Corps noted an unconfirmed report that troops from 4 Indian Division had moved from the Castle Hill area up to Hangman's Hill, Point 435, not far below the monastery.[28] By 9 p.m., after further reports through the day, NZ Corps was able to confirm this small piece of good news. Situation Report No. 53 included:

> SITREP 2100 hrs . . . one coy 1/9 GR [Gurkha Rifles] reported on pt 435 . . . no ground contact with coy possible during daylight(.) 2 NZ DIV(.) 6 INF BDE(.) little change in situation of fwd tps . . . own tks . . . contacted fwd inf . . . route [6] past r[oad] fork . . . in bad condition with numerous bomb craters . . . mov[ement] in fwd areas during day severely limited by accurate enemy SA and mortar fire . . . P[O]W . . . 39(.) IDENTIFICATIONS . . . 1 PARA BN . . . 2 PARA BN . . . 3 PARA BN [note these are Monastery Hill or town troops].[29]

Freyberg had rung General Galloway, of 4 Indian Division, earlier in the evening, and suggested that 5 Indian Brigade should quickly reinforce the Gurkhas on Hangman's Hill, and be prepared to assault the top of Monastery Hill. Galloway replied that he preferred not to divert Brigadier Bateman from his agreed plan, but he would give consideration to improving the firmness of the hold on Point 435 if circumstances permitted. Later in the evening, Galloway remarked that he thought the best way to clear Cassino was to put more infantry in: he seems to have regarded this as a prerequisite for further progress of the Indian Brigade on Monastery Hill.[30]

At 10.10 p.m. 5th Army's chief of staff rang Freyberg and stated the Army commander's disappointment that no attack was going in from the direction of Point 593.[31] He questioned whether tanks might be sent around the back. Freyberg pointed out the difficulties. 4 Indian Division was involved in a nine-hour attack and it was necessary for the NZ Division to continue slowly clearing Cassino. It was odd for Clark to ask about an attack in the hills above the Rapido Valley where the previous two attacks had come to grief, especially so in that he had approved NZ Corps' plan of 23 February, which involved no such diversion.

If the opening of the long and tortuous struggle of the March battle had been unexpectedly difficult for the attackers, it was as much a trial for the defenders. The bombing had reduced the numerical strength of II Battalion, 3 Parachute Regiment, in Cassino town. One of those survivors of the battalion remembered:

> One part of a company of 2/3 Parachute Regiment was above the Continental and the other in a building near the Botanical Gardens . . . when the bombing ended No. 5 Company was round the church to the south of Route 6, No. 7 was round the School below the Castle and No. 8 was in the Castle. 7 Company was completely overrun. We formed a line of survivors with 60 men between the Telegraph Pylon on the hill below the Castle down to Route 6; eventually from the Castle to the Continental. We had had twelve Mark IV Specials in houses round the Continental and all but one were destroyed by the bombing. We sent out many men on patrol that night to give the impresion of strength and to dig out buried men. We put the NZ troops on the defensive. On March 16th we had about 160 men in the town. On the night of the 16th/17th we got 80 fresh men. The New Zealand Infantry failed because they did not carry on past the Continental where there were no troops to hold them up. Our going back into the town was a bluff. There were only 40 men in the Continental in the afternoon of the 15th.[32]

If this was so, the garrison of the town area after the bombing was only slightly inferior in numbers to the attacking companies of the 25th Battalion, and given that these initially operated singly and somewhat out of touch with each other, it is hardly surprising that the NZ infantry should be brought to an early standstill. Split up into small groups, the tendency seems to have been to run into German sections not much smaller in numbers. Thus, the forty men mentioned in the Continental Hotel — who held a bastion as formidable as Point 593 had been in the hills — were in fact a much more serious obstacle than their numbers indicate. For one thing, they were under cover, while the attackers to advance had to expose themselves to fire. Also, the paratroopers were well equipped with automatic small arms — sub-machine-guns and machine-guns: proportionately more than the NZ infantry, whose machine-gun was the Vickers machine-gun, which could not be easily carried in rough terrain for more than 1,000 yards without difficulty.[33]

The paratroopers were ready. Even forty men, equipped sufficiently with automatic weapons, and still with an operational tank gun built in to the hotel lounge, represented a formidable obstacle to riflemen, bren-gunners and non-commissioned officers with Thompson sub-machine-guns. The numbers are in themselves less important than the salient fact that the bombing had the result that few troops could be brought to bear quickly. Those that did go in were infantry without tank support, with small arms and grenades, and with no way of ordering artillery and mortar fire directed on to enemy strong points. The New Zealand infantry were slow and their radios failed: the rubble, the craters, the rain, the mud, the snipers, the separation from the tanks and heavy-weapons support fire were all factors against a quick result. The Allied air support, while heavily damaging II Battalion of the 3 Parachute Regiment, had for the price reconstituted the urban terrain to suit an attritional defence. The other battalions of 1 Parachute Division remained largely untouched. Reinforcements began to slip through, infiltrating at night. Indeed both sides were to use the darkness to adjust, re-supply, and reinforce their positions, for such activities attracted opposition fire in daylight.

On the morning of 17 March, Freyberg's diary noted another fine day, which meant the weather was holding. The situation of elements of 5 Indian Infantry Brigade, strung out across the hillside of the eastern face of Monastery Hill from Castle Hill to Hangman's Hill, was unclear.[34] The NZ Division was having problems. Freyberg urged Parkinson to get on with sorting out the town area:

> GOC[Freyberg]: 'You have to work with great energy to get down to the station. Get them into the sunken road then work south. That is a first charge and should be got on with straight away. I don't want to bring in a brigade of 78 Div.' Comd NZ Div said it was quite unnecessary. GOC CONTINUED. 'Put great energy into cleaning it up on a broad front. It is essential that we should get through to the Gr's [Gurkhas on 435] tonight. We have . . . [to] establish a route through to the people on the hill for maintenance. Anywhere you can push in tanks do so . . .'[35]

This had been at around 8.20 a.m.; at 8.45 a.m., Clark rang Freyberg. Freyberg's diary recorded:

> Army Comd said 'You keep telling me you have plenty of infantry. I cannot see why the 78 Div cannot start.' GOC says Parkinson says

> there is a battalion of infantry doing nothing — no necessity for it [i.e., putting in more infantry]. 26 Bn are waiting to go in. Only very small area and we have a lot of troops in there already. GOC said we have more tanks than we can use . . . we have 350 waiting behind. At present it would not be a bit of use putting them in. Army Comd asked about the hook. GOC said it will not turn the scale. It is like the Anzio landing. It will only be some good when the front has gone, or when the thing looks as if it is going to bits. GOC said 'Nobody knows this better than you.' Army Comd said that if the enemy was hit from all directions he would become preoccupied. GOC said he would become preoccupied if he had his tanks bogged down over there. Army comd said 'With 400 I will replace them.' GOC said 'The thing is by doing it at the moment, it will give away surprise.' Army Comd said that GOC had indicated that the hook would be going in and he wondered what made him change his mind. GOC said that the hook would go in when the convent was taken and that has not happened. . .[36]

Clark clearly thought that Freyberg was dragging his feet about committing more infantry. He also clearly thought that armour should go round the back, and was not troubled about the likely losses. For Freyberg, Clark's intervention was an unnecessary distraction. Clark was trying to tell Freyberg how to run his battle. Clark seemed to fail to grasp how vital it was for NZ Corps to build up on Point 435 in order to assault the monastery and to clear the town area. Once the top of Monastery Hill was in 4 Indian Division's hands, and the town cleared, the armour would be able to drive through with impunity into the Liri — and the drive into the Liri was the goal.

According to NZ Corps Situation Report No. 56, at 9.30 a.m., the German counter-attack on Point 165 had forced the 1st Rajputana Rifles from their positions, though the 1/4 Essex were still firm on Castle Hill. 6 NZ Brigade had reorganized and two further troops of tanks had passed part way along Route 6. The real problems with craters and rubble further along still remained. At 6.30 a.m. the 25th Battalion had attacked an enemy strong point with preliminary support from tank guns, but the dust clouded accurate judgement of the situation.[37] The 25th Battalion, with 'B' Company, 24th Battalion under its command and 5 Troop, 19 Armoured Regiment, in support, worked forward in the area of the Botanical Gardens and Route 6, under heavy fire. The 75mm guns and the Browning machine-guns of the tanks made some impact on a stubbornly emplaced enemy. They reached within 200 yards of the Continental Hotel, in the face of fierce enemy fire. This heavy fighting had chewed into the German defences, but their defences were in depth, and any forward movement cost men. It was a room by room struggle, where each yard was viciously disputed.[38]

Behind this struggle, the 26th Battalion, also supported by tanks, dribbled rather than thrust towards the railway station. The 26th needed to be extricated from the town in the face of German rifle and spandau fire. The front company caught up with the tanks by accident, but any coherence in the move dissipated rapidly. The tanks helped clear the station area, and with a determined effort a platoon of 'C' Company went on to take the Hummock to the south-west. Three platoons then held the Hummock, the rest of 'C' Company held the Round House, and 'B' Company the area to the north of the station. The tanks were deployed out where they could bring fire support to the station area, and with the German minefield as protection, and close New Zealand machine-gun posts giving protective fire, the goal of the 28th Battalion in the February battle was secured. The infantry numbered around 100; but they had suffered thirty-three killed and fifty-eight wounded: perhaps 25 per cent casualties over the Battalion.[39] Distant enemy fire continued.

In the meantime, 'A' and 'D' Companies of the 24th Battalion had advanced into the gap between the 25th Battalion in the Route 6 area and the 26th Battalion in the station. This was not by design, but because a more elaborate plan for the two companies had dissipated in the face of fierce German resistance and fire over open ground, further advance meant annihilation.[40]

XIV Panzer Corps' evening report of 17 March reflected on the determination of the NZ infantry:

> South of the town the enemy fought our foremost posts to a standstill by weight of fire, and then occupied the station after hand-to-hand fighting.
>
> Attack after attack was launched on the eastern part of the town during the day. Bitter close-range fighting took place. The parachutists abandoned nothing but heaps of ruins to the enemy. The centre of town is still in our hands.[41]

If the infantry of the NZ 6 Brigade were exhausted by the evening of 17 March, the Germans were hard pressed. The town still held, and there was still good reason for being there: to hold Route 6. But Hangman's Hill had stayed in the hands of the Gurkhas, so had Castle Hill, and now the railway station was in NZ Corps control.

At 9.20 a.m. on 17 March the commander of NZ Corps went forward to NZ Tactical Headquarters, where he stayed watching the course of the battle with the divisional commanders, the BGS, and CRA, till some time after 1 p.m. At around 1.35 p.m., Freyberg rang the Army commander:

> . . . who asked whether any decision had been made about the attack from the north with the tanks and the Indians. He said 'I cannot help feeling that is the thing to do.' . . . Army Comd was frightened that

> reinforcements would come into the station and into the monastery unless we move fast. GOC said we would attack when Indians had their administration fixed.
>
> Army Comd asked about 78 Div. GOC 'I do not think there is any room for any [more] infantry. Army Comd thought it would be ____ [?] before 78 Div got across the river. GOC said 'But more infantry would increase casualties and achieve no more.' Re attack from the north GOC said we had 1200 casualties on last occasion. Army Comd replied that was when Cassino and Hangman's Hill were in the possession of the enemy. He would like to see a stimulated attack. GOC said it cannot be done owing to the timing . . . Army Comd asked whether he assumed attack from Hangman's Hilll would be tonight and the other [the north attack] in the morning. GOC said it depended on administration . . . Army Comds final comment was 'Well I hope she goes.'[42]

Later in the afternoon Freyberg rang Galloway of 4 Indian Division at around 3.15 p.m.

> . . . He [Galloway] considered that more infantry were needed to clear up the town. GOC explained that neither Gen Parkinson nor Bonifant desired it. Galloway said he was not taking the Monastery until the feeding position is right but that it was sure it would be done tonight if administration [ammunition, food, etc.] was in order. GOC suggested taking the hill and arranging maintenance by dropping from air. GOC then left for Tac to talk matter over.[43]

Neither the Army commander nor the commander of 4 Indian Division were in any position to estimate the Allied infantry strength in Cassino, yet they did so. Perhaps, they believed that if only there were more men in the town, the German defences might be swamped by weight of numbers. The senior officers in the Division did not agree. In the face of persistent small arms, and mortar, and artillery fire, it is hard to see how more troops would not have for the most part become more targets. The casualty figures were high (and the 26th Battalion's casualties speak for the dangers of quickly trying to move troops through the vicinity). Galloway's attitude is perhaps understandable, in his concern for the 5 Indian Brigade, strung out on the slopes of Monte Cassino itself, particularly Point 435. And for Clark, the suspicion lingers that his primary interest was a bigger demonstration to take the heat off Anzio; to that end he would not have been ruffled if a whole British Corps was broken.

If higher command was restive at the lack of spectacular thrusts through the German positions, the Situation Report of NZ Corps for 2100 hours on 17 March was unhelpful. While the redoubtable 1/9 Gurkhas still held out on Hangman's Hill, despite counter-attacks, and 1 Rajputana Rifles had retaken Point 165, the position uphill remained isolated in daylight. Although the railway station had been taken by the 26th NZ Battalion, and the 25th had made some gains in the town, the enemy strong points in houses and concrete emplacements on the western side of Cassino eluded reduction. The 26th Battalion's casualties were noted as 'considerable'.[44]

NZ Corps' Intentions, signalled to other formations for the night of 17/18 March, spoke of consolidation by the 4 Indian Division troops on Points 435, 165, and 193, porter parties to 435 being the night's priority.[45] Elements of 6 NZ Brigade were to move further on enemy strong points, aimed at the less likely clearance of Cassino. As Freyberg had said, 'it would be a slow business'.

'C' Company of the 24th Battalion had been left in reserve to the north of the town area. On the night of 17/18 March, the company moved up on to the face of Monastery Hill, where, via Point 165, they moved to take over Point 202 (another of the bends on the winding road to the abbey), taking over from Indian troops. They would attempt to take the Hotel Des Roses in the rear the following morning, 18 March, but were pinned down by heavy machine-gun fire.[46]

The abortive effort on the rear of the Hotel Des Roses came to nothing, 3 Parachute Regiment indulged in a sortie with even less chance of success. The Parachute Motor Cycle Company set out in the early hours of 18 March to attack the 26th Battalion in the railway station. Crossing the icy waters of the Gari in which they became thoroughly wet, they experienced what the Royal Sussex had undergone in the February battle — they were fired on by their own mortars, and took casualties. The 26th Battalion's historian recounted:

> . . . They rushed in, yelling that they were Indians but nobody was deceived. Instead both [26th] companies from their dugouts, shelters and houses poured a well-directed fire on them, inflicting heavy casualties . . . The action was over in a few minutes . . . [At the retreat of the attackers] the troops on the Hummock were waiting and, as the paratroopers ran across the mudflat towards the river, directed a steady fire on them. In the words of one officer . . . 'It was a pity they were so easily killed.'[47]

The attackers had been wiped out: three were taken prisoner, and perhaps nineteen of the Motor Cycle Company survived.[48]

The New Zealand infantry in Cassino town ground away against the determined and bitter defence of the paratroopers of the central strong points in the Hotel Des Roses, the Continental Hotel, and the ruins at the base of Castle Hill. The now thinly held paratroopers' perimeter was almost surrounded by Indian troops above on Monastery Hill, and by

New Zealand infantry in the town and the station. But NZ Corps was also thin in numbers, especially on the slopes. High on Hangman's Hill, the Gurkhas' commander, Major Nangle, observed the bloody work in the town:

> We watched, in one interval in the smoke, the New Zealanders below clearing one of the streets of Cassino. From our detached viewpoint we could appreciate the subtleties of the technique of both sides. The careful approach of the tanks, the searching for them by the German mediums, the blasting of each house in turn, the withdrawal of the Germans from house to house always covered by fire from another or from the street, the quick dashes of the supporting New Zealand infantry and the use of smoke by both sides.[49]

'C' Company of the 25th Battalion battered on at the enemy. After two attacks on a strong point, the last third attack took it, with fourteen of the paratroopers killed, three wounded, and three killed, and fourteen wounded for 'C' Company.[50] The main German defences held, and although the paratroops took severe casualties (No. 2 Company of 3 Parachute Regiment was reduced to its company commander), Heidrich was able to feed in sufficient troops to keep the fight going.[52]

Earlier in the day, Freyberg had:

> . . . almost made up his mind to order 5 Bde in but at 8.30 rang Gen Parkinson who still feels that he has sufficient troops and that the infantry want to do it their way. GOC said 'You must remember that the whole of the operation is being paralysed until Cassino is cleaned up.'[52]

At 8.45 a.m., Freyberg spoke to Keightley, of 78 Division, and told him to be ready to take over responsibility for the railway station area. At 9 a.m. he went to Tactical Headquarters and saw Galloway, Parkinson, and Keightley. The possibility of flooding the town strong points was raised, but the CRE, Brigadier Hanson, advised against it as the New Zealand infantry were in the lower part of the town.[53] At 4.15 p.m. Freyberg decided to move the weakened 28th Maori Battalion to Cassino. Although reduced in strength because of their reverse at the railway station in February, they were assault troops *par excellence.* The situation described in the General's diary for 4.30 p.m. was as follows:

> . . . 25 Bn reducing enemy strongpoints under 193 supported by tanks. They think they are getting troops behind enemy positions and are slowly getting control. 24 Bn after making progress pinned down. Tanks have reduced 5 enemy strongpoints. Situation has improved. 26 Bn hold present positions [station] with low coy strength. 28 Bn come

> under comd [6 Brigade] and [are to] attack west at 0300 [on 19 March]. Objectives: Buildings on west of town below 193 including the watch house at foot of Castle Hill.[54]

At 7.30 p.m. Freyberg spoke to Galloway, of 4 Indian Division, who said that in spite of reverses, the plan for the monastery attack was acceptable. Galloway would not put in the hook attack by tanks in the direction of Albaneta Farm unless the attack on the monastery was successful. Freyberg thought the attack — operation 'Revenge' — should go on in any case.[55]

At 5 a.m. on 19 March, Freyberg noted that although the work of the engineers had, as usual, been interrupted by enemy mortar fire, the 28th Battalion had made progress in the houses below 193. At 5.20 a.m., he rang Galloway who said that everything was ready, 'as far as he knew'. It was noted that the hook attack with the tanks was definitely to proceed. In forty minutes Galloway's optimism was to be abruptly dispelled. Freyberg's diary noted:

> *0600* Comd 4 Ind Div to GOC: He [Galloway] reported very tricky situation. Started about 15 minutes ago . . . Pts 193 and 165 have been attacked by Germans with hand grenades and 193 is very tricky. This affects strength of people attacking the monastery. It is disconcerting about the strength and a little . . . about . . . 193.[56]

The troops of 4 Indian Division were late in their preparations to attack from the vantage point of Hangman's Hill. As a company of Rajputanas were effecting a hand-over to an Essex platoon, three companies of I Battalion, 4 Parachute Regiment, descended on point 165 and onwards in the direction of the castle. The two companies of Essex outside the castle split apart, some returning in haste to the ruin, while others pressed on. The Germans advanced and with machine-gun, mortar and rifle fire, and grenades, assaulted the castle itself. A pitched battle for the castle developed. The paratroops pulled back, but returned to the attack at 7 a.m., but failed, despite showers of grenades and a smoke-screen. A last attack was mounted in the afternoon when the Germans blew out a section of the battlements and swarmed into the courtyard. They were cut to pieces. Both sides suffered heavy losses, the paratroopers having perhaps only forty men left out of 200.[57] There was a twofold result. The Indian Division's hold on the face of Monastery Hill was weakened, although the castle was held. The counter-attack by the Germans had dislocated Bateman's projected attack by troops of 5 Indian Brigade. The losses had been too severe, and the Indians were not strong enough to mount an attack on the summit of 516 (the monastery).

In the meantime, the armoured force heading for Albaneta Farm had left its rendezvous at Madras Circus to the west of Majola Hill, and ground its way forward. This force consisted of 7 Indian Brigade's Recce Squadron and the 760th US Tank Battalion of seventeen Honey tanks, 'C' Squadron of the 20 NZ Armoured Regiment with fifteen Sherman tanks, and three 105mm self-propelled guns from US Combat Command B.[58] The force moved off at around 7.30 a.m.:

> . . . up a grassy valley between rough bush-covered hills. The gradient was gentle and the track fairly good, although sown with S-mines ('One could see them going off like crackers under the tracks') and broken up with patches of very soft going between outcrops of rock.[59]

The appearance of this small armoured column in the rear of the enemy's positions was unexpected, and the paratroops of III Battalion, 4 Parachute Regiment, were disadvantaged and without anti-tank guns. A torrent of small-arms fire was poured on the armour, which had the effect of keeping the tank commanders' heads down; some of the Honeys were open-topped and were thus very vulnerable. Artillery shells were called down on the tanks, and the infantry's Panzerfausts (anti-tank grenade launchers) were brought into play. These weapons, the German equivalent of the American bazooka and the British PIAT, were most effective. Although the tanks broke through between Point 593 and Albaneta Farm, the road narrowed and the Shermans were hit or became stuck, one by one. The lighter tanks were even more vulnerable. Galloway opined that infantry should have moved with the tanks. Yet the Indians had proved in February that infantry could not live in daylight before 593, and given the fire the armour endured on 19 March, it seems unlikely that infantry in open ground with little cover could have stayed intact for long. The tank thrust ended, three Shermans and three Honeys were destroyed, and nine Shermans and seven Honeys damaged. Although eleven of the damaged tanks were recovered later, it was a blunt reverse.[60] By early afternoon the attack projected from Hangman's Hill was cancelled.

In the town far below the clamour in the hills, the New Zealand infantry continued to chip away at the strong points. The NZ Corps Situation Report No. 41 at 9 p.m., 19 March noted that the 28th Maori Battalion had moved up, with two Shermans for close support, and hammered away at the Continental Hotel.[61] The tank guns had dealt with two enemy tank guns inside the Hotel, and around 100 prisoners of war had been taken. Nonetheless, the western area of the town was not cleared. Neither was the Continental Hotel taken, in spite of the best efforts of the infantry and the armour. As this position held in a large arc the corner of Route 6, in conjunction with the enemy in the Hotel Des Roses and the Baron's Palace, the day's efforts came to little.

Given this stalemate it is hardly surprising that the commander of NZ Corps decided on regrouping on the night of 19/20 March. Already Freyberg had contacted Alexander's chief of staff, Harding, about relieving

4th Indian Division, which Freyberg had concluded had nearly come to the end of its endurance.[62] 7 Brigade had borne the brunt of the February battle, 5 Indian Brigade had been used extensively in this, and 11 Brigade had bolstered the effort with a costly involvement. Harding argued that Freyberg should use the 78th Division and insisted '. . . the longer you wait the more difficult it will be . . .'

There were too many chiefs and too few Indians! Perhaps this underlined to Freyberg the relative weakness of his role as commander of NZ Corps. There was no appeal to Clark, the Army Commander, as 4 Indian Division was a British Army Division and in any case Clark had little sympathy for NZ Corps. The idea of using 78 Division, which Freyberg had been careful not to push needlessly into the hills or the town, meant that in effect he was expected to fight the remainder of the March battle with a two-divisional corps: if 4 Indian Division was put back into reserve, there would only be the 78th Division at full strength, for the NZ Division had also taken a drubbing. When further crises arose, and reserve troops were needed now that the 78 Division was deployed, they would have to come from the worn down 4 Indian Division. His situation was in contrast to the German commander who, though short on the ground for troops, passed in fresh formations to replace worn-out units: the Parachute Division for the 90 Panzer Grenadier Division; and later troops of 115 Panzer Grenadier Division to leaven the load of the paratroops.

Whatever Freyberg thought about Harding's refusal, he resolved to fight on in his own way. Battalions from 78 Division could be put in where necessary. NZ Corps' Intentions were signalled on the night of 19/20 March. The regrouping ran as follows:

> . . . 78 INF DIV . . . relieve 2 NZ DIV CAV . . . 4 IND DIV . . . 6 RWK [Royal West Kents] to relieve tps at present on pt 193 . . . on relief by 6 RWK on pt 193 one coy 2/7 GR and one coy 1/6 RAJ RIF to occupy pt 175 . . . area pt 435 and pt 202 [map ref] to be held by 1/9 GR and one coy 4/6 RAJ RIF(.) . . . on relief . . . 2 NZ DIV CAV . . . relieve 23 NZ BN . . . 23 NZ INF BN to relieve 25 NZ INF BN in present positions [in centre of town](.) 25 NZ INF BN . . . to . . . come into bde reserve(.) . . .[63]

The New Zealand infantry brigade sectors were also to alter: 5 NZ Brigade would now look after the Cassino town sector north of Route 6; 6 Brigade would be in the south of Route 6. (This last measure was later revised by the General when he realized the increased enemy strength in the town area.) The next day he considered making the 78 Division responsible for the station by sending the 6 Buffs there. Even after this move, NZ Corps would still have over two fresh brigades of the 78 Division in reserve — the 11 and 38 British Brigades. The replacement of the Essex garrison on Castle Hill by the Royal West Kents was to secure the right flank of the attacking troops in the town. This security was only relative in that the top of 193 was in British hands. The face of the hill, strewn with ruins, rocks, and rubble, concealed what must have seemed to the New Zealand infantry in the town below, to be innumerable snipers and machine-gunners.

Monday 20 March was to be a day of hard work with little reward for NZ Corps. For the forward troops in the town it was slogging and more slogging. The strong points to take were only hundreds of yards away, yet the small distances involved bore no relation to the difficulties of the task. Shortly after 7 a.m. it was reported by NZ Division that communications within the forward battalions were limited. It was reported during the night that there were more Germans on the ground than earlier: the implication of this was that the stubborn paratroopers in the town had been reinforced.[64] Troops of the 24th Battalion on Point 202 were prevented from making contact with the Maori Battalion — German troops had cut them and the garrison on Hangman's Hill from the main forward areas.

In the face of these changes, Freyberg decided that the 78 Division would take over responsibility for the Station area on the night of 20/21 March. The 26th Battalion would have to join the other New Zealand infantry battalions in the town. If necessary, the New Zealand brigades could be merged together on a one battalion front, for the distances involved were very small. Freyberg then informed the chief of staff, 5th Army, that the Germans appeared to be firming up in their positions, and that 4 Indian Division would have to be relieved if the present situation persisted. He then tried, unsuccessfully, to contact Harding of Alexander's staff as well.[65]

The commander of NZ Corps spoke with Gruenther at 1.45 p.m., covering much the same ground — the difficulty of supplying the troops on 202 and 435, the heavy resistance in the town, and the need to relieve 4 Indian Division soon. It was arranged that Freyberg would meet Clark and Alexander at 3.30 p.m. on 21 March, although it was possible that certain decisions might have to be taken before then. Freyberg said that the New Zealand infantry would try to supply the troops on the high ground. Casualties estimated since 15 March were 500 for the NZ Division, and 700 for the Indian Division.[66]

By now the 23rd Battalion had joined the 28th Battalion in the fighting in the town. For the 23rd, the forward situation was appalling: it was as bad for other units in the area of the Continental Hotel and the base of Castle Hill. The concealment of the enemy was almost complete: the battalion companies took casualties before they even set eyes on a German.[67] For the 23rd Battalion it was a grim task:

> . . . the general complaint among the 23rd men was that they could see no enemy, no rifle or other flash to indicate the whereabouts of

> the enemy, who had perfect cover combined with perfect observation, and therefore complete mastery of the situation. Under these circumstances daylight attacks over ground so cratered and covered with debris that running was usually impossible did nothing more than give the enemy good targets.[68]

On 22 March, Private Bill Stirling of the 23rd found out why the German positions were so formidable. He slipped into a dug-out on the forward slopes of Castle Hill occupied by dead Germans:

> Inside, it was big and roomy and partially furnished for long-term occupation . . . A narrow fire slit gave a perfect view over Cassino town and the frontal approaches to the base of Castle Hill. In the foreground lay six dead Maoris in line, just as they had fallen in their attack. Farther along could be seen some of the 23rd dead from the earlier attack in the same sector.[69]

Under such circumstances, it is not at all hard to see why so little progress had been made in the ruined town area, where in places like the Continental Hotel, outstanding paratroop platoon commanders like Sergeant-Major Neuhoff could hold on and refuse to give an inch to all comers, including tanks![70]

On the afternoon of 20 March, Freyberg had a long talk to Burrows, the Commander of New Zealand Division's 5 Brigade.[71] Burrows did not think that the Continental had been taken. A tank was 15 to 20 yards away from it but could not proceed any further. Troops from the Maori Battalion in the area were no longer certain of the position of forward companies. They were not making any progress that afternoon. There was nothing for it but to plan to attack at night. For without cover or smoke nothing could live in the daylight.

Situation Report No. 55 at 9 p.m., on 20 March, developed Freyberg's conversation with Burrows.[72] Although an air drop brought supplies to the troops on 435, the story in the town was still the same. Heavy house-to-house fighting was reported but little progress was made during the day because of enemy mortar and artillery fire. Fire from 165 and 236 was difficult to stop because the Castle occupied by Allied troops was too close to the line of fire for the Corps artillery to engage those positions. Even the tanks with the 28th Battalion had had to withdraw because of the accurate observed fire of the opposing artillery: some were knocked out. A complicating factor now was that the German and New Zealand troops were so entangled in the ruins that fighter-bomber support would not be given even if it was available. From the air it was impossible to tell friend from foe.

The projected meeting of the NZ Corps commander with the Army commander and Alexander was to decide whether the fight should be continued or halted. The message for Freyberg read:

> The slow progress made so far in attacking the town of Cassino with the consequent delay in launching the attack on the Monastery, combined with the necessity of preparing the maximum forces for a full-scale offensive in the second half of April makes it essential to decide in the course of the next 24 or 36 hours whether (a) to continue with the Cassino operation in the hope of capturing the Monastery during the next three or four days or (b) to call the operation off and to consolidate such gains of ground as are important for the renewal of the offensive later. It is also necessary to decide when Eighth Army is to take over responsibility for operations on the Cassino front and when Headquarters New Zealand Corps is to be dissolved and replaced by Headquarters 13 Corps. In the commander-in-chief's view Eighth Army and 13 Corps should assume responsibility for Cassino front as soon as the Monastery has been captured and consolidated, or alternatively immediately it is decided to call off the present offensive.[73]

The battle was to groan on for a few more days. Freyberg realized that even though the situation looked grim, the taking of the German positions along the foot of Monastery Hill would almost immediately open up Route 6 through to the Liri. The tenacity of the Gurkhas on Hangman's Hill, and of 'C' Company, 24th Battalion, on Point 202, together with the 6 Royal West Kents on Castle Hill, showed that NZ Corps might have the sustained strength for assaulting the monastery heights, although until the town was reduced the opportunity was slim. If the Germans held out is could easily be a battle of diminishing returns, yet in terms of distance NZ Corps had nearly pushed the Germans from the town. Freyberg must fight on. To stop abruptly would invite a counter-attack on the troops on the heights: if there was to be a halt to operations, it would not be until those forces were withdrawn. Thus the pressure must be kept up.

The commander of XIV Panzer Corps, von Senger, was no more optimistic about the eventual outcome:

> . . . the enemy's air superiority, artillery superiority and . . . superiority in tanks all make it improbable that Cassino can be held for any length of time. It is likely that the wastage of the infantry in the town will compel us to pull back gradually to the line between the Abbey and the present left wing of the Machine Gun Battalion. The enemy has suffered heavily, but he is not exhausted, as he is only attacking at this one spot and has fresh reserves.[74]

This last point was somewhat ironic. The Allied forces held reserves and outnumbered the Germans in every capacity, yet Freyberg's request to Harding for the replacement of the 4th Indian Division had met with an oblique refusal: Freyberg must make do with the 78th Division. Both the Army commander and Alexander were waiting to see what would happen to Freyberg's Corps.

The assaults by NZ Corps continued. The Royal West Kents attempted to retake Points 236 and 165 on the night of 20/21 March, but this ended when a substantial minefield across the line of attack exploded. The enemy was forewarned and a further sally repulsed. Similarly, the 2/7 Gurkhas tried to wrest the enemy's grasp from Point 445, but were driven back by heavy enemy opposition. The attempt by the 21st NZ Battalion to make contact with the troops on Points 202 and 146 was held up by heavy enemy opposition.[75] The house-to-house, ruin-to-ruin battle in Cassino went on: an enemy tank was knocked out; an unsuccessful attack on a 'strongly defended house' was made; visibility deteriorated making the tank support fire impossible; the Buffs in the station were mortared during the morning; and the total number of prisoners taken now reached 248.[76]

The conference in the afternoon of 21 March was attended by Alexander, Clark, Leese of 8th Army, Kirkman of 13 Corps, and Freyberg of NZ Corps.[77] It was agreed that NZ Corps should continue the battle in the town for a few more days, to see if the matter could be brought to a conclusion.[78] On the early afternoon of 22 March, Freyberg held a conference with Keightley of 78 Division, with his CRA, and the Corps' BGS, Queree. An outline plan for taking the monastery was discussed, but no great enthusiasm for such an enterprise was shown by anyone. The idea was once again to assault Point 593, though Freyberg pointed out that any assault force on 593 could be shot at from all sides. The Corps commander agreed that it was a difficult operation 'without surprise, and that has been the history of this place for the last three months'. It was decided that 78 Division should prepare a plan, although Freyberg had little conviction that Cassino might be taken.[79]

Inside Cassino itself, the fighting continued, but with slow progress. Strong points below 193 were attacked, supported by tanks and artillery and counter-mortar fire, and enemy casualties were estimated. The fighter-bomber supply sorties continued on Point 435, as they had over the past days.[80] On the morning of 23 March a NZ Corps conference took place at 9 a.m., attended by Freyberg, Kirkman of XIII Corps, Galloway, Keightley, Parkinson, Weir, and Hanson. The problem of continuing operations was discussed. Freyberg considered that:

> 'It seems clear that the NZ Div is finished and has come to the end of its tether. They made no headway yesterday.' . . . Comd NZ Div reported that they had definitely come to the end of their tether.[81]

Various modes of attack were discussed. The river crossing had been too well disputed, and when 78 Division had tried to win footing, the enemy defences were found to be too strong. As to the heights, Freyberg said:

> Everyone says you can take them but when it comes to the point, they are not taken. 593 cost 1000 men to get 100 yards and looking at the ground . . . it was not certain that 100 yards was gained. One difficulty of attacking a point in the hills is that you cannot use the artillery.[82]

Parkinson advised that a frontal attack in the town should not be attempted:

> Comd NZ Div said they were losing men in the town all the time . . . The original job was to fight from house to house — that had been tried with a bn and did not come off. Then they tried with a lot of troops and still they had not found the answer . . . GOC commented that the troops in the town and the south were in the worst military position that he had ever seen troops in. It was because of the long term policy that they had to stay there.[83]

It was decided that the 78 Division would continue to prepare attack plans but that in the meantime Freyberg would advise Clark that the NZ Division could not go any further, and that the troops on the heights — Hangman's Hill — should be withdrawn.

At 11 a.m., Freyberg rang Gruenther:

> He said the general conditions are very difficult and I do not think we are making any headway. I do not think the NZers have any more offensive action in them. The administrative situation of the people on the hill will be very difficult tonight. I think I have to advise the Army comd that we cannot break through to the people on the hill.[84]

For the NZ Corps the March battle of Cassino had come to an end. The next few days were spent in extricating the garrison from Hangman's Hill and 202, and wiring, mining, and improving the defensive positions in the town and its environs. The hard-fought gains were not to be given up.

Given the largely lamentable litany of adverse factors, circumstances, and persons facing Freyberg at Cassino, the commander of NZ Corps did surprisingly well — within the limited sphere in which he was permitted to range. He kept his casualty rate low in aggregate: when his divisions became tired he asked for them to be replaced. He failed to win reinforcements for 4 Indian Division, but succeeded in having the Corps withdrawn in March. Freyberg planned his battles carefully, but because air support was not useful, or under his or his Army commander's control, co-ordination of attacks became dislocated. He was persistent in pursuing a tactical posture to break the German hold over the entrance to the Liri Valley, either through taking the heights and getting an alternative route for the tanks — the February battle — or through taking the town defences that cut Route 6 and also attempting to build up a force to take Monastery Hill, the dominant tactical feature — the March battle. It is a moot point that if the NZ Corps had come up against a tired 90 Panzer Grenadier Division in the town rather than the zealous élite fresh paratroopers, the result of the second battle may have been different, and perhaps opened up Route 6 at least for a time. Certainly 1 Parachute Division was pressed hard, and there was little left of 3 Parachute Regiment by the end of the March battle.

In the end though, Freyberg was utterly compromised by 5th Army at Cassino. He had to deal with unhappy subordinates, Tuker, Dimoline, and Galloway, who saw the terrible fate of 4 Indian Division. His own division, the New Zealand Division, was given an extremely unpleasant task under adverse circumstances. He could go neither forward nor back; Clark and Alexander had committed his Corps to battle at the strongest point on the Gustav Line. He had to fight on until they ordered his Corps to stop. Comparing his efforts with the American Corps and the later Polish Corps, it should be recalled that he had to fight twice, yet he managed to keep his casualties lower. He did not throw his troops away. Yet the defences were such that even to say he made the best of an adverse tactical environment makes sour reading.

In the Cassino battles, he was a trapped corps commander, with no room to show what his national command had been trained to do since El Alamein: a set-piece break-out followed by exploitation with armour and mobile infantry. It is perhaps a measure of the man that Cassino did not bury his reputation. Instead he went on to win further battles up the Italian peninsula, penetrating as far as Trieste, at the conclusion of hostilities in 1945. Crete was well behind. The New Zealand Government had no doubt that, at Cassino, he was the right man to lead the New Zealand Division.

Cassino was not taken, and the German attempt to snuff out the Anzio beach-head was still Kesselring's dominant concern. The Allies with their twenty divisions in Italy, to the German twenty-four, had not gained dominance — a dangerous situation given the closeness of 'Overlord', with its second front invasion of Europe. The last thing the Allied coalition wanted was to feed further reinforcements into Italy. The Italian campaign had become an expensive distraction.

With NZ Corps disbanded on 26 March, Freyberg reverted to Divisional Command. By mid-April 2 NZ Division had moved to the southern sector of X Corps' Appenine operational zone. Freyberg was now a participant in operation 'Diadem', albeit in a small diversionary role. 'Diadem's' aim was to destroy the right wing of the German 5th Army and to drive its remnants, together with those of the German 14th Army, north of Rome, and pursue them to the Rimini–Pisa line. The strategic aim was to inflict maximum German casualties with the likely repercussion of heavy

German reinforcement before the launching of 'Overlord' against Normandy.

Freyberg, despite his exhaused Division, was given the task of threatening the road to Atina. An artillery barrage at 0200 hours 4 May was followed by mortar and machine-gun fire to cover the right flank of a feint attack. A tank 'attack' was followed by a withdrawal, intended to persuade the enemy that the attack had failed. A second simulated attack was made towards San Biagio on 13/14 May. The German defenders were not drawn.

While the decimated 2 NZ Division was involved in this minor role the battle for Cassino was at last fought and won. Majdalany did not exaggerate when he described this last battle for Cassino as 'General Alexander's masterpiece; an operation in C major with full orchestra.'[85] Alexander threw two armies into the battle, to rupture the extreme right flank of the Gustav Line. The 5th and 8th Armies, no less than six corps, were gathered side by side on the 27 kilometre front between Cassino and the Mediterranean. Of the six corps no less than three were employed between the Liri and Monte Cairo — II Polish Corps, XIII British Corps, and I Canadian Corps. Alexander held a 3:1 advantage on the Cassino front, able to deploy over 1,600 guns, 2,000 tanks, and 3,000 aircraft.

The Polish Corps' task was to end the Cassino block to the advance along Route 6 to Rome. The success of this master plan depended on victory at Cassino. General Anders, the Polish commander, having been initially repulsed, launched his crucial attack on 17 May, in an assault that coincided with the crossing of the Rapido River and a final drive into the heart of the Aurunci mountains. A bloody and sustained German defence by the paratroopers was insufficient to stop the determined and sacrificial assault. The Poles hoisted their flag over the monastery's ruins at 1020 hours 18 May. The Polish Corps suffered nearly 4,000 casualties during the assault, of whom one-third were killed in action. It is doubtful whether the Polish Corps could have taken Cassino in isolation from the broad front actions of the 8th and 5th Armies.

The Gustav Line was finally broken and in the pursuit the second defensive barrier, the Hitler Line, was smashed through. Free city though it was, Rome fell on 4 June 1944 — albeit to the tactical disadvantage of the combined operations, though to the vainglory of General Mark Clark (with his concern to collect a Roman road sign and to assure his place in history as the conqueror of the city of the Caesars). The Allied pursuit, in which Freyberg's NZ Division participated, was next blocked by the Gothic Line, the barrier to the Po Valley and the Alps. In this pursuit, 2 NZ Division encountered heavy fighting on 1 and 2 August and participated in the capture of Pian di Cerri Ridge, the gateway to Florence, a city they entered on 4 August. In Florence the Division's discipline relaxed, unregulated dress, heavy drinking, and looting were commented on by the General in his diary entry of 8 August. Freyberg remarked:

> The shellfire was not heavy. If the German discipline was the same as ours, their forces under our shellfire would have been annihilated. There seems to be a slackness in leading and a slackness in battle discipline . . . You don't mess about in the open . . . I cannot help but think that casualties are due to lack of experience of junior leaders and the absence of battle drill. When you see a force going forward you see it straggling and not under command. You don't see any proper battle formation and I don't think in a lot of cases the men are properly under control.[86]

On 25 August 1944, 2 NZ Division was held in reserve on the coast, as the 8th Army crossed the Metauro River in the Adriatic sector. On 3 September 1944, Freyberg was seriously injured when his Stimson liaison aircraft overturned on landing. Until 14 October the General was relieved by Major-General C. E. Weir, and during this period 2 NZ Division took part in the advance on the Rimini corridor.

October was a month of disillusionment for 2 NZ Division. At a cost of 1,100 men killed and wounded the Division penetrated only 30 kilometres. The German Tiger tank, with its 88mm gun, now faced the Allied pursuers. Allied High Command had failed to respond adequately to the strength of German defence capability. John Strawson's comment is apt:

> What remains astonishing to those of us who fought in and survived the Gothic Line battles was: first, the amazing optimism displayed by the higher British commanders, who seemed not to have grasped after all the experience they had had that the German soldiers were masters of defence, would never give up lightly, were commanded by skilled, determined generals and the higher direction of the war by Hitler was such that he would never willingly give an inch of ground, as Kesselring had so ably and for so long demonstrated in his brilliant conduct of the Italian campaign: and secondly, given the great superiority of material, particularly of artillery and air power, and given also that indispensable commodity in war — time — why it was that we did not deploy our soldiers in the way the Germans did, in teams of tanks, infantry, anti-tank guns, artillery and sappers, making use of every skill and every ounce of fire power in co-ordinated and carefully prepared attacks, rather than driving forward with tanks, virtually unsupported by anything else, and simply writing them off as a result.[87]

On his return to duty Freyberg found 5th Army still confined in a corner of the Romagna Plain and the 8th Army held by the German defence. By December his troops were battling in snowstorms, advancing slowly to the Senio, with hard fighting. In January 1945 the Allied High

Command abandoned fighting for the winter, a decision that allowed the enemy to strengthen further its position.

In the spring offensive of April 1945, 2 NZ Division took part in Operation 'Buckland', to cross the Senio on 10 April. At an Orders Group at 1020 hours on 10 April, Freyberg ordered his Division to 'Get your tanks across and push on.'[88] His brigadiers were instructed to 'Give them a nasty time with tanks and air. Go for him, you must get the next flood bank and as much as you can of the far flood bank but don't push out into the blue without bridges. The limit is the Po.'[89]

Here was no cautious commander. By the close of 10 April, 2 NZ Division was in advance of the flanking divisions (8 Indian and 3 Carpathian Divisions) and Freyberg ordered a crossing of the Santerno. The pursuit of the retreating German army was now vigorous, and the 300 kilometres from the Santerno to Trieste was covered in only 22 days. The Po had been crossed on 24-25 April.

Although on 2 May 1945 the German High Command surrendered its forces in northern Italy, Freyberg's entry into Trieste was not undisputed. Marshal Tito's 4th Yugoslav Army was already in possession of some of the city and some German resistance continued. On 3 May 1945, 2 NZ Division received the surrender of the remaining German forces in Trieste, but increased tension with the Yugoslav communists made it necessary to prepare for another conflict — one ally against another. A show of armoured strength and some diplomacy prevented armed conflict and allowed a compromise to be reached.

The war in Europe was over. Freyberg's Division had come to the end of the road, albeit with some of his force to be conscripted for the Pacific War still in progress. Freyberg himself, Churchill's salamander, had survived the fires of battle, closing his military career with a pursuit as fierce as his cavalry dash to secure the vital bridge at Lessines in the last days of World War I. For Freyberg there were no more wars, but there were eighteen more years of honourable and distinguished public service, as Governor-General of New Zealand, as a Baron of the realm, and as Lieutenant-Governor of Windsor Castle.

CHAPTER 9

Conclusion

On 7 May 1945 the German High Command surrendered all German military forces to the allies. Freyberg's war in Europe had lasted over four and a half years, from 6 November 1939 when he addressed a letter to the New Zealand Government, outlining his appreciation of the capabilities needed in the commander of the 2nd New Zealand Expeditionary Force. Freyberg advised that:

> The GOC . . . should have commanded an Infantry Brigade, or similar Artillery Command, for the last years of the war. I suggest this because it is important that he should have practical experience of making and carrying out artillery fire plans in the various phases of battle. He should have actual experience in command during:
>
> (a) A retreat under heavy enemy pressure;
> (b) A counter stroke;
> (c) The forcing of a river line against opposition;
> (d) Operation in open warfare involving the co-operation of all arms.
>
> So much for the minimum requirements from a tactical and training point of view.[1]

Freyberg's advice was not without self-interest. He wanted the job and the qualities he advanced were mirrored in his personal profile. A brigadier in France at the age of twenty-nine years, Freyberg, in the course of World War I had multiple experience of his first two requirements — a retreat under heavy enemy pressure and a counter-stroke. In the advance to Germany he had won more limited experience of the forcing of a river line and open warfare. On 23 November 1939, M. J. Savage, Prime Minister of New Zealand, announced that Major General B. C. Freyberg would command 2 New Zealand Expeditionary Force.

From 1941 until 1945, in Greece, Crete, North Africa, and Italy, Freyberg was given every opportunity to test himself against his own measure. As a divisional commander in Greece he fought his New Zealanders 320 kilometres down the eastern seaboard, continuously harassed by Luftwaffe from above and armour threatening his flanks. Crete provided a second opportunity for retreat under heavy enemy pressure. Wavell, Auchinleck, Churchill, and Fraser all finally paid tribute to Freyberg's cool, calculated, and cautious conduct of two fighting retreats.[2]

North Africa gave Freyberg little opportunity to force a river line against opposition. In Italy, 9-10 April 1945, 2 New Zealand Division took part in a copy-book assault across the Senio River — building bridges for tanks and artillery before dawn, advancing 8 kilometres in twenty-four hours, and leaving behind the divisions on both flanks. Freyberg's well drilled and innovative NZ Division took the Po River in its stride, or at least with assault boats and amphibious craft. While his infantry engaged the retreating Germans, his engineers built a 90 metres folding boat bridge, to allow crossing for wheeled vehicles. By the close of 25 April 1945, his tanks were on the enemy side of the river; they had crossed on rafts. Padua was gained after a crossing of the broad Adige River on 27 April, and Trieste was entered on 2 May 1945, after a crossing of the Isonzo River, on 1 May. In Italy Freyberg's Division, from beginning until end, gained ample experience in the forcing of river lines against opposition.

But it is in his fourth requirement, the ability to conduct operations in open warfare, involving the co-operation of all arms, that Freyberg won his reputation as the 8th Army's most competent and aggressive divisional commander. In the Crusader battles (November 1941–January 1942) he was perhaps the first to perceive that success in desert warfare required the closest co-operation of armour and infantry, of ground and air forces, and a strategy whereby cruiser tanks would prevent Rommel's *Panzertruppen* from smashing into his infantry formations. It was here that Freyberg propounded repeatedly his doctrine of infantry–armour inter-involvement, contending that infantry must fight as divisions, not as fragmented columns, and that armoured corps must cease envisaging themselves as pursuit cavalry, and begin to act as partners in battlefield maneouvres wherein infantry, artillery, and armour, in unison, broke the enemy at his vulnerable placements. 8th Army commanders were slow to accept the wisdom of Freyberg's battle experience. On 14-15 July 1942, after a well-conceived and executed assault on Ruweisat Ridge, a prominance overlooking the El Alamein defence line, 2 NZ Division was finally driven from the tactically important heights, because no 8th Army armour or artillery was sent to support them. It was not until Montgomery's arrival as commander of the 8th Army that Freyberg's doctrine was accepted and the *Panzertruppen* were challenged by armoured corps ordered to support infantry advances at the risk of heavy casualties. The combination of air bombardment, artillery, armour, and infantry advance, in Tunisia, was vindication of Freyberg's fifteen months of advocacy.

That Freyberg was a most able divisional commander was not doubted after his Division's advances in Sidi Rezegh, and their relief of Tobruk. On 26/27 November 1941, Freyberg's New Zealanders succeeded 'where the tank men of XXX Corps had failed during the first five days of Crusader'.[13] Churchill's misgivings after Crete, prompted by the reports of Brigadiers Inglis and Hargest, Fraser's doubts that he and the recently deceased Savage had hired a loser, and the slight measure of doubt beneath the surface in the cables of support from British commanders, now and hereafter, gave way to praise and reliance.

Freyberg was by 1942 'indomitable', 'aggressive', 'experienced', and in Churchill's words 'a salamander'. Prickly with superiors who were less experienced in desert battle than himself, whether corps or army commanders, politically astute in using his charter to protect what he believed to be his Division's best interest, and demanding of maximum support in return for maximum divisional effort, Freyberg, by the second battle of El Alamein, had become something of an institution in the 8th Army. Even Montgomery thought it wise to deal with him directly, rather than through Freyberg's Corps commander, Horrocks.[4]

Whilst Freyberg's aptitude as a divisional commander is well vouched for, doubt was expressed by contemporary commanders and politicians about his performances as the commander of corps-sized formations. A fair test is to examine Freyberg's performances at Crete, Mareth, and Cassino against the definition of successful corps command propounded by Graham and Bidwell in their examination of Lieutenant-General Kirkman, who commanded XIII Corps, subsequent to Freyberg's March battle at Cassino. These eminent military historians argue that:

> His position is delicate, even ambiguous. He cannot, like an army commander, issue his orders, tour round the units to cheer up his troops and retire to his caravan to write letters or read books, leaving the details to his staff; resigned to the fact that he cannot usefully interfere until the battle reaches the crisis from which he hoped to pluck his victory. Divisional and brigade commanders are all busy with the minor tactics, techniques and mechanics of the battle they are about to fight and control from hour to hour. The corps commander has to ensure that all is going forward satisfactorily and that his divisional commanders are in his mind and can anticipate his moves, but without wagging them or 'breathing down their necks'; too close control may only serve to irritate or be interpreted as lack of confidence. The corps commander's position is very like that of the managing director of a firm. He is the executive who realises the army commander's aim and plan. He is personally responsible for the conduct of the battle. The detailed plan is his. The army artillery fire-plan, the mission given to the army engineers and the priorities given to the tactical air force have all been adjusted to meet his requirements.[5]

Creforce, an amalgam of New Zealand, Australian, British, and Greek forces, hastily deployed to repel a German invasion, known in size, method, and timing of arrival, was Freyberg's first corps command. With the men and material at his disposal, Freyberg deployed his force with every concern for the defence of sea and air landing zones, with attention to mobility and concealment, and in realization that air defence would be minimal. His orders were to hold Crete, and Crete was nearly held — despite his inadequacies in armament and ammunition. Freyberg's plan was sound as was his delegation of local initiative to his brigadiers, necessary because of the terrain, likely communication problems, and his overall corps responsibilties. It was 5 Brigade's commander's failure to comply with Freyberg's battle plan that in a large measure lost Maleme, and with it Crete. Freyberg can be blamed for giving Hargest a brigade, but only in hindsight. Until Crete, Hargest's reputation was that of a heroic World War I commander.

Crete gave Freyberg opportunity to show his capability not only as a corps commander, but as a *de facto* Army commander. Mareth, in the Tunisian campaign of early 1943, redressed the balance of previous defeat. Freyberg here commanded New Zealand Corps (2 NZ Division with the attachment of the British armour he had so long advocated, together with other units). Freyberg was now a master of the stratagem of a 'left hook' — an outflanking operation wherein mobility and surprise were used to win victories without the heavy casualties of frontal assault.

His third left hook (the first was at El Agheila on 11-17 December 1942, and the second near Tripoli in January 1943) involved passage around the southern end of the Mareth Line to the Tebaga Gap. NZ Corps broke through the enemy line on 26 March 1943. Freyberg's battle was a set-piece, a model of collaboration of close air and armour support, with a well planned breakthrough and well co-ordinated pursuit. On 29 March NZ Corps entered Gabes. He has been criticized for excessive caution. Given the intelligence available and his considerable experience in desert warfare he showed proper prudence in awaiting a reinforcement sufficient to secure his operational goal.

This was the crucial final victory in North Africa. The veteran German 90 Division surrendered to Freyberg in early May. The Italian 1st Army surrendered on 13 May. Freyberg's eighteen months in North Africa concluded with a demonstration of intricate combined-operation's control at corps level, with victory attained with a low casualty rate. In the seven months since the second battle of El Alamein, Freyberg's New Zealanders suffered one of their lowest battle casualty registers — 336 dead and 967 wounded.

To Freyberg's disadvantage his next major opportunity in corps command came with the creation of a NZ Corps — at Cassino. On 12 February 1944 the newly formed NZ Corps relieved the II US Army Corps after crossing the Apennines into the US 5th Army's area of responsibility. Freyberg's new command comprised his 2 NZ Division, an Indian division, and American troops. His operational goal was to clear the block to advance posed by the Cassino monastery, town, and hill, and thereafter break into the Liri Valley and push with speed to Rome. At Cassino,

Kippenberger, now a Major-General, commanded 2 NZ Division, while Freyberg, directly responsible to the American General Mark Clark, commanded the Corps.

NZ Corps failed to break through, despite attempts until 24 March 1944. The Corps was disbanded on 26 March. Freyberg's task was daunting — assault against veteran paratroop forces, with geographical and man-made features favouring the defenders. The weather, rain, and cold created a quagmire. The American divisions had failed to take the heights, and the Indian Division was unable to move to objectives with speed and effectiveness. Worse still, Clark was unsupportive, an advocate of heavy casualty frontal storming (quite unacceptable to Freyberg with his difficulty in gaining reinforcements), and the implementer of an agenda wherein Freyberg's disguised task was to take pressure from the Anzio offensive.

Freyberg's problems were worsened by inferior air–ground attack co-ordination, climaxing in timetables that released warplanes to fit lulls at Anzio, and in the inadequate bombings of the abbey and town. Graham and Bidwell's prerequisites — particularly that air support should meet the corps commanders' needs — were withheld.

The attrition at Cassino, wherein rugged terrain and rubble-covered streets replaced the open desert, demanded a new battle strategy from Freyberg. Tanks were of limited use, blocked by craters and bog. Artillery and air bombardment only provided new defences and road blocks for the garrison. Given a battered Corps, with morale reduced by Kippenberger's serious wounding, given Alexander's apparent lethargy and Clark's incapability in perceiving Freyberg's difficulties, it is small wonder he failed. His corps command in this operation was thorough in organization, but at Cassino he lacked the drive and charisma of Mareth. At Cassino he was confronted with a reminder of the battles of attrition of World War I, battles of frontal attack, maximum casualties, and defender's advantage. This was not the fighting Freyberg had trained his NZ Division to perform, and the losses that further effort would have required would have been quite unacceptable to the New Zealand Government. Cassino, with the entire Italian campaign, had become a vortex, swallowing allied manpower, weaponry, and supplies, to little strategic advantage.

Freyberg's tactical competence, as Cassino shows, must be assessed in the light of the political parameters allowed to him. His charter of 1940 made him responsible to the New Zealand Government, for the maximum usefulness of the Division to the allied war effort with the minimum of casualties.[6] He was loyal to this instruction and British and American superiors soon found that some orders, judged and weighed by Freyberg, were dismissed with the words, 'Well, I'll just have to let my government know that one.'[7] By the opening battles of Cassino, Freyberg, for all his protection of manpower resources, was reduced to a depleted 2 NZ

Division, with many veterans out of the line, on furlough, and with some less experienced new troops. New Zealand now faced a manpower shortage. Significantly, on the day NZ Corps was disbanded, 26 March 1944, the New Zealand Government determined to withdraw the two-brigade 3 NZ Division from the Pacific theatre, to allow more workers for home industry and sufficient reinforcements for Freyberg in Italy.

Prime Minister Fraser, who deliberately saved 2 NZ Division from the invasion of Sicily, had reluctantly agreed to participation in the Italian campaign, but assumed a speedy allied progress through Italy.[8] While Fraser was committed to victory in Europe, he had made plain to Freyberg the Government's continued concern over attrition.

Cassino gave Freyberg little opportunity to shine as a prescient commander, clear minded as to his role in future moves, and as clear minded over the moves best suited to the corps and army. It is a canard to suggest Freyberg was a general who had reached his pinnacle as a divisional commander. His appreciation of 4 January 1942, 'The New Zealand Division in Cyrenaica and Lessons of the Campaign', shows his perspicacity in assessing the enemy's tactical prowess, and using that analysis as a basis for the development of new tactics on the battlefield. This still eight months before the advent of Montgomery's arrival in Eighth Army. Freyberg's section on tanks, notes that the Panzer policy was to produce the largest number of tanks at the decisive moment. He noted:

— They understood the value of gun power.
— Most efficient organisation for maintenance and quick recovery [of] tank casualties.
— They avoid action unless conditions favourable, 'thus keeping their casualties lower than ours'.
— They won't attack without close support of arty, ATK guns, MGs. . .
— Tempo [of] German tank attack slow:— 'the tanks moving from one hull down position to another'.
— Direction of attack:— nearly always with sun behind them.
— Tanks took advant[age] of smoke and dust raised by bombardments. . .[9]

In his response to those effective German tactics, Freyberg on 4 January 1942 argued for maximum supporting fire to back armoured attacks, an aggressive attitude to anti-tank guns by Allied tanks, and night attacks by armour. Freyberg, in this paper, insisted that 'motorised infantry can and should use the *speed* of their *vehicles* to the full in attack to *gain surprise*'.[10]

His notes, when read in full, show systematic assessment of enemy method, and a clear set of alternatives. Though better suited by temperament to battle command than to staff work, Freyberg's intellectual capacity was quick and accurate. Successful generals need to be lateral thinkers, need to absorb the scenarios of military history and know how to adapt from these, need to use effectively the latest technology of war, and need to learn from the victories and defeats of their own campaigns. Freyberg's diary and note reflections, and the evidence of subordinates, suggest an alert commander, often ahead of his superiors. The General quickly perceived the failure of the armour at Alamein, and Freyberg's suggestion of an extension of 2,000 yards of the artillery barrage, was a key to the success of operation 'Supercharge'.[11] Freyberg's pertinent comment at the height of the second battle of El Alamein, that artillery would henceforth be the queen of the desert battle, and his advice to Montgomery, in favour of an inland attack, were proved to be well founded.

Freyberg was a fount of innovative tactics, a strength recognized by Montgomery. At Tebaga Gap his breakthrough utilized and adapted the basic concepts of the German *blitzkrieg*, with fighter-bombers used in place of dive-bombers, in front of an artillery barrage. This mix of tanks and infantry in that battle was a recipe for exploitation of the breakthrough, intended to maximize the armour's punch through the enemy's line.

Intelligent, innovative, and aggressive in corps battle command, Freyberg should have made good use of the highly accurate intelligence fed to him by the cryptanalysts of Bletchley Park, albeit without the uncloaking of their breach of German codes. At Crete his deployment of major formations gave close heed to the information received. In the desert, Ultra intercepts of German Enigma transcripts provided Freyberg, through Middle East command, with a close identification of enemy formation, supply, and general position, but for close location he needed to rely on radio and reconnaissance intelligence. Throughout, he gave the closest attention to movement intelligence. The Italian campaign gave Freyberg little help from Ultra. There were few possible German alternative strategies and tactics to be revealed in this campaign of attrition. Indeed, Ultra intercepts confused the allies in that part units, correctly identified by analysts, were taken to be whole units by the recipients of the Ultra transcripts.

All in all, Freyberg has emerged strong and impressive from the fire of this investigation — as a salamander should. It is not suggested that he is an undiscovered military genius — a new Alexander the Great, Napoleon, or Lee. It is argued, however, that he was not only a brilliant divisional commander, but also a highly able corps commander — albeit on two of these occasions the vanquished. At Crete and Cassino it is concluded that Freyberg could have done no more than he did. Loyal, sometimes beyond the call of duty, he did not later blame those who blamed him. The soundness of his planning, the economy of his casualties in an attritional cauldron such as Cassino, and his willingness to accept corps command (although his preference was for divisional) are marks of a successful professional commander.

This book is obviously not a complete life and times of Bernard Freyberg. Its concern has been limited to a study of the issues of innovative capacity, to his record of higher command, and his use of Ultra intelligence. Freyberg's consistent ability, tenacity, coolness, personal bravery, and humour have shone through the documents perused in the course of this study. He was never vindictive and he was horrified when others were, as demonstrated by his reaction to Montgomery's refusal to give his faithful chief of staff, Freddie de Guingand, a staff appointment in 1945 — 'the little bastard!'[12]

His personal modesty is well attested, particularly in his refusal to allow the publication of Montgomery's proposed foreword to a New Zealand Division training pamphlet. Its high praise deserves scrutiny:

> . . . What this pamphlet does not bring out is the magnificent leadership of Lt. General Sir Bernard Freyberg the commander of the New Zealand Forces in the Middle East. His splendid example, untiring energy, and infectious optimism were an inspiration to the whole army: wherever the battle was most intense, there was General Freyberg to be found. Such outstanding leadership can rarely have been seen in the history of the British Army.[13]

Chapter 1 — NOTES

1. A photograph exists of Freyberg as one of a group of 'Massey's Cossacks', taken at the time, in Sir John White's collection.
2. Auchinleck to Sir John Dill, Chief of the Imperial General Staff, 2 September 1941, in J. Connell, *Auchinleck,* pp. 275-6.
3. Mark Clark, quoted in J. Ellis, *Cassino: the Hollow Victory,* pp. 161-2.
4. W. G. McClymont, *To Greece,* NZ War History, p. 489; Hargest, quoted in J. McLeod, *Myth and Reality,* p. 175.
5. PRO PREM 3/109, Churchill minute to the Chiefs of Staff Committee, 14 June 1941.
6. Montgomery to Alan Brooke, the CIGS, 1 November 1942, quoted in N. Hamilton, *Monty — The Making of a General,* p. 836.
7. W. G. Stevens, *Bardia to Enfidaville,* NZ War History, pp. 183-4, 249-50.
8. F. Tuker, quoted in J. Ellis, op. cit., pp. 164, 178.
9. Churchill referred to Freyberg as 'the salamander'. He was recalling not only that Freyberg was like the mythological salamander enduring through fire, but also one of the generals of his famous ancestor, John Churchill, 1st Duke of Marlborough. Marlborough's sobriquet for Lord Cutts was the salamander, as Cutts was a fierce general of infantry, always in the thick of the fighting.
10. Montgombery to Alan Brooke, 1 November 1942, loc. cit.; Montgomery, in Barrie Pitt, *Crucible of War: Year of Alamein 1942,* p. 391.
11. Horrocks at the Battle of Tebaga Gap, and during the pursuit phase agreed to Freyberg's suggestions to alter the entire axis of advance in the follow-up operation.
12. F. M. Richardson, *Fighting Spirit: Psychological Factors in War,* Leo Cooper, 1978, p. 84.
13. Sir Leonard Thornton, interview with J. Tonkin-Covell, 16 July 1988.
14. F. W. von Mellinthin, *Panzer Battles* pp. 79, 84; ed. B. Liddell Hart, *The Rommel Papers,* p. 240.
15. Wavell to CIGS and Auchinleck, 27 August 1941, in J. Connell, *Auchinleck,* pp. 275-6.
16. H. Kippenberger, quoted in correspondence with Scoullar, Stevens, and Long, in J. McLeod, *Myth and Reality,* pp. 170-1, 179-80.
17. Ibid., pp. 170-85 *passim;* R. Lewin, *Ultra Goes to War,* pp. 158-9.
18. Robin Higham, *Diary of a Disaster,* p. 211.

Chapter 2 — NOTES

1. Freyberg's Report to the Minister of Defence (N.Z.), in Davin, p. 40.
2. Hinsley, vol. 1, pp. 137-8, 144, 391.
3. Calvocoressi, p. 68.
4. Hinsley, vol. 1, pp. 570-1, Calvocoressi, p. 68.
5. Hinsley, vol. 1, p. 571.
6. Ibid.
7. Ibid., pp. 221; 571-2.
8. Ibid., pp. 415-16.
9. Ibid., p. 417.
10. Ibid., pp. 415-17.
11. Ibid., p. 416
12. Ibid.,
13. Freyberg to Fraser, 1 May 1941, *Documents,* vol. 1, no. 388, p. 286.

14. PRO PREM 3/109, JIC (41) 181, 27 April 1941; GHQ, ME to War Office c. 2 May 1941, *Documents,* vol. 1, No. 393, p. 290.
15. Freyberg's Special Order of the Day, 1 May 1941, *Documents,* vol. 1, no. 390, p. 288.
16. Creforce Operation Order, no. 2, 29 April, 1941, PRO WO 169/1334A.
17. Ibid., Appendix A.
18. N.Z. Division, *War Diary,* WAII 1/21.1/1/17 vol. 3, Appendix 136, pp. 10-11.
19. Creforce Operation Instruction No. 10, 5 May 1941, issued 0200 hours, 4 May 1941. PRO WO 169/1334A.
20. Amendments to Creforce Operation Instruction No. 10, 5 May 1941, loc. cit.
21. Creforce Operation Instruction No. 10, 3 May 1941, loc. cit.
22. N.Z. Division, *War Diary,* entry 3 May 1941, WAII 1/DA 21.1/1/1-69.
23. GOC's diary, 4 May 1941, WAII 8/43; also 5 Brigade *War Diary* entry Sunday 4 May 1941, PRO WO 179/724.
24. 22 Battalion, *War Diary,* Maleme, PRO WO 179/735.
25. GOC's diary, 5 May 1941, loc. cit.
26. Freyberg to Wavell, 5 May 1941, *Documents,* vol. 1, no. 399, pp. 293-4.
27. Freyberg to Churchill, 5 May 1941, *Documents,* vol. 1, no. 398, p. 293; also PRO PREM 3/109, p. 133.
28. Hinsley, vol. 1, p. 417.
29. Ibid., p. 418.
30. OL302 of 1745 hours GMT, 13 May 1941, PRO DEFE 3/686.
31. OL278 of 2230 hours, 11 May 1941, PRO DEFE 3/687.
32. OL319 of 1840 hours, 14 May 1941, PRO DEFE 3/686.
33. 23 Battalion Operation Instruction, no. 3, 5 May 1941, in 23 Battalion *War Dairy,* PRO WO 179/736.
34. Ibid.
35. Ibid., entry for 15 May 1941.
36. Ismay to Churchill, PRO PREM 3/109, letter dated 2 July 1941 on the moon conditions on Crete at the time of the invasion.
37. Stewart, p. 96, quoted from G. Long, *Greece, Crete* . . . Canberra, 1953, p. 215.
38. N.Z. Division, *War Diary,* entry 7 May 1941, loc. cit.
39. W. Gibbons letter, 11 August 1978.
40. 23 Battalion, *War Dairy,* loc. cit.
41. 22 Battalion, *War Dairy,* loc. cit.
42. GOC's diary, 8 May 1941; *Documents,* vol. 1, no. 385, p. 283.
43. OL258 of 2105 hours, 8 May 1941, PRO DEFE 3/687.
44. OL262 of 1030 hours, 10 May 1941, PRO DEFE 3/687.
45. Creforce Operation Instruction No. 11, 11 May 1941, and Creforce Operation Instruction No. 13, of 15 May 1941, PRO WO 169/1334A.
46. Creforce Operation Instruction No. 11, 11 May 1941, PRO 169/1334A.
47. Freyberg to Fraser, 11 May 1941, *Documents,* vol. 2., no. 15, p. 10.
48. GOC's diary, 11 May 1941.
49. Freyberg to Smith, General Headquarters Cairo, 11 May 1941, *Documents,* vol. 1, no. 403, pp. 296-7.
50. GOC's diary, 11 May, 1941.
51. Prime Minister's Personal Minute to First Sea Lord, CIGS, and Chief of Air Staff, 10 May 1941, PRO PREM 3/109, Serial no. D164/1.
52. L.C. Hollis minute, Office of the Minister of Defence to the Prime Minister, 12 May 1941, PRO PREM 3/109.
53. OL268 of 1025 hours, 11 May 1941, OL277 of 2130 hours, 11 May 1941, OL278 of 2230 hours, 11 May 1941, PRO DEFE 3/687.
54. Brigadier Hargest's diary 10 May 1941, WAII DA52/10/10.
55. 5 Brigade, *War Dairy,* 11 May 1941, PRO WO 179/724.

56. 5 Brigade Operation Instruction No. 4, 18 May 1941, in Davin p. 66. Ross, pp. 62-3, Stewart p. 124.
57. Ibid.
58. Ross, p. 63.
59. Ibid.
60. Ibid.
61. Ibid.
62. GOC's diary, 12 May 1941.
63. J. Connell, *Wavell, p. 454.*
64. *BGS Appreciation — German Plan for Attack on Crete,* Force HQ, 12 May 1941, WAII 8/16 BGS file March to May 1941.
65. Hinsley, vol. 1, p. 418.
66. Baron von der Heydte, *Daedalus Returned,* Hutchinson 1958, pp. 40, 43; Stewart pp. 138-9.
67. CX/JQ911, OL302 of 1745 hours, 13 May 1941, PRO DEFE 3/686.
68. In Creforce Operation Instruction No. 10 of 3 May, the 5 May Amendment, the cable on the role of Greek troops, and the BGS Appreciation of 12 May 1941 for instance.
69. GOC's dairy, 14 May 1941.
70. Cox, p. 66.
71. Freyberg, comments on the Davin draft, 1952, Davin Papers, quoted in Stewart p. 128.
72. Brigadier Hargest's dairy, 13 May 1941, loc. cit.
73. GOC's diary, 15 May 1941.
74. OL319 of 1840 hours, 14 May 1941, PRO DEFE 3/686.
75. 22 Battalion *War Dairy,* May 1941, loc. cit.
76. General Conrad Seibt, The Crete Operation (XI Air Corps) MS 8-641 p. 35, Appendix C, in *World War II German Military Studies, vol. 13.*
77. Creforce Operation Instruction No. 13, 15 May 1941, PRO WO 169/1334A.
78. Creforce Operation Instruction No. 16, 18 May 1941, loc. cit.
79. 5 Brigade, *War Dairy* entry Thursday 15 May, loc. cit.
80. 22nd Battalion, *War Diary,* preamble, May 1941, loc. cit.
81. Ibid.
82. Ibid.; W.E. Murphy, pp. 110-11.
83. 22nd Battalion, *War Dairy,* May 1941, loc. cit.
84. Ibid.
85. Cox, p. 48.
86. 22nd Battalion, *War Diary,* May 1941, loc. cit.; Comeau, p. 61.
87. Freyberg to Wavell, 16 May 1941, *Documents,* vol. 1, no. 404, p. 297.
88. OL339 of 0805 hours, 16 May and OL341 of 1340 hours, 16 May, PRO DEFE 3/687.
89. General Conrad Seibt, loc. cit., pp. 19-20.
90. GOC's diary, 17 May 1941.
91. OL354 of 1045 hours, 17 May 1941, PRO DEFE 3/687.
92. GOC's diary, 18 May 1941; *Documents* vol. 1, no. 406, 18 May 1941, p. 298.
93. OL370 of 0150 hours, 19 May 1941, PRO DEFE 3/687.
94. Playfair et al., vol 2, p. 130.
95. Stewart, p. 142.
96. Ibid.
97. Hinsley, vol. 1, p. 419.
98. Report of AOC, Crete, p. 37, WAII 8/PART II C.
99. GOC's dairy, 19 May 1941.

Chapter 3 — NOTES

1. 22nd Battalion *War Diary,* PRO WO 179/735.
2. Davin, Appendix IV, p. 482.
3. 22nd Battalion *War Dairy,* loc. cit.
4. D. Richards, *Royal Air Force 1939-1945, vol. 1., HMSO 1953, pp. 331-2.*
5. Howell, in Stewart, pp. 148-9.
6. Ibid., pp. 146-7.
7. 22nd Battalion, *War Dairy,* loc. cit.
8. Ibid.
9. Stewart, p. 150.
10. Davin, p. 90 — perhaps as many as thirty gliders?
11. Ibid.
12. Ibid., pp. 90-4.
13. Gregory and Batchelor, p. 18.
14. Davin, p. 95.
15. Long, p. 221.
16. Creforce to General Headquarters, Middle East, 9 am 20 May, *Documents,* vol. 1., p. 299, fn. 1.
17. Stewart, pp. 200-1.
18. Report by Captain Watson in Davin, pp. 122-3.
19. W. Gibbons letter, 11 August 1983.
20. Davin, pp. 95-6; Stewart, p. 165.
21. Davin, p. 96.
22. 22nd Battalion, *War Diary,* loc. cit., entry 20 May 1941.
23. Report by Lt. J.W.C. Craig, 17 Platoon, D Company 22 Battalion, in Davin, p. 100.
24. 5 Brigade, *War Dairy,* 1030 hours 20 May 1941. PRO WO 179/724.
25. W. Gibbons, interview with JTC, 27 July 1988.
26. Ibid.
27. Battle Report of Fliegerkorps XI, *Einsatz Kreta,* Appendix II, para. 4, quoted in Stewart, fn. 17, p. 159.
28. 23rd Battalion, *War Diary,* entry 20 May 1941, PRO WO 179/736.
29. Ibid.
30. 5 Brigade, *War Diary* — report from 22nd Battalion at 10.09 hours 20 May 1941, loc. cit.
31. Ibid., 1030 hours, 20 May 1941.
32. Ibid., 1055 hours, 20 May 1941.
33. Colonel Andrew, comment, Davin Papers, in Stewart, pp. 170-1.
34. 22nd Battalion, *War Diary,* loc. cit.
35. 5 Brigade, *War Dairy,* 1140 hours, 20 May, loc. cit.
36. Stewart, p. 171.
37. Henderson, p. 46; Davin, p. 106.
38. Ibid.
39. 22nd Battalion, *War Diary,* loc. cit.
40. 22nd Battalion, *War Diary,* loc. cit.
41. W. Gibbons letter to P. Gibbons, 12 August 1978.
42. 5 Brigade, *War Diary,* 1455 hours, 20 May 1941, loc. cit.
43. Ibid, 1550 hours, 20 May.
44. Davin, p. 135.
45. Creforce Operation Order No. 2., PRO WO 169/1334A.
46. Ross, p. 67.
47. Ibid.
48. 22nd Battalion, *War Diary,* 1700 hours 20 May 1941, loc. cit.

49. Major Thomason, quoted in Simpson, pp. 174, 182.
50. Stewart, p. 125.
51. Both being appointed because their commanding officers had been posted back to Egypt: Falconer (23rd) and Macky (21st).
52. Colonel Andrew, Narrative, Davin Papers, quoted in Stewart, p. 172.
53. Davin, p. 110; Stewart, p. 172.
54. Stewart, pp. 172-3.
55. Davin, p. 67, also fn. 2.
56. Ibid.
57. Henderson, p. 73.
58. Ibid., pp. 73-4.
59. Ibid., p. 71.
60. Ibid., p. 73.
61. Ibid.
62. Ibid.
63. Ibid., p. 74.
64. Ibid., p. 73.
65. Gericke, in Stewart, pp. 172-4.
66. Davin, p. 110.
67. Ibid.; Stewart, p. 174.
68. Davin, p. 111; Stewart, p. 175.
69. W. Gibbons letter to P. Gibbons, 12 August 1978.
70. Freyberg to Wavell, 20 May 1941, *Documents,* vol. 1, no. 408, p. 299.
71. Cox, pp. 75-6.
72. Freyberg to Fraser, 20 May 1941, *Documents,* vol. 1, no. 409, p. 299.
73. GOC's diary, 20 May 1941.
74. Simpson, p. 195.
75. 5 Brigade, *War Diary,* 1825 hours 20 May 1941, loc. cit; Davin, p. 137; Simpson, p. 194.
76. Davin, pp. 112, 134; Stewart, p. 177; Simpson, p. 194.
77. 22nd Battalion, *War Diary,* loc. cit.
78. Ibid.
79. Ibid.
80. Ibid.
81. Colonel Andrew, Ibid.
82. 23rd Battalion, *War Diary,* loc. cit.
83. 22nd Battalion, *War Diary,* loc. cit.
84. Ismay to Churchill minute of 2 July 1941, PRO PREM 3/109.
85. 23rd Battalion, *War Diary,* 21 May 1941, loc. cit.
86. Stewart, pp. 232, 243-4.
87. Major Philp, narrative Davin Papers, in Stewart, pp. 255-6; Leckie's support for Hargest — let down by Andrew, Davin Papers, quoted in Stewart, p. 256.
88. Philp narrative in Stewart, p. 256.
89. W. Gibbons letter to P. Gibbons, 12 August, 1978.
90. NZ Division, *War Diary,* entry 0430 hours, 21 May 1944, loc. cit.
91. 5 Brigade, *War Diary,* entry 0500 hours, 21 May 1941, loc. cit.
92. Stewart, p. 185; Davin, p. 142. Less than three years later, Heidrich, Heilmann, and Neuhoff would be instrumental in holding Cassino against the NZ Division.
93. Davin, p. 140.
94. Ibid., pp. 140-1.
95. Ibid., p. 141; Stewart, p. 187.
96. *Einsatz Kreta,* Battle Report of Fliegerkorps XI, in Stewart, p. 201.

97. Davin, Appendix IV, pp. 480-1.
98. In Stewart, p. 206.
99. Ibid.; Davin, p. 179.
100. Davin, p. 180.
101. Ibid., p. 179.
102. Stewart, p. 210.
103. Ibid.; Davin, p. 174.
104. Stewart, p. 215.
105. Letter, Campbell to Stewart, 5 May 1960, in ibid., p. 217.
106. Letter, Campbell to Stewart, 1 May 1960, in ibid., p. 319.
107. Stewart, pp. 319-21; Davin, pp. 174-7.
108. General Student, quoted in Stewart, p. 253.
109. Ibid.
110. Gericke, letter to Stewart, 21 January 1960, in Stewart, p. 254.
111. Ibid., p. 262; Simpson, p. 203.
112. NZ Division, *War Diary,* 21 May, loc. cit.
113. Davin, p. 195; Stewart, p. 272; Simpson, pp. 201-2.
114. Long, p. 235, quoted in Stewart, p. 272.
115. Stewart, p. 264.
116. Captain J. N. Anderson, narrative in Davin, p. 188.
117. From Battle Report of *Einsatz Kreta;* in Simpson, p. 204.
118 Wenning, in Simpson, pp. 223-5: originally translated from diary.
119. Ibid.
120. W. Gibbons letter, 11 August 1983.
121. 23rd Battalion, *War Diary,* 21 May 1941, loc. cit.
122. Davin, p. 198.
123. Ibid.
124. Colonel J. T. Burrows, 4 Brigade Report, Appendix D, in Major-General Inglis' Papers, folder 45, Alexander Turnbull Library, MS 421.
125. Davin, pp. 222-3.
126. Gibbons' letter, 11 August 1983.
127. Simpson, note 42, Chapter 6, pp. 301-2.
128. Davin, p. 216.
129. Stewart, p. 299-300; Davin, p. 221-2.
130. Cox, quoted recollection, in Stewart, p. 307.
131. Message from Rear Admiral, 7th Cruiser Squadron, to First Lord of the Admiralty, PRO PREM 3/109 p. 12; D. A. Thomas, *Crete 1941: The Battle at Sea,* pp. 157, 173.
132. P. Smith, *Divebomber,* pp. 138-9.
133. OL404 of 0330 hours GMT, 22 May 1941, PRO DEFE 3/687.
134. OL411 of 1030 hours GMT, 22 May 1941, PRO DEFE 3/687.
135. GOC's diary, 22 May 1941.
136. W. Gibbons letter to JTC, 18 July 1988.
137. Davin, p. 238; Simpson, p. 236.
138. NZ Division Report, para. 97, in Davin, p. 239.
139. NZ Division, *War Diary,* 22 May 1941, loc. cit.
140. Ibid., 23 May 1941, loc. cit.
141. Freyberg to Wavell, 23 May 1941, *Documents,* vol. 1, no. 416, p. 302.
142. Freyberg to Wavell, 23 May 1941, *Documents,* vol. 1, no. 417, p. 302-303.
143. GOC's diary, 23 May 1941.
144. Freyberg to Wavell, 24 May 1941, *Documents,* vol. 1, no. 423, p. 305-306.
145. GOC's diary, 24 May 1941.
146. Freyberg to Wavell, 25 May 1941, *Documents,* vol. 1, no. 426, p. 307.
147. Kippenberger, p. 66.

148. Lieutenant Thomas' report in Davin, p. 317.
149. Colonel Gray in Simpson, p. 254.
150. Davin, p. 314; Simpson, p. 254.
151. GOC's diary, 25 May 1941.
152. Davin, p. 340.
153. Freyberg to Wavell, 26 May 1941, *Documents,* vol. 1, no. 428, p. 308.
154. Davin, p. 326 and fn. 2, Puttick's Report on Operations in Crete, Appendix A.
155. Davin, p. 339.
156. Brigadier Hargest's diary, 26 May 1941, loc. cit.
157. 23rd Battalion, *War Diary,* 0900 hours, 26 May, loc. cit.
158. 22nd Battalion, *War Diary,* 1100 hours, 26 May, loc. cit.
159. 5 Brigade, *War Diary,* 1420 hours, 26 May, loc. cit.; Davin, p. 350.
160. 4 NZ Brigade Report on Operations in Crete, 28 April–31 May 1941, Part III, 26 May, Major-General Inglis' Papers, MS421, folder 45.
161. 19 Australian Brigade, *War Diary,* 26 May 1941, WAII 1/DA364.4/1/1.
162. 0.181 NZ Division to Creforce, 26 May, Davin, p. 342.
163. 0.182 NZ Division to Creforce, 26 May, Davin, p. 343.
164. Ibid.
165. Stewart, pp. 402-3.
166. Freyberg, quoted in Davin Papers, in Stewart, p. 402.
167. Davin, p. 342; Stewart, p. 403.
168. Stewart, p. 406.
169. Davin, pp. 343-4; Stewart, p. 406.
170. 19 Australian Brigade *War Diary,* 26 May 1941, loc. cit.
171. Stewart, p. 401.
172. Lieutenant-Colonel A. Duncan to Stewart, 4 February 1963, in Stewart, p. 414.
173. Major-General Inglis letter, 16 May 1961, in Davin, p. 345.
174. 19 Australian Brigade, *War Diary,* 1900 hours and 1930 hours, 26 May 1941, loc. cit.
175. Ibid.
176. Kay, *27 Machine-Gun Battalion,* p. 111.
177. 4 NZ Brigade Report on Operations in Crete, Inglis Papers, MS421, folder 45.
178. Brigadier Hargest's diary, entry 26 May 1941, loc. cit.
179. Cody, *N.Z. Engineers,* p. 152, fn. 45.
180. Davin, p. 348.
181. NZ Division, *War Diary,* 20 May 1941, loc. cit; Davin, p. 360; Stewart, p. 408.
182. Davin, p. 359.
183. NZ Division, *War Diary,* 26/27 May 1941, loc. cit.
184. Brigadier Hargest's diary, 26 May 1941, loc. cit.
185. Ibid.
186. Ibid.
187. Ibid.; Stewart, p. 421; Simpson, p. 258.
188. Cody, *28 Battalion,* p. 119.
189. Captain F. Baker, A Company Commander's Report, in Davin, pp. 377-8.
190. Kippenberger, to Brigadier H. B. Latham, 27 August 1952, in Davin Papers, quoted Stewart, p. 372.
191. Davin, Appendix V, pp. 486-8; Appendix VIII, pp. 520-1.
192. Ibid., Appendix V.

Chapter 4 — NOTES

1. Brigadier Hargest's diary 2 June 1941, loc. cit.
2. McLeod, p. 175.

3. Ibid.
4. Sir John Colville's diary, 6 June 1941, in Martin Gilbert op. cit., vol. 5, p. 1103.
5. Ibid., 7 June 1941, in M. Gilbert, vol. 6, p. 1103.
6. Great Britain, Parliament. House of Commons. *Hansard* HMSO, 10 June 1941.
7. Kippenberger letter to Stevens, 8 April 1953, Department of Internal Affairs Files, IA 181/32/15; M. Gilbert, vol. 6, p. 1113; PRO PREM 3/109 D186/1.
8. PRO PREM 3/109 D186/1, Prime Minister to General Ismay for Chiefs of Staff Committee, 14 June 1941.
9. W. C. McClymont letter to Fairbrother, 14 May 1958, N.Z. Department of Internal Affairs Files IA 181/32/15.
10. Hinsley, vol. 1, p. 417.
11. McClymont, *To Greece,* p. 489.
12. Brigadier Hargest's 'short diary', 20 June 1941 loc. cit.
13. PRO WO106/3126, Report by an Inter-Services Committee on Operations in Crete (November 1, 1940, to May 31, 1941).
14. Ibid., part II, p. 10, no. 4.
15. Ibid., part II, p. 13, nos., 19-20, 23-4.
16. Ibid., part III, p. 15, no. 6.
17. Ibid., part III, p. 20, nos, 46, 47; the report noted of Force Reserve that 'Their efforts. . . may have done much to stem the tide.' p. 21, no. 50.
18. Ibid., part III, p. 21, no. 51.
19. Ibid., part IV, p. 29, no. 7.
20. Brigadier Hargest's 'short diary', loc. cit.
21. J. Connell, *Auchinleck,* pp. 275-6. CIGS to Auchinleck and Wavell, 20 August 1941.
22. Ibid., Wavell to CIGS, 21 August 1941.
23. Ibid., Wavell to CIGS and Auchinleck, 27 August 1941.
24. Ibid., Auchinleck to CIGS, 2 September 1941.
25. Horner, pp. 105, 108. Based on Gavin Long Notes 55 — interview with Brigadier W. G. Cremor, 30 July 1944, and G. Long Notes 44 — interview with Major-General G.A. Vasey, 21 April 1944.
26. Brigadier Hargest's diary, 25 May 1941; loc. cit.; Davin p. 341.

Chapter 5 — NOTES

1. H. Kippenberger, *Infantry Brigadier,* p. 81.
2. Fraser to Freyberg, 16 September 1941.
3. F. W. von Mellenthin, *Panzer Battles,* p. 68.
4. Ibid., p. 76.
5. Ibid., pp. 79, 84.
6. John Strawson, *El Alamein. Desert Victory,* p. 27.
7. Kippenberger, pp. 169-70.
8. David Irving, *Hitler's War,* pp. 169-70.
9. Kippenberger, p. 222.
10. Ibid., p. 226.
11. GOC's diary, 23 October 1942, N/A.
12. Ibid.
13. Ibid., 25 October 1941.
14. Ibid.
15. Ibid.
16. Nigel Hamilton *Monty. The Making of a General,* pp. 802-3.

17. Michael Carver, *El Alamein,* p. 137.
18. Strawson, p. 134.
19. GOC's diary, 2 November 1942.
20. Ibid.
21. Carver, p. 180.
22. Barrie Pitt, *The Crucible of War: Year of Alamein 1942,* p. 391.

Chapter 6 — NOTES

1. Montgomery's diary, March 1943, in Hamilton, vol. 2. p. 186.
2. W. G. Stevens, *Bardia to Enfidaville,* p. 160.
3. Freyberg, *Left Hook,* WA II 8/40.
4. Ibid.
5. Ibid.
6. Ibid.
7. Ibid.
8. Ibid.
9. Ibid.
10 Ibid.
11. Montgomery's Order for Operation Pugilist, 26 February 1943, in W. G. Stevens, *Bardia to Enfidaville,* p. 133.
12. GOC's diary, entries for 15 and 16 March 1943.
13. Ibid., 17 March 1943.
14. Ibid.
15. Ibid., 19 March 1943.
16. Ibid.
17. VM 6911 of 19 March 1943; CX/MSS/2291/21. Hinsley, vol. 2 p. 598; evening decrypt VM6845, 19 March; CX/MSS/2290/T10, Hinsley, vol. 2, p. 599.
18. GOC's diary, 20 March 1943.
19. Ibid.
20. Ibid., 20/21 March 1943.
21. Ibid.
22. VM6964 of 20 March 1943; CX/MSS/2294/T13, Hinsley vol 2, p. 599.
23. CX/MSS/T6, Ibid.
24. Montgomery's desert diary entry 20 March 1943, Hamilton vol. 2, p 187.
25. GOC's diary, 21 March 1943.
26. Ibid.
27. Montgomery to Freyberg, Main 8 Army to NZ Corps. 0.371, 21 March 1943, MOST IMMEDIATE, WA II 8/30 Turning of Mareth; GOC's diary 21 March 1943 notes receipt time as 2130 hours.
28. GOC's diary, 21 March 1943.
29. Sir Leonard Thornton, interview JTC, 16 July 1988.
30. PRO WO169/8519 No. 460 of 21 March 1943, in Hinsley, vol. 2 p. 600.
31. GOC's diary, 22 March 1943.
32. Ibid.
33. Ibid.
34. Hamilton, vol. 2, pp. 192-3.
35. Leese's unpublished memoirs, quoted in Hamilton, vol. 2, p. 193.
36. de Guingard, quoted ibid.
37. Ibid., p. 194.
38. Ibid., p. 195.
39. W. G. Stevens, *Bardia to Enfidaville,* p. 191.
40. GOC's diary, 23 March 1943.

41. Ibid.
42. Hinsley vol. 2, p. 601.
43. GOC's diary, 24 March 1943.
44. Ibid.
45. Ibid.
46. W. G. Stevens, *Bardia to Enfidaville,* p. 199.
47. Freyberg and Horrocks to Montgomery, Message 503, quoted ibid. p. 199.
48. Major-General M. St. J. Oswald, Interviewed by Nigel Hamilton 1 February 1983, in Hamilton vol. 2, pp. 197-8.
49. Montgomery to Freyberg and Horrocks, 24 March 1943, in W. G. Stevens, *Bardia to Enfidaville,* p. 200.
50. GOC's diary, 25 March 1943.
51. Ibid.
52. Ibid.
53. Ibid.
54. Ibid.
55. Ibid.
56. Ibid.
57. Ibid.
58. Ibid.
59. Ibid.
60. Sir Brian Horrocks in Hamilton op. cit. p. 201 fn.
61. de Guingand to Freyberg and Horrocks, 25 March 1943, in W. G. Stevens, *Bardia to Enfidaville* pp. 201-2.
62. Sir Harry Broadhurst, interviewed with Nigel Hamilton 20 Nov. 1979, in Hamilton op. cit. p. 200.
63. Ibid.
64. Ibid.
65. Sir Charles Richardson (Montgomery's GSO1 (Ops) at the time), interview with Nigel Hamilton, Ibid p. 201
66. F. H. Searl letter to Hamilton, 16 June 1981, Ibid p. 203.
67. GOC's diary, 26 March 1943.
68. Ibid.
69. Sir Leonard Thornton interview with JTC 16 July 1988.
70. Sir Sidney Kirkman, in Hamilton p. 753.
71. C. Messenger pp 28-31.
72. B. Pitt, *The Crucible of War: Year of Alamein* 1942 p. 101; also M. M. Poston, D. Hay, and J. D. Scott, *Design and Development of Weapons* HMSO 1964, p. 348.
73. de Guingand to Major-General McCreery, 25 March 1943 in Hamilton p. 199.
74. GOC's diary, 26 March 1943.
75. Air Historical Branch Monograph AHB/II/117/8 (c) pp. 211-213.
76. GOC's diary, 26 March 1943.
77. Freyberg to Fraser, 5 April 1943, in *Documents* vol. 2 no. 204 p. 171.
78. GOC's diary, 26 March 1943.
79. Ibid.
80. Ibid, 26/27 March 1943.
81. 21 Panzer Division *War Diary,* in W. G. Stevens, *Bardia to Enfidaville* p. 230.
82. GOC's diary, 27 March 1943.
83. Hinsley vol. 2 p. 602: PRO WO 169/8519, no. 465 of 26 March 1943; WO 208/3581, no. I/200 of 26 March; VM 7559 of 1345/26 March; CX/MSS/2324/T14.
84. GOC's diary, 27 March 1943.
85. Montgomery to Alexander, 10 p.m. 26 March 1943, in Hamilton, p. 201.
86. GOC's diary, 27 March 1943.
87. PRO WO 169/8591 X Corps *War Diary,* 28 March 1943.

88. GOC's diary, 28 March 1943.
89. Montgomery's desert diary 28 March 1943, in Hamilton p. 208.
90. GOC's diary, 28 March 1943.
91. PRO WO 169/8591 X Corps *War Diary,* 28 March 1943, X Corps Operation Order No. 15.
92. Ibid.
93. GOC's diary, 28 March 1943.
94. Hinsley vol. 2 p. 603, VM7733 of 0943/28 March 1943; CX/MSS/2335/T65.
95. Ibid, PRO WO 169/8591 X Corps *War Diary,* 28 March 1943.
96. PRO WO 169/8591 X Corps *War Diary,* 28 March 1943.
97. GOC's diary, 28 March 1943.

Chapter 7 — NOTES

1. Phillips, *Italy,* vol. 1, p. 178.
2. Ibid. p. 182.
3. Ibid.
4. Freyberg to Harding, 21 January 1944, from HQ SPADGER FORCE, in WAII/8/49.
5. Graham and Bidwell, p. 144.
6. Freyberg's address to Conference at N.Z. Division HQ, 1700 hrs, 22 January 1944, in WAII/8/49.
7. Molony, pp. 694-5.
8. Ibid. p. 694.
9. General Field Marshal Albert Kesselring, 'Concluding Remarks on the Mediterranean Campaign', 4 July 1948, in *German Military Studies World War II,* vol. 14 MS C-031 pp. 3-4; Molony, p. 479.
10. Kesselring, p. 5; Molony, p. 694.
11. Conclusions of Battalion and Company Commanders of 5th N.Z. Infantry Brigade from the Sangro battles of 28/29 November and 24 December, 1943, in January 1944, in WAII/8/49.
12. Ibid.
13. Kesselring, p. 14.
14. Ellis, p. 118.
15. Smith, p. 61.
16. Freyberg to officers and NCOs at 4th Armoured Brigade, 27 January 1944, in WAII/8/49.
17. Harding to Fifth Army, CGS no. 207, 30 January 1944, in WAII/8/50.
18. Smith p. 43; Ellis p. 94.
19. Ellis. p. 135.
20. Ibid., p. 161.
21. Trevelyan, pp. 83-4.
22. Clark, pp 283-4.
23. Clark's diary, in Blumenson, *Salerno to Cassino,* p. 402.
24. N.Z. Corps Outline Plan, 2 February, 1944, in WAII/8/50.
25. Conference at N.Z. Division HQ, 0900 hrs, 3 February 1944, in WAII/8/50.
26. Molony, pp. 705-6.
27. Ibid., p. 706.
28. Ibid.
29. Fifth Army Operations Instruction, 5 February 1944, in PRO WO204/6809.
30. Notes for a Conference on Air Support, 1000 hrs, 6 February 1944, in WAII/8/50.
31. Conference at N.Z. Corps HQ, 0800 hrs, 7 February 1944, in WAII/8/50.
32. Quoted in 'Telegram from Air Ministry to AFHQ', Algiers (Ref 02659) 5

February 1944, in PRO WO204/1454.

33. Alexander to Churchill, 8 February 1944, quoted in Molony, p. 705.
34. Freyberg, conversation with Harding, 8 February 1944, in WAII/8/50.
35. Cipher Message to External, Wellington from Main N.Z. Corps for Minister of Defence from Gen. Freyberg, 14 February 1944; CM to Main N.Z. Corps from Ext., Wellington for Gen. Freyberg from Minister of Defence, 16 February 1944, in WAII/8/50.
36. Ellis. p. 162.
37. N.Z. Corps Operation Instruction No. 4, 9 February 1944, in WAII/8/50.
38. GOC's diary, 9 February 1944.
39. Ibid.
40. N.Z. Corps Intelligence Summary No. 20, 10 February 1944, WAII 8/50, February 1944.
41. N.Z. Corps Intelligence Summary No. 21, 11 February 1944, WAII 8/50, February 1944.
42. GOC's diary, 11 February 1944.
43. Ibid.
44. Ibid.
45. Ibid.
46. Ibid.
47. Ibid.
48. Alexander's Operation Instruction, 11 February, quoted in Molony, p. 704.
49. N.Z. Corps Intelligence Summary No. 22, 12 February 1944, WAII 8/50, February 1944.
50. GOC's diary, 12 February 1944.
51. von Senger, *Neither Fear Nor Hope,* p.202.
52. Ellis p. 171; Graham and Bidwell, p. 181.
53. GOC's diary, 12 February 1944.
54. Ibid.
55. Notes of Taking Over Conference at HQ US 2 Corps, 0930 hours, 12 February 1944, WAII 8/50 February 1944.
56. GOC's diary, 12 February 1944.
57. Lieutenant-Colonel Glennie, 1st Royal Sussex, quoted in Graham and Bidwell, p. 197.
58. Graham and Bidwell, p. 198.
59. GOC's diary, 12 February 1944.
60. Ibid.
61. Letter, Tuker to Freyberg, 12 February 1944, WAII 8/50 February 1944. In addition to the other letter that urged a turning movement, Tuker also saw Freyberg and urged him not to compromise — Ellis p. 164.
62. GOC's diary, 12 February 1944.
63. Bishop Gregorio Diamare, Abbot of Monte Cassino (in Böhmler p. 177): 'In order to ensure the safety of the irreplaceable treasures and library, I had long before approved of their removal by German troops, who handed them over to the Vatican State.'
64. Graham and Bidwell, pp. 421-4, review the controversy succinctly.
65. Ibid., p. 422.
66. GOC's diary 12 February 1944.
67. Ibid., 13 February 1944.
68. Ibid.
69. Ibid., 14 February 1944.
70. Ibid.
71. Stevens, *Freyberg: The Man,* p. 91.
72. GOC's diary, 14 February 1944.

73. XIV Panzer Corps to Tenth Army, Appreciation of the Situation, 15 February 1944. XIV Panzer Corps Miscellaneous Appendices February 1944, p. 2 NA (MMS) Transl. from GMDS File 58199/20.
74. Ibid.
75. GOC's diary, 15 February 1944.
76. Kippenberger, p. 355.
77. Hinsley, et al. vol. 3, part 1, p. 193.
78. GOC's diary, 15 February 1944.
79. Molony, p. 713.
80. Hinsley, et al., vol. 3, part 1, p. 192.
81. Phillips, *Italy,* vol. 1, p. 226.
82. Ibid.
83. Ibid., pp. 226-7.
84. Ellis, pp. 184-5.
85. Stevens, *4th Indian Division,* p. 285.
86. GOC's diary, 16 February 1944.
87. Ibid.
88. Ellis, p. 186.
89. Majdalany, p. 148.
90. GOC's diary, 17 February 1944.
91. Ibid.
92. Ibid.
93. Ibid.
94. N.Z. Corps Intelligence Summary No. 27 of 1800 hours, 17 February 1944, in N.Z. Division, *War Diary,* loc. cit.
95. Colonel J. Showers, 1/2 Gurkhas, quoted in Stevens, *History of the 2nd Gurkha Rifles,* Gale and Polden, pp 102-3.
96. D. Pal, *Campaign in Italy,* Longman, 1960, p. 112.
97. Ellis, p. 193.
98. Molony, p. 718.
99. GOC's diary, 18 February 1944.
100. Phillips, vol. 1, pp 232-3.
101. Ibid., pp. 234-7.

Chapter 8 — NOTES

1. GOC's diary, 18 February 1944.
2. GOC's diary, 19 February 1944.
3. PRO WO204/10388 Outgoing message from AFHQ to Air Ministry for British COS, inf. Britman Washington for JCS, 20 February 1944.
4. Phillips, p. 246.
5. In Molony, p. 779.
6. Minutes of meeting at NZ Corps HQ, 1100 hours 21 February 1944, WAII 8/50 February 1944.
7. Phillips, p. 246.
8. Ibid., p. 252.
9. Sir Leonard Thornton, interview with JTC, 16 July 1988.
10. Molony, p. 780. It is important to note that 1st Parachute Division had recently taken casualties and was not up to full strength. Neither was NZ Corps.
11. Böhmler, p. 205-6.
12. von Senger's diary quoted in Ellis, p. 206.
13. General Weir, CRA, NZ Corps — comment on draft in Phillips p. 258.
14. 2 NZ Division Air Support Instruction, 11 March 1944, WAII 8/51, March 1944.

15. Molony, p. 785 — around 40 per cent hit the target. Had close to 100 per cent hit the town, perhaps the paratroopers *might* have suffered more casualties.
16. Böhmler, pp. 210-11.
17. Ellis, pp. 224-5.
18. Ibid., p. 222; Molony p. 786-7.
19. Ellis, p. 226.
20. Trevelyan, p. 201.
21. Ellis, p. 231.
22. Air Force Report in the Battle for Cassino, 14-24 March 1944, WAII 8/51, March 1944.
23. PRO WO204/7275 NZ Corps Operations 3 March to 26 March 1944 — Notes on Air Support for the Attack on Cassino.
24. NZ Corps Situation Report No. 44, 15 March 1944, NZ Division, *War Diary,* loc. cit.
25. GOC's diary, 15 March 1944.
26. NZ Corps Situation Report No. 46, 16 March 1944, NZ Division, *War Diary.*
27. Phillips, pp. 283-4.
28. GOC's diary, 0740 hours, 16 March 1944.
29. NZ Corps Situation Report No. 53, 2100 hours 16 March 1944. loc. cit.
30. GOC's diary, 1810 hours and 1950 hours, 16 March 1944.
31. Ibid., 2210 hours, 16 March 1943.
32. German paratrooper quoted in Graham and Bidwell p. 218; Böhmler's figures tend to agree.
33. Phillips, p. 171.
34. GOC's diary, 17 March 1944.
35. Ibid., 0820 hours, 17 March 1944.
36. Ibid., 0845 hours, 17 March 1944.
37. NZ Corps Situation Report No. 56, 0930 hours, 17 March 1944, loc. cit.
38. Phillips, pp. 292-3; Molony, p. 792; Ellis, pp. 242-3.
39. Phillips, pp. 294-7, Ellis, p. 244, Molony, p. 292.
40. Phillips, pp, 297-8.
41. XIV Panzer Corps Evening Report, 17 March 1944, Excerpts, p. 2, quoted in Ellis, p. 244.
42. GOC's diary, 17 March 1944.
43. Ibid.
44. NZ Corps Situation Report No. 64, 2100 hours, 17 March 1944, loc. cit.
45. NZ Corps Intentions night 17/18 March, 1944, No 66, loc. cit.
46. Phillips, p. 304; Ellis, p. 247.
47. Norton, p. 376.
48. Ellis, p. 247.
49. G. R. Stevens, *Fourth Indian Division* p. 309.
50. NZ Corps Situation Report No. 74, 2000 hours.
51. XIV Panzer Corps, *War Diary,* 18 March 1944 in Ellis p. 247.
52. GOC's diary 0740 and 0830 hours, 18 March 1944.
53. Ibid., 0845 and 0900 hours, 18 March 1944.
54. Ibid., 1615 hours, 18 March 1944.
55. Ibid., 1930 hours, 18 March 1944.
56. Ibid., 0600 hours, 19 March 1944.
57. Phillips, pp. 309-10; Ellis, pp. 250-1; Molony, p. 797.
58. NZ Corps Intentions night 17/18 March 1944, No 75, loc. cit.; Phillips p. 310.
59. Pringle and Glue, pp. 388-9.
60. Molony, p. 798.

61. NZ Corps Situation Report No. 41, 2100 hours, 19 March 1944, NZ Division, *War Diary.*
62. GOC's diary, 0710 hours, 19 March 1944.
63. NZ Corps Intentions night 19/20 March at 2130 hours 19 March 1944, No. 42, loc. cit.
64. GOC's diary, 0705 hours, 20 March 1944.
65. Ibid., 1345 hours, 20 March 1944.
66. Ibid.
67. Ross, p. 328-9.
68. Ibid, p. 329.
69. Ibid, p. 334.
70. Böhmler, p. 215.
71. GOC's diary 20 March 1944.
72. NZ Corps Situation Report No. 55, 0900 hours, 20 March 1944, loc. cit.
73. Molony p. 799; Phillips, p. 319.
74. XIV Panzer Corps, Appreciation of the Situation, 20 March 1944. XIV Panzer Corps, Miscellaneous Appendices pp. 3-4; GMDS File 58199/20.
75. NZ Corps Situation Report, 0900 hours, 21 March 1944, loc. cit.
76. NZ Corps Situation Report, 2100 hours, 21 March 1944, loc. cit.
77. GOC's diary, 21 March 1944.
78. Ibid.
79. Ibid., 22 March 1944.
80. NZ Corps Situation Report, 0900 hours, 23 March 1944, loc. cit.
81. GOC's diary, conference 0900 hrs 23 March 1944.
82. Ibid.
83. Ibid.
84. Ibid., 1100 hours, 23 March 1944.
85. F. Majdalany, p. 221.
86. Robin Kay, *Italy,* II, pp. 208-9.
87. J. Strawson, *The Italian Campaign,* p. 176.
88. GOC's Diary, WA8/67 and 68.
89. Ibid.

Chapter 9 — NOTES

1. Freyberg to C. A. Berendsen, Permanent Head of the Prime Minister's Department, 6 November 1939.
2. Fraser's communications with the CIGS: J. Connell, *Auchinleck,* pp. 275-6.
3. Richard Humble, *Crusader. The Eighth Army's Forgotten Victory, November 1941–January 1942,* p. 146.
4. Nigel Hamilton, *Monty: The Making of a General, 1887–1942,* p. 643.
5. D. Graham and S. Bidwell, p. 272.
6 See below, Appendix 2.
7. Major General M. St. J. Oswald, *Desert Diary,* 1942–1943.
8. F. L. W. Wood, *Political and External Affairs, (NZ in the Second World War, 1939–45),* pp. 284-6.
9. B. C. Freyberg, 'The New Zealand Division in Cyrenaica and Lessons of the Campaign', WA II/8 (Part II) E.
10. Ibid.
11. Personal Interview: Sir John White with JTC, 14 December 1988.
12. Nigel Hamilton, *Monty: The Field Marshal, 1944–1976,* p. 597.
13. NZ Army Training Pamphlet. 'Alamein Lessons'. Author's collection.

APPENDIX ONE

Table of Strength of the NZ Army 1938–1940

1938

1. *NZ Regular Force*
95 officers
20 officer cadets
395 other ranks, of whom some 340 were either NZ Permanent Staff or Artillery, i.e. no infantry!
Total: 510

2. *NZ Territorial Force*
(active list only)
745 officers
6367 other ranks, of whom some 2728 were infantry, 1956 mounted rifles, 1170 artillery.
With 294 infantry officers, infantry strength = 3022
Total: 7112

Army Total: 7,622

1939

1. *NZ Regular Force*
100 officers
15 officer cadets
478 other ranks, of whom some were NZ Permanent Staff or artillery.
Total: 593

2. *NZ Territorial Force*
(active list only)
778 officers
9586 other ranks
Infantry
305 officers
4426 other ranks
4731
Mounted Rifles
156 officers
2005 other ranks
2161

Artillery
121 officers
1863 other ranks
1984
Total: 10,364

Army Total: 10,957

1940

1. *NZ Regular Force*
143 officers
20 officer cadets
552 other ranks
sub total: 715
NZ Regular Force in NZEF and Overseas
55 officers
187 other ranks
sub total: 242

Short Service Appts.
14 officers
18 other ranks
sub total: 32

Temporary Personnel
152 officers
898 other ranks
sub total: 1050

Reservists Recalled
12 officers
46 other ranks
sub total: 58
Officer Total: 396
Other Ranks Total: 1701

Total: 2,097

2. *NZ Territorial Force*
(active list only)
755 officers
14,694 other ranks
Total: 15,449

Army Total: 17,546
[This does not include the National Military Reserve. Class II: 11,769 including this makes a total of 29,315]

Table for Defence Vote for Military Forces excluding Air, Naval Expenditure

Years	£
1933-4	215,950
1934-5	321,686
1935-6	378,181
1936-7	427,635
1937-8	529,632
1938-9	706,753

Compiled from *AJHR,* 1939, H19, Appendix 3

APPENDIX TWO

Freyberg's Charter

The formal authority vested in General Freyberg by the New Zealand Government was based on two communications from the then Prime Minister, Savage, and the Minister of Defence, Jones.

5 January 1940

The General Officer for the time being
Commanding the 2nd New Zealand
Expeditionary Force Overseas

The General Officer Commanding will act in accordance with the instructions he receives from the Commander-in-Chief under whose command he is serving, subject only to the requirements of His Majesty's Government in New Zealand. He will, in addition to powers appearing in any relevant Statute or Regulations, be vested with the following powers:

(a) In the case of sufficiently grave emergency or in special circumstances, of which he must be the sole judge, to make decisions as to the employment of the 2nd New Zealand Expeditionary Force, and to communicate such decisions directly to the New Zealand Government, notwithstanding that in the absence of that extraordinary cause such communication would not be in accordance with the normal channels of communication indicated in the following paragraph and which for greater clearness are also indicated in an attached diagram.
(b) To communicate directly with the New Zealand Government and with the Army Department concerning any matter connected with the training and administration of the 2nd New Zealand Expeditionary Force.
(c) To communicate directly either with the New Zealand Government or with the Commander-in-Chief under whose command he is serving, in respect of all details leading up to and arising from policy decisions.
(d) In all matters pertaining to equipment, to communicate with the War Office through normal channels, and through the liaison officer of the High Commissioner's office in London, the former to be the official channel.
(e) In matters of command, to adhere to the normal military channels between

the War Office and the General Officer Commanding the 2nd New Zealand Expeditionary Force overseas.

(f) To establish such administrative headquarters and base and line of communication units as are necessary for the functions of command, organisation [including training], and administration with which he has been invested.

(g) To organise, [train], change, vary, or group units and formations in such manner as he considers expedient from time to time.

(h) To fix and alter the establishment and composition of units and formations as the exigencies of service may in his opinion require from time to time.

After the Third Echelon has left New Zealand no officer above the substantive rank of captain will be sent overseas without the concurrence of the General Officer Commanding.

M. J. Savage
Prime Minister

[The references to training in square brackets in paragraphs (f) and (g) have been added at General Freyberg's request. They are not included in the text of the memorandum in the N.Z. Prime Minister's Department files, but were later put in at Freyberg's request.]

5 January 1940

Major-General B. C. Freyberg
General Officer Commanding
2nd New Zealand Expeditionary Force Overseas,
Wellington

The General Officer Commanding is hereby invested with the following powers:

(1) Authority to increase the scale of ration, if necessary.

(2) Authority to procure equipment (shown on equipment tables) that cannot be supplied through official channels. Such equipment to be bought through Ordnance channels where possible.

(3) Authority to incur expenditures which cannot be forseen at present, and which the General Officer Commanding considers necessary, for the protection of the health of the Force.

(4) Authority to incur expenditure, not exceeding £500 for any one transaction, for the recreation or other amenities of the Force.

(5) Authority to disburse, at the discretion of the General Officer Commanding, from an entertainment fund which will be provided, to an amount not exceeding £1,000 per annum.

F. Jones
Minister of Defence

APPENDIX THREE

Creforce appreciation of German attack plans

MOST SECRET EF/GSI/16

APPRECIATION — GERMAN PLAN FOR ATTACK ON CRETE

1. The following appreciation of possible German plan for attack on Crete, is based on previous German air attacks, and on Intelligence reports of German resources in the BALKANS.
2. The first objective will most certainly be the three aerodromes, HERAKLION, RETIMO and MALEME, the possession of which is an essential preliminary for the landing of troop carrying aircraft.
3. The second objective will be the seizure of SUDA BAY and HERAKLION ports to enable ships to land further troops and heavy equipment required for the complete occupation of the island.
4. The following is the probable sequence of events:
   - (a) *D-2 and D-1.* Heavy air attacks on RAF and troops, especially A.A. guns.
   - (b) *D 1 day.* Fighters and medium bombers low flying attacks on aerodrome perimeters to neutralise defences, to be followed almost immediately by parachutists.
   - (c) The first sortie of parachutists at each aerodrome will number about five hundred in five coys. of 100 each, dropped from 30 to 40 J.U.52. Height of jump will be about 300 feet. Parachutists will be landed all round the perimeter of the aerodromes and up to 1500 yards from the perimeter. Coys. will be formed up ready for action within 12-15 minutes of jumping. They will have LMGs MMgs and mortars, and will probably make extensive use of smoke.
   - (d) Within half an hour of the dropping of parachutists, the first batch of airborne inf. will arrive. They will have heavier weapons. It is expected that this operation will be carried out irrespective of the success or failure of the parachutists. An estimate of 5000 troops from 350 aircraft may be landed in the first sortie.
   - (e) The next step will be the landing of dive bombers, fighters and recce aircraft closely followed by aerodrome staffs, fuel and AA weapons.
   - (f) The JU 52s used to drop parachutists will probably return with another 1500 men which will be dropped at various key points to prepare the way for the Capture of HERAKLION and SUDA BAY ports, and to cause general disorganisation and confusion.
   - (g) *D.2.* Having seized and provisioned aerodromes, this day will be devoted to securing with the aid of further air borne troops, the ports of HERAKLION and SUDA BAY. Dive bombers will operate in close support of ground tps. *D.3 and subsequently*
   - (h) Ships will commence to arrive on this day, and the complete occupation of the island will follow as quickly as possible.
5. From the above appreciation, it will be noted that the entire plan is based on the capture of the aerodromes. If the aerodromes hold out, as they will, the whole plan will fail.
6. It is to be stressed to all troops defending aerodromes that the only danger is from the preliminary low flying air attack. Provided men are properly dug in, and where possible concealed, they have nothing to fear. It is important, however, that not only the men, but also their weapons must be protected during the preliminary air attack.

7. It is to be further noted, that up to the present, the aerodromes have not been bombed, nor have the ports been mined. The obvious deduction is that the Germans hope to use both themselves in the near future.
8. Although this appreciation has not mentioned sea landings on beaches, the possiblity of these attacks must not be overlooked; but they will be of secondary importance to those from the air.
9. WHEN READ, THIS PAPER WILL BE DESTROYED BY FIRE.

G. S. I.
FORCE HQ — Brigadier
12th May 1941 — General Staff

APPENDIX FOUR

CX/JQ911 (also called OL302) of 1745 hrs 13 May 1941

. . .COMMUNICATED TO YOU IN THIS SERIES HAS BEEN SENT TO MAJOR GENERAL FREYBERG PARA ONE STOP THE ISLAND OF CRETE (CRETE) WILL BE CAPTURED BY THE ELEVENTH (ELEVENTH) AIR CORPS AND THE SEVENTH (SEVENTH) AIR DIVISION COMMA AND THE OPERATION WILL BE UNDER THE CONTROL OF THE ELEVENTH (ELEVENTH) AIR CORPS STOP PARA TWO STOP ALL PREPARATIONS COMMA INCLUDING THE ASSEMBLY OF TRANSPORT AIRCRAFT COMMA FIGHTER AIRCRAFT COMMA AND DIVE BOMBING AIRCRAFT COMMA AS WELL AS OF TROOPS TO BE CARRIED BOTH BY AIR AND SEA TRANSPORT COMMA WILL BE COMPLETED ON SEVENTEENTH (SEVENTEENTH) MAY STOP PARA THREE STOP TRANSPORT OF SEA-BORNE TROOPS WILL BE IN COOPERATION WITH ADMIRAL SOUTH-EAST COMMA WHO WILL ENSURE THE PROTECTION OF GERMAN AND ITALIAN TRANSPORT VESSELS (ABOUT TWELVE SHIPS) BY ITALIAN LIGHT NAVAL FORCES STOP THESE TROOPS WILL COME UNDER THE ORDERS OF THE ELEVENTH (ELEVENTH) AIR CORPS IMMEDIATELY ON THEIR LANDING IN CRETE (CRETE) STOP PARA FOUR STOP A SHARP ATTACK BY BOMBER AND ((DIRECTOR FOR ALL ORANGE LEONARD THREE NOUGHT TWO)) HEAVY FIGHTER UNITS TO DEAL WITH THE ALLIED AIR FORCES ON THE GROUND COMMA AS WELL AS WITH THEIR ANTI-AIRCRAFT DEFENCES AND MILITARY CAMPS COMMA WILL PRECEDE THE OPERATION STOP PARA FIVE STOP THE FOLLOWING OPERATIONS WILL BE CARRIED OUT AS FROM DAY ONE STOP FIRSTLY STOP THE SEVENTH (SEVENTH) AIR DIVISION WILL MAKE A PARACHUTE LANDING AND SEIZE MALEME (MALEME) COMMA CANDIA (CANDIA) AND RETIMO (RETIMO) STOP SECONDLY STOP DIVE BOMBERS AND FIGHTERS (ABOUT ONE HUNDRED (ONE HUNDRED) AIRCRAFT OF EACH TYPE WILL MOVE BY AIR TO MALEME (MALEME) AND CANDIA (CANDIA) STOP THIRDLY STOP AIR LANDING OF ELEVENTH (ELEVENTH) AIR CORPS COMMA INCLUDING CORPS HEADQUARTERS AND ELEMENTS OF THE ARMY PLACED UNDER ITS COMMAND COMMA PROBABLY INCLUDING THE TWENTY-SECOND (TWENTY-SECOND) DIVISION STOP FOURTHLY STOP ARRIVAL OF THE SEA-BORNE CONTINGENT CONSISTING OF ANTI-AIRCRAFT BATTERIES AS WELL AS OF MORE TROOPS AND SUPPLIES STOP PARA SIX STOP IN ADDITION THE TWELFTH (TWELFTH) ARMY WILL

ALLOT THREE (THREE) MOUNTAIN REGIMENTS AS INSTRUCTED STOP FURTHER ELEMENTS CONSISTING OF MOTOR-CYCLISTS COMMA ARMOURED UNITS COMMA ANTI-TANK UNITS COMMA AND ANTI-AIRCRAFT UNITS WILL ALSO BE ALLOTED STOP WHICH IS NOW AWAITED COMMA ALSO AS THE RESULT OF AIR RECONNAISSANCE COMMA THE AERODROME OF KASTELLI (KASTELLI) SOUTH EAST OF CANDIA (CANDIA) AND THE DISTRICT WEST AND SOUTH WEST OF CANEA (CANEA) WILL BE SPECIALLY DEALT WITH COMMA IN WHICH CASE SEPARATE INSTRUCTIONS WILL BE INCLUDED IN DETAILED OPERATION ORDERS STOP PARA EIGHT STOP TRANSPORT AIRCRAFT COMMA OF WHICH A SUFFICIENT NUMBER DASH / ABOUT SIX HUNDRED (SIX HUNDRED) / DASH WILL BE ALLOTED FOR THIS OPERATION COMMA WILL BE ASSEMBLED ON AERODROMES IN THE ATHENS (ATHENS) AREA STOP THE FIRST SORTIE WILL PROBABLY CARRY PARACHUTE TROOPS ONLY STOP FURTHER SORTIES WILL BE CONCERNED WITH THE TRANSPORT OF THE AIR LANDING CONTINGENT COMMA EQUIPMENT AND SUPPLIES COMMA AND WILL PROBABLY INCLUDE AIRCRAFT TOWING GLIDERS STOP PARA NINE STOP WITH A VIEW TO PROVIDING FIGHTER PROTECTION FOR THE OPERATIONS COMMA THE POSSIBILITY OF ESTABLISHING A FIGHTER BASE ON SKARPANTO (SKARPANTO) WILL BE EXAMINED STOP PARA TEN STOP THE QUARTERMASTER GENERAL'S BRANCH WILL ENSURE THAT ADEQUATE FUEL SUPPLIES FOR THE WHOLE OPERATION ARE AVAILABLE IN THE ATHENS (ATHENS) AREA IN GOOD TIME COMMA AND AN ITALIAN TANKER WILL BE ARRIVING AT THE PIRAEUS (PIRAEUS) BEFORE MAY SEVENTEENTH (SEVENTEENTH) STOP THIS TANKER WILL PROBABLY ALSO BE AVAILABLE TO TRANSPORT FUEL SUPPLIES TO CRETE (CRETE) STOP IN ASSEMBLING SUPPLIES AND EQUIPMENT FOR INVADING FORCE IT WILL BE BORNE IN MIND THAT IT WILL CONSIST OF SOME THIRTY TO THIRTY FIVE THOUSAND (THIRTY TO THIRTY FIVE THOUSAND) MEN COMMA OF WHICH SOME TWELVE THOUSAND (TWELVE THOUSAND) WILL BE THE PARACHUTE LANDING CONTINGENT COMMA AND TEN THOUSAND (TEN THOUSAND) WILL BE TRANSPORTED BY SEA STOP THE STRENGTH OF THE LONG RANGE BOMBER AND HEAVY FIGHTER FORCE WHICH WILL PREPARE THE INVASION BY ATTACKING BEFORE DAY ONE WILL BE OF APPROXIMATELY ONE FIVE NOUGHT (ONE FIVE NOUGHT) LONG RANGE BOMBERS AND ONE HUNDRED (ONE HUNDRED) HEAVY FIGHTERS STOP PARA ELEVEN STOP ORDERS HAVE BEEN ISSUED THAT SUDA BAY (SUDA BAY) IS NOT TO BE MINED COMMA NOR WILL CRETAN (CRETAN) AERODROMES BE DESTROYED COMMA SO AS NOT TO INTERFERE WITH THE OPERATIONS INTENDED STOP PARA TWELVE STOP PLOTTINGS PREPARED FROM AIR PHOTOGRAPHS OF CRETE (CRETE) ON ONE OVER TEN THOUSAND SCALE WILL BE ISSUED TO UNITS PARTICIPATING IN THE OPERATIONS.

1745 13/5/41 GMT

APPENDIX FIVE

N.Z. Corps Operation Order for Supercharge, 25/26 March 1943.

N.Z. Corps Operation Order No. 2 (for night of 25-26 March, 1943) in the relevant extracts, ran as follows:

4. Air

From 15.30 hrs for a period of two hours R.A.F. is providing continuous fighter cover and direct air support for this operation. The following forces will be employed on this task:

Sixteen sqns fighter-bombers
One sqn tank-busters
One sqn Spitfires

INTENTION

5. N.Z. Corps will attack and capture the enemy position between Djebel Tebaga and Djebel Melab [Map references given].

METHOD

6. General

The attack will be made on a two bde front with 5 NZ Inf Bde on the right and 6 NZ Inf Bde on the left, 8 Armed Bde superimposed on the whole front. It will be supported by RAF and Arty. . .

8. Start Line Boundaries. . . .
   (f) Rate of advance.
   To first objective: 100 yds in 1 min.
   From first to second objective: 100 yds in 2 mins.

9. Timings
   (a) 8 Armd Bde cross ROMAN WALL at 1600 hrs at same time as arty bombardment commences.
   (b) 5 and 6 N.Z. Inf Bde cross inf start line immediately behind 8 Armd Bde at 1615 hrs.
   (c) There will be no pause on First Objective.

10. Arty
   (a) In addition to arty of N.Z. Corps, the attack will be supported by two fd regts and one med regt of 10 Corps.
   (b) Arty will support attack by a creeping barrage with timed concentrations on known enemy localities and hostile batteries.
   (c) Timings for arty barrage are shown in Trace 'A'.
   (d) To indicate final objective has been reached arty will fire smoke for 4 minutes, 200 yards ahead of objective.

11. Special Tasks
   (a) KDG: will maintain patrols as at present and be prepared to concentrate at short notice and pass through the bridgehead and exploit N.E.
   (b) Div. Cav: In support 6 N.Z. Inf Bde to move NE and assist in mopping up in foothills on western flank.
   (c) 8 Armd Bde: move in advance of inf during attack with heavy Sqnds leading, and regulating pace to the arty barrage. Regts will support bns as under:

Notts Yeo:	28 N.Z. (Maori) Bn
Staffs Yeo:	23 N.Z. Inf Bn
3 R Tanks:	24 N.Z. Inf Bn

   (d) Corps Res Gp: protection of Main N.Z. Corps
   (e) 'L' Force: Maintain present tasks.

12. Action on Capture of Final Objective
    (a) 8 Armd Bde: rally and form bridgehead and exploit to east and NE.
    (b) 5 N.Z. Inf Bde: reorganise and exploit high ground to the east.
    (c) 6 N.Z. Inf Bde: reorganise and complete mopping up of enemy pockets in foothills DJEBEL TEBAGA.
17. Recognition Signals
    (a) Ground to Air
        (i) Forward line of inf will burn orange smoke at the following times:
            15.30 hrs
            15.40 hrs
            15.50 hrs
            It is essential that orange smoke be shown ONLY BY FORWARD LINE OF TPs in order that R.A.F. will see continuous line of smoke indicating FDLs.
        (ii) Arty will fire smoke, rate one round per minute in general area of hostile batteries from 1530 hrs to 1730 hrs.
        (iii) To assist R.A.F., 5 N.Z. Inf Bde will establish a landmark letter 'A' at [point one mile east of Pt 201] by 0700 hrs and will burn RED and BLUE smoke on the site on approach of our aircraft. Between 1530 hrs and 1600 hrs the smoke will be shown every 60 seconds.
    (b) Ground to Ground
        Tracer fired vertically.
18. Zero Hour
    Zero hour wil be 1600 hrs, and is the time at which fire commences on the arty opening line.
19. Security
    It is imperative that NO mention of this operation be made by wireless, other than in high-grade cipher.
20. Codewords
    This operation will be known as SUPERCHARGE.
21. Synchronisation
    By B.B.C. time signal.

APPENDIX SIX

Freyberg's Report to Fraser on Mareth, 5 April 1943

Freyberg's account to Prime Minister Fraser, dated 5 April, 1943 followed closely on the heels of his 31 March cable:

I send this report from the battlefield just north of Gabes during a lull in operations...

The Eighth Army plan of attack was to carry out a two-pronged thrust by a frontal assault on the Mareth Line and an outflanking movement through the desert from an assembly area 80 miles to the south. Our force for this operation was known as the New Zealand Corps. Grouped with the New Zealand Division were the British 8th Armoured Brigade under Brigadier Harvey (3rd Royal Tank Regiment, Staffordshire Yeomanry and Nottinghamshire Yeomanry, 1st Battalion Buffs), King's Dragoon Guards, British medium field and anti-tank regiments, and Fighting French forces, under the command of General Leclerc, and a detachment of the Royal Greek Army.

Although the going was extremely bad and the country ill-suited for a flanking movement, the enemy was clearly very nervous about his flank, a result no doubt of our past activities at Agheila and Tripoli. Enemy reconnaissance planes were over the desert approaches each day. Despite the steps taken to ensure surprise, there is no doubt the enemy expected another 'left hook'. As organised, New Zealand Corps was an extremely fast-moving and hard-hitting formation admirably suited for making a surprise appearance on the battlefield. It relied for its striking power upon the Tank Brigade and its very powerful artillery group under our C.R.A. Brigadier C. E. Weir.

Since the enemy expected a flanking movement there was little chance of achieving strategic surprise. There is no doubt, however, that as a result of our manoeuvers round Rommel's flank since the Battle of Alamein, the enemy did not really know what was coming next. Added to this, they were short of trustworthy reserves, and there still appeared scope for again foxing Rommel. Our aim was to achieve the greatest degree of tactical surprise possible by dashing in quickly and delivering a sudden violent attack. We planned to lie up in a position that threatened two weak points in their defences — high ground at Matmata, south of Mareth, and gap farther west between Djebel Tebaga and the Matmata Hills, which led to El Hamma and Gabes.

In many ways the battle for the Mareth Line bears a close resemblance to the attack on Agheila, when your Division with a British armoured brigade carried out an outflanking movement and forced the enemy to withdraw to avoid encirclement. It involved moves by night of 27,000 men and 6,000 vehicles, tanks, and guns to an assembly area in the desert and a race to the objective across unknown and difficult country, followed by a series of quick but overwhelming attacks.

On 11 March New Zealand Corps began to assemble. The whole force was self-contained, with eleven days' food, water and ammunition and with petrol for 350 miles. By the 18th assembly was complete. Weeks of careful study of the ground from air photographs and patrol reports and detailed planning culminated in an explanation of the operation to all officers and N.C.O.'s on a plaster relief model of the area over which we were to move.

We moved all night on 19 March intending to make a surprise approach march by night on the 20th to coincide with the frontal assault on the Mareth Line. When, however, it seemed likely that the enemy were aware of our assembly, we decided to waste no further effort on deception but to rely entirely on speed. We therefore moved in daylight on the 20th in desert formation and raced north to break through to El Hamma and Gabes.

The going was never good and later it became so bad that no progress could be made by night, so that it was not until 3 p.m. on the 21st that armoured cars of the King's Dragoon Guards and light tanks of the Divisional Cavalry gained contact with the enemy. The enemy position, covered by a minefield, was astride the Kebili–Gabes road, close to where it runs through a narrow valley between the precipitous Djebel Tebaga range and the mountainous country which forms the right flank of the Mareth Line. With only three hours of daylight left, our artillery was deployed and registered before dusk. At 10 p.m., in full moonlight, the 25th (Wellington) Battalion and 26th (South Island) Battalion of the 6th New Zealand Infantry Brigade under Brigadier Gentry, accompanied by engineers of the 8th Field Company to clear gaps in the minefield and followed by a squadron of Sherman tanks of the 3rd Royal Tank Regiment, staged a brilliant attack which went through the minefield and captured Point 201. During this night attack 1500 Italian prisoners were captured. The early capture of Point 201 gave us secure entry through the enemy's prepared defences. We learned later that infantry of the 21st Panzer Division arrived next morning to take over the defences from their Italian allies, but they came twelve hours too late.

Although we had won a footing, the enemy still held high ground on either side of the pass, giving him observation for his artillery, and during the following days our troops were heavily shelled by a large concentration of enemy guns.

On 23 March Eighth Army's bridgehead on the Mareth Line was lost after a heavy German counter-attack, and General Mongomery decided to switch his main thrust to reinforce success on our front. The 10th Corps, including the 1st Armoured Division, was sent to join us. While they were making a three-day approach march through the desert, plans were hurried on to stage an attack as soon as the 1st Armoured Division arrived. To gain observation and gun positions a series of operations on both flanks were carried out. One of these was a brilliant attack at sunset on 24 March by the 3rd Royal Tank Regiment and Nottinghamshire Yeomanry of 8th Armoured Brigade, with most effective co-operation from massed artillery and R.A.F. fighter-bombers. This not only resulted in the capture of high ground on the left flank where German 88-millimetre guns had been sited, but also gained important observation points for our artillery.

Meanwhile we were making our plans to break through his defences. It was to be carried out in three phases:

> Phase 1: The capture of a mountain peak on our right flank to deny enemy observation of our assembly areas for attack.
> Phase 2: Blitz attack by New Zealand Corps to force a gap to El Hamma.
> Phase 3: Passing of 1st Armoured Division through the gap to capture El Hamma.

Phase 1 was carried out brilliantly by the 21st (Auckland) Battalion in the early hours of the morning of the 26th, when vital ground was taken in a moonlight attack.

Phase 2, which was given the code-name 'Supercharge II' was planned to start on the afternoon of the 26th. As usual, every effort was made to make this main attack a surprise. The 8th Armoured Brigade withdrew by dark and remained camouflaged in the wadis behind Point 201. The 23rd (South Island) Battalion and 28th (Maori) Battalion of the 5th Infantry Brigade under Brigadier Kippenberger and the 24th (Auckland) Battalion of the 6th Brigade assembled and lay up ready for the attack, while the 25th (Wellington) Battalion occupied a position on high ground on the left flank ready to advance with the other assault infantry. During the morning of 26 March the artillery of the 1st Armoured Division came in and by midday all preparations were complete. Our only anxiety was that the dust-storm might interfere with our air co-operation.

Meanwhile the enemy had also made his preparations and greatly reinforced his forces in the gap. The 21st Panzer Division had been joined by the German 164th Light Division, and on the day of the attack the 15th Panzer Division had been switched to our front from the Mareth Line.

At three o'clock on 26 March, as I drove up the valley in my tank, all was quiet except for occasional shellfire. There was no unusual movement or sign of coming attack. Exactly half an hour later, the first squadrons of the R.A.F. roared overhead and relays of Spitfires, Kittybombers, and tank-busters swept over the enemy positions giving the greatest measure of air support ever seen by our army. At four o'clock 200 field and medium guns opened their bombardment on a front of 5,000 yards. In an instant the attack developed and 150 tanks and three battalions of infantry appeared as from nowhere, advancing in the natural smokescreen provided by the dust-storm. It was a most awe-inspiring spectacle of modern warfare. The roar of bombers and fighters ahead of our advance merged with our barrage of bursting shells. Following close behind this intense barrage as it advanced came waves of Sherman tanks, carriers, and infantry and sappers on foot, preceded by three squadrons of Crusader tanks. Behind New Zealand Corps, coming down the forward slopes just in the rear of our front line, were 150 tanks of 1st Armoured Division, followed by their Motor Brigade in lorries, advancing in nine columns.

Hitherto all our big attacks had been by moonlight, and although the enemy was expecting us to attack we again achieved surprise by attacking in daylight.

Without check our armour swept through to the final objective, a depth of 6,000 yards. Enemy tanks were destroyed or driven back, anti-tank guns and artillery were overrun or captured. Meanwhile our infantry battalions, moving behind the armour, attacked the remaining enemy strongpoints, and fierce hand-to-hand fighting took place to clear the objectives and secure the high ground on both flanks. By dusk all enemy resistance had been overcome, except for the high ground at Point 209 and a strongpoint outside the left flank where the German garrisons still held out. During the night the 24th (Auckland) Battalion attacked and cleared the left flank, taking a large number of prisoners.

By moonlight on the night of the 26th, Phase 3 was completed when the 1st Armoured Division was launched from our bridgehead. Next morning they had reached the outskirts of El Hamma.

All day on the 27th mopping up of the enemy garrison continued. At Point 209 a bitter fight raged between the Maori Battalion and the 2nd Battalion of the 433 Panzer Grenadier Regiment, which finally ended by remnants of the German garrison, complete with commanding officer, surrendering.

The capture of the defile was a decisive defeat for the enemy and a triumph for our co-ordinated attack by tanks and infantry with powerful air and artillery support. It is true to say that all three German divisions as well as the Italian divisions opposed to us were severely mauled. A great many enemy killed and wounded were left on the battlefield and between 5,000 and 6,000 prisoners were taken, many being Germans from the Afrika Korps. Over forty tanks and a great many guns, MT, and all kinds of equipment were destroyed or captured. But the most important result of the battle was that the Mareth Line became untenable, and heavy casualties, which further frontal assaults would have involved, were avoided.

As soon as all resistance ceased in the defile, New Zealand Corps, led by the King's Dragoon Guards, New Zealand Divisional Cavalry, and 8th Armoured Brigade, fanned out north-east and east towards the coast road. Many prisoners were taken, including two battalions of Italian infantry who surrendered with all their equipment. The 8th Armoured Brigade dispersed the last rearguard of 15th Panzer Division, knocking out four more tanks and three 88-millimetre guns, and Gabes and El Hamma fell into our hands. . .

APPENDIX SEVEN

Freyberg's report to Fraser on Cassino, 4th April 1944

No. 319 4 April 1944

I have the honour to report on the part played by the New Zealand Forces in recent operations at Cassino. Reports of fighting from our war correspondents have been sent to New Zealand, and my purpose is merely to give a brief connected picture of our operations during the last two months.

In earlier cables I reported to you that we had temporarily become the New Zealand Corps under the Fifth American Army for operations with the 4th Indian Division, a British division, and with British and American armour and guns under command. As stated in my secret cipher message when our role was assigned to us, we had no illusions about the difficulties of the task ahead. I cabled then, 'We are undoubtedly facing one of the most difficult operations of all our battles.' [No. 317.]

The Cassino position is a formidable one, and not for the first time in history it has barred the way to armies advancing into the Liri Valley which leads to Rome. Cassino, once a substantial stone town, lies at the foot of Monastery Hill, which rises sharply out of the plain, not unlike the rock of Gilbralter in steepness and height. The road and railway to Rome pass through Cassino, the narrow plain over which we had to advance is flooded, wired and mined, and the entire defensive system is covered by the small but swift-flowing Rapido River. From the vantage point of the Monastery the enemy can watch and bring down fire on every movement on the roads or open country in the plain below.

This natural fortress of the enemy's Gustav Line held up the American advance earlier in the year, and it was from an American Corps that we took over after coming across from the Eighth Army front. As we drove forward we saw the ideal defensive country from which the American, British and French troops of Fifth Army had driven the enemy after months of heavy and most gallant fighting. At Cassino they attacked again and again, gaining important peaks to the north and a foothold in the northern edge of the town itself. These were the positions we took over, the 4th Indian Division moving into the mountains to the north while the 2nd New Zealand Division occupied the northern outskirts of Cassino.

Since the middle of February we have maintained pressure on the Cassino front. The enemy has been attacked from the air and bombarded by artillery and has been forced to deploy his reserves to meet the threat of a break-through. He put in his best available troops to hold Cassino and the heights above it. On 15 February the Benedictine Monastery was destroyed by heavy air bombardment, a step which was forced upon us because, despite enemy protests to the contrary, it was being used as an observatory for military purposes.

Prior to the main attack on Cassino itself, the 4th Indian Division fought a battle on the steep rocky slopes to the north of the Monastery. They gained ground on Point 593 and have held it ever since despite enemy counter-attacks and very difficult conditions. The enemy had prepared their positions in advance and their strongpoints blasted into rock had to be stormed at night with hand grenades and bayonet.

On 17 and 18 February the 28th (Maori) Battalion carried out an operation to cross the Rapido River south of the town. A bridgehead was won and the engineers were within an ace of getting demolitions repaired and bridges through after magnificent work, but dawn came an hour too soon. By daylight the enemy could pick out their targets from Monastery Hill and further work was impossible after continuous fire. Supporting arms could not be got up and our bridgehead was driven back by an enemy tank attack.

Meanwhile, plans were made for a full-scale attack supported by very heavy air and artillery bombardment. This was to be followed by an infantry assault which, if fully successful, would make a break for the armour into the valley beyond. The attack on Cassino and Monastery Hill by the 2nd New Zealand Division and 4th Indian Division, dependent as it was upon tank and air support, required firm going for the tanks and clear visibility for the bombers. This meant weeks of patient waiting since weather conditions in February and March in Italy leave much to be desired. At last on 15 March it seemed that the weather was right and the attack was launched.

Before dawn that morning the New Zealand troops on the northern outskirts of Cassino were withdrawn and at half past eight a terrific air attack began. For the first time heavy bombers of the Strategic Air Force, as well as medium and light bombers, took part in a close air support programme of unprecedented weight. From an observation post I watched already battered Cassino reduced to rubble. Squadron after squadron of Fortresses, Liberators, Mitchells and Marauders of the American Air Force came in, with short intervals between groups to allow the huge clouds of dust and smoke to clear. Flashes of flame from bursting bombs leaped from the buildings and from the slopes above the town, explosions reverberated through the hills and shook the ground under our feet. No enemy aircraft appeared during the attack. Enemy anti-aircraft guns were neutralised by artillery and none fired after half past ten.

At twelve o'clock precisely the last flight of medium bombers planted their bombs with impressive accuracy. Twelve o'clock was zero hour, when the Allied artillery (under our CCRA, Brigadier C.E. Weir) opened fire and the infantry attacked. Your Division (under Major-General Parkinson) had the task of storming Cassino. During the air attack there had been no artillery fire on Cassino as dust and smoke would have obscured the target for aircraft, but at zero hour between five and six hundred guns of all calibres opened on the Corps front, a bombardment heavier than at Alamein. Behind the creeping barrage infantry, engineers and tanks advanced into Cassino from the north.

The approach was a bottleneck restricted by massive mountains on the west and by the Rapido River on the east. Only one battalion could be deployed at a time, a factor which was a great handicap to our operations. The positions we had withdrawn from were occupied without trouble; our first objective, Castle Hill, a steep miniature of the Monastery feature just north of the town, was stormed and captured by the 25th Battalion, and the 26th Battalion, followed by the 19th Armoured Regiment, attacked Cassino itself. At first our attack met little opposition and casualties were very light. The prisoners taken were stunned and reported heavy casualties from the bombing. The town was completely wrecked, and the whole area was covered with wide, deep craters up to 60 feet across which could not be crossed by our armour. In some places where bombs had missed buildings or had not penetrated reinforced basements, there were snipers and enemy posts which were holding out, and on the western edge of the town the enemy position blasted into the base of the hill remained intact. From positions south on Monastery Hill enemy nebelwerfers and trench mortars came into action. Our artillery, bombers and fighter-bombers engaged these enemy mortar areas and continued the attack in depth on enemy positions on Monastery Hill and on gun areas in the valley beyond.

By evening good progress had been made and the stage was set for the next vital phase of the attack. This was to take advantage of enemy disorganisation during the moonlight. Cassino was to be mopped up by New Zealand battalions. Troops from 4th Indian Division were to take over Castle Hill from our 25th Battalion and then attack Monastery Hill. American and New Zealand engineers were to put a bridge over the Rapido on the main Rome road and clear routes forward through the town.

Up to this moment the operation had developed as planned. At nightfall, however, the weather broke and torrential rain fell throughout the night. Visibility was poor and the moon made little or no difference. It was impossible to keep control in the pitch dark and progress in Cassino was slow. When the 4th Indian Division moved, Cassino town had not been cleared. As a result they could not deploy on the precipitous slopes of Monastery Hill, and there was inevitable delay and loss of cohesion. In these conditions the achievement of the Gurkha Battalion in capturing 'Hangman's Hill', the point just below the Monastery, before dawn, was a magnificent one. But they were too thin on the ground to attack Monastery Hill.

The engineers' task of making routes and bridging gaps was also greatly hampered and slowed down by conditions. Owing to the low-lying nature of the ground, craters were full of water and mud and bridges had to be built across the gaps. Despite all difficulties, however, the engineers built steel bridges over the Rapido River before dawn.

On the morning of the 16th, Monastery Hill was still in enemy hands and Cassino had not been cleared; indeed, the enemy had had oportunity during the night to clear away debris and reorganise a number or strongpoints. It was clear that hope of obtaining full advantage of a surprise attack and breaking through with armour had gone and further progress would be slow. Cassino had to be cleared so that the New Zealand Division could link up with the Indian Division on Hangman's Hill.

At first light New Zealand infantry of 6th Brigade, with tank support, went on with their task.

Apart from isolated posts, the main enemy resistance was in the concrete defences in the south-west corner of the town, known as the Continental Hotel area, and at two points at the foot of Castle Hill, blasted into the face of the hill, where the enemy resisted fiercely. It was against these points that the New Zealand infantry concentrated during the following days. Close up behind the infantry the engineers built bridges, and with bulldozers and hand labour gradually cleared routes through. On the 17th, tanks of the 19th Armoured Regiment were brought into the town, and that morning our 26th Battalion, supported by a squadron of tanks, swung south and made an important advance, capturing Cassino railway station after fierce fighting. Enemy tanks and antitank guns attempted to intervene but were dealt with by our tanks and artillery.

From now on Cassino became the scene of most bitter fighting, and our battalions of 5th Brigade (under Brigadier Burrows) joined 6th Brigade (under Brigadier Bonifant) in the battle for the strongpoints. Our infantry, closely supported by our tanks, fought forward from one heap of rubble to another and dug out snipers in ones and twos. Walls of houses in the west of the town where the enemy held out were literally blown down in sections by our tanks. On the 19th 180 prisoners were taken from two strongpoints, but the enemy still held the western edge of the town securely and was able to supply and reinforce it by night. For a week, under cover of smoke by day and in waning moonlight by night, the battle went on. By day and night the town was shelled and mortared by the enemy, while our own guns were continuously in action masking enemy observation points on Monastery Hill with smoke and breaking up enemy formations and shelling his gun areas.

While your Division fought in Cassino, British and Indian troops of the 4th Indian Division fought back counter-attacks in the hills. We were forced off Point 165, but Castle Hill was firmly held by infantry from Essex and Kent. The garrison has already repulsed five counter-attacks made against it. The Gurkhas on Hangman's Hill and a company of our 24th Battalion on Points 146 and 202 became isolated but held on with great determination. They were supplied by air by American dive-bombers and fighter-bombers which dropped ammunition, water, and food in parachute containers with remarkable accuracy onto such difficult targets. The full success of our operation depended on our ability to clear Cassino and link up with these isolated garrisons so that the attack could go on to take the Monastery. This could not be accomplished and eventually the isolated troops had to be withdrawn by night.

In an attack against an enemy position such as this, the operation always divides itself into three phases: the break-in battle, the encounter battle, and the break out. Our plan was to reduce the second phase to a minimum by the violence of our initial blow, but blitz bombing proved a double-edged weapon and produced obstacles which made speedy deployment of our armour impossible. At Alamein, and in the battle of Mareth just one year ago, the third phase was reached after several days' heavy fighting and decisive battles were won. At Cassino the strong defence held, and we have not reached the third phase. We have, however, broken into his main defensive system, and in the fierce battles which ensued we have caused the enemy heavy casualties. We have won and now hold part of our objective. We have a bridgehead across the main Rapido River, and we hold Castle Hill and the bulk of the town and the railway station.

In this battle we have been fighting in the Fifth American Army. I would like to record here our pride in doing so and our deep appreciation of the help and co-operation we have had from General Mark Clark, his staff, and all the formations with which we have served. . . .

After the hard battle the troops were tired, but they are recovering quickly and are in good heart.

APPENDIX EIGHT

Tuker and Freyberg, 12 February 1944

SUBJECT: *OPERATIONS*

MOST SECRET
MAIN HQ 4 IND DIV
No 433
12 Feb 1944

Main N.Z. Corps (3)
1. I have today seen the officiating Comd 4 Ind Div and the Bde Comds at 4 Div HQ and there discussed the present situation in the 'Monastery' area of CASSINO in the light of our latest recces and the recent activities of the 2 American Corps.
2. From N.Z. Intelligence Summary No. 17 of 6 Feb para (C) it is apparent that the enemy are in concrete and steel emplacements on the 'Monastery' Hill.

From my wide experience of attacks in mountain areas I know that infantry cannot 'jump' strong defences of this sort in the mountains. These defences have to be 'softened' up either by being cut off on *all* sides and starved out or else by continuous and heavy bombardment over a period of days. Even with the latter preparation, success will only be achieved in my opinion if a thorough and prolonged air bombardment is undertaken with really heavy bombs, a good deal larger than Kittybomber missiles.
3. We have complete air superiority in this theatre of war but the softening of the Monastery Hill has not been started.

An attack cannot be undertaken till this softening process is complete. This has always been the view that I have voiced and it is now confirmed by what I later hear.

Already, three attacks have been put in and have failed — at some considerable cost, I am told. Another attack without *air* 'softening' will only lead to a similar result. The Monastery feature is a far more formidable feature than TAKROUNA, and resembles the higher parts of GARCI which were rightly deemed inaccessible to infantry attack once the first initial surprise had gone. At GARCI the enemy was in field defences and not in concrete emplacements.
4. If proper air 'softening' is not possible then the alternative remains:-
i.e. to turn Monastery Hill and to isolate it.

This course I regard to be possible as the enemy is, I believe still only in field defences in the mountain areas to the West and S.W. of MONTE CASTELLONI. Using MONTE CASTELONI [*sic*] and the area now held by the American 2 Corps as a firm base, and making it a firm base, we can attack in fast short jabs to the West and S.W. of CASTELLONI and cut No. 6 route West of MONASTERY HILL. With this, and an attack on CASSINO to keep that place quiet, the river can, I feel, be crossed lower down and the crossing joined up with the cutting from the North of No. 6 Road [Route 6], thus isolating MONASTERY HILL.
5. To go direct for MONASTERY HILL now without 'softening it' properly is only to hit one's head straight against the hardest part of the whole enemy position and to risk the failure of the whole operation.

(Sgd) Tuker,
Maj Gen,
COMD.

APPENDIX NINE

The plan for operation 'Dickens', 23 February 1944

OPERATION DICKENS: 2 NEW ZEALAND DIVISION AND 6 BRIGADE OPERATION ORDERS

SECRET
Copy No
23 Feb 44

2 NZ Div Operation Order No. 41
Ref Maps: 1/25,000 Sheets 160/II NE, 160/II NW,
160/I SW, 160/I SE.
1/25,000 Reproduction of German Map

INFORMATION

1. *Enemy*
   As contained in NZ Corps Intelligence Summaries.
2. *Own Tps*
   (a) Fmns flanking NZ Corps are to maintain present dispositions and exert pressure.
   (b) NZ Corps is to capture CASSINO and adv against the enemy line PIEDIMONTE–AQUINO–PONTECORVO.
   (c) 4 Ind Div is to
      (i) assist ops of 2 NZ Div by neutralising enemy posns on eastern slopes of M CASSINO with SA and mortar fire and by harassing enemy mov in CASSINO prior to zero;
      (ii) after capture of Pt 193 (G854213) by 2 NZ Div, take over and secure the feature;
      (iii) in conjunction with the adv of 2 NZ Div, attack south across eastern slope of M CASSINO feature;
      (iv) maintain pressure in sector NW of the Monastery to prevent the withdrawal of enemy reserves from that area.
   (d) Arty of CEF and 10 Brit Corps is to sp ops of NZ Corps by carrying out a CB programme in own sectors, and by neutralising enemy OPs in the vicinity of TERELLE G8127.
3. *Additional Tps under Comd*
   US CCB remains under comd 2 NZ Div for follow-up ops.

INTENTION

4. 2 NZ Div will capture CASSINO and break out into LIRI valley in vicinity of Highway 6.

METHOD

5. *General*
   (a) The op will consist of a daylight attack by inf and tks from the north, following an intense air bombardment, and supported by maximum arty effort.
   (b) The op will be referred to by the codeword 'DICKENS'.
   (c) After completion of Dickens, the ops included in 2 NZ Div Op Instr No. 21 dated 17 Feb (phases INSTEP, COBRA and JOINER) will be proceeded with as soon as possible.
6. *Groupings*
   Groupings within 2 NZ Div are shown in Appx 'A' att.

7. *Air Sp*
   (a) Air attacks on CASSINO will begin at approx zero minus 4 hrs, and will increase in intensity until zero.
   (b) It is expected that 360 hy and 200 med bombers will be available for the attack on CASSINO, and additional fighter-bombers for subsequent ops.
   (c) The safe bomb-line is shown in Appx 'B' att. NO tps will remain inside this line during air attacks on CASSINO.
   (d) NO attacks will be made on CASSINO after zero.
   (e) The following fighter-bomber targets have been prearranged for the adv from first to second objectives and will be 'called down' by a controller at Tac 2 NZ Div if required:

Rly st. . .	G860201
Amphitheatre	G853199
Pt 435	G847206

   (f) For ops by TFB on D plus 1 day, the following targets have been prearranged, and will be directed by the controller if required: On lower slopes of M CASSINO and along Highway 6 and rly line, behind arty barrage.

   Area G835205
   Wadi G831206
   Area G815215

8. *6 NZ Inf Bde Gp,* with in sp one additional armd regt and 7 NZ Fd Coy if required, will assault and capture CASSINO and Pt 193 from the north, then adv to secure a bridgehead into the LIRI valley.
9. *Preparation for the Assault*
   6 NZ Inf Bde will withdraw all tps to lying-up areas north of safety bomb-line immediately before first light on D day (see Trace in Appx 'B' att).
10. *Assault by 6 NZ Inf Bde Gp*
   (a) Details of arty sp are shown in appx 'B' att.
   (b) 6 NZ Inf Bde will make maximum use of ground smoke to cover fwd mov at zero.
   (c) First objective: Incl Pt 193 (G854213) — rd junc 854209
   — rd junc 860208
   Codeword: QUISLING.
   (d) Second Objective: rd junc 853197 — incl 55 ring contour
   G8519 — R GARI at 858192 - stream junc
   G861197 — rly at G862201
   Codeword: JOCKEY
   (e) Rate of adv: 100 yds in 10 mins.
   (f) Action on capture of first objective:
      (i) Reorg on Pt 193, but be prepared to hand over defence of this feature to tps of 4 Ind Div during night. D/D plus 1. Codeword for this relief is CROMWELL.
      (ii) Covered by arty 'stonks' for 15 mins, prepare to adv immediately for the capture of second objective.
   (g) Action on capture of second objective: Reorg to hold bridgehead JOCKEY until the passage of TFB.
11. *Arty:* NZA, with in sp II US Corps arty and 4 Ind Div arty, will
   (a) sp the attack by 6 NZ Inf Bde Gp in accordance with outline task table att at Appx 'B';
   (b) sp ops of TFB on D plus 1 day in accordance with 2 NZ Div Op Instr No. 21 dated 17 Feb.
12. *Engrs:* NZE, with under comd 48 US Engr Bn less one coy, will

(a) proceed at last light on D day with the construction of Class 30 br over R RAPIDO at Highway 6;
(b) clear and mark a route from this br to Highway 6 south of CASSINO;
(c) as soon as CASSINO rly sta has been captured, clear and repair rly route to give access to southern outskirts of CASSINO;
(d) proceed as soon as possible with the construction of a Class 30 br over R GARI on rly route and effect junc with Highway 6 in vicinity G853917;
(e) hold 7 NZ Fd Coy with a det mech eqpt in a suitable area east of the BARRACKS 8523, to come under comd 6 NZ Inf Bde if required for the clearance of routes through CASSINO.

13. *5 NZ Inf Bde* will
(a) carry out the following internal reliefs during night 23/24 Feb:
(i) relief of 2 NZ Div Cav Regt by one bn of 78 Brit Div;
(ii) relief of 23 NZ Inf Bn by 2 NZ Div Cav Regt;
(b) during night D minus 1/D, occupy fire posns well fwd with all weapons;
(c) from zero to zero plus 40 bring maximum neutralising fire to bear on enemy localities in CASSINO south of Highway 6. This will include the destruction of individual houses and suspected strongpoints by 17-pr fire;
(d) be prepared to take over defence of rly sta area, NOT beyond R GARI, after capture of second objective. Codeword for this op to commence will be HUNTER. Completion of take-over will be signalled by codeword OTAKI;
(e) provide immediate cover for engr parties working on RAPIDO br at Highway 6 and on rly route.

14. *CCB* will
(a) posn TD guns on Western slopes of M TROCCHIO during night D minus 1/D, sited to engage enemy localities in CASSINO south of Highway 6 and to harass enemy mov on rds south of the town:
(b) engage houses, enemy mov and suspected enemy localities in these areas from zero to zero plus 40 on D day;
(c) be prepared to est TC system at two hrs notice from zero hr;
(d) at 1900 hrs on D day, assume a one-hr alert to pass TFB through bridgehead JOCKEY for the capture of objective LIBEL as already ordered in 2 NZ Div Op Instr No. 21 dated 17 Feb.

15. *4 NZ Armd Bde* will
(a) hold one armd regt in readiness as from zero to move from present area to come under comd 6 NZ Inf Bde Gp if required;
(b) be prepared to proceed with phase COBRA after success by TFB.

16. *Pro*
(a) 2 NZ Div Pro Coy will be prepared to est red lights on one fwd route from M TROCCHIO to objective JOCKEY at last light on D day.
(b) Codewords for routes will be:
CARUSO: present route to FDLs of 6 NZ Inf Bde via BARRACKS 8523
MILTON: Highway 6
DISNEY: Highway 6 to rd junc 872205, thence by rly route.
(c) APM 2 NZ Div will maintain liaison between Tac 2 NZ Div and TC post.

17. *Zero*
(a) Zero will be the time at which arty opens on barrage opening line.
(b) time and date are dependent upon flying conditions but zero will NOT be before 1200 hrs on 24 Feb.
(c) It will be promulgated on the evening before the attack by the codeword BRADMAN followed by a time and date.

ADM
18. Normal.
INTERCOMN

19. *Bdys*
    (a) *Inter-Div:*
        (i) Right with 4 Ind Div:
            Incl to 2 NZ Div: Pt 175 G854218, Pt 193 G854214
        (ii) Left with 46 Div:
            Excl to 2 NZ Div: CLE CECRO [*sic*] sq G9014; RIVOLO LADRON to G877131, line of R GARI to G875126; G864123, thence line of F LIRI.
    (b) *Inter-Bde:*
        Incl to 5 NZ Inf Bde:
        rd S PASQUALE G868221 to rd and river junc G862216.
20. *Locations*
    (a) See NZ Corps Location statement as at 1800 hrs 18 Feb 44.
    (b) Tac HQ 2 NZ Div will open G914197 at a time to be notified.
    (c) (i) Tac HQ 6 NZ Inf Bde: G858225
        (ii) Main HQ 6 NZ Inf Bde: G885228.
21. *Wireless*
    All sets in 2 NZ Div will break silence and commence normal working at zero minus two hrs.
22. *Recognition*
    Ground to Ground
    (a) By day: Rifle held vertically, muzzle uppermost and/or one RED tracer fired vertically.
    (b) By night: One RED tracer fired vertically.
23. *Passwords*
    Challenge: MOTOR
    Answer: JEEP
24. *Codewords*

(a) Codeword for op	DICKENS
(b) Cancellation of op	ALEXANDER
(c) FIRST objective — 6 NZ Inf Bde	QUISLING
(d) SECOND objective — 6 NZ Inf Bde	JOCKEY
(e) Handover of Pt 193	CROMWELL
(f) Present 6 NZ Inf Bde fwd route	CARUSO
(g) Highway No. 6 through CASSINO	MILTON
(h) Rly route	DISNEY
(i) Zero hr	BRADMAN
(j) Arty tasks	TILDEN
	MAROON
	LENTIL
	TROTSKY
	GHANDI

ACK

L. W. Thornton
Lieutenant-Colonel
General Staff
2 New Zealand Division

Time of Signature: 0140 hrs
Method of Issue: Copies 1-4, 21-23 by LO.
6, 7, 9, 10, 11, 13, 16, 17-20 by Runner.
5, 8, 12, 14, 15 by SDR

APPENDIX TEN

Chronology of Freyberg's career

1889	Bernard Cyril Freyberg is born in London.
1891	Freyberg family migrates to New Zealand.
1905	Freyberg wins New Zealand junior swimming title.
1910	Freyberg wins New Zealand senior swimming title.
1911	Begins practice as a dentist in Morrinsville.
1912	Gazetted a Second Lieutenant in 6th Hauraki Regiment (Territorial Force).
1912	Moved to Levin.
1914	Commissioned in the British army and posted to 7th 'Hood' Battalion, Royal Naval Brigade.
1915	Awarded DSO for exploits in the Dardenelles.
1916	Commander of the 'Hood' Battalion. Awarded Victoria Cross.
1918	Brigadier-General in 29 Division in France.
1922	Marries Barbara Maclaren.
1929–31	Commander of 1 Battalion, Manchester Regiment.
1934	Retires from army.
1939	General Officer Commanding Salisbury Plains.
1940	Appointed Commander of New Zealand Expeditionary Force. In Egypt and Britain.
1941	Greek and Crete campaign. Commander Creforce. 1st Desert battles.
1942	Promoted Lieutenant-General. Crusader battles, 1st battle of E1 Alamein, 2nd battle of El Alamein. Awarded KCB and KBE.
1943	Mareth. Commander 10 Corps. Moves to Italy.
1944	Gustav Line. Appointed NZ Commander NZ Corps for Cassino battles. Gothic Line. Injured in aircraft accident.
1945	Trieste at war's end. V.E. Day.
1946	Awarded GCMG
1946–52	Governor-General of New Zealand.
1951	Created Baron Freyberg of Wellington and Munstead.
1952	Deputy Constable and Lieutenant-Governor of Windsor Castle.
1963	Died on 4 July.

GLOSSARY

AABty	Anti-aircraft battery
Arty	Artillery
ANZAC	Australian and New Zealand Army Corps
AOC	Air Officer Commanding
AIF	Australian Imperial Forces
A/Tk	Anti-tank
Army Y	Generic term for intercepted wireless traffic
AFV	Armoured Fighting Vehicle(s)
Bde	Brigade
Bde Gp	A battle formation used in the early desert campaigns
Bn	Battalion
Bty	Battery (of guns)
BGS	Brigadier, General Staff
Boniface	Early cover name for Ultra, before June 1941
Bletchley Park	British code breaking centre
Bofors guns	Light anti-aircraft weapons
Blitzkrieg	Lightning attack
Coy	Company
Creforce	Freyberg's Corps in Crete
CIGS	Chief of the Imperial General Staff
CBME	Combined Bureau Middle East
COO	Creforce Operation Order
COI	Creforce Operation Instruction
C-in-C	Commander-in-Chief
Cryptanalysis	Code breaking operations
CX	Ultra Code Prefix to Communiques to Head of British Secret Service
COS Committee	Chiefs of Staff Committee (British)
CRA	Commander Royal Artillery
DAK	Deutsche Afrika Korps
Div Com	Divisional Commander
Div Cav	Divisional Cavalry (armour)
Enigma	German Code deciphering machine
Einsatz Kreta	Fliegerkorps' battle report
FEC	French Expeditionary Corps
FFF	Free French Forces
Fliegerdivision	Luftwaffe air landing division
Fliegerkorps	A major Luftwaffe unit
Gr	Ghurka
GOC-in-C	General Officer Commanding in Chief
GSO1	General Staff Officer, 1
G2	General Staff Officer 2
GHQME	General Headquarters Middle East
HILL 107	Kavzakio Hill, Maleme, Crete
Inf Bd	Infantry Brigade
'I' Tank	British Matilda Infantry support tank
IGS	Imperial General Staff (British)
Ju	Junkers (a German military aircraft description)
JIC	An intelligence sub-committee of the British Chiefs of Staff
KDG	King's Dragoon Guards
L Force	General Leclerc's Force

'Left hook'	An outflanking movement aimed at turning the enemy's position
Luftwaffe	German military airforce
Luftflotte	A German air group
LO	Liaison Officer
Me	Messerschmidt (a German Military aircraft designation)
MNBDO	Mobile Naval Base Defence Organisation
MO	Medical Officer
MG	Machine-gun
Main 8th Army	8th Army's main headquarters
NZEF	New Zealand Expeditionary Force
NCO	Non-Commissioned Officer
OL	Orange Leonard (an Enigma summary designation)
Pz	Panzer
RASC	Royal Army Service Corps
RE	Royal Engineers
RTR	Royal Tank Regiment
RT	Radio telephone
RWK	Royal West Kent Regiment
Sqn	Squadron
'Soft skinned'	Non-armoured vehicles
Staffel	A Luftwaffe minor formation
Sit rep	Situation report
Spadger Force	The cover name for NZ Corps prior to Cassino
SNO	Senior Naval Officer
Schwerpunkt	The vital ground
Tac HQ	Tactical Headquarters
Tp	Troop
Ultra	British summaries of German coded signal traffic
Very flares	Coloured flare for signalling or temporarily illuminating part of battlefield. Invented by E. W. Very (also known as verey flares).

BIBLIOGRAPHY

ARCHIVE MATERIAL

United Kingdom

- Public Record Office
- Cabinet Papers
  - CAB 106/366 Operations of NZ Corps 3 February–26 March 1944
- Prime Minister's Office
  - PREM 3 Operational Papers
  - PREM 3/109
- Headquarters Papers
  - WO 201 Middle East Forces
  - WO 204 Allied Forces in North Africa, Italy and France 1942–1945
    - WO 204/4354 Lessons from the Cassino Operation
    - WO 204/6809 5 US Army Operations Memoranda
    - WO 204/7275 NZ Corps Operations 3 February to 26 March 1944
    - WO 204/7566 Fifth Army — Cassino Operations: Lessons Learnt 15–24 March 1944
    - WO 204/8287 Operation Dickens
    - WO 204/8289 2NZEF Operations Report November 1943–November 1944
- War Office Directorates
  - WO 106 Directorate of Military Operations and Intelligence
    - WO 106/3126 Report by an Inter-Service Committee on Operations in Crete, 1st November 1940 to 31st May 1941
- War Diaries
  - WO 169 Middle East Forces
    - WO 169/1334 Creforce *War Diary*
    - WO 169/8591 10 Corps *War Diary*
    - WO 169/8677 1st Armoured Division *War Diary*
  - WO 179 Dominion Forces
    - WO 179/724 5 NZ Brigade *War Diary*
    - WO 179/734 21 NZ Battalion *War Diary*
    - WO 179/735 22 NZ Battalion *War Diary*
    - WO 179/736 23 NZ Battalion *War Diary*
- Ministry of Defence
  - DEFE 3 Intelligence from Enemy Radio Communications, 1939–1945
    - DEFE 3/686 Crete March 14–May 29 1941, OL 1–500 (incomplete)
    - DEFE 3/687 Crete March 14–May 29 1941
    - DEFE 3/891 Signals to Allied Commands Conveying Special Intelligence Crete Series, from March 1941
    - DEFE 3/894 Signals to Allied Commands Conveying Special Intelligence. Cairo and AOC Crete Series, 1941, April 28–May 28

New Zealand

- National Archives
  - Freyberg Papers
  - WA II Series 8
    - WA II/8/9 War Diary, Anzac Corps 1940–41
    - WA II/8/10 General Historical Papers 1940–41
    - WA II/8/16 BGS' file March–May 1941
    - WA II/8/17 Historical Papers, Orders, etc May 1941

WA II/8/18 Crusader July–November 1941
WA II/8/21 General January–December 1941
WA II/8/24 Minquar Qa'im and Ruweisat Ridge 1942
WA II/8/25 Battle of Alamein September–November 1942
WA II/8/25a General Papers, Lightfoot and Supercharge
WA II/8/27 Turning the Agheila Position 1942
WA II/8/28 Nofilia to Tripoli December 1942–February 1943
WA II/8/29 Medenine 1943
WA II/8/30 Turning the Mareth Line 1943
WA II/8/31 Akarit to Enfidaville 1943
WA II/8/40 Left Hook, 1942–1943
WA II/8/41 Conference in Tripoli February 1943
WA II/8/43 GOC's Diary — Part I 1939 to September 1941
WA II/8/44 GOC's Diary — Part II September 1941 to September 1942
WA II/8/45 GOC's Diary — Part III September 1942 to September 1943
WA II/8/46 GOC's Diary — Part IV September 1943 to October 1944
WA II/8/67 GOC's Diary — Part V October 1944 to January 1945
WA II/8/68 GOC's Diary — Part VI January 1945 to October 1945
WA II/8/48 Miscellaneous collected jottings
WA II/8/49 Historical, Operational January 1944
WA II/8/50 Historical, Operational February 1944
WA II/8/51 Historical, Operational March 1944
WA II/8/54 Historical, Operational August 1944
WA II/8/57 Historical, Operational November 1944
WA II/8/58 Historical, Operational December 1944
WA II/8/60 Historical, Operational February 1945
WA II/8/61 Historical, Operational March 1945
WA II/8/62 Historical, Operational April 1945
WA II/8/63 Historical, Operational May 1945
WA II/8/Part II C Report by AOC in Crete
WA II/8/Part II D Miscellaneous Formation Reports, Crete
WA II/8/Part II E Unexpurgated copy of Report on Operation Crusader, 1941
WA II/8/Part II O Correspondence with CGS NZ
WA II/8/Part II EE Reports on Battle of Cassino
WA II/8/Part II AAA GOC's Powers

Other WA II Series I, selected unit war diaries, including
WA II DA 52/10/10 Brigadier Hargest's diaries and letters
WA II/1/DA21.1/1/1 — 69 2nd New Zealand Division *War Diary*
WA II/1/DA364.4/1/1 19th Australian Brigade *War Diary*

Alexander Turnbull Library
Maj-Gen L. M. Inglis Papers MS421
New Zealand Parliament, House of Representatives, Appendices to the Journals.

BOOKS

Christopher Andrew, *Secret Service*, Heinemann, 1985
Laurie Barber, *Redcoat to Jungle Green*, INL Print, 1984
Martin Blumenson, *Mark Clark*, Jonathan Cape, 1985
Rudolf Bohmler, *Monte Cassino*, transl. R. H. Stevens, Cassell, 1964
C. A. Borman, *Divisional Signals*, NZ War History Branch, 1954
Peter Calvocoressi, *Top Secret Ultra*, Sphere, 1981
Michael Carver, *El Alamein*, Batsford, 1962
Anthony Cave-Brown, *Bodyguard of Lies*, Star, 1977
Mark Clark, *Calculated Risks*, Harper, 1950
J. F. Cody, *21 Battalion*, NZ War History Branch, 1953
J. F. Cody, *28 (Maori) Battalion*, NZ War History Branch, 1956
M. G. Comeau, *Operation Mercury*, Kimber, 1961
John Connell, *Wavell — Scholar and Soldier*, Collins, 1964
John Connell, *Auchinleck*, Cassell, 1959
Mathew Cooper, *The German Air Force 1933-1945*, Janes, 1981
Geoffrey Cox, *A Tale of Two Battles*, William Kimber, 1987
Charles Cruickshank, *Greece 1940–1941*, Newark, 1977
D. M. Davin, *Crete*, NZ War History Branch, 1953
B. L. Davis, *German Parachute Forces, 1939–1945*, Arms and Armour Press, 1974
D. S. Detweiler, C. B. Burdick, and J. Rohwer, ed., *World War II German Military Studies*, vols. 13, 14, 23, Garland Publishing, 1979
Documents Relating to New Zealand's Participation in the Second World War 1939–1945, NZ War History Branch, vol. I, 1949, vol. II, 1951
John Ellis, *Cassino: the Hollow Victory*, Sphere, 1985
Noel Gardiner, *Freyberg's Circus*, Richards and Collins, 1981
Martin Gilbert, *Winston S. Churchill*, vol. 6, Heinmann, 1983
Dominic Graham and Shelford Bidwell, *Tug of War: the Battle for Italy 1943–45*, Hodder and Stoughton, 1986
Barry Gregory and John Batchelor, *Airborne Warfare 1918–1945*, Phoebus, 1979
Nigel Hamilton, *Monty — The Making of a General: 1887–1942*, Hamish Hamilton, 1981
Nigel Hamilton, *Monty — Master of the Battlefield: 1942–1944*, Hamish Hamilton, 1983
Nigel Hamilton, *Monty — The Field Marshal: 1945–1976*, Hamish Hamilton, 1986
D. Hapgood and D. Richardson, *Monte Cassino*, Angus and Robertson, 1984
Jim Henderson, *22 Battalion*, NZ War History Branch, 1958
John Hetherington, *Airborne Invasion*, Oswald-Sealey, 1944
Robin Higham, *Diary of Disaster*, University Press of Kentucky, 1986.
F. H. Hinsley, E. E. Thomas, C. F. G. Ransom, and R. C. Knight, *British Intelligence in the Second World War*, HMSO vol. 1, 1979, vol. 2, 1981, vol. 3 pt 1, 1984
D. M. Horner, *High Command — Australia and Allied Strategy 1939–1945*, Allen and Unwin, 1982
Richard Humble, *Crusader: The Eighth Army's Forgotten Victory, November 1941–January 1942*, Leo Cooper, 1987
W. G. F. Jackson, *The Battle for Italy*, Batsford, 1967
H. A. Jacobsen and J. Rohwer, ed., *Decisive Battles of World War II: the German View*, transl. E. Fitzgerald, Michael Joseph, 1972
Robin Kay, *Italy, vol. 2*, NZ War History Branch, 1967
John Keegan and Richard Holmes, *Soldiers*, Hamish Hamilton, 1985
Major-General Sir Howard Kippenberger, *Infantry Brigadier*, Oxford University Press, 1949
G. C. Kiriakopoulos, *Ten Days To Destiny: the Battle for Crete*, Franklin Watts, 1986
Robert H. Larson, *The British Army and the Theory of Armoured Warfare, 1918–1940*, University of Delaware Press, 1984

Ronald Lewin, *Ultra Goes To War*, Hutchinson, 1978
B. H. Liddell Hart, *History of the Second World War*, Cassell, 1970
B. H. Liddell Hart (ed), *The Rommel Papers*, Collins, 1955
Gavin Long, *Greece, Crete, and Syria — Australia in the War of 1939–45*, Series I, Vol. II Canberra, 1953
John McLeod, *Myth and Reality*, Reed Methuen, 1986
W. G. McClymont, *To Greece*, NZ War History Branch, 1959
Fred Majdalany, *Cassino — Portrait of a Battle*, Longmans, 1957
F. W. von Mellenthin, *Panzer Battles*, University of Oklahoma Press, 1971
Samuel Mitcham, *Hitler's Legions*, Secker and Warburg, 1985
C. J. C. Molony, *The Mediterranean and the Middle East*, vol. V, HMSO, 1973
W. E. Murphy, *2nd New Zealand Divisional Artillery*, NZ War History Branch, 1966
Williamson Murray, *Luftwaffe*, Grafton, 1988
J. North, ed., *The Alexander Memoirs*, Cassell, 1962
N. C. Phillips, *Italy, vol. 1, The Sangro to Cassino*, NZ War History Branch, 1957
Barrie Pitt, *The Crucible of War: Western Desert 1941*, Jonathan Cape, 1980
Barrie Pitt, *The Crucible of War: Year of Alamein 1942*, Jonathan Cape, 1982
I. S. O. Playfair, et al., *The Mediterranean and the Middle East*, HMSO, vol. 2, 1956, vol. 4, 1966
D. J. C. Pringle and W. A. Glue, *20 Battalion and Armoured Regiment*, NZ War History Branch, 1957
K. Sandford, *Mark of the Lion*, Hutchinson, 1962
J. L. Scoullar, *Battle for Egypt*, NZ War History Branch, 1955
Frido von Senger und Etterlin, *Neither Fear Nor Hope*, transl. G. Malcolm, Macdonald, 1967
Tony Simpson, *Operation Mercury*, Hodder and Stoughton, 1981
D. W. Sinclair, *19 Battalion and Armoured Regiment*, NZ War History Branch, 1954
Peter Singleton-Gates, *General Lord Freyberg, V.C.*, Michael Joseph, 1963
E. D. Smith, *The Battles for Cassino*, Ian Allan, 1975
P. C. Smith, *Divebomber*, Moorland Publishing Co., 1982
P. C. Smith, *Impact — the Divebomber Pilots Speak*, William Kimber, 1981
Sir John Smyth, *Leadership in War: 1939–45*, Purnell, 1974
Theodore Stephanides, *Climax in Crete*, Faber and Faber, n.d.
G. R. Stevens, *Fourth Indian Division*, McLaren, 1948
W. G. Stevens, *Bardia to Enfidaville*, NZ War History Branch, 1962
W. G. Stevens, *Freyberg, V.C.: the Man*, Reed, 1965
I. McD. G. Stewart, *The Struggle for Crete*, Oxford University Press, 1966
John Strawson, *El Alamein: Desert Victory*, Dent, 1981
John Terraine, *The Right of the Line: the Royal Air Force in the European War, 1939–1945*, Hodder and Stoughton, 1985
David A. Thomas, *Crete 1941: the Battle at Sea*, New English Library, 1972
Ronald Walker, *Alam Halfa and Alamein*, NZ War History, 1967
Robert Wallace et al., ed., *The Italian Campaign*, Time-Life Books, 1978
I. McL. Wards, 'Operation Pugilist and Supercharge II — a Study of Command', Unpublished MA Thesis: Victoria University of Wellington, 1946
Gordon Welchman, *The Hut Six Story*, McGraw-Hill, 1982
Nigel West, *G.C.H.Q.*, Coronet edition, 1987
Nigel West, *M.I.6.*, Panther, 1983
Charles Whiting, *The Battle for Twelveland*, Corgi, 1975
M. C. Windrow, *Luftwaffe Airborne and Field Units,* Osprey, 1972
T. H. Wisdom, *Wings Over Olympus*, Allen and Unwin, 1942
F. L. W. Wood, *Political and External Affairs*, NZ War History, 1958
Peter Young, ed., *Decisive Battles of the Second World War*, Barker, 1967

SUBJECT INDEX

PERSON INDEX